"Our entire way of life in this country is being revised and remolded by the nine Justices of the Supreme Court," a California Congressman complains, and a bumper sticker in his constituency reads: FLUORIDATE EARL WARREN.

"The judiciary is an intrinsic part of this fast-moving world," says the Chief Justice, "and like all of the other parts, it must be properly geared and attuned to the realities of our time."

A native of Washington, D.C., John D. Weaver worked for various government agencies in the early days of the New Deal, then spent five years on the Kansas City (Mo.) *Star*. A free-lance writer since 1940, he has written short stories and articles for most of the country's leading magazines, as well as two novels; a humorous work about his multi-talented wife; a book on Lincoln for young readers; and THE GREAT EXPERIMENT, a witty, informative account of everyday workings in the Federal Government.

Books by John D. Weaver

Fiction

WIND BEFORE RAIN

ANOTHER SUCH VICTORY

Nonfiction

AS I LIVE AND BREATHE

THE GREAT EXPERIMENT

WARREN: THE MAN, THE COURT, THE ERA

Juvenile

TAD LINCOLN: MISCHIEF-MAKER IN THE WHITE HOUSE

WARREN

The Man
The Court
The Era

WARREN

The Man
The Court
The Era

by JOHN D. WEAVER

LITTLE, BROWN AND COMPANY · BOSTON · TORONTO

Published simultaneously in Canada
by Little, Brown & Company (Canada) Limited

PRINTED IN THE UNITED STATES OF AMERICA

*For
Harriett,
of course*

Contents

WARREN

The Man
The Court
The Era

1

The Storm Center

Our entire way of life in this country is being revised
and remolded by the nine Justices of the Supreme Court.
— CHARLES H. WILSON, *Member of Congress*[1]

No tribunal on earth is as powerful as the Supreme Court of the
United States. Five of its nine Justices, acting in concert, can
strike down a law passed by the five hundred and thirty-five members of Congress or an executive order issued by the President,
perhaps the same President who appointed them to their lifetime
jobs. They serve without ever having to look a voter in the eye,
shake his hand or kiss his progeny. Dressed in the black robes of
their priesthood, they sit like tribal elders in a white marble temple
dedicated to the ideal incised above the main entrance: EQUAL
JUSTICE UNDER LAW.

At the time Earl Warren packed his belongings in Sacramento,
turned in his key to the Governor's Mansion and flew to Washington
to preside over the opening of the October, 1953, term, American
justice under law was something less than equal for — among
others — a Negro child, a penniless prisoner, a naturalized citizen
and a metropolitan voter. The Warren Court proceeded to throw
open the doors of public schools to all children, to give impecunious
defendants the right to counsel when brought to trial in a state
court on a criminal charge, to permit the foreign-born to go abroad
on the same terms as other American citizens, and to order the
equalization of malapportioned legislative districts which for years
have kept a nation of city dwellers under the thumb of rural politicians.[2]

"Our entire way of life in this country is being revised and remolded by the nine Justices of the Supreme Court," complains Representative Charles H. Wilson of California, and a Virginia colleague, the Honorable William M. Tuck, has seen fit to compare the Chief Justice to Samson: "He is not a synthetic Samson. He is genuine, for like Samson he is not only blind, heedless, desperate and destructive, but he has also pulled down the temple . . ."[3]

In spite of Congressional assaults, the Court's Corinthian temple is still standing on Capitol Hill, where it was built in the early 1930's following the jovial regime of Chief Justice Taft, who passed along to the designer a bit of wifely counsel: "Mrs. Taft says it should be easy to keep clean."[4] It is still clean and outwardly quiet, but as Mr. Justice Holmes observed in 1913, it is "the quiet of a storm center."[5]

Like its predecessors in times of dynamic growth and change, the Warren Court is accused of usurping the power of Congress, trampling the rights of the states, and meddling in matters that are none of its business. It is charged with coddling Communists and criminals, snuggling up to atheists, and remaking the law of the land to fit its own warped notions. It has made the Republic safe for French films, contraceptives and *Fanny Hill* (just so long as it is not mailed with a sensual leer from some such place as Intercourse, Pennsylvania, or Middlesex, New Jersey).[6]

The Court sent shivers down Madison Avenue spines when it outlawed television commercials designed to deceive viewers with phony demonstrations purporting to prove a product's merits,[7] and, in another opinion written by the Chief Justice, it rocked Capitol Hill inquisitors by defining the boundaries imposed on the power of Congress to conduct investigations (". . . the power to investigate, broad as it may be, is also subject to recognized limitations. It cannot be used to inquire into private affairs unrelated to a valid legislative purpose").[8]

A hurricane was loosed in 1962, when the Court prohibited the New York Board of Regents from subjecting children in public schools to an official prayer.[9] The spectacle of schoolchildren in tax-supported classrooms reciting a prayer composed by bureaucrats might appear to be an intolerable intrusion by the state on the most intimate of family relationships, but, oddly enough, the loudest denunciations of this particular decision came from those who are most disturbed by encroachments of government on their everyday affairs.*

"No decade in American history has brought to the Supreme Court such a diversity of deeply troublesome and controversial questions . . ." the Washington *Post* declared on the tenth anniversary of Warren's appointment, and back home in California the San Jose *Mercury* praised the Chief Justice for having "provided leadership in a Supreme Court that has brought on a revolution in the field of human rights."[11]

Not since the turbulent days of Chief Justice John Marshall (1801–1835) has the Court made so many bold, basic changes in the legal, social and political structure of the United States. The poor are getting a heady taste of justice once reserved for the rich. Negroes have not only moved up from the back of the bus, but are also swimming in public pools, serving on Southern juries and voting in local, state and federal elections. Congressional seats that once were safe for elderly rural spellbinders are now thrown open to young city slickers, and in the selection of state legislators, a suburban housewife is no longer outvoted by an upstate cow.

"Under the present Chief Justice, the Court has undoubtedly done more to strengthen the rights of the individual than it ever did in all the years up to his appointment," the San Francisco *Chronicle* declared in March, 1966, when Warren celebrated his seventy-fifth birthday, and the Washington *Post* reminded its readers: "Earl Warren came to an angrily divided Court in 1953. His robust, healthy good humor, goodwill and good sense did much to unify the Court in spirit if not in opinion and to give it a sense of direction and force in meeting emergent social issues made dangerous by a failure of executive and legislative leadership."[12]

Under the Constitution, Congress controls the nation's purse, the President its sword. The Court, in its early years, seemed to have

---

* A Louis Harris survey, published in mid-November, 1966, indicated that less than half (48 per cent) of the American people would rate the Court's performance as "Good" or "Excellent." The pollsters reported that "younger people, Negroes and the better educated tend to back the Court while white Southerners, older people and the less well-educated tend to be the Court's severest critics."[10]

been left with nothing more than a bit of parchment. As Hamilton had predicted, it was "the weakest of the three departments of power."[13] It was Marshall who made the Court a coequal partner with the legislative and executive branches of the Federal Government. In *Marbury v. Madison* (1803), he enunciated the doctrine of judicial review by which the Court exercises power to declare an act of Congress unconstitutional.[14]

The Marshall Court, expounding the Constitution in favor of a central government sufficiently strong to preserve the Union, made a nation of the disparate and mutually suspicious states spilling west from the Eastern seaboard, encompassing a population of from seven to fifteen million. The Warren Court has used the same flexible document to protect the basic rights of some two hundred million individuals scattered across the North American continent and a string of volcanic islands in the Central Pacific.

"Because of the size and complexity of our society," says Representative James C. Corman of California, "the individual would be submerged if it were not for the Warren Court."

Change has come so quickly that the highly combustible rulings of the McCarthy era already seem as remote as Chautauqua orations on the free coinage of silver, but flag-waving, hellfire-breathing evangelists of the radical right continue to deplore the Court's application of constitutional privileges and immunities to political heretics. They seem to feel that these unalienable rights, like salvation, should be extended only to people of their sort.

"I don't accuse him of being a Communist, but there is something radically wrong with him," the late Senator Joseph McCarthy said of Chief Justice Warren, and the Senator's political heirs still denounce the Court as "one of the most important agencies of the Communist Global Conquest . . ."[15] In their minds, the only question to be settled is whether the Chief Justice should be impeached or lynched.

"Earl Warren has sinned too grandly for impeachment," L. Brent Bozell writes in *National Review*. "He has defiled our jurisprudence and made war against the public order. He has not stolen chickens."[16]

Philip B. Kurland, a professor of law at the University of Chicago, prefers to quote the old frontier saloon sign: "Don't shoot the piano player. He's doing his best." Writing in the *Harvard Law Review*, Professor Kurland goes on to add: "It is still possible, however, to wish that he would stick to the piano and not try to be a one-man band. It is too much to ask that he take piano lessons."[17]

Outwardly, Earl Warren appears the least likely man in Washington to be presiding over a revolutionary tribunal that has inflamed so many bigots, crackpots and law professors. He is a big, friendly man; a Mason and a Moose; a deeply religious, Bible-reading father of six children, who is "Grandpa" to some sixteen youngsters, "the C.J." to his wife of forty-odd years, "The Chief" to his law clerks, and "Governor" to California cronies who share his enthusiasm for sports, hunting, fishing and politics.

Visiting him in his hushed chambers, where no sound from the outside world intrudes, it is difficult to believe that prejudice, paranoia and pedantry should have concentrated so much fury on this hearty septuagenarian who comes lumbering out from his lawbooks with the enveloping friendliness of Smokey the Bear. As has always been his custom, he shows callers the courtesy of coming forward at once to greet them rather than waiting until they have reached his desk.

He has a remarkable faculty for putting a stranger immediately at ease. Young law school graduates, during their first interview before assuming their duties as clerks, are astonished at how quickly their initial nervousness disappears. Within minutes, they are chatting freely about hobbies, books, ambitions. Later, on Saturday afternoons, they usually lunch with the Chief, then take in a ball game, go for a brisk walk or, in bad weather, sit around the University Club listening to anecdotes about old political campaigns in California.

"He'll work your tail off," says a former law clerk, "but he works just as hard himself, usually harder."

He sets his alarm for 7 A.M., but is likely to awaken before it has a chance to ring. He works for an hour or so in bed, reading and making notes before eating the light breakfast his wife fixes for him. In recent years he has begun to watch his weight ("more for curiosity than anything else"), but on the eve of his seventy-fifth birthday he admitted he had begun to backslide from the ritual of setting-up and stretching exercises that used to precede his breakfast.

"I never could keep it going," he said. "I'm not that methodical in my ways."[18]

However, he still tries to walk a mile or two every day, either on his way to the Court, which takes him down Connecticut Avenue toward the White House, or when he heads for home at the end of his workday, which is generally around six-fifteen. He likes to wait until the traffic starts to thin.

"He never leaves without taking home a stack of bench memos, briefs, and petitions to grant certiorari," says another ex-clerk, "and he reads them, too. You can tell from the questions he asks next morning."

Clerks are expected to answer with complete candor, but at times they are so awed by the eminence of their employer that they start indulging in respectful evasions, using what the Chief Justice calls "weasel-words." Warren tends to become snappish when they obviously disagree with him but are afraid to speak up. He likes them to argue forcefully until he has reached a decision, and then he expects absolute loyalty. The clerks are never supposed to forget that they are part of his team.

"Yes," says one of his early-day clerks, "we were always members of the Chief's team, and naturally we'd root for our man to write the big decisions. When the Chief Justice sides with the majority of the Court, he is responsible for assigning the writing of the opinion to an Associate Justice or, of course, he can take it himself. He's so damned fair that he bends over backwards to avoid even the slightest suggestion of seeming to hog the good ones."

"He took the school desegregation case because he felt that an opinion of such magnitude should come from the Chief Justice, speaking for the entire Court," says a confidant who happened to be chatting with Warren one day during the period he was mulling over the wording of his historic ruling in *Brown v. Board of Education.*

"You know how I feel about segregation," the Chief Justice said. "It isn't a question of what I'd like to say, but of what the Constitution will permit me to say."

A passionate commitment to law and order lies at the core of his being. Chatting with a luncheon guest one day, he got to talking about some of the cruelties visited on suspected lawbreakers by officers sworn to uphold the law. His large frame trembled, his face flushing a darker pink as he mentioned a case where a Negro of limited intelligence had been sentenced to death on the basis of a "confession" he had signed after having been beaten into insensibility, then strapped in the state's electric chair for further questioning.

"What are we supposed to do in the face of a thing like that?" the Chief Justice said, his big hands clenching.

"He's the fairest man I've ever met," says a former law clerk, "and the most direct."

When a lawyer starts buttressing his client's case with a formidable array of legal precedents, the Chief Justice may break in to ask, "Yes, but were you *fair?*" Once, when a Southern attorney general, arguing a civil rights case, alluded to his segregated state as "the people," Warren interrupted to ask, "Just what people are you referring to?"[19]

After years of stumping his native state, shaking hands and talking over local problems, Warren often feels lonely in what he calls "this marble mausoleum." The stillness at times is overwhelming. When a young California Congressman spoke to him about the excitement of Washington, the Chief Justice said, "Yes, it's different over there where you are. You deal with people. We deal with records."

When he administered the oath of office as a Sacramento municipal judge to thirty-six-year-old Earl Warren, Jr., in December, 1966, he expressed envy of his son's work in a trial court, where he would "see witnesses, hear them talk and judge their truth and honesty." In more than thirteen years as Chief Justice, he said, "I've never seen a witness or a litigant or a jury or any of the other things which make the administration of justice a human experience."[20]

He welcomes any chance to escape, to be once again in a crowd. He turns up regularly at large funerals, cornerstone-layings, graduation exercises and world peace forums.

"He's always loved people," said the late Mrs. Ethel Plank, the Chief Justice's sister, who remembered him as a lively, good-natured youngster in knee-pants, trotting around the streets of Bakersfield, California, selling newspapers, delivering ice, riding his pet burro.

"He made friends with everyone. Mama used to say that if she missed him, she'd just look for a group of people and he'd be in the middle of it."

Even before he was old enough to go to school he had begun to demonstrate that spongelike capacity to absorb facts, which was later to leave such an indelible impression on a succession of staffs in Oakland, Sacramento and Washington.

"He was quite precocious," Mrs. Plank told a friend shortly before her death in June, 1966. "I remember Dad started to teach me the states and capitals and the rivers they were on. I couldn't have cared less, but Earl picked them up, and by the time he was three or four he could recite them all."

Bakersfield, in the years of Earl Warren's growing up, still had something of the lusty, brawling, lawless atmosphere of the frontier. On Saturday nights the streets crawled with cowhands and sheepherders, with working stiffs from the oil fields and railroad yards. It was a time of drinking and fighting, gambling and whoring. When violence spilled over into the courts, young Warren used to stop by the county courthouse on his way home from Kern County High School, park his bicycle outside and go in to enjoy the drama of the law.

"My determination to become a lawyer goes back so far that I can hardly remember ever having been without it," he has often remarked to friends.[21]

He was not a brilliant student of the law. A classmate remembers him as "ebullient, youthful, immature." He developed slowly, but he demonstrated an extraordinary capacity for growth. He learned law through enforcing it, administering it, interpreting it. A tough prosecutor, he evolved into a progressive governor and, at an age when most men are making plans for retirement, into a just judge.

"He's a late learner," says Judge Robert W. Kenny, the charming, freewheeling California Democrat who had the historic misfortune of running against Warren in 1946. "He learns abdominally. He isn't reading it or hearing it; he's picking it up by osmosis."

"He's always been a good listener," says another California politician. "He doesn't sit there thinking up what he's going to say when you get through talking; he *listens*."

"Yes, he learns by listening," says a former law clerk. "Some judges depend entirely on what they read in the briefs, but oral arguments mean a lot to the Chief. When he's making up his mind on a case, he'll frequently play a tape recording of the oral presentation."

Aside from three years with a private law firm after leaving the University of California (B.L., 1912; J.D., 1914), Warren has spent his entire working life in public service. He managed to rear six children on salaries that never seemed to stretch far enough. After the family moved to Sacramento, taking over the gingerbread mansion assigned the governor of California (it was Lincoln Steffens's boyhood home), Mrs. Warren continued to wash and iron her husband's shirts. She still does.

"Mom hasn't changed a bit," says Jim, the oldest of her three sons. "She's always in motion, always with something in her hand — a dustcloth, a glass of orange juice. Something's going on all the time. She's baking a cake, writing letters, ironing a shirt."

Although the Chief Justice could well afford to send his shirts out if his wife cared to have them professionally mangled, he has amassed no large private fortune. He lives pleasantly at the Sheraton-Park Hotel on an annual salary of $40,000 plus the $12,500 a year he receives under California's contributory retirement system.[22] His pay would be larger by $4,100 a year if he had stuck with his old job.

In 1965 he might have been given a $3,000 increase if some of the decisions of the Warren Court had been more palatable to certain members of the House of Representatives. Congress, the year before, had raised its own pay to the tune of $7,500 a year, but had given the Supreme Court Justices a boost of only $4,500. A proposal to make up the discrepancy led to an ill-tempered display of pettifoggery.

One representative suggested that Congress "reduce the salaries of these people to the amount that legislators make since they have assumed the legislative role."[23] Another complained about the Court's long vacation from the insufferable heat and humidity of the summer months in Washington.

"Whatever the length of their vacation is," grumbled Representative Laurence J. Burton, a Utah Republican, "it is not long enough."[24]

"Many of the members of this House say they want an independent judiciary," Representative Sidney R. Yates of Illinois declared. "Yet it is apparent from the debate that the contrary is true. They want a judiciary that is independent but not too independent. They want a judiciary which agrees with their views. They want the Court to avoid controversy in an explosive time when controversy is a part of our way of life."[25]

The $3,000 increase was rejected by the House, but not before Congressman Corman had told his colleagues that, in denying the members of the Court their rightful salary, "we do not demean them, we demean ourselves."[26]

As governor, in addition to a large staff to handle his mail, appointments, speeches and press relations, Warren had grown accustomed to having a mansion, limousines, planes and highway patrolmen put at his disposal. As Chief Justice, he found he not only had to do most of his own work but also had no official residence and no car.

"One night," as an old friend in Congress tells the story, "Earl was invited to a reception at the White House. When he got back to the hotel that evening, he told his wife he'd decided to rent a limousine. She said she thought it was a needless extravagance, but he insisted it wouldn't look right for the Chief Justice to call on the President in a taxicab. They're both great sticklers for protocol, so Mrs. Warren gave in without an argument.

"Earl changed to white tie and tails. When the desk called to tell him that their car had arrived, he escorted his wife downstairs to the lobby, then out to the main entrance where the limousine was waiting. On the side facing them, in enormous white letters, they saw the words: NATIONAL AIRPORT. It was too late to make other arrangements and, besides, they'd have to pay for the thing, so they climbed in and rode off to the White House."

Once the story got around Washington, two members of the California delegation in Congress quietly tucked an item in a pending appropriations bill providing a limousine for the Chief Justice. Although Congress and the Court are within easy walking distance of each other, they do so little visiting back and forth that ten years after the Chief Justice got his limousine, a member of the House Appropriations Committee was amazed to learn that the eight Associate Justices still shared one official car. They had asked Congress for $4,000 to trade in their six-year-old Chrysler.[27]

Among the power centers of Washington, the Supreme Court is unique. It is quiet. In the Capitol, the White House, and the paneled throne rooms of the major federal agencies, the daily crises of government are dealt with in an untidy environment hostile to reading and reflection. Phones ring constantly. Pressures pile up. Each day is another frantic race against the clock and the first coronary. Only in the Supreme Court Building is there time for thought in an atmosphere conducive to contemplation.

"I've found the quiet of my chambers and of the library a very soothing thing after the hectic years I've put in as an executive," Warren said at the end of his first term as Chief Justice.[28]

He had been called upon to preside over a divided, drifting Court that had fallen behind in its work. Not since 1850 had so few cases been decided as in 1950.[29] The Warren Court has been accused of many things, but no one has ever charged it with indolence. A born administrator, with a remarkable ability to get strong-minded associates to work together, Warren has refurbished every public office he has ever held, leaving it more orderly and more efficient than he found it.

As a district attorney in the San Francisco Bay area (1925–1939), he built up a first-rate investigative staff, schooled his deputies in the preparation of trial briefs, and never had a conviction reversed on appeal. As California's attorney general (1939–1943), he took over a musty institution that had made little effort to keep abreast of the times and modernized it. As governor (1943–1953), he streamlined cumbersome, overlapping departments, put them in the hands of experts, and eliminated waste and duplication.

"His administration of state government was far and away the finest in modern American politics," says Senator Thomas H. Kuchel, who served as state controller during several years of the Warren administration.

When the Governor moved to Washington, he found himself in an institution where break with tradition comes slowly, but during his years as Chief Justice change has visited the Supreme Court. Although it is still one of the last appellate courts in the country to deliver its decisions orally, the opinions are no longer handed down only on Monday. Now, to accommodate the press, they are announced when ready,[30] and copies are distributed to reporters by page boys wearing long pants instead of knickers.

"When I became Chief Justice in 1953," Warren says, "the docket entries were still being made in longhand. It wasn't until the 1957 term that we began using a typed loose-leaf docket."[31]

"How do you like the new Chief Justice?" a prominent California businesswoman asked a Negro attendant who was escorting her from the marshal's office to Warren's chambers one afternoon early in his first term.

"In all the years I've been here," he said, "it's the first time I've been treated like a man."

"He hadn't been there two days," says one of Warren's intimates, "before he knew every guard and every messenger by name. He even knows the names of their kids."

The Court is a warmer, less forbidding place because of the Chief Justice's instinctive courtesy. In the old days, when a lawyer filed an application to practice before the Supreme Court, he paid his twenty-five-dollar fee, got someone to vouch for his qualifications, shambled past the bench with a covey of self-conscious colleagues, and received an ornate certificate that has always been more impressive than meaningful, because few lawyers ever expect to argue a case before this awesome tribunal.

Warren has never forgotten the cordial reception he received from Chief Justice Hughes when he was admitted to practice before the Court in 1932.[32] It left such a lasting impression on him that when he took over the high-backed center chair, he turned the cold, cheerless admission ceremony into a warm and personal experience, greeting each lawyer by name and welcoming him to the Court with a friendly smile.

"He really runs that place," says a former clerk. "I first went to work there in July, while he was off somewhere salmon-fishing, and then one day the atmosphere of the building began to change. The guards, the messengers, the other clerks, everybody seemed to perk up. Word had gone out that the Chief was coming back."

"As an administrator," says a former member of his gubernatorial staff, "he had one glaring fault. If you did something wrong, he'd sure as hell let you know it, but when you did a good job, he'd never bruise your back patting it."[33]

"He's a very cautious, prudent man," says another of his old Sacramento associates. "He moves slowly, studying each step. 'Let's pick this thing up by the four corners and take a look at it,' he used to say when a new problem came along. Sometimes it seemed to take forever for him to make a move, but when he made it, it would invariably be the right move at the right time. His sense of timing is uncanny, almost mystical."

"He has the memory of an elephant," says still another associate. "He never forgets, and if anybody double-crosses him, he seldom forgives."

He has never outgrown the friends of his early days. Whenever he is in the San Francisco Bay area, he heads for the Oakland apartment of Johnny Mullins, a retired civic leader who, in 1925, rounded up the votes by which the Board of Supervisors appointed him district attorney of Alameda County. It was this appointment that diverted Warren from private practice to public service. In the entrance hall of Mullins's apartment, facing the front door, is a 1953 photograph of the Chief Justice inscribed to "the first sponsor and for thirty years the most loyal supporter in public life of his friend . . . Earl Warren."

"He brought that to me the first Christmas after he was appointed to the Court," Mullins says, and his wife likes to tell the story of a wedding reception to which they were invited but were unable to attend because her husband's arteriosclerosis makes it difficult for him to get around.

"One of the Warren girls was getting married in San Francisco," Mrs. Mullins says.* "We've known the children all their lives, so naturally we wanted very much to go, but we couldn't. We were sitting here reading, when suddenly the doorbell rang, and in came the Warrens. They'd brought us the whole top part of the wedding cake."

In Sacramento the Chief Justice drops by a shoe repair shop on H Street to chat with Randall R. Butler, who took care of the family

---

* Virginia, the oldest daughter, married John Daly, the television personality, December 22, 1960. The reception was held in the Venetian Room at the Fairmont Hotel.

footwear when the Warrens lived down the street in the Governor's Mansion. Since then, the Governor — as Butler still thinks of him — has traveled to some of the most remote reaches of the earth, where he is known and respected as the author of the decision ending segregation in public schools, and wherever he and his wife have gone, they have usually found time to drop the Butlers a line and to hunt up an addition to their collection of silver demitasse spoons, each representing some exotic place no Sacramento cobbler is ever likely to visit.

"Earl Warren is honest, likable, and clean," John Gunther wrote in 1947; "he will never set the world on fire or even make it smoke; he has the limitations of all Americans of his type with little intellectual background, little genuine depth or coherent political philosophy; a man who has probably never bothered with abstract thought twice in his life . . ."[34]

Gunther found the Governor a kindly, stable, well-balanced man, devoted to his family, a joiner but "not a politician of the raucous, grasping kind that has despoiled so much in the United States . . ." Warren was dismissed as "a friendly, pleasant, average Californian; no more a statesman in the European sense than Typhoid Mary is Einstein; and a man who, quite possibly and with luck, could make a tolerable President of the United States."

In 1947, when Governor Warren was a contender for next year's Republican Presidential nomination, it didn't occur to Gunther that he might end up at the opposite end of Pennsylvania Avenue as Chief Justice of the United States. Even when his appointment was announced in the early fall of Eisenhower's first year in the White House, it was impossible for anyone, including his sponsor, to predict just what direction he would take after he had slipped into his new black robe. It would have to be new because he had never worn one before.

"Does a man become any different when he puts on a gown?" the late Justice Felix Frankfurter was often asked, and he liked to reply, "If he's any good, he does."[35]

"For a justice of this ultimate tribunal, the opportunity for self-discovery and the occasion for self-revelation are unusually great," Abe Fortas wrote some months before he was appointed to the Court. "Judging is a lonely job in which a man is, as near as may be, an island entire. The moment is likely to come when he realizes that he is, in essential fact, answerable only to himself."[36]

"He has to live with what he puts in those books," Warren tells visitors, indicating the volumes of Supreme Court decisions that line one wall of his chambers, where he sits in a red leather chair with a pleasant view of the Library of Congress.[37]

"He's happy as hell up there," says a veteran of the California political wars who has remained close to the Chief Justice. "He told me once, 'Look,' he said, 'this is better than being President. There have been thirty-some Presidents, but only fourteen Chief Justices.' He loves that job. And why not? You can't beat it. If he'd gone to the White House in '52 instead of Eisenhower, he'd have been out of work for the last five, six years. And he doesn't like golf."

"He's one hell of a lucky guy," says another member of the inner circle. "Anywhere along the line he might have sunk from sight. During the Depression, when he had all those kids to feed, he might have disappeared into a big law firm or gone on the bench. When he got to be attorney general in 1939, he liked the job and might have stuck with it the rest of his working life, like his predecessor, but the Democratic governor started giving him a bad time, so Warren ran against him and beat him. He might have quit after two terms and never been heard from again if the lieutenant governor hadn't been so damned anxious to take his place. Nobody's ever going to push that stubborn, square-headed Scandinavian around."

Old friends disagree as to the timetable of Warren's political ambitions. Some say it was inevitable that after a couple of terms as attorney general he would have run for governor. They also insist he would never have bowed out after two terms. This would have meant being politically unemployed in 1952, when he would have his best chance to lay claim to the White House. Some of those closest to him still think he might have wound up as the Republican candidate had it not been for the machinations of Richard Nixon, who left the convention with the Vice-Presidential nomination as his door prize.

Ironically, in the summer of 1964, a dozen years after Warren seemed to have reached the end of the road politically, he was participating in reapportionment decisions that may prove to be the most far-reaching action taken by the Supreme Court in the last hundred years. Nixon, in the meantime, had moved out of California, defeated in his race for governor, and Eisenhower was sitting on the sidelines at the Goldwater convention in San Francisco, a virtual stranger. Republicans hadn't even shown him the courtesy of hanging his picture in the cave of winds the party had selected for the site of its suicide pact.

To make the General's cup even more bitter, the *New York Times Magazine* in the summer of 1962 had published the results of a poll taken by Professor Arthur M. Schlesinger, Sr., of seventy-five American historians.[38] Asked to rate the Presidents, the panel had placed Eisenhower number twenty-two, just behind Chester A. Arthur. (Truman finished in ninth place.) At the same time, it was being suggested that future historians might consider the appointment of Earl Warren as Chief Justice to be Eisenhower's most important act as President.[39] Privately, according to Washington gossip, Eisenhower was denouncing it as the biggest damfool mistake he made in the eight years of his Presidency.

2

A Poor Clarinet Player

I, Earl Warren, will to Lorraine K. Stoner my ability to
slide through, doing as little work as possible . . .
— WILL OF THE CLASS OF '08,
KERN COUNTY HIGH SCHOOL,
BAKERSFIELD, CALIFORNIA[1]

THE Chief Justice enjoys telling the story of his first political
speech in Los Angeles as a candidate for state office. A native
son in a city of outlanders, he lost no time in letting his audience
know that he had been born near the Union Station.

"I thought that would go over big," he says, "but I got no response
at all. I thought maybe they hadn't heard me, so I said it again, and
again no response. Then a little later on I just happened to mention
that my father came from Iowa, and that raised the roof."[2]

Methias H. Warren was brought in infancy from his native
Norway to the New World, coming to rest in Eagle Grove, Iowa,
shortly after the end of the Civil War.[3] The family name, "Varran,"
was anglicized,[4] and later, to complete the simplification, "Methias"
became "Matt." Unhappy at home after the remarriage of his
widower father, Matt Warren dropped out of school and roamed
the Middle West, working as a farmhand in summer, a mechanic in
winter.

He fell in love with a pretty Swedish girl named Christine
Hernlund (she preferred to call herself "Chrystal").[5] They were
married February 14, 1886, in Minneapolis, and a year later their
daughter Ethel was born. Seeking a warmer, drier climate for his
family, Matt set out for California in 1889, settling first in San
Diego, then moving to Los Angeles, where he rented a five-room

frame house at 457 Turner Street, near the old depot.[6] Here, on March 19, 1891, Earl Warren was born. The midwife, Mrs. A. Mueller, listed him on the city's records as an unnamed, male American, the son of "Warn, M" and "F. Warn," a mistake which was to make trouble sixty years later when the Governor of California applied for a passport.[7]

"Son," Matt Warren explained when the boy asked why he had no middle name, "when you were born, we were too poor to enjoy any luxury of that kind."[8]

Los Angeles, at this time, was second to San Francisco both in population and in political power. The northern city was heavily Catholic and pro-labor. Its southern rival was Protestant and anti-labor.[9] A shameless creature of the Southern Pacific, which paid Matt Warren seventy dollars a month to repair its rolling stock, Los Angeles took the company's bribes, ran its errands, and did its dirty work. Middle-class Christian businessmen supported local ordinances closing the saloons on Sunday and placing in safe hands the selection of surgeons called on to testify in damage suits involving injuries suffered on Southern Pacific trains.

Across the continent, in the spring of 1892, the Amalgamated Association of Iron and Steel Workers set out to negotiate a new contract for skilled workmen at the Homestead, Pennsylvania, works of Carnegie Steel. A deadlock over wages developed. The workers were locked out. When Pinkerton agents were brought in, they were met by armed strikers. Three Pinkerton men and seven strikers were killed. At the company's request, the governor dispatched the state militia to escort strikebreakers into the plant. The strike was crushed.

It had demonstrated, in the words of Gene Debs's biographer, that "a modern corporation could destroy with one stroke the strongest craft union in America."[10] In Chicago the following year Debs announced the formation of the American Railway Union, a new concept in organized labor. It was an industrial union, the forerunner of the Congress of Industrial Organizations. Instead of limiting membership to skilled craftsmen, as the American Federation of Labor had done in providing a private club for the aristocracy of labor, the A.R.U. welcomed the lowliest man working on the railroad, just so long as he was "born of white parents."[11]

Negro co-workers were offered "sympathy and support," but not membership in the A.R.U.

Matt Warren joined the new union, paid his one-dollar initiation fee and in the early summer of 1894, when the A.R.U. came to its moment of truth with management, he was one of the more than one hundred thousand men who quit work. President Cleveland's attorney general applied to the courts to crush the upstart union. An omnibus injunction against the leaders was issued in Chicago by two federal judges, one of whom had recently declared: "The growth of labor organizations must be checked by law."[12] Debs went to jail. Matt Warren, fired and blacklisted, managed to scrape along on his savings, while other A.R.U. members walked the streets, lined up at soup kitchens, vanished in hobo jungles, or crawled back to work on the company's terms.

After working for a while in lonely desert towns, living in enforced exile from his family, Matt headed a hundred miles north of Los Angeles to Bakersfield, where the Southern Pacific was moving its yards. The company's need of skilled labor was so great that Matt was removed from its blacklist and put to work as a car repairer. He installed his wife and two children in a rented house on the eastern reaches of Bakersfield in a railroad town originally called Sumner, then Kern, and finally Kern City.[13]

"They were quite young parents," Ethel recalled when she was in her late seventies, "and now when I look back, I think of how much wisdom they showed in bringing us up. They didn't spoil us, but they were so self-denying. Everything was for the children."

"Father would always buy me any book I wanted," Governor Warren said in 1948, and he very early bought his children the Century Encyclopedia which sat in the bookcase in the dining room.[14]

Matt was never much of a reader, but neither Earl nor Ethel would ever lose the vivid memory of their father huddled over his desk in front of the coal oil stove in the dining room, applying himself to his International Correspondence School lessons. He was a practical man, boning up on bookkeeping and accounting, preparing to accumulate an estate to leave his family.

"He wasn't very robust," Ethel said. "I think he always had a fear he wouldn't live to raise his family."

He was determined to enable his children to get the formal education he had missed. While their mother saw to it that they were well fed and neatly dressed, their father prodded them to pay attention in school and take advantage of their opportunity to learn, to make something of themselves. He was the family disciplinarian.

"We learned obedience," Ethel told a Bakersfield *Californian* reporter in 1958. "I think learning this as a child makes life easier, for one has to learn to get along with other people. We had only to be spoken to once and, although Earl was a little more daring than I, he never went too far and seemed to know just exactly where to stop in defying parental rule."[15]

"Never had any trouble with him," says Leo G. Pauly, who was principal of the Washington School when the future Chief Justice attended it in the 1890's. Mr. Pauly was still a spry, familiar figure on the streets of East Bakersfield in the mid-1960's when he passed his ninetieth birthday. He was still walking along Baker Street at regular hours each day, running up a total of three miles on his two round trips between home and office.

"Earl was an average student," he said of his most famous pupil, "a very docile little fellow who attended strictly to business."

He could have led his class with ease if only he had worked a little harder, his mother was convinced, and when he was graduated from high school at the age of seventeen, a year or two younger than most of his classmates, three mischievous young ladies wrote in the class will: "I, Earl Warren, will to Lorraine K. Stoner my ability to slide through, doing as little work as possible . . ."[16]

Although his mother was disappointed in Earl's report cards, she was impressed by the early intimations of his administrative ability. If he had a chore to attend to, kindling to split or a toolshed to tidy up, he would assemble a group of youngsters from the neighborhood and entertain them while they did his work. In the hours between school and odd jobs, he played ball in the dusty streets of Kern City with Jean Phillip, rode along the rim of the China Grade Bluffs on a burro named Jack, trotted off into the hills to hunt and fish.

"It was wide-open country in those days," he says. "It was an outdoor life. I rode my burro all over town. He was my friend. In fact, I was the only friend Jack would acknowledge. Other kids couldn't do a thing with him."

To Ethel's amusement, her mother at times would say one thing to the children, quite the opposite to the neighbors. "You children argue more than any two children I've ever heard," she used to tell them, and then they would hear her purring over the back fence, "The children never argue." One particular argument was fastened in Ethel's memory because her father used it to teach her a lesson.

"We were never allowed to strike each other," she recalls. "I used to say to Earl, 'I wish I could hit you.' Well, it seems I said it once too often. My father said, 'All right, you want to hit your brother, go ahead and hit him.' He took us out to the woodshed and I started crying. I never made that remark again."

The two Warren children played with youngsters representing a variety of national origins, many of them speaking with accents picked up in homes where English was a foreign language. Like all children, Ethel went through a time of self-scrutiny when she was searching for an identity, something to establish and explain the uniqueness of being Ethel Warren.

"We'd come home from school after we'd heard the other children boasting that they were Italian or French or German, and I'd say, 'What are we?' and my father would say, 'You're Americans.' I felt I'd been cheated."

One Sunday morning in the spring of 1903, just a month after Earl's twelfth birthday, the Sabbath quiet of the town was shattered by a gun battle that left three men dead. About ten o'clock that morning Bakersfield peace officers had received a tip that Jim McKinney, a bandit who had been terrorizing the San Joaquin Valley, was holed up on L Street, south of Twenty-first. The two-story brick building was a Chinese joss house in the heart of the city's notorious tenderloin district.

Nine lawmen set out from the town jail to bring McKinney in. Among them were City Marshal Jeff Packard and the two Tibbett brothers, Will and Bert. When they reached the hideout, Packard and Will Tibbett went inside to search the building while the others stood guard outside. Suddenly shots rang out. The officers ran across the yard as Packard staggered toward them, his arms limp and bleeding. Then Bert Tibbett spotted the outlaw and cut him down with his shotgun, firing both barrels. At almost the same instant Bert saw his brother sprawled on the ground.

"Immediately after the battle," the *Daily Californian* reported next day, "the most intense excitement prevailed in the city. This was accentuated when Marshal Packard was brought in a buggy along Nineteenth Street on his way to his home, bleeding profusely, and still further a few minutes later when a bus arrived at Baers' drug store with the prostrate form of Will Tibbett. The wounded man was taken into Baers' drug store and physicians summoned, but it took but a glance to show that the officer was wounded unto death. A rifle ball had entered his right side penetrating the abdominal cavity. The wounded man was perfectly conscious, directed those present as to where he was wounded, but was suffering the most intense agony. A half hour later he was taken upstairs to the Southern Hotel and there surrounded by his family he died shortly before one o'clock."[17]

Will Tibbett left a widow and four children, including a six-year-old son, Lawrence, who went on to make something of a name for himself as a singer. The boy's father, it was quickly discovered that bloody Sunday, had not been killed by McKinney's shotgun, as his colleagues had at first assumed. The fatal shots had been inflicted by a rifle. Suspicion fastened at once on Al Hulse, a stonemason who had sheltered the outlaw in his room. Hulse was arrested and hustled off to jail.

By this time angry crowds had collected along the streets. Their mood was so unfriendly that when a jail cell was unlocked for Hulse, he gladly flung open the door himself, darted inside and slammed it shut. Young Warren, hearing of the excitement, had jumped on his burro and trotted into town. He arrived too late to see the prisoner, but when he was told of the man's deadly accuracy in firing at the deceased officers, he was reminded of a turkey shoot he'd watched a few days earlier. One contestant had managed to get a turkey with almost every shot.

"Here, son," the man had said at one point, tossing a wild white turkey to Earl, "take this one home with you."

When Al Hulse was brought to trial, Earl Warren was among the spectators in the packed courtroom. As he had suspected, the defendant was the same man who had given him the turkey. The

trial resulted in a hung jury, and Hulse was left to languish in jail.
Finally, more than three years after the Sunday morning shoot-out,
he did himself in by slitting his throat with a razor.[18]

Both of the Warren children were put in the hands of a music
teacher who hoped to make a pianist of Ethel, a clarinetist of Earl.
Brother and sister appeared in an occasional matinee performance
at the local opera house ("actually," the sister pointed out, "it was
just a little theater up over a store"), but after a while Ethel decided
to leave a clear field to Paderewski. The teacher had better luck with
her brother.

"I played clarinet in the town band," he says, "and at about the
age of fifteen I was one of the charter members of the musicians'
union. It wasn't my music. It was their need for members."

Local 263 was chartered March 1, 1906 (Warren turned fifteen on
the 19th). In 1952, when the International Federation of Musicians
held its convention in Santa Barbara, Governor Warren greeted the
delegates with the reminder that membership in the Bakersfield
local had started him "in the race of life."[19] A year later, at the
bottom of a letter acknowledging the congratulations of Federation
President James C. Petrillo, the newly appointed Chief Justice
added a postscript in his own handwriting: "My regards to the
brothers of the federation. Their kindness to me has always been
more than a one-time poor clarinet player deserved."[20]

"He didn't play in our school orchestra," says one of his high
school classmates, now a conservative Republican businessman who
disapproves of the landmark decisions of the Warren Court in the
field of civil rights. "He was always rather evasive on the subject,
but I think it was because of his union membership. Playing in the
town band carried a small honorarium, so that was all right with the
union, but nobody got paid for playing in the school orchestra.[21]

"Earl was strong for the unions. I don't remember him getting
into any arguments, especially during his first two years, when we
had a pretty rough crowd in school, but most of them were
eliminated by Earl's junior year, so he had an easier time of it. I
don't mean to say he was belligerent about unions. But he was
obviously very sympathetic. He favored them."

Earl worked during his summer vacation, saving his money for college. He put in one summer on an ice wagon. Next year, when he was eleven years old, he took over two paper routes, distributing the Los Angeles *Herald* in the morning, the Bakersfield *Californian* in the afternoon. For two summers he drove mule-drawn grocery wagons.

"Son, never let yourself be caught broke," his father used to say, illuminating the warning with the precept: "Saving is a habit, like any other, and once established will last a lifetime. If you are earning only a dollar a day, make sure to save a penny of it."[22]

For the boy, insolvency came to be equated with death after hearing his father tell of a wretched winter in Chicago when a tubercular brother had died in his arms. With money for medicine and doctors, Matt was convinced, his brother's life could have been saved. In later years, if any single disillusioning experience ever served to alienate Earl Warren from the wealthy reactionaries in the Republican party, it was their successful fight to block the compulsory health insurance program he proposed to the California legislature at the start of his third year as governor. The episode illuminated the gulf between their world and his.

Warren was thirteen years old when he entered Kern County High School in Bakersfield. The undersized, towheaded teenager was smaller than most of his classmates and still in knee-pants.

"He was so little none of the girls wanted to go out with him," an alumna (Class of '07) recalls, and one of his '08 classmates says, "I never knew him to ask a girl for a date."

Then as now, he never missed a ball game or a track meet if he could help it. He tried out for the high school baseball team, but as Omar Cavins remembers it, "I beat him out for right field." Matt Warren discouraged his son from playing football, a game he considered too rough for the youngster (in his senior year he got in a minor game as right end).[23]

"He was a meek, mild boy," says Mrs. Ruth Smith Henley, a K.C.H.S. classmate.

"He was not very conspicuous, didn't seek publicity or class office," says Francis Vaughan, another '08 graduate. "He was neither aggressive nor retiring, but well-balanced, cautious."

In physics class, during his senior year, he was teamed for

laboratory work with Minnie Mae Robinson, Ethel Said and Mary Ashe (in those days she was called "Minnie"). When they got stuck on a difficult problem, Miss Mary recalls, the three girls usually had to solve it by themselves without any help from Earl, who was bored by physics. In *The Oracle,* the class yearbook, Miss Mary was described as: "A merry heart that laughs at care." Earl Warren was given the needle in a line purporting to be autobiographical: "I know many things, but nothing distinctly."

"He was not a particularly good student," says Vaughan. "He didn't have the curiosity of a scientist. He seemed to be looking around for something to do. More interested in history, I suppose, than anything else."*

"He still likes to read history," says Earl Warren, Jr. "We used to have quizzes at the dinner table, and he was always fascinated by his lack of knowledge of science. If he had it to do over again, he says he'd study chemistry and physics. He never liked Latin, by the way. I think it's because it's a dead language."

"Our Latin teacher wasn't very inspiring," says Vaughan. "Even Ethel Robesky dropped out after taking the required two years of it."

Ethel Robesky, the bright, pretty valedictorian of the Class of '08, later married Willie Simpson of the Class of '09, who went on to become district attorney of Los Angeles County. Willie, like Ethel, was a good student. He was also editor of the K.C.H.S. yearbook and a star debater, outshining Earl Warren, who is credited with only one major appearance. In the fall of 1907 he joined Warren Stockton in upholding the affirmative side of the question, "Resolved: That it is not for the best interests of Bakersfield and Kern to consolidate." The negative side was argued by two girls. The boys won.[25]

"He had quite an analytical mind," his sister said. "At home Dad and Earl used to take opposite views of things. I think Dad was drawing Earl out to see what he was thinking."

In the summer following his junior year, young Warren worked

---

* "History, particularly of our own country," Warren replied in April, 1947, when a young journalism student asked which public school subject he considered most valuable. "In our history," the Governor explained, "we find the origins of all our governmental institutions, and by knowing their story, we are in a better position to understand and perfect them."[24]

for the Southern Pacific as a call-boy. He was paid twenty-two cents an hour to corral the crew when a train was scheduled to start its run. He put in a twelve-hour day, covering the town on bicycle, flushing crewmen from a front-porch swing, a neighborhood bar, a floating crap game, or a crib in Jap Alley, where Japanese girls smiled at male passersby from windows hung with colorful paper lanterns.

A few blocks away, John Withington's saloon near Nineteenth and K streets was a hangout for the town's politicians. On election day party workers would round up the hobos strung out along the Southern Pacific tracks and herd them to the polls, where they cast ballots in the name of the dead men still listed as registered voters. A dormant propriety awakened in the saloonkeeper one day when he called out to a derelict about to palm himself off as a dead Withington: "No, you can't vote in the name of my father!"[26]

"It was a wild, wild town," Omar Cavins recalls. "There was always a poker game going on in the back room at the Arlington saloon. I've seen twenty-dollar gold pieces stacked on the table as high as a player's head. There were three dance halls — the Owl, the Standard and the Palace. They charged two-bits a dance, and the Johns were encouraged to buy the Janes a glass of colored water — cold tea, I suppose. I used to stuff myself on the free lunches, and if I had a nickel, I'd buy a beer. They didn't pay any attention to kids. You could help yourself."

Barging in and out of saloons and poker parlors, tracking down an elusive engineer, young Warren was soon on the best of terms with local dealers and croupiers. They took professional pride in demonstrating the technique of dealing from the bottom of the deck and slipping a pair of loaded dice into a friendly crap game. This technical information was filed away in the boy's memory, to be drawn on later when he started tidying up Alameda County.

In late May, 1908, while the honor students at K.C.H.S. were putting the finishing touches on their graduation speeches ("All the World's a Stage," "Build in Mountain Fastness," "American Supremacy"), Earl Warren was rehearsing his role in the senior class play, "What Became of Parker?," a farce starring his sister's pretty friend, Helen Campbell.[27]

"The character of Fred Parker was played by Earl Warren and his scenes with Miss Campbell were well acted," the *Californian* reported after commenting that "the acting of the young amateurs was a delightful surprise to their many friends."[28]

"One rehearsal ran late," Miss Mary Ashe recalled in the fall of 1966, "and Earl and several others were quite late to school the next day, so they were expelled."

As Warren remembers the incident, the expulsion hit only three students — Reg Stoner, Tim English and himself. "We decided that if we weren't going to graduate with the class, there wasn't much point in appearing in the play. The Scribner Opera House was sold out, so the board of education held an emergency meeting and reinstated us."[29]

In the graduation picture of the Class of '08, Warren is standing in the center of the front row, his hair parted in the middle, his hands behind his back. The same picture of the senior class (eleven girls, six boys) appeared on the front page of the *Californian* on September 4, 1958, when the surviving members assembled for their fiftieth reunion.

"It was Omar Cavins's idea," says Ruth Smith Henley. "He came up to me one day and said, 'We ought to have a big reunion this year,' and then he left town and turned all the work over to me."

Earl and Ethel Warren both came home for the big doings at the Stockdale Golf and Country Club. The Chief Justice shook every hand within reach, astonished old acquaintances by calling them by their first name, posed for a picture with Mrs. Millie Munsey, who gloried in the distinction of having taught him in the third grade,[30] and then made an after-dinner talk which at least one classmate found dull and disappointing.

"It was all about how this fellow had gone around the world looking for a diamond mine or something, and all the time it was right there in his backyard at home."

The Chief Justice had drawn on the memory of an evening when he was still in short pants and his father had taken him to hear a famous lecturer on the Chautauqua circuit. The subject was "Acres of Diamonds." As the youngster sat spellbound, the lecturer spun his tale of a prosperous Persian farmer who had learned from a passing stranger of the wealth to be had in diamonds. The farmer sold his land, parceled his family out among his kinsmen, and left to roam the world in search of diamonds. He ended up ill, penniless and alone. Meanwhile, the farm back home had turned out to be one of the world's richest diamond mines.

"I remember that this lecture was delivered at the time when so many of our people were rushing up to Alaska in search of gold," the Chief Justice says. "I saw a number of them return empty-handed to our little city. In the meantime, the great oil fields of Kern County had been discovered, and water had been brought to the arid soil making a garden spot out of what had been desert."[31]

The lecture was still fresh in his memory during his freshman year at the University of California, when he heard Lord James Bryce, author of *The American Commonwealth*, predict that California would someday have a population of fifty million.[32] It had been one million at the time of Warren's birth. Fifty-five years later, when he was starting his second gubernatorial campaign, it was nine million. In Los Angeles that spring, he revisited his birthplace, chatted with the current occupants of the house, Mr. and Mrs. Harry Woo, and then spoke at the Jonathan Club, taking the state's explosive growth as his theme. Plans for California, he said, should anticipate a population within twenty years of twenty million.[33]

"That figure shocked some of my friends who believed that it was extravagant," he says. "They said that the experts did not forecast such a tremendous growth, and that I would do better to say fifteen instead of twenty million. I refuse to change my figure, saying that the growth of California should be predicted by optimists, not by experts."

When he set out for the University of California with eight hundred dollars saved up from his odd jobs, Warren was a gangling adolescent who had never spent a night away from his parents.

"I was young, immature, very much the Freshman, and I was known by that name," he later recalled. "No book or professor had a profound influence on me, not even in the law school. Companionship was the greatest thing I found at the University, and it still stands out in my mind today as more important than anything I learned in classes."[34]

In the minds of its members no doubt exists that the Class of '12 is the greatest in the history of the University. It includes not only a Chief Justice, but also two outstanding conservationists, Horace M. Albright and Newton B. Drury, both of whom served as directors of the National Park Service; Dr. Tracy I. Storer, the distinguished zoologist; Herman Phleger, the prominent San Francisco attorney who was legal adviser to the State Department during the Eisenhower administration; Ray Gidney, who was in Washington at the same time as Comptroller of the Currency; two Superior Court judges, Chris B. Fox and Thomas J. Ledwich; and Shirley Temple's father-in-law (James B. Black also happened to be board chairman of the Pacific Gas and Electric Company).[35]

"Yes, it's quite a class," Horace M. Albright says. "On December 7th, when those Jap planes came in over Pearl Harbor at dawn, there was a little private plane flying around above the naval base. It surprised the hell out of the Japs, but it was certainly no surprise to us that the pilot was a member of the Class of 1912."

Warren made no athletic team, set no academic record, held no class office. "He never ran for anything himself," a classmate recalls, "but he was very active politically. A bit *too* active for my tastes. He was always backing somebody for some kind of office. He'd come up to you and say, 'Now, Jim, you know John's a good fellow. I'm sure you're going to vote for him.' Some of us resented his approach."

"He was a very popular fellow," another classmate says, and most agree that he was a friendly, unsophisticated youngster from the small, back-country high school which had given the university baseball team its flashy battery, Reg Stoner behind the plate, Will Forker on the mound.

During his six years in Berkeley, Warren lived at La Junta Club, which became a local chapter of Sigma Phi Fraternity. He put on thirty pounds gorging Bill the Dog Man's frankfurters, hitting the free lunch counter at the Waldorf Bar, and drinking mugs of beer at Pop Kessler's restaurant. Among his friends he was known as "Pinky," a nickname often attributed to his pink complexion, but the Chief Justice says he acquired it from a nurse when he was in the infirmary with a case of pinkeye.

"Some of my friends heard her say, 'Come on, Pinky, it's time for your medicine.' They picked the name up and it stuck."

After three years at the University, majoring in political science,

Warren entered Boalt Hall, the law school. He had managed to do well in classes that held his interest (political science, history, English), but had been bored by subjects for which he could see no useful application. He was a practical young man. He was also stubborn. Early on, he clashed with William Carey Jones, Boalt Hall's colorful dean. The twenty-year-old freshman didn't like the way Dean Jones and his staff taught law.

"The law school made a fetish of discouraging the acquisition of practical knowledge," he says; "and they were so committed to the case system that they denied you the opportunity of seeing things in perspective. They started off on antique English language from Old English law, and didn't want anybody to read on the outside. I didn't approve of their methods of teaching and didn't like them; I said nothing, either to my fellow students or the professors, but I suppose my attitude must have been apparent."[36]

At the end of his first year at Boalt Hall, when he received his bachelor of law degree but still had two years to go to get his doctor of jurisprudence, he was bluntly told by Dean Jones: "Warren, I don't like to have to tell you this, but I think you should be prepared for the fact that you will never graduate."

"Why?" Warren asked. "Haven't I passed my examinations?"

"Yes, you passed the written examinations, but you have never once all year volunteered to speak in class."

"Is it obligatory that one volunteer to speak in class, Dean?"

"No, it's not exactly obligatory."

"Was I ever informed that I would have to volunteer in class in order to graduate?"

"No, we simply assumed that you knew."

"Well then, Dean, as I was never told, and it is not obligatory and I am passing my examinations, I am going to graduate."

The dean reminded him that if he failed any of his five remaining subjects, he wouldn't graduate, and Warren told him, "I haven't the slightest intention of flunking any of the five remaining subjects." In the dean's constitutional law class the following year, Warren was never called on to recite and he never once volunteered, but he got a good grade on his written examination.

Because he liked to learn by doing, he took time from his studies to spend his afternoons clerking in a local law office. In the spring of

1914, right on schedule, he turned in his J.D. thesis ("The Personal Liability of Corporation Directors in the State of California").[37] On May 6th it was officially approved by Dean Jones. Perhaps providentially, the dean never lived to see the day when Boalt Hall would be overshadowed by a magnificent annex, The Earl Warren Legal Center, and his former student would be saluted by the President of the United States as "the greatest Chief Justice of them all."[38]

3

The Crusader

. . . if you asked him about a point of law, he'd sweep his arm past the lawbooks lining the wall, and he'd say, "There's your answer."
— A FORMER DEPUTY DISTRICT ATTORNEY
OF ALAMEDA COUNTY, CA. 1935

A FEW days before President Johnson paid an unscheduled visit to the Chief Justice on the evening of his seventy-fifth birthday, giving him among other presents a handsomely inscribed photograph, some of the most dazzling ornaments of the bench and bar gathered for an informal ceremony at the National Lawyers Club in Washington, D.C. A bust of Warren, his first likeness in bronze, was to be unveiled.

"By very diligent research," Attorney General Katzenbach said of the club's guest of honor, "I have found a short period which is unaccounted for before he served his country in the First World War, a period of perhaps two years, a period of which I have with all the research facilities of the Department of Justice not been able to find out what he was doing for his country. But knowing this man you may be sure that he was doing something, for from that period of time on he has served with the greatest distinction."[1]

During this period, the Chief Justice explained, he had been making do on the prevalent rate of fifty dollars a month for young lawyers just out of law school. When the First World War came along, he said, some young lawyers who were about to starve went into service. In fact, it was the war that saved their lives.

Actually, Warren went off to war three years after he left Boalt

Hall, not two. Professionally, they were the dullest, least rewarding years of his life, and the only ones following his graduation not devoted to public service. After he was admitted to the bar, he got a job in the law offices of the Associated Oil Company in San Francisco. A year later he moved across the bay to Oakland, where he clerked in the office of Robinson & Robinson. His salary barely took care of his lunches and carfare.[2]

"Pinky would like to get married too," a member of the Class of 1912 wrote a newly married classmate at this time, "if he could find a girl willing to live on air."

He could always count on a good dinner from his sister, who had settled in Oakland after her marriage to Vernon Plank, a Southern Pacific storekeeper. Vernon was immensely fond of his brother-in-law but amused by his indifference to clothes. Earl didn't seem to care what he wore, as long as it was a double-breasted blue suit. When it got shiny, he bought another one. It got to be a family joke at the Planks'.

"My husband used to kid him about it," Mrs. Plank later recalled, "and so he decided to buy something different. He came home one day with a black-and-white checked suit. My goodness, you never saw such a thing in your life. I think he went into the Army to avoid having to wear it. While he was gone, we gave it away."

In August, 1917, Private Warren was dispatched to Camp Lewis, near Tacoma, Washington, where he was assigned to Company I, 363rd Infantry, 91st Division. He was made a first sergeant after his four weeks of basic training. A few months later, in January, 1918, he was admitted to officers' training, and eventually landed at Camp Lee, Virginia, where he was commissioned a second lieutenant and put in charge of running recruits through bayonet school.[3]

"That outfit's got to be the biggest in the history of the American Army," says Jim Warren. "Every time I'm introduced to anybody anywhere near Dad's age, they tell me, 'Oh yes, I was in the Army with your father.'"

When the war ended, he was serving as a first lieutenant at Camp MacArthur in Waco, Texas. Discharged a month after the signing of the Armistice, he returned home to Bakersfield to spend Christmas with his parents, then went back to Oakland, where he moved in with Ethel and Vernon. He was still in uniform, trying to figure out just how he could readjust to civilian life on his sixty-dollar bonus.

"I remember rather distinctly going back to Oakland to purchase my new civilian clothes," he recalled in 1943. "I remember the personal shock occasioned by being asked sixteen dollars for a shirt."[4]

On his first morning in Oakland he walked downtown and ran into Leon Gray, a friend from his Robinson & Robinson days, who had just been elected to the state assembly. He offered Warren a staff job at five dollars a day. When they got to Sacramento, they bumped into Assemblyman Charles Kasch, a classmate of Warren's. Kasch insisted they should do better by old Earl. He got him appointed clerk of the Judiciary Committee. The job paid seven dollars a day.[5]

Warren roomed with Gray at the Hotel Sequoia, where he struck up a warm friendship with Frank Anderson, a young Oakland legislator who suggested he serve an apprenticeship in the office of Ezra Decoto, the district attorney of Alameda County, before setting out to make his fortune as a trial lawyer. The idea appealed to Warren and, without saying anything to him about it, his friends decided to make a deal.

When Decoto showed up in Sacramento, seeking legislative authority to add another man to his staff, he was told he could have an additional hired hand but it would have to be Earl Warren. Decoto demurred. He already had a man trained for the job, he protested, but the legislators insisted it was to be Warren or nobody. When Warren got word of the impasse, he sought out Decoto and explained that he would like to work for him but not under these circumstances. He told Decoto to go ahead and hire his own man.

"I appreciate that, Warren," Decoto said. "If there should ever be an opening in the district attorney's office, I'll keep you in mind."[6]

The opening cropped up a year later. Warren, meanwhile, had put in three months with the legislature and saved enough money to buy civilian clothes. On his return to Oakland he had started to form a partnership with Gray, but had passed it up to accept a job in the city attorney's office. He had been paid two hundred dollars a month and left free to engage in outside practice, but had been too busy handling the city's public affairs to take on a private client.

On May 1, 1920, he walked over to the old frame County Courthouse on Broadway, between Third and Fourth streets, and climbed the wide stairway to the second floor.

"There was no elevator," a colleague later recalled. "The district attorney's office on the second floor was very overcrowded. The office was on the right-hand side of the building and the caller went into an office with a counter where a clerk took the callers' names and interviewed them to find out whom they should see. They were then directed down a dark corridor to the office of the appropriate deputy or the district attorney. The investigators were officed in a room in the attic on the top floor of this old building."[7]

Warren's new job cost him fifty dollars a month in reduced wages. "The drop in salary bothered me not at all," he says. "I thought I would work in the district attorney's office for about a year and a half, and at the end of that time I would go into private practice and become a great trial lawyer. So I worked sixteen hours a day for the first five years, and ended up by remaining eighteen years, often working until midnight at least five nights a week."[8]

"When Earl Warren came into my office as a deputy," Decoto used to say, "I would frequently ask him on Saturday morning if he could find me some law on a case in the office in the course of the next few days. Monday morning there would invariably be a memorandum on my desk setting forth all the law on the subject involved."[9]

He has always been a hard worker, with a prodigious capacity for accumulating, absorbing and analyzing facts. Even old friends are taken aback at times by the oddments tucked away in his memory. It is like the attic of a family that has been for some generations in the business of producing almanacs.

"I keep trying to trap him on sports, and I always fall flat on my face," says Jack McDermott, a Sacramento businessman who attends the World Series every fall with the Chief Justice. "For years I've been a referee for high school football games. Well, one night we were sitting around the hotel room after dinner, talking, and I got to describing a game I'd refereed.

"I mentioned a penalty I'd assessed for pass interference, and he cut in on me. 'You certainly blew that one,' he said, and I said, 'What do you mean?' He insisted I'd brought the ball back to the wrong line. I always carry rule books with me for just this kind of argument with him, so I said, 'All right, let's look it up.' He said, 'You assessed the correct penalty for college competition, but it's different for high school games.' I looked it up, and he was right."

Whenever one of his deputies resigned, as frequently happened during the boom years of the early 1920's, Decoto would throw up his hands and ask, "My God, who knows anything about his cases?" Invariably the reply would be, "Warren."[10] In 1923 Decoto named Warren his chief deputy, and assigned him to the Board of Supervisors, where he caught the eye of John F. Mullins, who had first been elected to the board in 1908 and served for nearly twenty years.

"He was our legal adviser," Mullins says. "This brought him into close contact with county problems. He was very active and studious on both civil and criminal matters. I trusted him completely."

In January, 1925, when the governor appointed Decoto to the State Railroad Commission, it was up to the county supervisors to name a successor to serve until the next regular election in November, 1926.* Warren wanted the job, but seemed to have little chance against Frank Shay, the personable chief deputy in charge of criminal cases. Shay had the support of the Mike Kelly machine, which could usually be relied on to deliver at least three of the five votes on the Board of Supervisors.

Running into Warren at the courthouse one day, Kelly explained that he had nothing against him personally but he had promised the job to Shay, whose friends had been supporting him for years. Warren declared his candidacy anyway, and word soon got around that he and Shay each had two sure votes. The deciding vote was Johnny Mullins's. To cast it for Warren would be political suicide. This, Mullins announced, was precisely what he intended to do.

"You'd have thought hell had broken loose," he recalled forty years later. "But I stood my ground. I know of no man ever elected or appointed to public office with as free a hand as was given Earl Warren. That's why he succeeded. He went in clean and he remained clean."

Mullins managed to obtain a unanimous vote of the board for

* Decoto resigned from the Commission in 1930 and returned to the private practice of law. In November, 1943, Governor Warren appointed him to the Superior Court in Alameda County. He died in 1948.[11]

Warren. When the announcement was made on January 12, Frank Shay handed in his resignation and gave up the practice of law. He never even returned to the courthouse to clear out his desk. He moved to a ranch near Gilroy and became a leader in the state's prune and apricot industry. If the vote had gone against him, Warren probably would have resigned and entered private practice as a trial lawyer.*[12]

"I don't believe there was any one time I decided on public life," he says, "but it became my preoccupation. I think I would have left in 1932 if it hadn't been for two things — the Depression and a sheriff who'd been elected in 1926 and was a thorough corruptionist. I'd been trying to throw him out. If I'd quit, with an election coming up, it would have looked as though I hadn't meant what I'd been saying."

Sheriff Burton F. Becker took office in January, 1927, supported by the Kelly machine and its underworld affiliates in charge of bootleg gin, girls, gambling, skin games and narcotics. It was a classic conflict between the black hats and the white hats. Inevitably, as could have been predicted by any red-blooded, right-thinking admirer of Tom Mix and Tim McCoy, there was a showdown between the crooked sheriff and the crusading young district attorney. The sheriff was driven from office and the D.A. was reelected by the largest majority in the county's history. And, of course, he got the girl.

One Sunday morning in 1921, when he turned up for a birthday party at the old Piedmont Baths, Warren spotted a radiant face among the bathers splashing about the pool. He asked his hostess to introduce him.

"She was in the water, and I could see only her head," he says, "but she looked wonderful to me."[13]

Like Warren's mother, Nina Palmquist had been born in Sweden and brought to Iowa as a child. Her parents had moved to California seeking a mild, beneficent climate. Her mother had died when Nina was three years old, her father when she was thirteen.

---

* The breach between the two men was officially closed in April, 1943, when Governor Warren appointed Shay to the Farm Production Council.

She had been self-supporting ever since. At the time she met Earl Warren ("I spotted him just as quickly as he spotted me"),[14] she was the widow of a musician, Grover Meyers, who had died when their son, James, was three weeks old. She had gone back to work, managing a chain of women's clothing shops.

The least impulsive of men, Warren made haste slowly in his courtship of the attractive widow. They went out together only on Saturdays, usually dinner dancing or to the local stock theater. One night he took her to his sister's for dinner, where she met his mother. She interpreted this as a promising omen.

But Warren proceeded with all deliberate speed. It was two years after they met that they became engaged, and another two years went by before they were married. In the meantime, he had moved up to the office of district attorney, where he was being paid $7,000 a year instead of $5,000. On October 14, 1925, after a noon wedding, the couple set out on a honeymoon trip to Portland, Oregon, and Vancouver. As a wedding present the Board of Supervisors gave the bridegroom a thirty-day leave of absence. He accepted half of the gift.[15]

On their return to Oakland, the Warrens moved into a five-room flat where their first child, a girl, was born in 1928. Jim, who was nine years old at the time, had already been adopted by his stepfather before Virginia's birth, and claims credit for her name.

"There was a kid I went to school with, Bob Jones, who had a sister that was the prettiest girl I'd ever seen. Her name was Virginia."

In 1929 the Warrens moved into a three-bedroom house on Larkspur Street, and began adding bedrooms and children: Earl, Jr. (1930), Dorothy (1931), Nina Elizabeth (1933) and Robert (1935).

Warren talked his wife's obstetrician into letting him accompany her into the delivery room when each of the five children was born.

"He got as white as the surgical gown they gave him to wear," Mrs. Warren says, "but he stayed right with me. And it helped."[16]

In 1935 they acquired an old commodious house on Vernon Street which remained the Warren home until the family moved into the Governor's Mansion.

"I'll never forget Earl and those kids at our twenty-fifth reunion," says Horace Albright of the Class of '12. "We had a picnic up in

Contra Costa County, and Earl spent the whole time chasing after those kids. It was like trying to pick up leaves in a windstorm."

"They were good youngsters," their Aunt Ethel said, "but they took liberties with him that they didn't take with their mother. He never put a hand to one of the children. He'd talk to them, so they knew he meant business. He had a nice way of handling them, never yelled at them. He was really a good father."

Sunday was Nina Warren's holiday. Her husband packed the children off to their Aunt Ethel's for a visit or turned them loose in the park or at the zoo. On pleasant evenings, after a dinner at Fisherman's Wharf, he would shepherd them through the scented streets of San Francisco's Chinatown. He taught them to swim and to ride, and the boys learned to handle firearms on hunting trips before they were old enough for high school. They were also imbued with their father's love of sports. The boys went in for football, the girls for swimming and tennis.

At one time the Warrens had a child in five of the first six grades of an Oakland elementary school. Mrs. Warren delivered and picked them up in shifts, fixed their lunches, and took care of them when they had the measles, whooping cough and chicken pox. Whenever one came down with spots or a fever, all caught it.

"Gave me a good time to houseclean," Mrs. Warren said when asked how she managed.[17]

The children were expected to earn their allowance (twenty-five cents a week) by making their beds each morning before breakfast, hanging up their clothes and keeping their rooms neat. Mrs. Warren made the daily inspection and disbursed the funds.

"Once, when they were small," she recalls, "I found that none of them but Jim had tidied up their rooms. So I put a stack of six quarters on the table and said, 'Well, the pot goes to Jim.' After that, believe me, I had no more trouble."[18]

None of the children was ever spanked or sent to bed as punishment. "Dad used to talk things over with us," says Honey Bear (Nina, the youngest daughter, acquired the nickname in infancy and it is still used by the family). "It hurt more than a spanking."

"You were always on your honor," says Earl, Jr., a Sacramento municipal judge with four children. "If you did something wrong, the punishment was in knowing you had broken the code."

After smoking cigarettes in secret for a while, Virginia turned herself in to her mother, who doesn't smoke or drink. Mrs. Warren expressed the opinion that it was up to Virginia to decide whether she wanted to smoke or not, but that if she did, there was a proper time and place for it. Even after she had been graduated from college, Virginia still wasn't smoking cigarettes in public.[19]

"I never heard a jury bring in a verdict of guilty but that I felt sick at the pit of my stomach," the Chief Justice is often quoted as saying.[20] In recent years he has explained that the quotation is accurate in regard to capital crimes, but that it has been exaggerated by frequent repetition. "I was a hard prosecutor," he says, "and a lot of times I would have felt badly if the defendants had not been convicted."

"He was both vigorous and fair," says Willard W. Shea, who was working the other side of the street in those days as the county's first public defender. "In a trial, he'd take every legal advantage, but he seldom went ahead with a prosecution until he had all the bags covered. As public defender, I had no investigators, no funds for that sort of thing. I remember one case where the defendant said he couldn't have committed the crime, he was in Los Angeles at the time. I believed him. I went to Warren and told him the story. He sent one of his investigators down there and checked out the information. Then he went into court and asked to have the case dropped."

"Warren never ducked the tough cases," Frank Coakley, his successor, said in 1948. "He threw the book at them. He hated a bunco man worse than a burglar, and never lost a case against these swindlers."[21]

In 1926, facing the voters for the first time in his life, the thirty-five-year-old district attorney pitted his record against the $25,000 slush fund he said had been raised to defeat him. "We have secured convictions in 414 of the 499 felony cases disposed of in the Superior Court," he announced. "This is an average of 83 per cent convictions as compared with an average of 66 per cent throughout the state."*[22]

---

* According to a statistical study published in 1936, more than 86 per cent of the defendants prosecuted on felony charges in Alameda County were convicted. In Los Angeles County the total was 74 per cent; in San Francisco County 67 per cent.[23]

"I managed to win that election," he said later, "by meeting and talking to more voters than any candidate had ever talked to before."[24]

The United States was the most lawless civilized nation on earth, Warren said at the time he took office.[25] After expressing his feelings about gambling and bootlegging ("I believe that a man should take his pay home with him, and not leave it at some bootlegger's or gambling place"),[26] he later explained to a group of Oakland businessmen: "The only way the racketeers can get control in any community is by alliance with politics, and control of your public officials, your courts, your sheriff, your police chief, your district attorney, and other law-enforcement agencies."[27]

Warren ran a tight, honest ship, free of political favoritism. He broke up a bail-bond ring that had enjoyed cordial relations with City Hall. He packed the principals of a paving-contract scandal off to prison, although one of them happened to be a city commissioner of considerable wealth and influence. The same impartial justice was handed out to gamblers, petty crooks and rumrunners.

Warren himself gave up drinking during Prohibition.

"How can I drink bootleg liquor at a party on Sunday night," he explained, "and then on Monday morning send my deputies to prosecute bootleggers?"[28]

"He's never been much of a drinker," says one of his friends, "but he likes a drink before dinner. It used to be bourbon, now it's Scotch. As for Prohibition, it wasn't something he favored. It just happened to be the law, and he was being paid to enforce the law."

"He's always operated on the theory that nobody can criticize a man for doing his job," says Judge Kenny. "He was a strict prosecutor. Now he's Chief Justice, and he's no longer dealing with gambling and prostitution ordinances, but with the Bill of Rights, and he's enforcing it."

Toward the close of a routine workday in the late 1930's, he lumbered into the office of Helen R. MacGregor, his personal secretary. She has never forgotten the incident. "He said, 'I've got to make a speech on the Bill of Rights.' He dictated some notes, taking each of the rights and telling how it hampered him as district attorney. But then he went on to say that he wouldn't have any one of those rights diminished in any degree 'for my sake, my children's sake, or my children's children's sake.' "

A Boalt Hall graduate (Class of '22), Miss MacGregor had served as law clerk for United States District Judge Frank H. Kerrigan in San Francisco before going to work for Warren in April, 1935. During her four years with Judge Kerrigan, she had come to appreciate the meticulous care with which Warren prepared a case for trial.

"His investigative work was carried out within constitutional limitations," she says. "Judge Kerrigan often commented that cases from Alameda County did not fail on motions to suppress because proper constitutional steps had been taken."

The restraints of the Bill of Rights had not yet come to be gradually imposed on the states by the Supreme Court. Thus, a prosecutor could obtain a conviction in a state court through the use of methods which would have been unacceptable to a federal judge. Warren trained his staff to respect a defendant's right to due process of law regardless of whether the case was to be tried in a state or federal court.

"I never saw an involuntary statement taken from a defendant," says an ex-deputy district attorney. "We didn't advise him of his right to counsel and to silence, because that wasn't the law at that time. But if a man didn't want to talk, that was OK, and whenever he asked for a lawyer, he got one."

"We used to get away with all sorts of things before Warren took over," says a former investigator. "Hell, I'd have a pocketful of search warrants, and just fill in the name and date as I went along. He sure put a stop to that. And no more free turkeys at Thanksgiving and no more Christmas presents. You should have seen the loot we used to get."

Professor Raymond Moley of Columbia University described Warren in 1931 as "the most intelligent and politically independent district attorney in the United States."[29] Later, when Warren was rounding out his first year as governor, Moley explained: "The reason I spoke of him as a district attorney as I did was the calm and efficient way in which he organized his office, carried on the important business of law enforcement without thought of immediate political considerations, stayed by it a long time, built up a fine organization and when he moved on . . . left the office in good hands."[30]

It struck Warren as strange that no one had ever bothered to write a book about the business of being a district attorney. In a holograph preface to a proposed manual, he pointed out that the district attorney "has become the most powerful officer in local government; he has developed from a mere advocate to a powerful executive and legal officer who declares and determines the law enforcement standards of his county, and, through the exercise of quasi-judicial functions, determines, in the main, who shall be prosecuted and who shall not be subjected to our criminal procedure."[31]

"This rise in power has gone hand in hand with the decline in power and importance of other law enforcement officers — particularly the sheriff, with the result that all of the agencies concerned with the administration of criminal justice — even the jury and the courts — have been relegated to a position of comparative unimportance." (In the margin opposite this statement is a question mark.)

"As could be expected," the preface continues, "abuses have crept into the system, perhaps not so grave in California as in other parts of the country, but sufficiently serious to challenge the attention of all persons interested in the proper administration of justice. These abuses are caused more by a lack of understanding of the true responsibilities of the position and a failure to realize the importance to the public of the manner in which many of the functions of the office are performed. This lack of knowledge is understandable. There is no school or university where men may be trained for such public service, and even the shelves of our libraries are almost totally devoid of information bearing directly upon the subject.

"In California at the general election of 1930, twenty-eight (?)* new D.A.'s were elected in the fifty-eight counties of the State. Almost without exception these men were totally without experience as a District Attorney. Most of them had never practiced criminal law, and some were young men only recently out of college, with little or no experience in the practice of law."

Warren set out to build a bridge of understanding between those

* The question mark appears in the MS.

who enforced the law and those who simply abided by it, usually paying little attention to it as long as they were not inconvenienced by its operation. Day after day, night after night, he talked to Lions and Rotarians, Soroptimists and the Council of Jewish Women, and to fellow-members of the Exchange Club, American Legion, Elks, Native Sons and Moose, striking variations on the theme of crime and punishment:

"It is impossible to cage up men like animals and expect them to become better."[32]

"When a man enters the Alameda County prison, he does not touch his feet on the ground again until he is freed. He sits and broods, and becomes more bitter towards society responsible for his incarceration."[33]

"The State owes an obligation to its prisoners to see that they are not discharged from the penitentiaries in worse condition than they came in."[34]

"Once a boy has a crime record his opportunities for success are cut 75% and he loses 90% of his self-respect. Those are hard odds to fight against."[35]

"If people have money, they are likely to escape punishment. It is a shame to think that there should be one law for the poor and one for the rich, but the present methods are leading toward that result."[36]

Miss MacGregor could find no simple answer when a graduate student in the summer of 1965 wrote to ask her why Earl Warren had developed such great popularity as district attorney, but as she looked back, certain qualities stood out as contributing factors.

"He created a favorable impression," she replied. "A big, good-looking, friendly, unpretentious man, he inspired confidence.

"He selected a staff of unusual competence and inspired their devotion. They were both skillful and scholarly. Trial briefs and research always preceded trials. Investigation of facts was of paramount importance. He had his own investigative staff to work with police departments. The homicide squad of lawyers and investigators went to the scene of a crime immediately — any hour of the night. In any serious situation the office swung into action with precision."[37]

The loyal, closely knit staff was recruited largely from among young law school graduates caught up in the Depression. They often served without pay until a vacancy occurred. The arrangement gave them a place to go every morning at eight o'clock. They worked a long, hard day in exchange for a desk, a telephone and secretarial help. They were allowed what one of their number refers to as "a marginal private practice."

"I was sworn in after I got out of law school in 1932," he says, "and had to wait sixteen months before I got on the payroll. You had to sweat it out until somebody quit, and in those days jobs were so hard to come by, you didn't let go once you'd landed one."

"The Chief had a good thing going for him," says another ex-deputy. "Whenever an old friend asked him to put a young law school graduate to work in his office, he could say, 'I'd love to do that, but you see I've got this fellow who's been working for me ever since last spring and he hasn't been drawing any pay, so it wouldn't be fair to give the next vacancy to somebody else, now would it?' That office, by the way, was the best organized I've ever been acquainted with."

In the easygoing days of the Decoto regime, deputies had hacked away at their own caseload, paying little attention to the work of their colleagues. Warren introduced a daily conference system which kept each man in touch with all the others. Every Thursday afternoon deputies from outlying towns would be called in for a general meeting. A weekly review of pending cases and policy problems, both civil and criminal, was conducted for the entire staff every Saturday morning at eight-thirty.

"And God help you if you showed up at eight-forty," says a former deputy. "The Chief would greet you with those cold blue eyes and a booming, 'Well, well, good afternoon, Mr. So-and-So. It's nice of you to drop by.'"

"He was a hard man to work for, most exacting, took long hours for granted, and you never expected any praise," says another alumnus. "He could lay you out colder than a mackerel. But anger never stayed with him. Incidentally, I never heard him apologize. I doubt that he ever apologized to anybody for anything."

The young lawyers Warren rounded up during the Depression and the New Deal are now senior partners, judges and law professors, some in retirement. They speak of the Chief with affection, respect (despite their differing views on his judicial opinions) and, at times, with amusement:

"It was a bruising experience to go to a football game with him. He was in on every play, and if you sat next to him, you could end up with a cracked rib or two."

"He had three great qualities: The ability to make decisions, an unerring sense of timing, and an infinite capacity for remembering names."

"When he became district attorney, the office had one investigator. He built up a real investigative staff, 'the crime-crushers' we used to call them. They had to read law, engage in firearm practice, study new techniques in law enforcement."

"The Chief had a characteristic gesture I'll never forget. At those Saturday morning meetings, he'd answer any question you put to him about a policy matter, but if you asked him about a point of law, he'd sweep his arm past the lawbooks lining the wall, and he'd say, 'There's your answer.'"

"Yes, he'd expect you to go look up the law yourself. If you suggested asking the attorney general for an opinion, he'd glower at you and ask, 'What did you study in school?' and you'd say, 'Law, sir,' and he'd say, 'All right, you're a lawyer. Now what is the attorney general? Just another lawyer.'"

"If a deputy went to him and said, 'I'm not sure this man is guilty,' he would be removed from the case, and we'd discuss it at our Saturday conference. If we all felt the man was not guilty, the case would be dropped. None of us was ever asked to prosecute a defendant if we weren't sure of his guilt."

As district attorney in California's third largest county, Warren worked routinely with violence, but close associates say he has never quite got over his horror of it. "It offends his sense of order, his love of the law," says a former member of his staff. Warren's earliest memory, still vivid, is one of mock violence, the hanging in effigy of a railroad official by a group of strikers. Thirty-odd years later, on a Sunday morning in the spring of 1938, he was suddenly forced to relive this childhood trauma.

"We'd gone to a Masonic breakfast meeting at the Claremont Hotel in Berkeley," says Oscar Jahnsen, his chief investigator. "I saw him get up and leave the room, then I was called out. He said, 'Oscar, someone has murdered my father.'"

In East Bakersfield, where the two Warren children grew up, retired railroad men taking their ease in Sumner Street bars remember Matt Warren as a hard worker who stood for no nonsense in his shop. He worked his way up on the Southern Pacific from a mechanic to master car builder. He never drank or smoked, lived frugally, put his money in a savings-and-loan company and in dozens of modest rental properties in working-class neighborhoods.

At the time of his death, five years after he retired from the railroad, he was living alone in a small frame house on Niles Street. His wife was in Oakland, recuperating from an operation for cataracts. Sometime between 8 P.M. Saturday, May 14th, when a tenant came to pay his fifteen-dollar rent, and 9:30 A.M. on the following day, when a handyman discovered the body of his seventy-three-year-old employer, Matt Warren was killed by a blow on the left temple as he sat in a large chair facing the open oven of the gas stove in his kitchen.

At the foot of the back steps, just fifteen feet from the old man's chair, were several lengths of two-inch pipe about two feet long. A groove in the grass indicated a missing piece which was found in the yard next door. It was spattered with blood and bits of hair. The killer apparently had dragged his victim from the chair, where he had been mortally wounded, to the bed, where the contorted body was found, the face covered by a blanket. A bruise on the left arm suggested an attempt to ward off the blow.

"The old man knew who hit him; I'm convinced of that," says Jahnsen, who flew to Bakersfield at once to help Chief of Police Robert Powers with the investigation.

"It was a clear case of robbery," Power still maintains, but Jahnsen has never been convinced that this was the only motive. His principal suspect, who had done business with Matt Warren, clammed up abruptly when he seemed on the verge of a confession. The suspect is dead now, and the murder remains unsolved. Around East Bakersfield, it is generally accepted that someone, possibly a tenant or a transient, had heard the neighborhood gossip of the large sums of money the old man was rumored to have hidden in the house, and killed him to get it.[38]

"Reports that he was wealthy have been greatly exaggerated,"

Warren said when newspaper stories began to refer to his father as a "millionaire" and a "capitalist" living the austere life of a recluse. "Since he was seven years old, my father worked hard, much of his life with his hands. He took no pleasure for himself. He tried to give that to his children and their children."[39]

The old man had been haunted by a fear of poverty, underscored by the memory of the penniless brother who had died in his arms of tuberculosis, unable to afford a hospital bed. Poverty, to Matt Warren, was a disease with a high mortality rate. To immunize his family, he worked and scrimped all of his life, indulging only one luxury — his children. He left an estate officially valued at $177,653,[40] but when his body was found, both of his wallets were missing (one contained business papers, the other cash) and he had two cents in his pockets.

4

The Politician

A Progressive is a man who is afraid to be a Democrat and ashamed to be a Republican.
— A CALIFORNIA DEMOCRAT, 1931[1]

WHILE Warren was making a name for himself as Alameda County's livewire district attorney, Ulysses S. Webb was coasting along comfortably as California's attorney general. His long tenure had made the office a personal, haphazardly operated institution. His salary was frozen at $5,000 a year by the state constitution, but he was permitted to accept fees from his private practice. Californians, in short, were making do with the services of a part-time lawyer as their chief legal adviser and law-enforcement officer.[2]

As secretary of the state's District Attorneys' Association and a past president (1931), Warren was in close touch with law-enforcement officials throughout the state. In 1934 he called on them to support a series of amendments to the state constitution designed to modernize the antiquated methods of catching and convicting criminals. One of the proposals would strengthen the office of the attorney general. He was to be made a full-time employee of the state, cut off from outside practice and paid the same salary as an associate justice of the State Supreme Court ($11,000 a year at the time). The attorney general was to occupy an office second only to the governor's in power and influence.

"To convict criminals we must first catch them," Warren wrote in urging adoption of the amendment. "The vast majority of felonies committed in this country go down into history as unsolved crimes. Even when we know who the criminals are it is not only difficult but often impossible to arrest them, and the manner in which the

Dillingers, the 'Baby Face' Nelsons, the Machine Gun Kellys, the Tuohys and numerous other criminal gangs have been playing hide-and-seek with the public authorities has truly become a national disgrace.

"This is not the fault of any one agency or of any one State. The fault lies largely in the lack of organization of our law-enforcement agencies. We are operating under a system of law enforcement which was established centuries ago when our population was small, our colonies separated by wilderness, when there were no repeating firearms and when the fastest mode of transportation was the horse and buggy. That system which gave to every county, city and town the right to regulate its own police affairs without supervision or interference from anyone could function efficiently in the simple society that existed in those days, but in our present complex society of one hundred and twenty-five million people, geared up as it is with railroad trains, automobiles, airplanes, machine guns and automatic pistols, that system has become inadequate.

"The law-enforcement business of California is a gigantic business costing the people of the State thirty million dollars a year, and it is being run in a most unbusinesslike manner. There are in this State 276 incorporated cities and 58 counties, each of which is handling its law-enforcement work in its own way without supervision. Any private business operated in this manner could result in but one thing — bankruptcy."[3]

In Alameda County, as Warren kept pointing out, there were eleven separate police departments, "and the sad part is there is no power to make them work together."[4] Each department was a stubborn, self-contained island, suspicious of its neighbors, and often more interested in staying in office than in apprehending lawbreakers, particularly those who had strong political connections. It was not unusual for Warren's investigators to raid a bookie joint and find the premises deserted, thanks to a friendly tip from a rival law-enforcement office.

"He managed to break down the walls between police officers, deputy sheriffs and district attorneys," says a California judge whose legal career began in Warren's Oakland office. "He got law-enforcement people to work together, to pool their information. The exchange depended on mutual confidence. They trusted Warren."

California voters bought the entire crime-busting package put before them on the 1934 ballot, including a constitutional amendment which was struck down by the Supreme Court in 1965 (*Griffin v. California*).[5] Having worked to broaden the powers of the attorney general and more than double his salary, Warren was accused of creating a plush job for himself. He made no secret of his ambition to succeed the elderly incumbent, but as he had already explained to the attorney general, not until Webb chose to retire.

"A man should never be in a hurry for a political job," he says; "when he starts pushing, he thinks and does things he would never do under normal circumstances."[6]

Finally, early in 1938, when Webb was in his seventy-seventh year, he sent for Warren, thanked him for his patience and courtesy, then told him he didn't intend to run again. Warren declared himself a candidate on February 17th.[7] He was warmly endorsed by district attorneys, sheriffs, police chiefs, probation officers and judges, the men with whom he had worked most closely in the last dozen years.

"As a lawyer he has been sound and diligent in his practice," said Chief Justice William H. Waste of the California Supreme Court. "As an administrator he has been capable and cooperative, and he has ever been known as a fearless and efficient, yet eminently fair, prosecutor."[8]

In an eight-page mailing piece, Warren spoke of the increasingly complicated and expensive problems presented by the state's youth and rapid growth. He discussed organized crime, but pointed out that the attorney general should be more than a policeman. He was California's chief counsel, the legal adviser of its top officials, the protector of the individual's personal rights and the state's property rights. "In doing so he should interpret the laws in keeping with the purpose of the legislature and the principles of constitutional law." If elected, he pledged, the office would be conducted on a nonpartisan basis.[9]

As district attorney, Warren was already running a nonpartisan office. In 1928, when he stumped the Bay Area for Herbert Hoover, one of his deputies, Frank Coakley, spent his free time beating the drums for Al Smith.*[10] As might have been expected in the late 1920's, when the country seemed to have achieved not only permanent prosperity but also permanent Republican possession of the White House in Washington and the Governor's Mansion in Sacramento, Warren's staff was predominantly Republican.

"Well," suggested a former deputy district attorney when asked how the office had reacted to the coming of the New Deal, "let's say it was 'tolerated.'"

"There was a lot of grumbling about the alphabet-soup agencies," says a colleague, "but the Chief kept saying, 'Give 'em a chance, give 'em a chance.'"

One February morning in 1935, when a young lawyer in the office was bent over his desk making notes for a brief, with open lawbooks spread as far as his arms could reach, Warren came striding in, his face flushed with indignation.

"He started slamming the books shut," the ex-deputy recalls. "'Throw 'em away,' he said. 'Forget 'em. They're no good now. Contracts don't mean anything any more.' He'd just got word of the Supreme Court's decision on the Gold Clause Cases."

Congress, in June, 1933, had approved a joint resolution voiding the clauses in public and private bonds pledging redemption in gold. Instead, government obligations were to be discharged with legal tender. Thus, purchasers of Liberty Bonds containing a promise to pay in gold would be paid in dollars. They would receive face value ($1.00) rather than the full gold value ($1.69). By a five-to-four vote the sovereign privilege of the state to welch on its debts was affirmed by the Court. Such is its power that a switch of one vote would immediately have added $100 billion to the nation's debt and, in the words of F.D.R., would have invalidated "the chief foundations of the whole recovery program."[11]

In 1936, rounding out his two-year term as chairman of the Republican State Central Committee, Warren led the California delegation to the national convention that chose Governor Landon of Kansas as the party's sacrificial offering to the electorate. In an effort to kidnap the delegation, William Randolph Hearst had fielded a slate of delegates headed by Governor Frank Merriam and

* Coakley later succeeded to the office and still holds it.

pledged to Landon. Warren had successfully countered this ploy by putting his own name at the head of a rival ticket technically committed to his candidacy but, in reality, unpledged.[12] In the battle between the two sets of Republican delegates, Warren had spared the party pain by fighting Hearst rather than Landon.

"The Landon sentiment, which has been sweeping the country, has moved from the East and Middle West into the Pacific Coast States and is making itself felt in California," he dutifully declared in July,[13] two months after he had gone to San Francisco to participate in a celebration of the first anniversary of the Supreme Court's "sick-chicken" decision killing NRA (National Recovery Administration).

"We are celebrating today the anniversary of that great pronouncement of our Supreme Court nullifying the first major effort to change by stealth, and under the guise of recovery legislation, the greatest free government of all time into a totalitarian state wherein men are but the pawns of a dictator, and of the mock government which clothes dictators and their bureaucracy with an air of benevolence and respectability."[14]

And some weeks later, in September, 1936, he continued the attack: "People in all sections are realizing more and more the fallacies of the Roosevelt regime of impractical experimentation and the unbridled waste of public funds which come from every wageearner through hidden taxes, as well as from the pockets of taxpayers on property and income."[15]

Nearly a year after Roosevelt's devastating victory (only Maine and Vermont were Electoral College dropouts), Warren stood among the Republican ruins and stoutly maintained, "The Republican party still stands for every humanitarian principle, and its rehabilitation into a living, vibrant organization will enable it to speak for the people."[16] The party's major campaign contributors seem to have accepted the statement as nothing more than a ritualistic chant, the sort of thing a politician was expected to say. Apparently they had no idea the words might ever be taken seriously.

"He's a Democrat and doesn't know it," Truman said in 1948,[17] but Warren is a Bull Moose Republican who came of age in a time of reform, when the first Roosevelt was shaking a big stick at the trusts and the Progressives were reclaiming California from the railroads and returning it to the residents. *

At the start of his junior year at the University of California, Warren heard a bully Charter Day address by Colonel Roosevelt, who had just come home from potting large African animals. "I always pictured him as a great big robust man," the Chief Justice says, "but he was a short fellow with a high-pitched voice." The following year, while Warren was working on his J.D. thesis, Governor Hiram Johnson was redeeming the platform pledges of the Progressives.

The state constitution was rewritten to eliminate corrupt political machines by providing for popular, nonpartisan government. To the confusion of outlanders, who regard the workings of California politics as a mystery beyond the comprehension of the uninitiated, the basic reforms of Governor Johnson and the Lincoln-Roosevelt League are still the law of this bizarre land.

The voters continue to do their own lawmaking by means of the initiative and the referendum, and if they get fed up with a public official before his term expires, they can use the recall procedure to remove him. The initiative and the referendum enable Californians to enact laws the legislature fails to pass or prefers to submit directly to the people. The initiative is brought into play to amend the state constitution or simply to put a new law on the books. The referendum permits the people to pass upon an act of the legislature.[19]

By paying the market price for the number of signatures required to place a proposition on California's bewildering ballot, any crackpot with enough money (or, in the case of pension promoters, enough disciples) may submit the idiocy of his choice to the electorate. Fortunately for the state's solvency and sanity, the voters — with a few distressing exceptions — have usually faced up to their ignorance of the complicated proposals put before them and have sensibly voted No. But the same voter who turns down greyhound racing is equally inclined to reject an initiative measure calling for modernization of California's unwieldy constitution, and

---

* "Warren may be a Democrat under Truman's definition," the late Henry Wallace said in the 1948 campaign, "but Roosevelt would never have called him one."[18]

on the same ballot he is likely to express routine approval of some elderly, unimaginative officeholder simply because the man already has the job and, by law, his name heads the list of candidates.

Bernadette Doyle, a Communist organizer, once ran up 450,000 votes on a Democratic ballot containing the name of two Doyles. This was the result of another Hiram Johnson legacy, California's unique cross-filing primary law. Designed to do away with party bosses, the law permitted a candidate for public office to file in the primary of any political party. Until 1954 it was not even necessary for an office-seeker to inform the voters of his actual party affiliation.[20]

In order to run in the general election, a candidate had to win the nomination of his own party in the primary, but in a state heavily populated by newcomers who didn't know the names of local politicians, and by old settlers who kept moving from one legislative district to another, it was not too difficult for an active, personable campaigner to walk away from the primaries as the candidate of both major parties, as generally happened with incumbent secretaries of state, controllers, treasurers, attorneys general and members of the Board of Equalization.

More than half of the California Congressional races were decided in the 1940 primary, and four years later 90 per cent of the candidates for state senator won the nomination of both major parties. Governor Warren got a free ride in November, 1946, after emerging from the June primary as the candidate of the Democratic party as well as the Republican.

"In the West no one is barred," Warren said in 1948. "We have a sort of wild and woolly political arena. Everyone is on his own — and the devil takes the hindmost. Everyone is a potential candidate for every office. Everyone runs on every ticket. Our people register one way, and usually vote another. Even carpetbaggers are not resented — that is, if they tell us they're going to stay."[21]

Cross-filing reached its ultimate absurdity in the Thirty-sixth Assembly District in 1948 when the Republicans nominated a Democrat and the Democrats nominated a Republican, but both candidates were rejected by the voters of their own parties. As a result, neither was eligible to run in the general election. In 1959 a Democratic legislature repealed cross-filing, despite the opposition of incumbents of both parties who felt that its retention would help keep them in office.

Originally, cross-filing professed to serve only the idealistic cause of nonpartisan government. In practice, it was used by Republican reformers to thwart obstructionists within the party's ranks. When a Johnson Republican ran for the legislature, he registered as a Progressive and cross-filed as a Republican. With luck, he might win both nominations and in the process knock off a Republican reactionary. If he failed to make the grade as a Republican, however, he could still run in the general election as a Progressive.

"He comes from the loins of labor," an enthusiastic union leader said in 1942 when Warren was campaigning for governor,[22] but a more accurate political genealogy has been supplied by George E. Mowry, the historian of the Progressive movement in California. After describing the middle-class professional men, mostly lawyers and journalists, who put Hiram Johnson in the governor's office, Mowry sketched a composite portrait of a 1910 Progressive, which might have served equally well for Earl Warren a generation later:

"He was educated, intelligent, able. A man of unquestioned sincerity and public integrity, he was also benevolently aware of the underprivileged groups around him."[23]

In the six years of Progressive government under Hiram Johnson (1911–1917), California enjoyed the most enlightened administration it had ever seen, but in the 1920's conservative Republicans came back into power. By the time Warren first began to make a splash in state politics, Johnson was a remote, ill-tempered voice in the United States Senate, fulminating against the Yellow Peril. The Progressive party had grown old and tired, its proud prewar banners stained and shabby.

"A Progressive is a man who is afraid to be a Democrat and ashamed to be a Republican," one of the Assembly's three Democrats said during a 1931 debate on a proposal to abolish cross-filing.[24]

The bill was defeated. Seven years later, when Warren ran for attorney general, he filed as a Republican and cross-filed on the Democratic and Progressive tickets. The Assembly, meanwhile, had become so heavily infiltrated with Democrats that at the 1937 session they had achieved a majority (47 out of 80). The Senate was still safely in Republican hands (40 to 16), but the Depression and the New Deal had radically altered the state's political composition.

In 1930, midway in Herbert Hoover's luckless administration, registered Republicans in California enjoyed a three-to-one edge over Democrats. Two years later, when F.D.R. was swept into the White House, the gap had narrowed (1,556,264 Republicans; 1,161,482 Democrats). By 1934, the Democrats had pulled ahead (1,555,705 to 1,430,198). In the general election of 1932, California Democrats had elected a United States Senator (William Gibbs McAdoo), but had not been given an opportunity to vote for a governor. When their big chance came in 1934, a funny thing happened to them on the way to Sacramento. They ran into Upton Sinclair and something called EPIC (End Poverty in California).[25]

"Gentlemen — and ladies — this is not politics," the Los Angeles *Times* thundered a few weeks before the election. "It is war."[26]

George C. Creel, who handled Woodrow Wilson's relations with the press during World War I, looked forward in the early spring of 1934 to becoming the first Democrat to be elected governor of California in the twentieth century. His only opposition was Upton Sinclair, a Socialist writer newly turned Democratic politician. It was perhaps fitting that Creel, who had come to national notice as a propagandist, should be undone by a pamphlet.

This remarkable document, *I, Governor of California and How I Ended Poverty; A True Story of the Future,* gave Sinclair's campaign its title, EPIC, and helped bury Creel in the primary (436,000 to 288,000). Among other things, Sinclair proposed to use scrip to finance new state undertakings and to soak the rich to provide pensions for the elderly, the incapacitated and the widowed. The state would also establish land colonies and operate idle factories, producing for use rather than for profit.[27]

"Sinclair's plan is a false lure to the voters," Warren said when he visited Los Angeles in early October, a few days after Republican leaders meeting in Sacramento had elected him chairman.[28]

He was drowned out by the shrill voice of the *Times:* "The threat to sovietize California is as much a call to militant patriotism in defense of the State as would be the appearance of a hostile fleet off our coast."[29] The editors were too busy holding back the red hordes to give much space to Warren, but he was approvingly identified as "one of the younger progressive Republicans."[30]

Warren's friends among California lawmen were susceptible victims to the EPIC hysteria. While Sinclair was being denounced as a Moscow agent, the anti-Christ, a vegetarian, a pacifist, a believer in telepathy and a millionaire, the police chiefs of Los Angeles and San Francisco were addressing the Fourteenth Annual Convention of the California Peace Officers Association in Pasadena, explaining how the Communists were warping the minds of the American people in their efforts to put radical leaders in public office.

"It is our job to go out and enlighten the general public and tell them who and what Communists are . . . " the San Francisco police chief said,[31] and his Los Angeles counterpart, who also professed to be an expert Marxman, explained how the Communists were recruiting Negroes.

"They say to the ignorant Black of the South, 'Under Communism marriage is not a necessity. If you want the mistress in whose home you work, the lady of the house, she can be your possession under Communism. If you want to live with a white woman one day, a week, a month or a year, that is your right and privilege under our form of government. If you want to live with three hundred and sixty-five different white women in a year, that is your right under Communism, our form of government.' "*

"The issue is between Americanism and extreme radicalism," Warren said in a radio talk at the height of the campaign to save California from a program he denounced as "a foreign philosophy of government, half Socialistic and half Communistic."[32]

With Sinclair as governor, it was feared, California would become an open-air asylum for the aged and indolent, the ill and the indigent. Vagrants would swarm across the golden land like an infestation, stripping it naked. Already taxpayers were supporting

---

* One of the paragraphs in the resolution adopted by the peace officers has a strangely contemporary ring: "Communists recognize constituted authority and police departments in particular as definite deterrents and barriers to the fulfillment of their program of force and violence, and therefore, are organizing public sentiment in opposition to the police, alleging 'police terror,' 'police brutality,' and other charges, thus diverting attention from the actual situation, as has happened in other nations prior to the time the Communist uprisings occurred . . ."

some 1,250,000 Californians living on relief. The majority of them (70 per cent) were residents of Southern California, where the latitude for lunacy has always been generous, particularly when it has taken the form of an eccentric religious, political or economic faith.

When leaders of both major parties gathered in Sacramento in late September to organize for the 1934 campaign, the Republicans had no choice but to unite behind the affable, uninspiring incumbent, Governor Merriam. In a good-natured, back-slapping mood, the delegates sang out their approval of Earl Warren as state chairman. Down the street, the Democrats were snarling at one another, torn apart by Sinclair's candidacy. When the bloodletting was over, the new state chairman was a tall, white-haired Los Angeles attorney, Culbert L. Olson.

In November, after one of the most bitterly fought campaigns in the state's history, Sinclair was sent home to write a sequel (*I, Candidate for Governor and How I Got Licked*), but his friend Olson was elected to represent Los Angeles County in the state senate. He looked like the man to beat in 1938, when the Democrats would get another chance to take over the Governor's Mansion.

5

The Red Harvest

. . . where you have a Mexican camp and they tell you
to keep out, a couple of these vomiting candles just
tossed over the fence will start them going . . .
— A CHEMICAL WARFARE GAS MANUFACTURER
TO THE CALIFORNIA SHERIFFS
ASSOCIATION, 1934[1]

ONE evening in the late spring of 1938, when Judge Robert W.
Kenny was driving home with a Superior Court colleague,
Judge Fletcher Bowron, the two men got to talking politics, and
Bowron, a Republican, asked Kenny, a Democrat, if he would
cross party lines and support Earl Warren for attorney general.
Although he was raising money for the state ticket headed by Cul-
bert Olson and was a candidate for his seat in the state senate,
Kenny agreed to endorse the Alameda County Republican.

"I was probably the only active Democrat in Southern California
that he knew personally," Kenny recalls. "I'd met him some years
earlier when we were both in Sacramento lobbying against a bill
that would have had the effect of granting a ninety-day leave of
absence for bail-bond jumpers. He came down to Los Angeles and
we had lunch together. I told him it would be a lot easier for me if
he'd make some kind of statement on civil rights."[2]

Warren made his statement on July 20th in a handwritten letter to
Kenny, who endorsed him three days later as "the only candidate I
can support for attorney general."[3]

"I believe," Warren wrote, "that the American concept of civil
rights should include not only an observance of our Constitutional

Bill of Rights, but also the absence of arbitrary action by government in every field and the existence of a spirit of fair play on the part of public officials toward all that will prevent government from using ever present opportunities to abuse power through the harassment of the individual."

In California during the 1930's the individual most in need of relief from the abusive power of government was the migrant farm worker. His ranks had nearly doubled, rising from 190,000 in 1930 to 350,000 by the end of the decade when *The Grapes of Wrath* was published. As Carey McWilliams points out in *California: The Great Exception,* it was essential for employers to see that this mobile labor pool should be large (to protect farmers from having to bid against one another for stoop labor) and unorganized (to provide continued control of wages and working conditions).[4]

When organizers began to turn up in the fields and orchards and vineyards where illiterate Mexicans were working as peons, living in innocence of modern sanitation and the United States Constitution, they were put under surveillance by members of the California Peace Officers Association, whose interpretation of the First Amendment right to speak freely and assemble peaceably was constricted by a professional prejudice against anyone bent on disturbing the established order. Union organizers were indiscriminately regarded as Communists (as some of them unquestionably were). In the lexicon of law enforcement, "Communist" and "radical" were usually synonymous.

"It was around 1929, I think, that we first became conscious of the fact that Russian Communists were beginning to infiltrate California," says a former member of Warren's staff who worked closely with the Peace Officers Association in keeping tabs on the migrant labor camps. "We were having a lot of trouble, strikes in the fields, groups of labor being organized that had never been organized before. Mexicans were being organized. The people who were organizing them were radicals. It was an open challenge to law enforcement. We began to build up the first record of Communist activity in California."

A representative of Warren's office, attending the 1933 convention of the California Peace Officers Association, urged the delegates to forward information on the movement's leaders to Clarence

Morrill, chief of the State Bureau of Criminal Identification and Investigation. "They move around a great deal," he said, stressing the importance of keeping files up to date.[5] When Morrill queried Warren about an Alameda resident in the summer of 1938, one of his inspectors was able to reply promptly that the man "was reported as a subscriber to *People's World*."[6]

Following a series of agricultural strikes in 1933, California's large industrial interests got behind a move to combine local and regional farm associations into one powerful organization. In the past, farmers had joined together to promote the interests of one crop or one valley. On March 28, 1934, with the formation of the Associated Farmers of California, they united against the common enemy, the organizer (or "agitator") preaching the alien gospel of collective bargaining.[7]

"You would be surprised how those fellows hang together," the Glenn County sheriff said in May, 1938,[8] after the organization had regrouped its forces to wage guerrilla warfare against the National Labor Relations Act, the Magna Carta of the labor movement, popularly known as the Wagner Act.

As Commissioner of Immigration and Housing in California for four years, with responsibility for inspecting some five thousand agricultural labor camps, Carey McWilliams came to be an expert on the machinations of the Associated Farmers. He viewed the organization with admiration and revulsion, struck by its efficiency and its ruthlessness.

"Carefully coordinated from the top, the organizational network functions with clocklike precision, policing entire crop industries, enforcing uniform decisions, holding recalcitrant employers in line. When the need arises, the full weight of this powerful apparatus can be brought to bear upon any threatened sector of the agricultural front with crushing force and effectiveness. Local, county, state, and, on occasion, federal officials jump when the Associated Farmers crack the whip."[9]

The Associated Farmers attracted the interest of the Senate subcommittee selected in June, 1936, "to make an investigation of violations of the right of free speech and assembly and undue interference with the right of labor to organize and bargain collectively."[10] Under the chairmanship of Senator Robert M. La Follette, Jr., the subcommittee began its California investigation in October, 1938, and a year later held twenty-eight days of hearings in the state over a period of three months (November and December, 1939; January, 1940). In February, 1942, somewhat shaken by what it had seen and heard, the La Follette Committee reported that its California findings were "almost beyond belief."[11]

"Unemployment, underemployment, disorganized and haphazard migrancy, lack of adequate wages or annual income, bad housing, insufficient education, little medical care, the great public burden of relief, the denial of civil liberties, riots, strife, corruption, are all part and parcel of this autocratic system of labor relations that has for decades dominated California's agricultural industry."[12]

Among its exhibits, the subcommittee included a hardsell sales pitch for chemical warfare gas given the California Sheriffs Association at its 1934 convention. "Any time any of you people want any information, we will be glad to have you call on us," said a genial spokesman for the Lake Erie Chemical Company of San Francisco.[13] Along with ordinary tear gas, he recommended the use of vomiting gas in special situations. For example, he said, "where you have a Mexican camp and they tell you to keep out, a couple of these vomiting candles just tossed over the fence will start them going and your two or three thousand Mexicans will decide to move and move very suddenly and you will never have them back in your county again."

In November, 1938, after his election as attorney general (he won it in the August primary by getting the nomination of both major parties), Warren was preparing to turn his Oakland office over to Ralph E. Hoyt, his chief assistant, when the La Follette Committee wrote him a letter asking if Alameda County happened to have any ordinances on its books regulating the use of public sidewalks and highways, the distribution of handbills, and the holding of parades on public streets and meetings in public parks.[14] The lame-duck district attorney sent the committee copies of Ordinances 281 and 282.

"These two ordinances were enacted as part of a definite program to improve the working conditions of our migratory workers and to avoid the riots and other disturbances which resulted in bloodshed in many counties of California during the year 1933-34," Warren wrote. "In this county we have a perishable pea crop in the spring; in fact, it is so perishable that if the pea crop is ripe in the morning and it is not harvested until afternoon it is not marketable. This crop has been harvested for years by migratory workers, and we have from four to six thousand workers engaged in that employment, depending upon the acreage to be harvested.

"While over 99% of the workers came to the county in good faith to harvest the crop, yet there was a mere handful of agitators who followed them for the purpose of creating disturbances and to see that the crop was not harvested. This handful of men adopted a very well-defined technique. Briefly, their method was to drive automobiles on the highways in such a way as to block the highway in the neighborhood of a farm where pea pickers were working, and when the highway was so blocked up, this group would start a disturbance for the purpose and with the intent to frighten the workers and to create a general breach of the peace."[15]

Along with the two county ordinances, Warren sent the La Follette Committee copies of three editorials which had appeared in the San Francisco *News* in the spring of 1934, headed: "Keep Our Valleys Smiling," "Two Ways of Fighting Reds" and "Better Than Violence." The editors appealed both to growers and to responsible labor leaders, "who too long have left our agricultural workers to their fate or to the leadership of Communist agitators more interested in revolution than in reform."[16]

In the first editorial, Warren was praised for having arranged a meeting of local growers and peace officers on the eve of the 1934 harvest. They had met in Centerville, the heart of the pea-growing district, and listened to a federal official who had just concluded an investigation of a strike by lettuce-pickers in the Imperial Valley. The government man had signed a report which the *News* approvingly quoted:

"We recommend that federal and state governments exercise every power and authority to maintain in fact the rights of free speech, free press and free assembly, and that men, either citizens or aliens, shall not be harassed by permanent, temporary, amateur, or self-appointed officers of the law.

"We recommend that the federal government encourage the

organization of workers, in order that collective bargaining may be effective in matters of wages and conditions, both working and living, and that the right to strike and peacefully picket shall be maintained."[17]

"In the Imperial Valley," the second editorial observed, "attorneys representing the strikers have been kidnapped, beaten up, and thrown out on the desert many miles from the nearest town." This violence was contrasted with a letter from R. H. Chamberlain, an assistant district attorney in Warren's office, written toward the end of the 1934 pea harvest: "There has been no disorder whatever and the workers appear to have been satisfied with prevailing conditions — both as to pay and as to living accommodations. The latter have been better this year than ever before . . ."[18]

The third editorial quoted at great length a letter Warren had written to Simon J. Lubin, author of the law establishing the Commission on Immigration and Housing, which had been working to improve the lot of the migrant worker. In his letter, Warren told how peace had come to the county's pea fields:

". . . we advised the farmer that the problem of avoiding violence and disorder was not a one-sided affair; that the question was not alone to assure to the growers a profitable harvest, and that it would be necessary to provide proper living conditions for the pickers and pay them an adequate wage. We emphasized the fact that there must be no 'vigilante' group formed, nor would any private citizens be deputized as sheriffs . . .

"I desire to say that subsequent events have confirmed the splendid spirit in which the farmers have cooperated with us throughout the harvest. With very few exceptions — and they occasioned no trouble whatever — the leading farmers of Alameda County have provided the drinking water and other facilities suggested and required by Mr. Edwards of the State Housing Commission . . .

"One of your suggestions to Mr. Chamberlain was that we use every effort to prevent dishonest labor contractors from complicating the situation. We have endeavored to put this suggestion into force and I am glad to say that the pickers have in each case received what they earned without the possibility of any labor contractor retaining a large share of the wages . . .

"Although more than four thousand migratory workers have been in Alameda County this year, assisting in the pea harvest, not a single violation of the law has occurred and not one arrest has been necessary or has been made. Of course, as was expected, a handful of Communist agitators made their appearance when the harvest first got under way and they have constantly attempted to foment trouble among the pickers. Due to the fact that every precaution had been taken to insure, as I have said, proper living conditions and adequate compensation, they made no impression. We have records of instances in which the occupants of a camp merely laughed and jeered at the Communist agitators who were trying to persuade them to quit work and go on strike. In every quarter the pickers have expressed themselves as satisfied with conditions."[19]

"I congratulate you heartily," Lubin replied.[20]

After Warren left the district attorney's office, a search of its records failed to turn up a single prosecution under the two county ordinances he had sent the La Follette Committee.[21] Similar anti-picketing laws had been passed in other counties and in other states. In the spring of 1940, the Supreme Court struck down two such ordinances, one from Shasta County (*Carlson v. California*). In both instances Justice Murphy spoke for the Court, declaring that "publicizing the facts of a labor dispute in a peaceful way through appropriate means, whether by pamphlet, by word of mouth or by banner, must now be regarded as within that liberty of communication which is secured to every person by the Fourteenth Amendment against abridgement by a State."[22]

"As for the Constitution, it does not seem too much to say that it is gone," Justice McReynolds extemporized in dissent when five of his brothers decided the *Gold Clause Cases* (1935) in favor of the New Dealers.[23]

In another five-to-four ruling a year earlier, Chief Justice Hughes had spoken for the Court in upholding a Minnesota law designed to help farmers hold onto their farms by putting off the foreclosure of mortgages. "While emergency does not create power," he wrote, "emergency may furnish the occasion for the exercise of power."[24] The same squeeze put on Minnesota lawmakers by depressed farmers (mobs were forming to prevent foreclosures) had been applied by dairymen to the New York legislature, which had passed a milk-control law establishing a board to set minimum retail prices.

Leo Nebbia, a Rochester grocer, stumbled into the history of constitutional law by selling two quarts of milk and a five-cent loaf of bread for eighteen cents, the price of the milk alone. He was tried and convicted. By another five-to-four vote, the Court sustained the price-fixing law on grounds staked out in a 1927 dissent of Justice Stone in a case involving the prices New York brokers were charging for theater tickets: "Self-interest is not permitted to invoke constitutional protection at the expense of the public interest . . ."[25]

Whatever hopes the Minnesota mortgage and New York milk decisions may have aroused in New Deal breasts in 1934 were dampened early the following year. In January, the Court voted overwhelmingly (only one dissenter) to strike down the section of the National Industrial Recovery Act which delegated to the President the power to regulate interstate shipments of petroleum produced in excess of quota limits.[26] The "hot oil" case was followed a few weeks later by an adverse ruling on a railroad retirement scheme setting up a pension plan for superannuated employees. Justice Roberts, a former railroad lawyer, wrote the five-to-four opinion doing the elderly railroad workers out of their pensions.[27]

Finally, on "Black Monday" — May 27, 1935 — the Court decided *Schechter Poultry Corp. v. United States,* testing the constitutionality of the law establishing the National Recovery Administration.[28] Among other violations of the NRA code for the live poultry industry, the four Schechter brothers had been charged with undercutting their competitors by selling diseased chickens at four to eight cents a pound below the market price.

Chief Justice Hughes, speaking for a unanimous Court, found the law an unconstitutional delegation of legislative power. Also, in the Chief Justice's opinion, the sick chickens sold by the Schechter brothers "had come to a permanent rest within the state,"[29] and, as a consequence, were not involved in interstate commerce. It was this aspect of the decision which prompted F.D.R. to comment that "we have been relegated to the horse-and-buggy definition of interstate commerce."[30]

In 1937, following the Roosevelt-Landon election returns and the President's proposal to lighten the judicial burdens of the "Nine Old Men" by giving them the assistance of some younger brothers, the Court began to see the New Deal in a more favorable constitutional light. As the current joke had it, "A switch in time saves nine." A state minimum wage law similar to one held invalid in June, 1936, was found to be acceptable the following March.[31] Two weeks later decisions in five National Labor Relations Board cases upheld the constitutionality of the Wagner Act,[32] which had goaded the Associated Farmers into such a violent struggle against collective bargaining as to bring the La Follette Committee scurrying out to California.

"The Nation faces again the periodic necessity of restating our national ideals and determining the place to be occupied by agricultural workers in a democratic society," the Committee declared in its final report, after having described its mission as an attempt "to throw full light and understanding upon the task of making the adjustments that a democracy must make when men who work the land are largely separated from rights of property in it."[33]

By the time the La Follette Committee got to California in the fall of 1939, its ears had been bent by every imaginable variation on the cry of "Communism" as an excuse for the use of unconstitutional methods to suppress the legitimate activities of organized labor. But it had heard nothing to compare with the shrieks of rage and pain which arose in the feudal valleys ruled by the Associated Farmers whenever their economic nerve-ends were touched by any mention of fair wages and flush toilets. The Committee sought to reason with this hysteria in its report:

"If the legislative bodies of this Nation had declared membership in the Communist party or sympathy with its objectives to be contrary to law, depriving the guilty person of his rights under our Constitution, and that law had been declared constitutional, then the charge of Communist affiliations in labor bodies or strikes would be a pertinent subject of inquiry for a body given the responsibility of investigating violations of labor's rights.

"But beliefs and political affiliations are not unlawful under our present system of laws. And so, regardless of their political affiliations, strikers, strike leaders, outside sympathizers or union organizers were possessed of rights to meet and discuss their grievances with employers, to organize into trade unions for the lawful purpose of collective bargaining, and to conduct lawful activities, including the use of strikes and picketing, to bring economic and moral pressure on employers to meet their demands.

"Undue and unlawful interferences with the lawful exercise of these rights will not be condoned or excused by true adherents of democratic government under our Constitution because of unpopular and misguided political affiliations of the victims. There are laws on the statute books for the detention and punishment of treason, criminal conspiracy, sabotage, violence, and crimes against the state. They should be vigorously enforced against offenders. But that, as yet, is a separate question from the right to organize into trade unions, bargain collectively, strike, and picket peacefully.

"Yet this issue of the allegedly communistic character of some of the leaders of agricultural unions in some of the strikes was constantly adverted to by employers and their spokesmen throughout the course of the investigation. It is a material factor in the thinking of many people about the whole problem and charges the atmosphere of [the] California agricultural labor struggle with a bitterness, distrust, and hatred that beggars description."[34]

The bitterness, distrust, and hatred were so deeply rooted in the thinking of California peace officers that twenty-five years after the La Follette Committee hearings, one of Warren's former "crime-crushers" could say with complete conviction: "The committee was infiltrated with Commies."

The fight to keep California out of the Kremlin's clutches took a judicial turn in the summer of 1940 when Governor Olson selected Professor Max Radin to fill a vacancy on the State Supreme Court. A liberal Democrat, active in politics, he had supported Olson in his gubernatorial campaign and had been commuting from Boalt Hall to Sacramento to serve as one of his advisers during his first year and a half in office.[35]

"Concerning Prof. Radin's intellectual equipment and knowledge of the law there appears to be no question," the Los Angeles *Times* declared, "but, unfortunately, the same cannot be said of his political and social views."[36]

"I am not a Communist, as everyone knows," Radin insisted.[37]

His nomination was submitted to the Judicial Qualifications Commission, composed of the state's chief justice, its senior appellate justice and Attorney General Warren. Ordinarily approval was a routine matter, but in such feverish times, when Europe was falling to the Nazis and the United States seemed to have been captured by left-wingers and one-worlders, the appointment of a liberal law professor to the state's highest bench was cause for patriotic concern.

While the San Francisco *Chronicle* was urging Radin's confirmation, "with no more of the scurrilous attack that arises from inability to distinguish between liberal faith and subversive character,"[38] the professor was being denounced by the American Legion as a supporter of radical doctrines, and as "an extreme leftist" by the San Joaquin County Bar Association and the Stockton Chamber of Commerce.[39]

"He has spoken at radical meetings and he has been warmly defended (without protest on his part) by Communists of the reddest hue," according to the Los Angeles *Times*, which seemed to feel the professor's viewpoint was "out of line with the requirements of the times."[40]

"Today only men who are above suspicion should be permitted to hold important government positions," said Assemblyman Sam W. Yorty,[41] who was later to tangle with the *Times* when he became mayor of Los Angeles and the paper passed into the enlightened hands of a new generation of owners.

Yorty, in 1940, was presiding over a legislative committee investigating allegations of subversive activity on the part of State Relief Administration employees. Eighteen of them had been arrested on contempt charges after refusing to answer questions about Communist affiliations. Also, nearly twenty years before the Warren Court invoked the protection of the Constitution for the National Association for the Advancement of Colored People when it was up against a similar situation in Alabama,[42] the defendants had refused to put their CIO union membership list in the hostile hands of the Yorty committee.

"If they should be found guilty," Professor Radin had written the city attorney prosecuting the cases, "I wonder if it would not be proper to suggest to the judge that a nominal fine or suspended sentence would fully meet the needs of justice . . ."[43]

He had also written to a friend in Stockton who had formerly practiced law with the judge trying the cases. Radin had asked the attorney to "speak a word for a light sentence to the judge," after first pointing out that the young defendants had already been severely punished. They had been fired, blacklisted and hauled off to Stockton's notorious jail, where they had been held under "vastly too great bail." As the professor explained, he was simply trying "to soften the blow I'm afraid will be delivered at the poor youngsters."[44]

In retrospect, Radin's letters may seem merely a gentle expression of compassion, but they were regarded as improper, even inflammatory, by his right-wing critics and as injudicious by others who admired the professor but questioned the wisdom of his appointment on the basis of his temperament rather than his politics.

"A great shock to me," Governor Olson said in late July[45] after Attorney General Warren emerged from a lengthy meeting of the Judicial Qualifications Commission and announced: "We have considered all the facts in connection with the nomination, including the report from the board of governors of the State Bar, and we have come to the conclusion that the nomination should not be confirmed."[46]

In Berkeley, where Radin is remembered with great affection by former students and colleagues, there is a residual feeling of disappointment that the brilliant writer and teacher, the son of immigrants, never achieved his lifelong ambition to sit on the bench, but there is little evidence of resentment against Warren for his part in blocking the appointment.

"Max was charming," says one of his former colleagues. "He discoursed volubly and well on all subjects, often with a scanty background. He was possessed of such an active imagination that he had trouble at times distinguishing fact from fantasy. I would rather have had him as a companion than as a judge."

"A very fine man," said Stephen W. Downey, a prominent Sacramento Democrat whose brother, Sheridan, served two terms in the United States Senate (1939–1951). "A little bit woosey, like some of the rest of us are probably, but a good man, an honest man."[47]

"I think Max Radin was a marvelous character," said Jesse W. Carter, the fighting liberal on the state Supreme Court from January, 1939, until his death nearly twenty years later. In Carter's view, Radin was "a wonderful lawyer and wonderful man," who was blackballed by Warren for, among other reasons, his criticism of the way Warren had handled the prosecution of a waterfront killing aboard the S.S. *Point Lobos* in 1936.*[48]

Radin was rejected without being given a chance to answer the charges brought against him, or even to know what the charges were and who had made them. Olson wanted him to make a fight for his seat on the bench, but neither the diminutive professor nor his wife had the stomach for it. Reluctantly, his name was withdrawn but not before the governor had asked him if he could recommend some other outstanding professor of law for the job.

"Yes, of course," he said. "Roger Traynor."[49]

Traynor was not only distinguished as a teacher and scholar, but also as an authority on taxation. He had drafted the Retail Sales Tax Act of 1933, and had recently been brought into Warren's office to organize a tax division and to take charge of tax cases in state and federal courts. At forty, he was a full professor of law at Boalt Hall, a part-time deputy attorney general and a tax consultant to the Secretary of the Treasury.

"It was a complete surprise," Traynor says of his nomination, which breezed through the same commission that had turned down Radin.

Traynor, a gentle dynamo with a quiet voice and a roaring laugh, is now Chief Justice of the California Supreme Court, and in the view of Justice Walter V. Schaefer of the Illinois Supreme Court "he has been for many years our number one judge."[50]

Before Olson ornamented it with Carter, Traynor and Phil Gibson, the California Supreme Court had been a traditional sanctuary for legal mediocrity and political conservatism. If a piece of liberal legislation passed the assembly, which was apportioned on the basis of population, it risked sudden death in the senate, where a rural majority had the whiphand. If it slipped past the senators, its opponents could count on a friendly welcoming committee of right-thinking judges when it got to the Supreme Court.

"After you had served the vested interests in the state for years in fighting labor unions, defeating social legislation in the courts and

* Justice Carter had a low opinion of Warren's ability as a lawyer. "He couldn't find his way to a courtroom door," he grumbled to intimates, but he lived to change his mind after Warren had served five terms as Chief Justice.

squabbling over water rights," Carey McWilliams once wrote, "tradition dictated that your last years should be spent, in semi-retirement, serving these same interests on the Supreme Court."[51]

Ironically, at the time his nomination was turned down, Radin was drafting an amendment to the state constitution, backed by Olson, calling for the abolition of the state senate and the creation of a unicameral legislature apportioned on the basis of population.[52] If the proposal had been adopted in 1940, when Attorney General Warren voted against its author, California senators would not have been forced to sign their own political death warrants twenty-five years later, as required by the ruling handed down by Chief Justice Warren in *Reynolds v. Sims* (1964).

6

At Sea with the Law

I won't give up the ship!
— TONY CORNERO, 1939[1]

AFTER taking the oath of office as attorney general in Oakland at the county courthouse, Warren moved across the bay to his new, oak-paneled, sixth-floor office in the State Building facing the Civic Center in San Francisco. He had hardly walked into the office at nine o'clock Monday morning, January 2, 1939, before he got a tip from a Sacramento banker on the State Board of Prison and Paroles that some hankypanky had apparently been going on in the issuance of paroles. The private secretary of the outgoing governor — a Republican — was suspected of having put them up for sale. Warren also learned that in the last hours of his administration the governor had appointed this same young man to the bench. In fact, he was to serve as a Superior Court judge in Warren's own bailiwick, Alameda County.

This bit of Republican skulduggery gave the incoming attorney general a chance to make good at once on his campaign pledge of an honest, efficient, nonpartisan system of law enforcement. He hurried over to Sacramento, where the first Democratic governor in forty-four years was being inaugurated. Once he had laid the charges before Olson, Warren returned to San Francisco to interview a tavern-keeper who was reported to have made a five-hundred-dollar payoff for the commutation of a life sentence imposed on a convicted killer. Governor Merriam's ex-secretary ended up in court as a prisoner rather than as a judge.[2]

"When I came into office there were seven tracks holding dog races," Warren later recalled. "There was no supervision over these tracks; the odds were fixed, and so were the dogs. It was just a plain racket and I made up my mind that this open violation must stop. Every track had its own season, so they did not conflict with each other, and the track which happened to be open at the time was El Cerrito, run by Black Jack Jerome, a former San Francisco strike-breaker. Our office worked up the whole case, and when we were ready to go into court, I asked Jerome to come to see me. He asked if he might bring his lawyer. I said yes, and when they arrived I told them, 'I don't want to put you out of business the hard way, but you're breaking the law, and you'll have to go.' Jerome asked, 'Are you going to treat all the tracks the same, or are you just picking on us?' When I replied that all tracks would be treated the same, Black Jack asked permission to confer with his lawyer in the outside hall. When they returned a few moments later, he said, 'This is Wednesday. Can we operate through Saturday night, and then close?' "

"I cannot give you permission to continue an illegal activity," Warren said, "but I hardly think this office would be prepared to issue an order until Monday morning, and so if you shut down Saturday night, we would have no reason to issue that complaint."[3]

A few months later, when the operators of two dog tracks in San Mateo County threatened to reopen, Warren shrugged, "If they do, I'll have a lot of dogs on my hands."[4] At the same time, along with slot machines and bingo games, he was making a frontal attack on bookmaking establishments. "Every time you see such a place you can be sure they are paying someone for the privilege to operate," he told California businessmen.[5] Addressing a convention of the state's district attorneys, he said, "There are some business people who will stand for anything as long as it means money in their pockets."[6]

In Southern California, "the greatest single nuisance" confronting the new attorney general was a fleet of four gambling ships operating off the coast.[7] The action was being blatantly advertised over the radio, in newspapers, on billboards and even by skywriters using letters two miles high. This nose-thumbing defiance of the law was too much for Warren. In late July, he descended on Los Angeles fighting mad.

"It is unthinkable that California should tolerate this," he said.[8]

The ships were separating the public from millions of dollars a year, none of which was being returned in the form of taxes. To Warren, the floating casinos were not only "a source of constant temptation" to the public, but also an encouragement to "other law violators to traffic in narcotics and similar evils."

"It is my plan to wipe them out, as I hope to wipe out all other illegal gambling in California," the attorney general told Los Angeles reporters.

"How?" they asked.

"We will find ways and means," he said. "The State is not impotent to put an end to this illegal barricade of our waterfronts."⁹

"This ship is operated by courageous, open-minded, fearless American citizens," said Antonio Stralla, alias Tony Cornero, commanding the fleet's flagship, the *Rex*. (He had lost his interest in one of the other ships, the *Tango*, on a single cut of the cards.)

Warren sent Oscar Jahnsen out to the *Rex* to have a look around and talk to Cornero.

"I'd had a little shooting scrape with Tony about 1922, '23," Jahnsen says. "It was in Los Angeles, at Sunset and Fairfax. I was working for the Treasury then, and he was smuggling Scotch up from Mexico. Well, I took my wife and two schoolteacher friends out to the ship. We had a nice dinner, then I got to gambling. A crooked cop put the finger on me. Tony came up and tapped me on the shoulder. 'Mr. Jahnsen,' he said, 'what can I do for you?' I said, 'Tony, don't you remember Sunset and Fairfax?' and he said, 'Oh yes, of course.' He asked me what I was doing on the ship, and I told him, I said, 'Tony, you're violating the law, you've got to stop.'

"He said, 'No, I'm beyond the three-mile limit. You can't touch me.' Then he took us all over the ship, all four of us. He was particularly proud of his ship-to-shore phone, and at one point he opened up a desk drawer and let me see a big .41 Colt. The Chief told me to tell Cornero he could have a safe escort for all of his gambling equipment, get it across California into Nevada, where it would be legal. Otherwise, he was going to put the ship out of business and the stuff would all get busted or dumped in the ocean."

After two days of conferences with the district attorney and the sheriff of Los Angeles County, along with the police chiefs of Los

Angeles, Long Beach and Santa Monica, Warren suddenly made his move on Friday evening, July 28.

"The time for talk has passed," he said. "Now is the time for action."[10]

Tony Cornero was vacationing in Texas when the lawmen were piped aboard the *Rex* at 7:45 P.M. Some eight hundred customers had taken water-taxis out to the ship for an evening of cards, dice, roulette and bingo. They went on playing as the head of the sheriff's vice squad descended to the lower deck and handed the skipper a five-page legal document ordering him to desist at once.

"We are law-abiding citizens," protested a man identified as the ship's "trustee," and sent word back to Warren that the *Rex* intended to stay in business.[11]

The same orders were given at the same time to the men in charge of the other three ships. The armada's lawyers insisted the vessels were anchored on the high seas, outside the territorial waters of California and beyond the reach of the state courts.

"I do not care whether the four ships operate within or without the so-called three-mile limit," Warren said. "We shall proceed against them regardless of this and regardless of what action is taken in Congress or elsewhere."[12]

A bill outlawing gambling ships was getting a sympathetic hearing from the House Judiciary Committee, but while the lawmakers discussed it in Washington, the lawbreakers continued to operate off the California coast. In fact, business seemed to pick up over the weekend following issuance of the abatement orders. Warren called in Jahnsen and Warren Olney III, assistant attorney general in charge of the criminal division. A battle plan was drawn up.

"It was like a military operation," Olney told Bill Davidson years later.[13] "Since we had only five investigators in our office, we had to use deputy sheriffs from the county of Los Angeles. We knew that many of them were in the pay of the gamblers, so Earl ran the whole thing with the utmost secrecy to avoid a tip-off to the ships. On D-Day, we locked up forty cops and eight accountants in Patriotic Hall in Los Angeles, and the Chief briefed them. Then we transported them to the waterfront in sealed busses, and loaded them directly into waiting patrol boats from the state Fish and Game Authority. The raids went off like clockwork. I later became

an officer in the Marine Corps, but I always remember my experience with Warren's Commandos as my first amphibious operation."

Olney took command of the task force that set out from the
harbor at San Pedro to subdue the *Tango* and the *Mount Baker*
(also known as the *Showboat*), which were anchored off Long
Beach. Jahnsen assembled his forces at the Santa Monica pier for an
attack on the *Rex* and the *Texas*. Warren, along with the sheriff and
the district attorney of Los Angeles County, directed the operation
from a command post established at a beach club on a bluff overlooking the ocean. It was equipped with telescopes and shortwave
radiophones. Officers on motorcycles were standing by, ready to
deliver messages and help take prisoners into custody.

Olney encountered no resistance from the *Tango* and the *Mount
Baker*. The startled skippers quickly capitulated. "My God, cops!"
Olney heard one man say. "And they're not ours!"[14] The *Texas*
also surrendered without a fight, but the *Rex* met the seafaring posse
with fire hoses and heavy steel doors blocking the gangway.

"All right," Warren said when this Mexican standoff was reported
by radiophone, "if they won't let us on, we won't let anyone off. It's
a process of attrition. They've got women aboard whose husbands
don't know they're out gambling, and they've got husbands aboard
whose wives don't know they're out with other girls. Let's see what
happens."[15]

After one night of the blockade, Cornero was begging for mercy.
Warren agreed to spare him the disagreeable death of being ripped
apart by angry customers. A deal was made whereby the customers
were permitted to come ashore and a guard was placed on the ship's
anchor chain to prevent its escape.

"I won't give up the ship!" Cornero was quoted as shouting one
evening,[16] but by the end of the fourth day the men in the patrol
boats were confident that he would soon exhaust either his food or
his patience. Word reached the admiral's flagship at this point that
the House of Representatives had just passed a bill making it a
federal crime to operate a gambling ship off the coast of the United
States.

"It ain't right," Tony was heard to say. "It's unconstitutional."*[17]

"He is sitting out there, cut off from shore and unable to operate,"

* The bill was killed in the senate by a parliamentary maneuver before it
was brought to a vote.

Olney told reporters Saturday afternoon, as the fifth day of the blockade ended. "As far as we're concerned, he might as well be in Alcatraz."[18]

Cornero managed to hold out for ten days, then he surrendered unconditionally. The attorney general clambered aboard a Fish and Game patrol boat and rode out to the *Rex*.

"It was like General Grant taking General Lee's sword," Olney says.[19]

When Cornero was brought ashore, shortly before noon, he was booked at the Santa Monica police station. Asked to give his occupation, he replied, "Mariner."[20]

Meanwhile, back at the office, Miss MacGregor had been digging into the lawbooks. In a long memorandum, she called attention to an interesting quirk of maritime law dating back to the early seventeenth century.[21] The gambling ships, it seemed, were anchored in wide, sweeping bays. True, they were more than three miles from the nearest point of land, but measured from headland to headland, as sanctioned by ancient precedents, it could be argued that they were actually within California's territorial limits.

In any event, the Supreme Court had ruled in *New Jersey v. City of New York* (1931) that a state had power to abate a nuisance even when the act creating it had occurred at sea more than twenty miles from the state's shores.[22] Finally, the water-taxis serving the ships were subject to state regulation as a public utility. No licenses had been applied for or issued. Thus, they were operating in violation of the law.

Not at all, argued the fleet's lawyers. Even if the gambling ships were held to be within the state's territorial waters and not on the high seas, traffic between the shore and the ships fell within the admiralty and maritime jurisdiction of the Federal Government and was not subject to regulation by the states.

A Superior Court judge in Los Angeles County disagreed with this contention, citing the historic hassle between the State of New Jersey and the City of New York. For years, the city had been dumping "noxious, offensive and injurious materials — all of which are for brevity called garbage — into the ocean"[23] at points of from ten to twenty-two miles from the New Jersey shore, polluting adjacent waters and menacing public health.

It was of no importance where the acts creating the nuisance took place, whether within or without the United States, the Supreme Court had held when its jurisdiction was challenged by New York City's lawyers. What mattered was whether the damage caused by the nuisance lay within the court's territorial jurisdiction, as was clearly the case in New Jersey. Similarly, the courts of California had jurisdiction over the nuisance being inflicted on the state and its residents by the illegal acts taking place on the gambling ships.

"The waters off Santa Monica, between Point Dume and Point Vicente, constitute a bay," Judge Emmet H. Wilson ruled, echoing Miss MacGregor's memorandum, "and the State's jurisdiction extends three miles to sea from a straight line drawn between the two headlands."[24]

Having obtained a court injunction putting an end to the offshore action, Warren fired another broadside at the gambling ships on November 1. He wrote a letter to J. H. O'Connor, Los Angeles County counsel, and sent a carbon copy to his old friend and college classmate, John R. Quinn, county assessor.

"Ordinarily," Warren wrote O'Connor, "I am not inclined to exact penalties but these people as you know are racketeers who have not only flouted the laws of the State but have beaten and oppressed citizens who visited the gambling ship and have even taken innumerable relief checks issued by the County of Los Angeles for the care of poor families in the operation of their illegal gambling games."

"I think this is an opportunity for the County of Los Angeles to recover some money which could be well used for the solution of your relief and other problems," he wrote Quinn in a covering letter,[25] and four weeks later, on advice of counsel, Cornero gave up the fight.

He agreed to the destruction of all the gambling paraphernalia aboard the *Rex*, to the payment to the State of $13,200 for expenses incurred in putting him out of business, settlement of county taxes in the amount of $4,200 and the production of all books and other papers of the *Rex* for examination by state income tax officials. He also compromised for $7,500 a claim brought against him by the California Railroad Commission for operating a public conveyance without a license.[26]

Jahnsen was put in charge of a detail armed with axes and crowbars. They boarded the *Rex* and proceeded to destroy 120 slot machines, 20 dice tables, 20 roulette outfits and 25 blackjack tables, together with Chinese lottery layouts, bingo apparatus, and equipment used for betting on horse races. It was one of the most professionally satisfying experiences in Jahnsen's long career in law enforcement.[27]

After serving as a casino manager in Las Vegas during the war, Cornero suddenly bobbed up off the Southern California coast again in 1946, commanding the *Lux*, a war surplus vessel he had managed to convert into a gambling ship.

"He has been able to obtain the necessary steel, lumber and other materials that cannot be secured in this state for veterans' homes and other essential construction," Governor Warren wrote President Truman on August 6,[28] and quoted Cornero as having declared, "Any molestation of persons or equipment aboard ship will be treated by us as piracy."

"I desire to make a personal appeal to you to assist the State of California in ridding our coastline of these continuous law violations which amount to a public nuisance against the law-abiding people of our state," the Governor continued, and copies of his letter were sent to the secretary of the treasury and the attorney general.

Federal agents seized the *Lux* on a technical charge, and Cornero was relieved of his command. On April 28, 1948, Truman signed a bill sponsored by Senator Knowland prohibiting the operation of a gambling ship in the territorial waters of the United States. Cornero returned to Las Vegas where, in July, 1955, he dropped dead of a coronary thrombosis after an all-night crap game. He died a loser, $10,000 in the hole.[29]

7

Murder Most Foul

Malice, which distinguishes murder from manslaughter,
is implied "when the circumstances attending the killing
show an abandoned and malignant heart."
— CALIFORNIA PENAL CODE, SECTION 188

W ARREN had waited so long to take over the attorney general's
refurbished office that he wanted to stick around for a while
and enjoy it, but Governor Olson kept egging him into a fight, forcing him to make the race for governor. The feud came out in the
open in October, 1940, when Olson dropped by San Quentin to
visit three prisoners Warren had prosecuted in the liveliest, most
controversial case of his fourteen-year career as district attorney.[1]

It began on Sunday, March 22, 1936, when the body of George
Alberts, chief engineer on the S.S. *Point Lobos,* was found slumped
in his bunk just before the freighter was to pull out from the Encinal
Terminals in Alameda. His skull had been bashed in, and one leg
almost completely hacked loose by a large knife. In one corner of
the stateroom blood was four inches deep.

The following November four men were put on trial in Oakland.
A fifth had managed to flee the country. Three of the defendants
were officers of the Marine Firemen, Oilers, Watertenders and
Wipers Union. Earl King was the union's chief executive, Frank
Conner its ship's delegate aboard the *Point Lobos,* and Ernest G.
Ramsay one of its patrolmen. The state charged that these three
men had hired the fourth defendant, George Wallace, and the
missing man, Ben Sakovitz — both members of the same union — to
beat up Alberts, who had run into trouble with Conner and King

after firing a fellow-member of the Marine Firemen without paying him all the money due him for overtime work. Wallace testified that he had stood guard while Sakovitz proceeded to turn what was to have been a routine waterfront beating into murder.[2]

"The union officials told Sakovitz to beat the engineer within an inch of his life," according to Bob Kenny's often-quoted remark, "but he forgot to take a ruler."[3]

The ship murder case came into court at a time when the ports of the United States had been shut down by a strike which, according to the Shipping Merchants Association, was costing the Pacific Coast some $7,000,000 a day. The anti-labor Los Angeles *Times* put the blame squarely on Harry Bridges, "the alien radical," who had led the maritime unions in the eighty-six-day strike of 1934. He was still out to achieve the same objective, the *Times* reported, "to bring the State under radical, Socialized control."[*4]

In its running account of the trial, the *Western Worker* ("Western Organ of the Communist Party, U.S.A.") consistently referred to the proceedings as "the framed murder conspiracy case." An anonymous pamphlet, *The Ship Murder: The Story of a Frameup*,[5] pinned the crime on Wallace, who was accused of fingering the three Marine Firemen in order to save his own skin. Warren was pictured as a ruthless tool of the shipping interests, packing three innocent men off to prison as part of a scheme to break the maritime unions and curry favor with the Los Angeles *Times*-Oakland *Tribune* axis by getting Bridges deported.

"I had good labor connections," says Oscar Jahnsen, who handled the investigation for Warren's office. "They tipped us off that Alberts had been firing Communists and that this was a Communist murder."

According to Jahnsen's sources, at least one of the killers had recently been in touch with Albert M. Murphy, assistant secretary and treasurer of the Marine Firemen, the man just below King in the union hierarchy. Jahnsen moved in next door to the hotel room occupied by Murphy and Matthew Guidera. He listened to their

---

* In the same issue of the *Times*, word was flashed from "authoritative quarters" that "King Edward VIII has been persuaded to abandon his romance with Wallis Simpson and will marry a hand-picked princess."

conversations by applying a stethoscope to the wall between the two rooms, then used a skeleton key to gain entry when the two men were out. In the top dresser drawer he found a letter from George Wallace, postmarked Brownsville, Texas. Wallace wanted money to get across the border into Mexico.

"That was our first big lead," says Jahnsen.

The letter was photographed, then returned to the dresser drawer. At the same time a microphone was concealed under a table to provide better reception than Jahnsen had been getting from the stethoscope. When Murphy got back to the hotel that evening and fell into conversation with Guidera, Jahnsen and another investigator on Warren's staff were waiting next door with a stenographer from the district attorney's office.

"Murphy's language was pretty foul, but Florence didn't bat an eye," Jahnsen says. "She got it all. Around one o'clock next morning I figured we'd heard enough. I knocked on Murphy's door, and he said, 'What do you want?' 'I want to talk to you,' I told him, and he said, 'What about?' I said, 'I have to arrest you for being an accomplice in the murder of George Alberts.' He opened the door, but he insisted he didn't know a thing about the Alberts case, so I asked him, 'What about that letter from George Wallace in your top dresser drawer?' His face went white."

Murphy's circulation didn't improve when Jahnsen casually repeated the substance of recent conversations, then suggested to Murphy that he reach up under the table. Murphy's fist closed around the microphone. He yanked the wires loose, then began to pace the floor, muttering to himself. He had no idea how long his room had been bugged, or whether his talks with King had been overheard and recorded.

"Mr. King has left you holding the bag," Jahnsen told him. "You got the safety deposit box in your name. You've been paying out the money. Why don't you tell us all about it? I can't promise you anything, but you're not going to get hurt telling the truth."

Jahnsen says he advised Murphy he could call a lawyer, if he wanted to, but by this time Murphy had begun to see himself caught in a frame-up. He was only too happy to make a full statement. Afterwards, Jahnsen warned him to stay away from his old union associates, or he might find himself suddenly dead. Finally, to protect his witness, Jahnsen arrested him.

"I arrested King at the same time," he says. "We brought the two of them in together, and Murphy wanted to make his plea look good, so he put on quite an act for King's benefit. He even accused us of stealing twenty dollars from him while he was being searched. A cop got mad and hit him in the stomach, said he'd be damned if anybody was going to call *him* a thief. King started yelling, 'Police brutality!' and leaped to Murphy's defense."

Ramsay was locked in a different jail, kept apart from the others. He gave Warren's office a statement, then repudiated it. Conner was brought back from Seattle by the FBI and refused to talk until he had seen his lawyer. He asked for a Seattle attorney, who declined to take the case. Conner, during this period, had been put up at a hotel by the district attorney's office.

According to the authors of *The Ship Murder,* Conner spent the night of September 2 "handcuffed to a chair, undergoing a third degree that finally became cold-blooded torture. He was threatened with violence, although never actually struck, being told over and over, hour after hour, that King and Ramsay (whom he barely knew) had 'confessed' and named him as Alberts' murderer."[6]

"On the contrary," says Jahnsen, "he was given good treatment in the hotel, all he could eat, cigars, whatever he asked for except booze. We told him that Murphy had given us the full story. He was afraid he was going to be left holding the bag. He confessed."*

Wallace, meanwhile, was still in Brownsville, where he was found hiding in a boxcar. He was hungry and frightened, his clothes in rags. Two men from Warren's office escorted him back to the Bay Area. Jahnsen told them to treat him gently, buy him some clothes, stake him to a good dinner, win his confidence. By the time Wallace reached the Hotel Whitecotton in Berkeley, where a delegation from the district attorney's office was waiting for him, he had come to

---

* Thirty years later, in *Miranda v. Arizona,* Chief Justice Warren quoted a police training manual to demonstrate the constitutionally unacceptable advice being given peace officers on the art of conducting an official interrogation. A typical example: "Where emotional appeals and tricks are employed to no avail, he must rely on an oppressive atmosphere of dogged persistence. He must interrogate steadily and without relent, leaving the subject no prospect of surcease."[7]

regard his armed escort as his only protection against the homicidal distrust of his recent employers in the Marine Firemen, Oilers, Watertenders and Wipers Union.

"When he was brought in," Jahnsen recalls, "I walked up to him, stuck my hand out and said, 'Well, well, Mr. Wallace, how are you? Everything OK? These fellows been treating you right?' Then I introduced him to everybody in the room, and I told him he could hire a lawyer, if he wanted to. 'All we want is the truth,' I said. 'Now why don't you tell us what happened? Start at the beginning.' "

Wallace's account of the crime confirmed the statement made by Murphy and the confessions Ramsay and Conner had repudiated. The story of the ship murder started on Saturday morning, March 21, 1936, when Conner telephoned King at the Marine Firemen office in San Francisco to inform him that Alberts had fired Edward Widmer, a union brother, without paying him all of the overtime money he had coming to him. Conner asked King to send a patrolman over to the *Point Lobos* to straighten things out.[8]

Wallace happened to be in the union office around the time of Conner's call. King asked him if he wanted to go on a job, and Wallace refused the offer, then left. Shortly afterwards he met Ramsay and Sakovitz, who told him he had better go back to King's office, King wanted to see him. The three men proceeded to King's private office, where Ramsay was heard to say of Alberts, "That Goddamn fink, he belongs to some company union and he needs a lesson."

"Go over and beat him up," King said, and walked to the outer office, where he instructed Murphy, the union treasurer, to give Ramsay thirty dollars for an "expedition across the bay."

When Wallace and Sakovitz got outside, Sakovitz asked if Wallace had anything he could use in case of trouble. Wallace said no, and Sakovitz suggested he go see the janitor, who gave him a piece of rubber, later described as half of a printing roller about eighteen inches to two feet long and about four or five inches thick. Wallace turned the bludgeon over to Sakovitz.

Wallace, Sakovitz and Ramsay, accompanied by a sailor whose name is not known, headed for the Howard Terminal in Oakland, where the *Point Lobos* was docked at that time. They reached the dock around noon and hung around for nearly four hours. During this time Ramsay twice left the others and boarded the ship. "That God-damned fink," he said after his first visit, "I talked to him and I could not get him off." Conner joined the group and Ramsay again went aboard and again failed to lure the chief engineer ashore. Before Ramsay could make a third try, Alberts left the ship with a companion, crossed the dock, entered a car and drove off.

"That God-damned fink got away," Sakovitz said.

"You had better beat it," Ramsay said, "split up."

During the night the *Point Lobos* moved to the Encinal dock in Alameda, where Wallace, Sakovitz and the anonymous sailor arrived next morning. They picked up two more sailors from the steamer *Arctic* before they were joined by Conner. Taking the battle stations assigned by Sakovitz, Wallace went to the starboard side of the ship near the passageway in which Alberts's stateroom was located and Sakovitz proceeded to the forward end of the passageway close to the chief engineer's door, where he was facing Conner. The others took various positions about the ship's deck.

Alberts came aboard with the captain and entered his stateroom. Conner gave Sakovitz a hand signal. A few moments later Wallace heard a noise in Alberts's stateroom which he described as sounding like "ugh, ugh, ugh." Seconds later, Sakovitz emerged with blood on his hands.

"You had better beat it," he told Wallace, and when the group later met at a nearby warehouse, he said, "It is all over with — beat it."

King, in a subsequent conversation with Murphy, expressed his annoyance at the way the job had been bungled, explaining that he had sent Sakovitz and Wallace to the *Point Lobos* to "tamp up" on the chief and the damn fools had gone too far and killed him. In conspiring to do violence to the deceased, King, Conner, Ramsay and Wallace had acted with malice, which distinguishes murder from manslaughter. Their crime, in the language of the law, had been carried out under circumstances which showed "an abandoned and malignant heart."

They were brought to trial in Superior Court, Judge Frank M. Ogden presiding. The judge, a protégé of Warren's, had served under him as a deputy district attorney. Lawyers defending the three labor leaders got nowhere in their efforts to get a different judge or to have their clients tried separately instead of with Wallace. Meanwhile, Wallace had insisted on putting himself in the hands of the public defender rather than hire his own lawyer with the $5,000 offered him by the King-Ramsay-Conner Defense Committee.

Objection was also raised to the lists from which the jurors were selected. The names had been supplied by banks, business establishments and industrial plants, but not by any labor organizations. One of the jurors, it developed later, had lent $3,200 to a deputy in Warren's office before the trial, and subsequently advanced him more than $24,000. No evidence was ever produced to indicate that Warren knew of these transactions, but they reinforced the conviction of the Defense Committee that "the district attorney's machine was in complete control of the situation . . ."[9]

The trial began in mid-November, a few days after F.D.R. had disposed of Alf Landon. Pickets paraded back and forth in front of the old courthouse in downtown Oakland, while most of the seating inside was taken up by prospective jurors. When the defense attorneys asked about their politics, it developed that most of them were Republicans.

"I'm surprised that Roosevelt got elected," King's attorney grunted.[10]

Once the trial got under way, Conner's attorney set out to demonstrate that his client's "confession" had been extorted during his stay at the Hotel Whitecotton. Warren succeeded in having the statement read to the jurors, then he was called to the stand by the defense. The confession, he testified, had been "freely and voluntarily given," and he pointed out that when Conner had asked to see the attorney he wanted to handle his case, arraignment proceedings had been discontinued to permit him time for a conference.

"'These fellows are not going to leave me out,'" Warren quoted Conner as having said. "'The whole bunch of them are Communists except me and they're not going to pin this thing on me.'"[11]

"Murphy also put the blame on the Communists," Jahnsen says, "but he had trouble with words. Used to call them 'those damned Commicals.'"

The twelve members of the jury and the two alternates (eight men, six women) spent Christmas and New Year's at the Claremont Hotel in Berkeley, guarded by deputy sheriffs. The four defendants were in the county jail. Warren and his staff were busy packing the office files, getting ready to move to the new courthouse at Twelfth and Fallon. In the late afternoon of January 5th, after being out four hours and twelve minutes, the jury filed back into the courtroom. On their first ballot they had reached a verdict. The four men were found guilty of second-degree murder. They got twenty years.

"Only when the people of California and the United States put *their own men* into office will these frameups stop and the victims be turned loose," readers of *The Ship Murder* were warned. "Labor and progressive people can and must put men into Earl Warren's place and Judge Ogden's place who will take orders from the people, not from shipowners and their brother millionaires."[12]

In December, 1938, however, the District Court of Appeal affirmed the judgments of conviction. "From a consideration of the whole record we are convinced that no prejudicial error was committed in the rulings of the court and that all questions of fact involved were submitted to the jury under proper instructions."[13]

Sakovitz, the actual killer, was never brought to trial but he wrote a curious footnote to the case. After fleeing the country, he joined the French Foreign Legion, then turned up in 1943 as a private in the United States Army in North Africa. Identified by his fingerprints as a fugitive from justice, he was being brought back to the States in the brig of an army transport when he vanished again, this time for good.[14]

After his chat with King, Ramsay and Conner in San Quentin in the fall of 1940, Governor Olson infuriated Warren by remarking at a press conference that he was thinking of extending clemency to the three men.*

"I can't figure them out as the type of men who would deliberately participate in the murder of anyone," Olson said.[15]

"Heretofore," Warren snapped back, "I have never said one word against the Governor on any of his official acts, but silence on my

---

* Wallace's case was different. Because of prior convictions, he could be pardoned only on recommendation of a majority of the state Supreme Court justices.

part in this matter would be cowardice. These men are assassins — proved to be so."[16]

So far," the Governor said, "my impressions are that the evidence relied upon to convict these men with the actual murder of Alberts seems thin."[17]

"These men were fairly tried and honestly convicted," Warren insisted. "They are now in the penitentiary as convicted murderers; they are also revolutionary radicals — Communists."[18]

Politics, in Warren's opinion, had inspired the Governor's trip to San Quentin. The legislature had recently passed a bill introduced by Assemblyman (later State Senator) Jack B. Tenney, removing the Communist party from the ballot. Olson had signed the measure, with — as Warren put it — "an apology to all the radicals in the state."[19] The Communist party, the Governor had declared, was foreign-controlled, "and for that reason should not be entitled to legal recognition in the political life of America."[20] His subsequent hint of clemency for King, Ramsay and Conner was interpreted by Warren as "an appeasement to the Communists for signing the Tenney bill."[21]

The Advisory Pardon Board had considered the case of the three men in May. With no advance notice to most board members, including Warren, the hearing had been shifted from the office of the lieutenant governor to a nearby assembly room. "The place was jammed full of Communists," Warren said afterwards.[22] The board voted four-to-one against a recommendation for a pardon. The lone dissenter was Lieutenant Governor Ellis Patterson, a Democrat who believed King, Ramsay and Conner were not guilty and should be set free at once.

"I liked Mr. Warren very much," Patterson said in 1962, "but at that time he was playing to the press and to the reactionary and conservative business interests who were opposed to labor organizations in any form whatsoever. He developed, I presume as district attorney, a very sadistic view on life. The main thing was to win cases, no matter who died or who hung. We had quite a disagreement on this. I notice as a Supreme Court Justice he has become more liberal, and, in my opinion, a better man. So I forgive him his shortcomings then because I think that he was playing politics and not his conscience."[23]

As attorney general, serving on the Advisory Pardon Board, and later as governor, charged with the life-or-death responsibility of executive clemency, Warren was strongly inclined to abide by the decisions of the courts. Patterson took the view that the Advisory Pardon Board was set up "to catch the mistakes of the courts." Warren, he recalls, finally stormed out of a board meeting, vowing never to return, and he kept his word.

"'If I ever become governor, I'm going to have this body abolished!'" Patterson quoted him as having said, and then added, "He did just that when he became governor. But he did set up an Adult Authority, which is probably a better organization."

Instead of pardoning King, Ramsay and Conner, Governor Olson left the matter up to the Board of Prison Terms and Paroles, which released them on parole in late November, 1941.

"An outrage to public decency," Warren snapped.[24]

"Labor's long battle for the freedom of these maritime union leaders, framed on a murder charge and serving twenty-year sentences in San Quentin Prison, was won today . . ." Vern Smith wrote in *People's World*.[25]

"The murderers are free today," Warren said, "not because they are rehabilitated criminals but because they are politically powerful communistic radicals."[26]

Warren's attitude toward the use of the Governor's pardoning power was revealed during his first week as attorney general, when Olson announced his intention of pardoning Tom Mooney. After studying the voluminous records of the case, the Governor was convinced the labor leader was "wholly innocent"[27] of the July 22, 1916, Preparedness Day parade explosion in San Francisco which had killed ten persons and wounded forty others. Extremely sensitive at this time to any talk of an anti-labor frame-up, Warren expressed his opinion to the Governor:

"I realize that an application for pardon is addressed to the conscience of the Governor and that there is no requirement in the law that he give consideration to any particular fact or to any legal decision involving the applicant. I trust, however, that in any action you may take on Mooney's application for a pardon you will bear in mind that today law enforcement is, at best, difficult of accomplishment and that you will neither cast any unwarranted reflection upon the agencies charged therewith, nor lend any encouragement to those forces that are opposed to the enforcement of our laws and to the maintenance of security of life and property."[28]

Much the same sentiment would crop up twenty-five years later in bumper stickers distributed by the John Birch Society: SUPPORT YOUR LOCAL POLICE, a slogan which at the University of California campus in Berkeley became HELP THE FUZZ and in Los Angeles, SUPPORT YOUR SUPREME COURT — IT SERVES AND PROTECTS YOU.

8

The Road to Sacramento

Everything we have in California is better than it is any-
where else. Even our Republicans are better than the
Republicans anywhere else.
— ROBERT W. KENNY, *describing*
Earl Warren to F.D.R. in 1943[1]

I N August, 1940, Attorney General Warren went to Washington
to take part in a federal-state conference on law-enforcement
problems related to national defense. When he got home, he spread
the latest word from the capital among California peace officers,
then summoned them to join other interested state and local officials
in a conference attended by spokesmen of the Army, Navy and
FBI.[2]

"One thing we have to avoid is the stampeding of highways for
places of safety in the suburbs in case of bombing or sabotage in the
San Francisco and Los Angeles areas," Warren said nearly a year
before the attack on Pearl Harbor.[3]

"If bombs and devastating panic ever come to this country," he
continued in the late spring of 1941, "it will be the law-enforcement
officers who will restore order. Without proper planning in advance
it will be too late. Even next month may be too late."[4]

Having already predicted that "in all probability we will be in this
war before long,"[5] Warren reverted to a favorite theme, the lack
of support given law-enforcement officers by politicians and the
public.

"We must have higher standards of law enforcement. The very
nature of our democracy allowing equal freedom for both bad and
good presents a situation that the totalitarian powers are not over-

looking. Do not be deceived that they are not attempting to exercise fifth column activities or sabotage in this country. They would like nothing better than to create the same situation here that they developed in France, Denmark and Holland prior to their capitulation."[6]

In speech after speech, Warren warned Californians of the dangers inherent in a heavily industrialized state where water and power supplies had to be carried great distances through unpopulated territory. He rounded up local peace officers for a three-day crash course given by the FBI on how to deal with fifth columnists, spies and saboteurs.[7] He plumped for passage of the state's first law directed specifically against sabotage.

"This war is different from other wars in that sabotage is artfully and extensively used upon nations by the enemy, and for that reason particularly we need this law," Warren testified when the Uniform Sabotage Prevention Act was before the judiciary committee of the state senate in March, 1941.[8] The bill was opposed by organized labor, largely because of how it might be interpreted by "some two-by-four judge." Once the law was enacted and anti-labor judges tried to use it against permissible union activities, Warren quickly set them straight on the legislative intent of the measure.

California was divided into nine districts, each with its own emergency organization. District heads served on the State Civil Defense Council, which gave the various cities and counties a chance to coordinate plans for home defense. Warren had already helped put a Mutual Assistance Act through the legislature, enabling lawmen and firemen to cross local borders. A house was no longer to be allowed to burn to the ground while fire trucks of a neighboring jurisdiction stood helplessly by on the opposite side of an invisible boundary line.[9]

To a suspicious Democratic Governor, the activities of the energetic Republican Attorney General suggested the beginnings of a political campaign to unseat him. An irreparable break between the two men was inevitable. It came shortly after Pearl Harbor when Olson issued a "state of emergency" proclamation which omitted any specific role for the attorney general. Warren, in blistering terms, challenged Olson's authority.

"Warren's attack might have been avoided if the Governor had consulted him freely and sought his advice," Robert E. Burke writes in *Olson's New Deal for California*. "But one of the things Olson never was nor could have been was truly diplomatic. Each man was wilful and determined to play his proper role in the state's war effort, and each distrusted the other."[10]

Six weeks after Olson pocket-vetoed an appropriation of $214,000 to meet the additional costs of running the attorney general's office because of the war, Warren announced his candidacy for governor. In the statement he made to the press on April 9, the Attorney General said the times called "for a unity of purpose and action that rises above every partisan consideration. They demand a nonpartisan administration of our state government. If elected, I will give such an administration."[11]

"His hypocrisy is only equaled by the fraudulent nonpartisanship of the Republican predatory interests and their newspapers, which sponsor and support him," Olson said next day at his press conference,[12] and toward the end of his campaign he continued in the same vein: "Anyone who is so cowardly as to put on the cloak of nonpartisanship in an election like this, either acknowledges that he is a political eunuch and does not know what it is all about, or that he is a political hypocrite."[13]

"I believe in the party system," Warren had said at the outset, "and have been identified with the Republican party in matters of party concern, but I have never found that the broad questions of national party policy have application to the problems of state and local government in California."[14]

For more than thirty years, ever since the high tide of the Progressive Era, Warren reminded the electorate, Californians had lived with nonpartisan city and county offices, as well as nonpartisan courts and schools. During this period, he said, legislators and other elected officials had come to look at the state's needs without regard to partisanship.

"These officers deal with problems such as security of the people in their homes, the administration of our schools, business methods in government to prevent overtaxation, civil service to prevent the spoils system, conservation of our resources, both human and natural, to prevent exploitation, the social services to raise living standards, co-operation with the agencies of the Federal Government to carry out national policies, and now civilian protection to further the war effort.

"None of these problems permits of solution through partisanship. They cut entirely across party lines."

Taking "Leadership, Not Politics" as his campaign slogan, Warren proposed to end "petty partisan politics."[15] He promised to treat the legislature as a political equal. Together they would work to improve the state's defenses, tidy up its welfare programs, eliminate its wasteful expenditures and — this being California — increase its old-age pensions.

Still nettled by the release of the three *Point Lobos* prisoners, Warren attacked the Olson administration's handling of paroles as its "darkest chapter." Of the 5,904 prisoners paroled during Olson's term, Warren continued, 207 had been convicted of rape and 285 of other sex crimes. The Governor hit back at this emotional use of statistics as a reflection of the inhumane feelings of a man "who has been a prosecutor during his entire life, and whose capacity for bias and prejudice against his fellow men is unlimited."[16]

"Earl Warren is a shrewd politician with a well-developed ability to conduct a campaign on his own issues, avoiding questions of a highly controversial nature and emphasizing his own most decisive arguments," Richard Foote Pederson wrote in the thesis he submitted at Stanford for his Master of Arts degree in 1947.[17]

Despite pressure from Olson, Warren refused to commit himself on the politically sensitive subject of "hot cargo" and "secondary boycott." The question had been heatedly debated in the 1941 legislature, when rural lawmakers used the national emergency as an excuse to pass what union leaders referred to as a "Slave Labor Bill." It outlawed two effective weapons of organized labor: The refusal of employees to handle goods or perform services for one employer because of a union dispute with another and the use of a boycott under such circumstances. When the legislature overrode Olson's veto, the AFL and CIO proceeded to put the Hot Cargo Act to a vote of the people on the referendum ballot.

"I am taking a neutral position on the hot cargo bill because I believe it is absolutely imperative that bitterness and controversy should be avoided at this time on any issue which tends to divide our people,"[18] Warren said, happy to dispose of the matter by leaving it to the voters. They approved it.

In the campaign's only face-to-face debate, held in San Francisco on October 11, the Attorney General at one point found himself skating on constitutionally thin ice.

"Why did you veto the bill requiring schoolchildren to salute the American flag, sir?" Warren asked.

"I did so because it had been ruled unconstitutional by the Supreme Court," the Governor replied.

"That is a deliberate distortion of the truth. On the contrary, the Supreme Court upheld the constitutionality of that proposal and I think you must know so."

"Well, at any rate," Olson said, "I did not believe it was constitutional myself, and I thought it more important to have children learn to love the flag than to force them to salute it."[19]

Technically, Warren was correct, but in this particular round Olson outpointed him. The Court in June, 1940, more than two years before the Olson-Warren debate, had sustained the constitutionality of a compulsory flag salute in public schools despite its conflict with the religious beliefs of Jehovah's Witnesses (*Minersville School District v. Gobitis*).[20] Justice Stone had registered a strong, eloquent dissent, but no other voice on the Court had been lifted against this abuse of the First Amendment.

Two years later the Witnesses were back before the Court, this time protesting a city licensing tax imposed on their sale of religious books and pamphlets (*Jones v. City of Opelika*).[21] In June, four months before the Governor and Attorney General squared off in San Francisco, a majority of the Court had upheld the tax. Again Stone had dissented, but this time he had been joined by Black, Douglas and Murphy, who recanted their *Gobitis* votes and now declared their belief that the case had been wrongly decided.

These four dissents so shortened the life expectancy of *Gobitis* as a precedent that, just a few days before Warren needled Olson on the subject, a three-judge federal district court had refused to be bound by the ruling in issuing an injunction against the West Virginia Board of Education, restraining it from requiring children to salute the flag in the state's schools.*[22] On this issue, Governor

---

* It was not until May, 1943, after Stone had become Chief Justice and Byrnes had been replaced by Rutledge that the wrong done in *Gobitis* was righted by *West Virginia State Board of Education v. Barnette*.[23]

Olson was closer to the law as it has been laid down by the Warren Court than was Attorney General Warren.

The San Francisco debate, taking place just three weeks before election day, was something of an anticlimax. It was obvious even to the Governor's closest friends that he was going to be clobbered. In the August primary, Warren had not only collected 635,000 Republican votes, but had also picked up 400,000 more from registered Democrats. Olson had not cross-filed. Running only on the Democratic ticket, he had received 513,000 votes, less than half of Warren's combined total.[24]

"Warren's strength was a welcome surprise even to his friends," the San Francisco *Chronicle* stated editorially. "Olson's weakness was greater than his sternest critics expected."[25]

Among other mistakes, Olson had put too much faith in the political arithmetic of California. Warren was a Republican in a state with 2,300,000 registered Democrats and 1,370,000 registered Republicans. While the Governor conducted a bumbling, lackluster campaign (one and one-quarter million Democrats didn't even bother to come to the polls in the primary), the Attorney General took to the hustings, making effective use of the radio, shaking every hand in sight, bounding into remote villages no candidate had bothered to visit before. No one had ever traveled so many miles, talked to so many voters and, afterwards, remembered so many of their names.*

"The Governor would go into a town, shake hands with half the people, make a talk, shake hands with the other half, then we'd be on our way," says Ray McCarthy, his driver.[26]

Among the Democrats who switched to Warren was George Creel, who had campaigned for Olson in 1938 after having been sideswiped four years earlier by Upton Sinclair. Creel got three phone calls from the White House, where Marvin McIntyre had been given the job of persuading him to withdraw his endorsement. Despite the increasing chill in the air as they talked, Creel refused.

"Not only was Earl Warren, the Republican, a vastly superior

---

* Like President Kennedy, who never forgot how each Boston precinct voted in his congressional races, the Chief Justice can still tick off the final returns from the most obscure crossroads polling places.

person in every way," he wrote in his autobiography a few years later, "but I had sickened of the crackpot demagoguery that passed for liberalism."[27]

On election eve, while Olson warned Democrats to be chary of "cross-filing Republicans," Warren declared in a state-wide radio broadcast: "The next governor of California will face some of the gravest problems ever encountered by any of his predecessors. He will also face great, and possibly greater, opportunities."[28]

Warren ended up with 1,275,285 votes to Olson's 932,995, and was assured of Republican majorities in both houses of the legislature. Among the Democrats who went down to defeat was Lieutenant Governor Patterson, who had given him such a rough time on the Advisory Pardon Board. Patterson remained convinced that one-third of the people who voted for Warren thought he was a Democrat.[29] Patterson was understandably bitter about cross-filing. In 1936, when he was a registered Republican, he had won the Democratic nomination for an assembly seat, only to be disqualified because the voters of his own party had rejected him.

Senator Bob Kenny, who had conducted an active, independent campaign for attorney general, was the only Democratic candidate for state office to survive the victory Warren had given the minority party. During Christmas week the Governor-elect invited his successor to have luncheon with him.

"He was most gracious and explained to me the capabilities and assignments of the various members of the staff," Kenny recalls. "Although there was no civil service then for the office of the attorney general, I reappointed all of Warren's deputies."[30]

A few months later, when Kenny had his only personal meeting with F.D.R., the President asked him what kind of a fellow the new governor was. "Mr. President," Kenny replied, "I'm just a California booster at heart. Everything we have in California is better than it is anywhere else. Even our Republicans are better than the Republicans anywhere else."[31]

Even by the exotic standards of California politics, Warren and Kenny make a strange pair. Kenny comes from an old, well-off California family. The blood of bankers flows in his veins. Warren was born into a working-class family, and brought up to regard the stock market as a form of gambling. Warren has the commanding build of a section foreman. Kenny has the contours of a snowman and the look of a mischievous cherub.

A worldly wit, Kenny enjoys sophisticated company, vintage wines and French sauces. Warren is an outdoorsman, who likes football and duck-hunting, and leans more toward Bob Hope than Mort Sahl. Kenny is a sparkling conversationalist (when John Gunther asked him where a former governor was living, he said, "East Oblivion").[32] Warren is a man of boundless good humor, radiating great personal warmth, but he is no wit.

After making his way through the three hundred and thirty prepared speeches Warren delivered during his first eight years as a state official, Pederson observed in his master's thesis that humor was "very noticeably absent." In fact, only once had the texts of the speeches indicated an attempt to get a laugh. At a University of Southern California banquet, Warren had suggested that the coach should be restrained under the antimonopoly laws from winning so many track championships.[33]

"That big, broad smile is deceptive," says a former member of his staff who used to help draft Warren's speeches. "Actually, he's a very serious man, not given to facetiousness. He used to tell us to put more zing into his speeches. We tried. It just didn't work. He could warm up an audience with little stories about the kids, but once he got down to business he was deadly serious."

When the Governor was appointed Chief Justice, a San Francisco lawyer grumbled, "I can guarantee that every one of Earl Warren's decisions will sound as if he's running for President or assistant God."[34] Earlier, in a politically inspired opinion he would now just as soon forget, Pierre Salinger declared, "He can pronounce publicly a platitude with a reassuring tone of discovery as if here, with the help of God, he has stumbled upon a hitherto unsuspected but eternal verity."[35]

"Yes," an old friend admits, "he can be stuffy as hell at times."

No stuffiness was in evidence, however, the day Louis Unter-meyer was introduced to the Chief Justice for the first time. They met in the spring of 1962 at a midday ceremony in Washington, D.C., where Robert Frost and Justice Douglas addressed a group gathered in a Georgetown meadow to pay tribute to Thoreau on the centennial of his death. When Secretary of the Interior Udall made the introductions, Warren beamed at Untermeyer, pumped his hand, and expressed admiration for his poems and anthologies. Untermeyer responded with equal warmth, then suddenly gave way to an impish impulse.

"Mr. Chief Justice," he said, "how is your impeachment proceeding coming along?"

Without blinking an eye, Warren smiled and said, "Fine, thank you."

"I don't know," Untermeyer continued. "I keep writing letters to the editor and signing petitions, but our program doesn't seem to be getting anywhere."

"Oh, I wouldn't worry about it, Mr. Untermeyer," Warren said. "They tell me it's doing quite well."[36]

Untermeyer was completely captivated, not merely by what the Chief Justice said but by the man himself. He exudes goodwill, good fellowship, a sense of well-being. Unlike Untermeyer, who delights in verbal play, Warren is the born advocate, choosing his words carefully, with no stylistic embellishments to distract from the orderly arrangement of facts. His speeches and opinions are usually more notable for their simplicity and sincerity than for their literary distinction, but at times — as in his eulogy for President Kennedy — his words achieve the eloquence of an emotion strongly felt and clearly expressed.

"I'd never characterize him as a man with no sense of humor," says one of his former law clerks. "He certainly enjoyed Kennedy's humor, for instance. But he isn't a clever man or malicious. Part of what seems to be a lack of humor may be due to his political training. He may feel that humor can be dangerous to a man in public life."

"His humor often takes the form of a deadpan ironic comment," says a former member of his gubernatorial staff. "We had a petite and very young messenger in the early days of the administration. She told me she wanted to quit because she was pregnant and so was her mother, and the girl wanted to help her mother. When I told the Governor, his comment was: 'And *grandmother?*'"[37]

During the four years they worked together as governor and attorney general, Warren used to warn Kenny: "Watch out, Bob, you might be hitting into a double play." It was Kenny's nature to play a bold, dashing game. Warren, on the other hand, has never been flashy. He is a workhorse, a clutch-hitter. In his last year as attorney general and his first year as governor, when he finally did swing at a bad pitch, he hit into the same double play that had caught up virtually every political and civic leader on the West Coast, not to mention the President of the United States, the Congress and the Supreme Court.

9

Exodus, 1942

It was just something that happened.
— MRS. SHIG NISHIO[1]

"I HAVE come to the conclusion that the Japanese situation as it exists in this state today, may well be the Achilles' heel of the entire civilian defense effort," Attorney General Warren said a few weeks after the attack on Pearl Harbor,[2] and then, in one of his rare gaffes, he told a conference of sheriffs and district attorneys on February 2, 1942: "It seems to me that it is quite significant that in this great state of ours we have had no fifth-column activities and no sabotage reported. It looks very much to me as though it is a studied effort not to have any until the zero hour arrives."[3]

Ten days after Warren cited the sinister innocence of the Japanese-Americans as evidence of their perfidy, Walter Lippmann came out in favor of their evacuation from the West Coast. Four days later, Westbrook Pegler concurred, and the deed was done by President Roosevelt in an executive order and by Congress in a law that F.D.R. signed and the Supreme Court later upheld.[4]

"It was the first event in which danger to the nation's welfare was determined by group characteristics rather than by individual guilt," Morton Grodzins writes in *Americans Betrayed: Politics and the Japanese Evacuation.* "It was the first program in which race alone determined whether an American would remain free or become incarcerated."[5]

One American citizen, a man named Korematsu, refused to leave California. He was arrested, tried and convicted. His conviction was upheld by a six-to-three vote of the Supreme Court. The opinion supporting this massive assault on the civil liberties of 110,000 men, women and children — 70,000 of them citizens of the United States — was written by one of the greatest libertarians in the Court's history, Mr. Justice Black.[6]

"Attorney General Warren's record is characterized, on one side, by a scrupulous regard for the legal status of resident Japanese and, on the other, by a determination to foster the evacuation by every possible lawful means . . ." Grodzins writes.[7]

On February 5, 1942, a Bay Area assemblyman wrote the Attorney General inquiring about the legality of a State Personnel Board order barring from civil service examinations anyone descended from nationals of countries with which the United States was at war. The board had also directed its staff to refuse to certify such outcasts for state jobs and to investigate those already on the payroll. The order included citizens of German and Italian descent, but it was obviously intended only for Japanese-Americans.

"It attempts to establish different degrees of loyalty and in so doing discriminates against naturalized citizens and citizens by birth of the first generation, in favor of those citizens whose forbears have lived in this country for a greater number of generations," Warren wrote in reply. "Such distinctions are neither recognized nor sanctioned by any provision of the Constitution or by any law, and unquestionably constitute a violation of the civil liberties guaranteed to all citizens by the fundamental law of our land. . . .

"A substantial portion of the population of California consists of naturalized citizens and citizens born of parents who migrated to this country from foreign lands. They have in the past and do now represent the highest standards of American citizenship. Many of them are now in the armed forces of our government. Some have already given their lives in our cause. Many of them — the naturalized citizens — left the countries of their birth for the express purpose of acquiring American citizenship because of their hatred of the tyrannies which we are now fighting. This has intensified their appreciation of American citizenship and increased their loyalty. To question that loyalty or place them in a category different from other citizens is not only cruel in its effect upon them but is also disruptive of the national unity which is so essential in these times."[8]

Two weeks later, Warren testified before a House committee headed by his Alameda County friend and neighbor, John H. Tolan. The committee had come to California to gauge the pressure building up behind proposals to evacuate Japanese-Americans from the West Coast.

"We believe that when we are dealing with the Caucasian race we have methods that will test the loyalty of them [*sic*]," Warren testified before the Committee, "and we believe that we can, in dealing with the Germans and the Italians, arrive at some fairly sound conclusions because of our knowledge of the way they live in the community and have lived for many years. But when we deal with the Japanese we are in an entirely different field and we cannot form any opinion that we believe to be sound. Their method of living, their language, make for this difficulty."⁹

At a recent meeting of some forty district attorneys and forty sheriffs, the Attorney General continued, he had asked whether any of them had ever received information on subversive activities or disloyalty from anyone of Japanese descent, regardless of whether he was born in the United States (Nisei) or in Japan (Issei). The answer was no.

"Now that is almost unbelievable," Warren told the visiting Congressmen. "You see, when we deal with the German aliens, when we deal with the Italian aliens, we have many informants who are most anxious to help the local authorities and the State and Federal authorities to solve this alien problem. They come in voluntarily and give us information. We got none from the other source."¹⁰

The Attorney General produced maps of California indicating areas where the Japanese-Americans owned, occupied or controlled land. "An inspection of these maps," he said, "shows a disturbing situation. It shows that along the coast from Marin County to the Mexican border virtually every important strategic location and installation has one or more Japanese in its immediate vicinity." "It will interest you to know that some of our airplane factories in this State are entirely surrounded by Japanese land ownership or occupancy. It is a situation that is fraught with the greatest danger and under no circumstances should it ever be permitted to exist."¹¹

"I noticed a telegram this morning with reference to the civil rights of these people," Representative John J. Sparkman of Alabama commented, then asked, "What do you have to say about that?"

"I believe, sir, that in time of war every citizen must give up some of his normal rights," Warren replied, after having first emphasized his belief that all decisions regarding "the solution of our alien enemy problem" should be made by the military rather than by civil authorities.[12]

This put the matter up to Lieutenant General John L. DeWitt, commanding general of the Western Defense Command, who had already (February 14th) made his recommendation to the Secretary of War, stating the racist rationale for evacuating Japanese-Americans but not their fellow-citizens of German and Italian descent: "The Japanese race is an enemy race and while many second- and third-generation Japanese born on United States soil, possessed of United States citizenship, have become 'Americanized,' the racial strains are undiluted."[13]

"The fundamental question is not one of race discrimination," Attorney General Webb had argued in 1923, defending California's Alien Land Law before the Supreme Court (*Porterfield v. Webb*). "It is a question of recognizing the obvious fact that the American farm, with its historical associations of cultivation and environment, including the home life of its occupants, cannot exist in competition with a farm developed by Orientals with their totally different standards and ideas of cultivation of the soil, of living and social conditions."[14]

"We're charged with wanting to get rid of the Japs for selfish reasons," the secretary-manager of the Grower-Shipper Vegetable Association of Salinas told Frank J. Taylor of the *Saturday Evening Post*. "We might as well be honest. We do. It's a question of whether the white man lives on the Pacific Coast or the brown man."[15]

Warren had grown up with agitation against the Japanese, who first began to appear in California around the turn of the century. In January, 1907, Kern County High School debaters took on the subject, "Resolved: That the action of San Francisco in regard to the Japanese school problem is justifiable." The board of education had segregated Japanese pupils, who numbered ninety-three out of a total school population of 29,000. In October, at the start of Warren's senior year, debaters had argued the question of whether Japanese should be permitted to become naturalized citizens.[16]

"A Jap's a Jap," General DeWitt testified in 1943. "They are a dangerous element, whether loyal or not."[17]

Loyal or not, the Japanese-Americans by this time had been hustled off to concentration camps run by the War Relocation Authority. Its director, Dillon S. Myer, later wrote in *The New Republic:* "Our experience has shown us that living in camps, cut off from the main currents of American life, does things to people. It saps the initiative, weakens the instincts of human dignity and freedom, creates doubts, misgivings and tensions."[18]

"Have you ever heard an Army or Navy man advocate release of these Japs?" Warren asked his fellow-governors in June, 1943, when they convened in Columbus, Ohio. "Have you ever heard anyone connected with the FBI indicate such action would be consistent with the national security? What do state and local law-enforcement officers believe? I can tell you. They believe they cannot long be responsible for the safety of their communities if these people are released and scattered throughout the country.

"If the Japs are released no one will be able to tell a saboteur from any other Jap. We are now producing approximately half of the ships and airplanes of the country on the Pacific Coast. To cripple these industries or the facilities that serve them would be a body blow to the war effort. We don't want to have a second Pearl Harbor in California. We don't propose to have the Japs back in California during this war if there is any lawful means of pre-venting it."[19]

Suddenly, on Sunday, December 17, 1944, the War Department announced without warning that the Army orders excluding all persons of Japanese ancestry from the Pacific Coast would be rescinded as of January 2, 1945, and only internees known to have a "pro-Japanese attitude" would remain in detention. The others would be free to make a "gradual and orderly return."

"There's going to be plenty of trouble," a Sacramento assembly-man predicted, and Mayor Bowron of Los Angeles reiterated the warning he had given government officials in Washington, "If you send them back in numbers, you'd better send the Army with them."[20]

Calling on Californians to "join in protecting constitutional rights of the individuals involved," Governor Warren pointed out in his official statement: "Any public unrest that develops from provocative statements or civil disturbances that result from intemperate action will of necessity retard the flow of needed materials to our boys in the Pacific who are moving steadily but at great sacrifice toward their ultimate goal — Tokyo.

"Most California families have a boy or girl in the armed forces. Military decisions such as these are designed for their ultimate success and speedy return to the homeland. As civilians, it is our duty to comply with such decisions as loyally and cheerfully as they do."[21]

"We Shan't Pretend to Like It," the Los Angeles *Times* slugged a lead editorial, decrying the order as "a grave mistake, due to snap judgment under political pressure from some nonmilitary source."[22] The editorial writer's snap judgment made under pressure of a deadline was contradicted in the news section of the same edition by a *Times* reporter filing from Washington: "Signs multiplied that the Army acted on the basis of a tip that the Supreme Court would order release of all loyal Japanese-Americans from WRA centers . . ."

The first of the three evacuation cases to be decided by the Court was *Hirabayashi v. United States*,[23] which was argued on May 10 and 11, 1943. Gordon Hirabayashi, a United States citizen, was a senior at the University of Washington in February, 1942, when General DeWitt ordered the evacuation of Japanese-Americans from West Coast military areas. Hirabayashi defied the exclusion orders. He not only failed to present himself at the assembly center designated for his removal, but he also violated the 8 P.M. to 6 A.M. curfew imposed on all enemy aliens and on "all persons of Japanese ancestry." He was found guilty on both counts.

Speaking for an anguished majority, Chief Justice Stone confined the Court's ruling on Hirabayashi's appeal to the curfew order, which was sustained as a military necessity. "We need go no further here than to deny the individual the right to defy the law," Justice Douglas wrote in a separate concurrence after a lively argument with his former law professor.[24] In Douglas's view, as privately expressed to Stone, there should be some sort of appellate procedure open to loyal internees. "Otherwise, if the military commander knows there are only 10 per cent of the group who are disloyal he can nevertheless hold the entire group in confinement for the duration without any opportunity on the part of the 90 per cent to prove that they are as loyal to the United States as members of this Court."

Murphy and Rutledge also filed separate concurring opinions, making it clear that military acts were subject to the same judicial scrutiny given a questionable use of power by civil authorities. As Justice Murphy warned, *Hirabayashi* "goes to the very brink of constitutional power."[25] A year later, in his *Korematsu* dissent, he declared the Court had gone over the brink in upholding the mass evacuation of the Japanese-Americans in the absence of martial law.[26] Justice Roberts agreed that "the indisputable facts exhibit a clear violation of Constitutional rights."[27]

The Court was not unmindful of the hardships caused the internees, Justice Black wrote for the majority in *Korematsu*, and then observed that "hardships are a part of war, and war is an aggregation of hardships."[28] In a strongly worded reply, Eugene V. Rostow, former dean of the Yale Law School, declared: "The idea of punishment only for individual behavior is basic to all systems of civilized law. A great principle was never lost so casually. Mr. Justice Black's comment was weak to the point of impotence."[29]

On the same December morning that the Court decided in *Korematsu* to go along with the military in the removal of the Japanese-Americans, it balked at their detention beyond a reasonable length of time required to screen out potential spies and saboteurs. Mitsuye Endo, an American citizen, had sought release from a relocation center in a habeas corpus proceeding. When her case got to the Supreme Court, she won her freedom. Justice Murphy cited her internment as "another example of the unconstitutional resort to racism inherent in the entire evacuation program."[30]

While the Justices were keeping the final text of *Ex parte Endo* under lock and key for the weekend, the War Department was hurriedly announcing that the West Coast no longer appeared to be in serious danger of enemy attack. As a result, trustworthy Japanese-Americans were to be released from the relocation camps. The generals managed to get the gates opened voluntarily just a few hours before the Court interpreted the Constitution in such a way that, solely because of race, a loyal, law-abiding citizen of the

United States could be dispossessed and publicly humiliated but could not be indefinitely locked up. Meanwhile, during the detention and debate, there had been 1,300 deaths in the camps and 4,300 births, and on the mainland and in Hawaii some 13,000 Japanese-Americans had joined the armed forces.[31]

"We don't want Japs here," an American Legion post commander said in Salinas,[32] where Caucasian farmers were spending a profitable Christmas on land taken from their Nisei neighbors at forced sales, and the project director of one of the internment camps reminded Californians who had done the Japanese-Americans out of their farms and fishing boats, their shops and homes, their cars and furniture that "only a relatively few have anything to go back to."[33]

After getting word of the War Department's announcement rescinding the evacuation order, Warren conferred by phone with the governors of Oregon and Washington, and sent for Walter F. Dexter, State Superintendent of Public Schools, instructing him to break in on the Christmas holiday of school officials and call a meeting as soon as possible.

"Certainly," Warren said, "we want no untoward incidents in the schools, and a little preparation in the vacation period will prevent this, I believe."[34]

He also called a meeting of the law-enforcement advisory committee of the State War Council, which could see no difficulties ahead "unless incidents are provoked by intemperate words and thoughtlessness."[35] During the course of this meeting, as one of the committee members recalls, "He asked us, 'What are we going to do with them? How are we going to protect them from bigots?' It was suggested that we adopt a resolution condemning the placing of these people in the concentration camps and declaring our intention of doing whatever we could to protect them from violence. 'No, it's no good,' Warren said. 'Why not?' he was asked, and he explained, 'Because at the time of their exclusion not one of us raised a voice against it. We can't condemn it now.' "

"But," says one of his closest associates, who worked with him during the war, "you've got to put this thing in the context of the times. How did we know whether enemy submarines were landing spies along the coast? Or whether we were going to be bombed at any minute? We kept getting tips that saboteurs were going to set fire to our redwoods, knock out our power lines, blow up our bridges, and God knows what else. And, remember, we were civilians. We weren't about to contradict a three-star general."*

By historical happenstance, Warren now sits to the left of Justice Black, who wrote *Korematsu,* turning the Court's back on the notion that punishment is to be meted out only to a demonstrably guilty individual. To the right of Justice Black sits Justice Clark, who in the early days of the war was dispatched by the Department of Justice to coordinate the Alien Enemy Control Program on the West Coast.

"You will find him a very approachable fellow," Warren advised the fiercely anti-Japanese members of the California Joint Immigration Committee when Clark first turned up in California a few weeks after Pearl Harbor.[37]

"I have made a lot of mistakes in my life," Justice Clark told the editors of the San Diego *Union* when he revisited California in the summer of 1966, "but there are two that I acknowledge publicly. One is my part in the evacuation of the Japanese from California in 1942 and the other is the Nuremberg trials. I don't think that they served any purpose at all . . ."

"Wouldn't you say the Japanese evacuation was influenced by wartime hysteria?" Clark was asked, and he said, "We should not let those things influence us."

As for his own participation, "I didn't pick them up physically and move them out, but I issued the orders. The reason I say that I think it was bad is because, well, even way back a citizen always had preferred position. In the Bible it says 'I am a Roman citizen — A subject of Rome and am entitled to this and that and the other.' It's the same with an American citizen in my book. We picked up these people — they were, of course, of foreign extraction, but they were our citizens — our fellow citizens. We picked them up and put them in concentration camps. That's the truth of the matter. And as I look back on it — although at the time I argued the case — I am amazed that the Supreme Court ever approved it."[38]

* "There is something about standing on the shores of California and seeing Jap submarines sink our coastwise ships or fire at shore installations that has a sobering influence," Warren had told his fellow-governors when they met in 1943.[36]

The Japanese-Americans were rousted and swindled, shamed and robbed, but when they returned to California, they were given the full protection of the law. With an innate dignity that served as the ultimate reproach to their persecutors, the older evacuees went back to work while the younger generation went to school. In 1950 only one out of twenty-two Japanese-American men was working in a professional field in California. Fifteen years later it was one out of six.[39] Among them was John F. Aiso, a Harvard Law School graduate who spent six years in the United States Army before he was appointed to the Municipal Court of Los Angeles by Governor Warren in 1953. He was later elevated to the Superior Court bench.

"There is no bitterness now," Mrs. Shig Nishio née Esther Takei told Jack Jones of the Los Angeles *Times* in the fall of 1965, twenty-one years after she had boosted the blood pressure of white Christian chauvinists by being the first of the young evacuees to return home and go back to school. She had been nineteen years old at the time. "It was just something that happened," she continued. "We must work to keep it from ever happening again."[40]

10

The Corner Pocket

. . . a prime, ripe, sun-kissed man . . .
— *Time*, May 1, 1944[1]

WHEN Warren moved into the governor's corner suite in the Capitol (legislators called it "the corner pocket"), Oscar Jahnsen dropped by to have a look at the Chief's new digs. Poking around, he discovered the place had been so thoroughly bugged that it took three days to trace the elaborate wiring system linking eight offices with an automatic recording device in an upstairs room. Meanwhile, Warren had invited the lieutenant governor, the attorney general, and the presiding officers of the senate and assembly to stop in and see for themselves.

"I assured them that they or any others could come into these offices any time without feeling they were being spied upon or their conversations were being made the object of eavesdropping," he told reporters.[2]

He showed them how his predecessor had been able to record conversations in his office by switching on a microphone hidden under his desk. A flick of the switch enabled him to record telephone conversations picked up through the use of induction coils. Jahnsen's search of the premises turned up only the wiring. The microphones were missing. In a loud, angry voice, Charles W. Lyon, the assembly speaker, asked what had happened to them.

There was nothing mysterious about the wiring system, Olson explained.[3] It had been used to record testimony given at hearings and conferences. Speaker Lyon still wanted to know where the microphones had been stashed. Next morning he got a call from the State Finance Department. It had been informed by Olson's former press secretary that the missing microphones could be found in a box in the janitor's closet of the governor's suite. Accompanied by the Capitol superintendent, the janitor and Miss MacGregor, Warren's secretary, Speaker Lyon proceeded to the closet and found the box. It contained what appeared to be five telephones. On examination they turned out to be dummies, each containing a microphone. On the base of the phones was a bureaucratic warning: "Not for outside calls."[4]

Downtown Sacramento office workers soon got accustomed to seeing the Governor walking to and from the Capitol. Crossing the spacious grounds, he would greet a gardener by name, then pop into some state office where no governor had ever set foot before. After introducing himself to flustered stenographers, he would chat for a while, then lumber off, booming a loud "Hello, there!" to a passing newspaperman.

During his campaign, his nonpartisanship had been questioned by Democratic disbelievers who remembered his partisan activities on behalf of the Republican party as state chairman and national committeeman. When he was accused of not having appointed any Democrats to key jobs in the attorney general's office, he had promptly pointed out that of the five most important appointive posts — the assistant attorneys general — three had gone to Democrats (William T. Sweigert, Jess Hession and Hartwell Linney) and two to Republicans (Warren Olney III and Everett Mattoon).

"They were appointed to these places by me on the basis of their experience, training, ability and integrity," Warren said,[5] and continued the same practice as governor, taking his Democratic associate, Bill Sweigert, along with him as his executive secretary.

Lawrence Arnstein, a tireless worker in the field of public health, was in Sacramento during Warren's first days in office. "Mr. Public Health," as he had come to be known, testified before the state budget committee, asking for $160,000 to be shared by a school of public health, a venereal disease laboratory and crippled children. Warren listened to what he had to say, then fell into conversation with him. As they talked, Arnstein dropped the name of Dr. Wilton Halverson, the health officer of Los Angeles County. Warren's eyes lighted up.

"I want him as my health director," he said, but Dr. Halverson had no intention of leaving Los Angeles County, where he was being paid considerably more than Warren could offer him. However, like many another appointee who followed him into the service of the state, he was powerless against the Governor's charm and persistence.

"Afterwards," Arnstein recalled, "when he was at my house one evening to dinner, he told me that when Warren sent for him, he talked quite a while and then told him he wanted him to be health director. Halverson asked the Governor why he wanted him; he hadn't asked him whether he was a Republican or a Democrat, or what his religion was. Warren said, 'I'm not interested in what your religion is. I'm just interested that you were recommended by a committee that I have a great deal of confidence in.'"

The same procedure was used when Warren came to appoint his director of welfare, Charles Schottland. As Arnstein tells it, "He was interviewed by Warren for about eight hours, and he told me that he had never been so thoroughly cross-examined by anybody. He was surprised to find out how much Warren knew about welfare in the state. When he finished, Warren said, 'Well, I'd like you to take the job.' Schottland said, just as Halverson had, 'You haven't asked me what my religion or my politics are.' Warren again said, 'I'm not interested in that. I'm interested in the fact that after talking to you for a whole day I feel you know the subject, and I want you to be my welfare director.'"*6

Harold Anderson was happily running Palo Alto's Municipal Department of Light and Power when the Governor tapped him for Commissioner of Public Utilities. Anderson demurred at first, then gave in.7 Charles Purcell, the Department of Public Works engineer who had designed the Bay Bridge, expected to be introduced to his new Republican boss when he was summoned into the presence of the Governor-elect in mid-December, 1942. Instead, he was told he had been selected to run the department.

"I damn near fell over," he later told a friend.8

"Warren's cold scrutiny of candidates for appointment has been so impersonal and so scientifically applied to the qualifications of the applicant that there are literally hundreds of job-hungry citizens

* Dr. Halverson was a Republican and a Seventh-day Adventist; Schottland, a Democrat and a Jew.

who can't muster the courage to approach him directly," Kyle Palmer wrote in the Los Angeles *Times* at the end of Warren's first sixty days as governor.[9]

Warren kept some of Olson's appointees, but lost no time in sacking Carey McWilliams, the liberal, articulate Commissioner of Immigration and Housing, whose concern for migratory workers had placed his name at the head of the Associated Farmers' purge list. McWilliams retaliated with nearly four pages in *The New Republic*, depicting Warren as "the darling of the Associated Farmers."[10] The Governor was characterized as "essentially grim and hard-boiled," "mean-natured and vindictive," a man who "reveres policemen, deputy sheriffs and investigators." While purporting to be "the Liberal Statesman," McWilliams declared, he was in truth a reactionary trained to mouth such phrases as "old-age security," "collective bargaining," and "social planning."

"Warren let himself be taken in by what the Associated Farmers told him about Carey," says a California politician friendly to both men. "It's a pity they never got to know each other. They were never as far apart as they thought."

Warren had been governor only six months when street fights broke out in Los Angeles between servicemen and Mexican-American youngsters in "zoot suits" (long coats, peg-top pants). McWilliams called Attorney General Kenny in San Francisco and told him the situation was more serious than the newspapers had reported. Kenny drove over to Sacramento to see Warren and suggested that he appoint a citizens' committee headed by the Auxiliary Bishop of the Roman Catholic Church in Los Angeles. Warren acted on the suggestion at once. Kenny never told him that it was McWilliams who had proposed the bishop.[11]

Sacramento newspapermen, for the most part, liked the new governor. They found him friendly and frank, with a sense of personal dignity that forbade the wearing of funny hats and the striking of outlandish poses. He often spoke about his children, but refused to let them be politically exploited. The Governor's Mansion was the Warren home, reserved for family and friends, and off-limits to press agents and politicians. At times, however, Warren would interrupt a news conference to relate a family anecdote, and he frequently translated legislative proposals into domestic terms.

"I think of my daughter Virginia walking home from a cannery at two in the morning and I realize that I don't want this for anyone's daughter," he said when Santa Clara Valley canners were seeking legislation to permit young girls to work through the midnight shift.[12]

The bill was sponsored by anti-labor lawmakers who hoped to use the wartime emergency as an excuse to cripple trade unions and undermine the legislative ground they had gained.

"It has taken years of struggle to place humanitarian statutes like the eight-hour law for women and children on the statute books, and, as far as I am concerned, I do not propose to be a party to their repeal," Warren said, and as his executive secretary later recalled, he went on to suggest that "all groups get together and work out a sensible wartime measure under which working conditions of women and children could be relaxed under careful state supervision during wartime without abandoning the underlying principle of this kind of legislation."[13]

"We must return to the fundamentals which brought our nation into being . . ." Warren told an American Legion audience in August, 1943, delivering one of the God-Home-and-Mother speeches which distressed his more sophisticated admirers. "We must reattach ourselves to the old moorings — the family, the home, religion and free government . . ."[14]

But he had also told the legislature, "This state has never been afraid to be progressive,"[15] and for openers he had proposed pension, parole and civil service reforms, along with a tax cut and the establishment of a War Council and a food-and-fiber agency to help make better use of the state's agricultural machinery and manpower.

"We have seen the signs of confusion arise over the slowness of democracies to function," he said in his first inaugural address. "Ours is an opportunity to restore confidence in those who have become distraught and misguided."[16]

When Warren first took temporary title to the white, three-storied Executive Mansion at Sixteenth and H streets, the seventy-year-old gingerbread house was shabby and sagging, the cupola tilting, the paint peeling, the front porch chewed up by termites, the steps patched with pieces of tin. With characteristic prudence, the Governor-elect inspected the premises and refused to let his family set foot in the firetrap until something was done about repairing the steps and providing fire escapes.

In April, 1943, three months after their father's inauguration, the children were transferred from the Vernon Street home in Oakland to their new quarters in Sacramento. Mrs. Warren handled the logistics, managing to find time between packing and unpacking to lay in a supply of groceries and arrange her newly painted kitchen (cream and red). She let the cook and housekeeper help her wash and dry two complete dinner services, one for twenty-four, the other for twelve, along with the pots and pans, and a dozen varieties of glasses, each of which came in a set of twenty-four.

"It sure is good to find some life around this old place," a guard told Virginia Coontz of the Oakland *Tribune* when she dropped by to see how the Warrens were making out.[17]

The two youngest children, Honey Bear, nine (nobody ever called her by her real name, Nina), and Bobby, eight, had found a lovely tree to climb. Dottie, eleven, was playing basketball with one of the guards. Virginia, fourteen, a sophomore at McClatchy High, was answering a letter from an admirer. Thirteen-year-old Ju-Ju (the family's nickname for Earl, Jr.) had taken up taxidermy. He was busy stuffing a bat. Jim, newly married, had gone off to the wars, but his photograph, in his Marine Corps uniform, was prominently displayed.

The Warrens, Miss Coontz reported, were having the same trouble with wartime food shortages as their neighbors. They had not tasted meat for five days, but with company coming for dinner Mrs. Warren had acquired a leg of lamb, which she served with rice, zucchini, a peach and cottage cheese salad, and a custard.

"It looked pretty good to five hungry children," Miss Coontz wrote.

Once the family moved in, the Mansion was so full of Warrens there wasn't even a guest room. The Governor and Mrs. Warren took over the room formerly reserved for guests after Honey Bear laid claim to what had been the governor's bedchamber. She wanted it because it had a shower, and she usually got what she wanted, including a pinto horse named Peanuts, jointly owned with Bobby.

It was the children's father who bought Peanuts. Their mother thought Honey Bear and Bobby were too small to ride, but she didn't dissent. Later, when the two youngsters began to work out on jumpers, she couldn't bear to watch them take the hurdles, but again she entered no demurrer. She went along with the head of the house who is fond of saying: "Being alive at all is a perpetual gamble. Too much fear is defeat in advance."[18]

Honey Bear remembers the grotesquely charming old Governor's Mansion as a happy place, overrun with dogs and children,* cluttered with ice skates, tennis rackets, fishing rods and baseball gloves. This was where Ju-Ju took over the lot next door for a Victory garden, where Dottie entertained her Girl Scouts and Bobby practiced on his secondhand cornet, where Honey Bear ("a born housekeeper," her mother said when the child was nine years old) used to sweep out the guards' quarters when she couldn't find any work to do in the big house.

It was also where Virginia, decked out in her first formal, waited nervously upstairs for the young man who was to take her to a high school dance. He was met in the front hall by Jerry, a Dalmatian more accustomed to Ju-Ju's bluejeans and T-shirts than to dinner jackets. The dog snapped at the seat of the boy's trousers, then ripped one sleeve from his coat. Virginia burst into tears, Mrs. Warren ran downstairs with a needle and thread, and the young couple got to the dance an hour late. Jerry was turned over to the armed forces for military duty, and replaced by three springer spaniels.

"Jerry was Earl's dog," Bobby says. "Strictly a one-man dog. If Earl and I got to wrestling on the lawn, he'd take after me. And he meant business."[19]

When Bobby first tried out for the McClatchy High School football team, one of the players made the mistake of suggesting, "Go easy on him, guys. That's the Governor's kid." On the next play, Bobby hit the youngster so hard his teeth rattled.[20] By the time he was graduated, Bobby was looked on as one of the best defensive linemen in the Sacramento Valley League. In the meantime, he had

* But never cats. As a child, Mrs. Warren was badly burned when her dress caught fire. While she lay swathed in bandages, unable to move her head or arms, a cat jumped up on her and started toward her eyes. The horror of that helpless moment has never left her. She can't bear to be in the same room with a cat.

injured his knee and made a lasting contribution to the sizable body of family anecdotes.

"It's a story Dad loves to tell," Jim Warren says. "You see, he didn't want to forbid Bobby to play anymore, but at the same time he didn't want him to end up with a permanent injury, so he finally told Bobby, 'We'll leave it up to the doctor.' Bobby was allowed to pick his own doctor. After the examination, the doctor said, 'Well, Bobby, all I can say is that if you were my boy I'd never let you play again.' Bobby was crushed. Then he went to another doctor who looked him over and said he saw nothing wrong in his playing. 'Now *there's* a doctor that knows his business,' Bobby said, and Dad was very much amused. Bobby was allowed to go on playing."

"I can never recall him giving a flat no as the response to any question we put to him," Bobby says of his father. "He'd talk it over. If you went up to him and said, 'Dad, I think I'd like to do such-and-such a thing,' he'd say, 'Well, son, that sounds interesting.' Then he'd start asking you questions about why you wanted to do it, and by the time you got through explaining, you'd decided it wasn't such a good idea after all. He's a master at letting people make their own decisions in a way he regards as desirable."

The Warren family was a microcosm of a free, diverse and democratic society in which each member was able to grow in his own way, according to his own ambitions and abilities.

"There was a special interest in encouraging development of the *differences* in our interests," says Jim Warren. "None of us was ever given any feeling of obligation, implied or otherwise, to follow Dad into law."

But on New Year's Day, 1930, when Earl Warren, Jr., was born, his father told Oakland reporters: "He'll be dedicated to football and law, and there is no question that California will beat Stanford when my boy plays."[21] The boy's preoccupation with all living creatures, however, took him into animal husbandry instead of law, and he went to the University of California agricultural college at Davis instead of the Berkeley campus. After his graduation in 1952, he put in a year on a sheep and cattle ranch, then went to work as a farm adviser in Alameda County, specializing in matters relating to livestock, dairy cattle and forage.

"Many of us look to the county farm adviser to help us with problems that mean a great deal to our present and future," a ranch owner said in the fall of 1954. "Frankly, when we found out the son of a famous man had been given the job, we were concerned about it. But we didn't give it a second thought once we saw Warren go to work. Ask him to come up to your ranch and check a problem at nine in the morning and he's there. And that same night you'll find Warren up past midnight talking to ranchers at their association meeting."[22]

After spending three years on the job, he resigned and, in the fall of 1957, turned up in Berkeley as a freshman law student. "There's a need in this day and age to know law," he said.[23] He was twenty-seven years old, with a wife and two children to support, at the time he made the change. His wife went back to work as a fashion coordinator to supplement the money he had saved and borrowed to pay for his legal education.

"Earl played his cards his own way," says his brother Jim. "It was by virtue of establishing a respected reputation in his own field that he justified or vindicated, if you will, the decision that brought him into law."

In January, 1962, while practicing law in Sacramento, Earl created something of a stir in California politics by changing his registration from Republican to Democratic.

"I just think the Republican Party today is drifting away from rather than toward Dad's brand of Republicanism," he said,[24] and proceeded to campaign vigorously against Richard Nixon when the former Vice-President ran for Governor of California. ("With both eyes firmly focused on Washington, he staggers blindly around the state, promising the moon one minute and threatening to drag us back to the nineteenth century the next.")[25]

Archibald M. Mull, Jr., a former president of the California State Bar and an old family friend of the Warrens, paid tribute to Earl, Jr., in December, 1966, when he took office as a municipal judge in Sacramento. Young Warren, in Mull's words, "seems to be compelled to do everything well."[26] While rearing four children, he had not only been active in trial and appellate work, but had also participated in forty civic and professional organizations and committees, written a book on agricultural law, served on the governor's advisory board on mental health, and worked as a deputy director of the Chile–California Alliance for Progress program.

"Dad was always intensely and actively interested in helping his sons develop their individual pursuits as soon as the first spark of interest glowed long enough to justify fanning it into flame," Jim Warren recalls. "For instance, Bob's absorption with athletics brought him close to a decision to become a coach. His first job — with the State Department of Corrections — bore out the sincerity of his interest. His work in rehabilitation was, in fact, the coach of the Soledad Prison teams in Salinas. I'll never forget his comment one year that his basketball team was really loaded. 'I've got a burglar, two rapists, an embezzler and an arsonist in the starting lineup!' "

Jim's childhood hobby of copying the funny papers (later he sketched the family portraits for the Warren Christmas cards) led him into an advertising agency. Some years after the war, he found himself sinking into a corporate quagmire in San Francisco. He was a popular, talented executive in a large firm, well on his way to a vice-presidency and an ulcer. But it wasn't what he and Maggie really wanted to do with their lives. They talked of chucking it, finding a place in the Napa Valley, and going into business on their own. Jim thought of opening a real estate office, maybe getting hold of an old winery. However, there were three boys to be fed, clothed, and put through college.

"I talked it over with Dad," Jim says, "and never once did he let on how he felt about it. He just made sure that we considered every angle. After we made the big move, I received a letter from him that said, 'When you first spoke of doing it, I offered no advice because only the person whose career is involved can evaluate all the factors necessary to such a decision.' And later in the letter, he said, 'For one thing I am happy, and that is that when you made up your mind what you wanted to do, you had the courage to do it.' "

As a youngster, Jim got caught skipping Sunday school to practice diving at an athletic club in Oakland. Warren took him aside one day, spoke of the pleasure and the physical benefits to be derived from swimming, and then asked Jim if he felt that these things — important as they were — were more important than neglecting to do what his parents expected of him.

"He asked me what I thought of it," Jim later recalled, "and first thing you know I was arguing against myself."[27]

When the subject of an appropriate punishment was brought up,

Jim said he supposed he should be forbidden the use of the pool for a while. "No," his father said, "swimming is a good thing for you." So it was agreed that the boy was not to go to the movies for a month.

"And that was a real punishment," Jim says. "I loved the movies."

As a teen-ager, too young for a learner's permit, Jim charmed Elizabeth, the maid of all work, into teaching him to drive. On his sixteenth birthday, when he asked permission to apply for a learner's permit, his father asked if he had ever driven a car. "Yes," Jim said. "Elizabeth let me." Warren beamed. "Good. If you'd said no, I wouldn't have let you get the permit." A generation later, Jim ran into the same problem with John, his youngest son, who had not only taken a turn at the wheel of the family car but had even driven on a freeway. It happened to be the Earl Warren Parkway.

Edgar (Pat) Patterson, a parole officer in Sacramento who put himself through college while working for the California Highway Patrol, likes to reminisce about the years he was assigned to the Governor's Mansion. He used to drive Honey Bear and Bobby to school, then share a wedge of Mrs. Warren's devil's food cake and a glass of milk with them in the afternoon.

"The kids were so nice," Pat says. " 'Come on now, get in this car and let's go to school,' I used to tell them, and they'd mind me right off. But they didn't like to be driven in the big black Cadillac. They preferred the Chevrolet. If I was in the big car or wearing my uniform, I'd have to let them out a block away, so the other kids wouldn't see them."

"The Chevrolet was fairly inconspicuous," Bobby says, "but when you have a police officer driving the car, it's pretty uncomfortable for a kid. At that age you want to be like everybody else."

"I remember how the Governor used to kiss Bobby good-bye every morning," Pat says. "Then as he got older, Bobby began to get embarrassed. He'd duck away. The Governor got the point. I'll never forget the first time he stuck out his hand to Bobby instead of kissing him."

"Mother and Daddy were so unselfish," Honey Bear says. "They gave so much of themselves. We had love and warmth and security. We were always able to speak to them at any time about anything. Parents don't have time for their children now. Life is too fast."

"As far back as any of us can remember, Dad was 'always there,'"
says Jim Warren. "He never missed a game, for example, that any of
us played in, if it was humanly possible to make it. And when you
consider the span between my first high school game and Bob's
graduation from college, with Earl in between, a dutiful father can
wear out a lot of tires and get pummelled in a lot of hard and
uncomfortable bleachers over seventeen years."

"He's a complete family man," Pat says. "When I'd pick him up at
the Capitol, first thing he'd say was, 'Well, Pat, how're they doing?'"

"He never brought his work home from the office," Honey Bear
says. "When he walked in that front door, he belonged to us. He was
all ours."

Once Warren had moved into the Governor's Mansion, he set out
to improve the odds against his remaining in residence long enough
to get the children through high school. Only one governor in the
state's history, Hiram Johnson, had ever been elected to a second
four-year term. After spending forty-eight months in the capital's
rotting Mansion, fighting lawmakers by day and rodents by night, it
was traditional for a California governor to take to the hustings and
explain to coldly silent audiences why he hadn't made good on his
campaign promises. Determined to lengthen his political life expectancy, Warren began by treating the legislature as his executive
equal.

"Ours is an opportunity to strengthen faith in men's ability to
work together for the common good," he told a joint convention of
the senate and assembly in his first inaugural address,[28] and
when he set up shop in the governor's corner office he pointedly left
the door open, inviting the lawmakers to stop in any morning for an
informal visit.

"There isn't a man in the legislature who does not feel free to go
down and see the Governor any time on any matter," a capital
correspondent reported.[29]

In February, when the legislature was about to recess, Warren
turned up on the floor of both houses, going from desk to desk,
shaking hands, calling each member by his first name, startling them
at times by his detailed knowledge of conditions in their districts. A
month later, when the lawmakers returned, the Governor was on

hand again, welcoming them back to the Capitol in a brief, friendly exchange of political small talk.

When he found that individual legislators were hesitant in accepting his open invitation to come see him, he started asking them in as members of standing committees. With each group — agriculture, taxes, crime — he listened more than he talked, and ended by saying, "You fellows write the bill."* In four months, they managed to pass 1,290 bills, including all of the Governor's major measures.[31]

"Working with a person like that, you learned that nothing is impossible," says Heman G. Stark, director of the California Youth Authority.

Called to the Governor's office one morning, Stark found him in a dark mood, his face flushed, his fists clenched. He teed off on the shocking state of civil defense in California. He wanted something done about it and, as new associates came quickly to learn, when he wanted something done, he meant today, or preferably yesterday. Stark was sent to Los Angeles with orders to set up a civil defense office.

"You have it running by Monday morning," Warren said.

"That was on Thursday," Stark says. "I went down there that afternoon and found space in an old building at Second and Hill. We started painting the place Friday morning, moved the furniture in on Saturday, got the phones put in on Sunday, and at nine o'clock Monday morning I got a call from Sacramento. He wanted to know if I was in business. I was."

Stark was brought to Sacramento in the early days of the Warren administration when the Governor raided the Los Angeles Probation Department. Karl Holton, the county's chief probation officer, was appointed director of the state's new Youth Authority, and Stark, who had worked for him for years, was placed on his staff. Stark succeeded him as director in 1952 when Holton returned to Los Angeles County for another twelve years of distinguished public service. The California Youth Authority, meanwhile, had served as a model for other states in modernizing their correctional programs for the wayward young.

---

* "The Governor is a good listener, but he does not say much," a union official told a Los Angeles newspaperman in December, 1944.[30]

"This is one of the greatest social experiments we have ever undertaken in this state," Warren said of the Youth Authority Act, which had been signed into law by his predecessor.[32]

The Youth Authority developed from a plan drawn up by the American Law Institute "to protect society more effectively by substituting for retributive punishment methods of training and treatment." The first state to adopt the proposal was California, where peace officers, prosecutors and prison officials had been educated by the pioneer work of August Vollmer, Berkeley's enlightened police chief. Among other things, Vollmer served as president of the Prison Association, a group of citizens interested in raising the standards of correctional institutions.

The Prison Association drafted the bill setting up the Youth Authority and escorted it through the 1941 legislature. Young lawbreakers were no longer to be committed to the care of Dickensian warders. Instead, the courts would deliver them to the Authority, where their difficulties could be examined, their abilities gauged, and their lives redirected. Each case would be studied with a view to determining whether the young offender should be paroled or placed in a YA camp for training and, if necessary, treatment.[33]

"We have made a wrong approach to the crime problem," Warren told the legislators. "We have been willing to spend lots of money on police, prosecutors and prisons, but very little on crime prevention. The solution is to prevent these boys and girls from becoming habitual criminals."[34]

Warren called for the consolidation of existing agencies within the administrative borders of the Youth Authority, making it responsible for "all services in the interests of youth in dire need of a helping hand."[35] He also asked that the Authority be directed to concern itself with the prevention of delinquency as well as with the training and treatment of young delinquents.

"Young people between the ages of fifteen and twenty-one years constitute only 13 per cent of our state population," he said in the fall of 1946, "but a recent California study based upon police and sheriff's records disclosed that during one year more than 40 per cent of all serious public offenses in the state were committed by persons within this age group."[36]

In picking Karl Holton to run the Youth Authority, Warren selected a probation officer who had put the agency's humane philosophy in practice by setting up forestry camps in Los Angeles County for boys in trouble with the law. Holton had come to realize that long before most youngsters turned up in court for sentencing they had already been punished by the sort of world into which they had been born. The world had to be changed as well as the children it spawned. Warren concurred.

"Regardless of the shortcomings of the homes from which the prisoners come, or of the sordid social conditions in the communities where they were reared, or of the failure of society to look out for its underprivileged members, or of a politically controlled prison, the parole system is held responsible for those it sends out into the world under its supervision," the Governor had said as attorney general,[37] and in his first confrontation with the legislature he declared his intention of taking "every bit of politics out of the parole system and the pardoning power."[38]

As attorney general, he had stamped out of a meeting of the Advisory Pardon Board, threatening to have it abolished if he ever became governor. Once in office, he did away with the board as part of a sweeping reformation of the parole, pardon and prison systems. It was a toss-up as to which was in worse shape, California's prisoners or its prisons. Both had to be taken in hand.

"At the time I became governor in 1943," he later recalled, "the basic law covering the California penal system had not been changed substantially since 1879. We had two major prisons for men, loosely supervised by a part-time prison board. We had a women's prison, supervised by another part-time board. We had three youth correctional institutions operated by a different Department of Institutions. We had a sentencing and parole board distinct from the Prison Board. We had a Youth Correction Authority without supervision over youth institutions."[39]

Working with Karl Holton, he designed a streamlined, centralized Department of Corrections, which did away with obsolete, politically manipulated boards and agencies. Responsibility for the development and execution of a coherent policy of penology was placed in the hands of a director appointed by the Governor. Warren chose Richard A. McGee who, like Stark, continued to serve under subsequent governors. Along with the Youth Authority, the department was put in charge of a new Adult Authority which set forth its philosophy in gratifyingly clear and simple terms:

"The Adult Authority subscribes to the doctrine that the protection of society is the aim and purpose of the penal system. It does not believe that punishment alone is truly protective. Only when prisoners are rehabilitated as well as punished, does the penal system solve its problem."[40]

"The one relic that we have of barbarism," Attorney General Warren had said in 1939, "the one relic that we have of medievalism, is our belief that we can take men who are weak in character, men who have got into trouble not because they are desperate or vicious, but perhaps because they are indolent, hold them in jail for a period of time with absolutely nothing to do except to commune with other people with the same or greater weaknesses, and then turn them out on society and expect them to be better."[41]

One day when members of a crime-and-correction committee of the legislature were seated at the big conference table in the Governor's office, Warren made a suggestion he had been mulling over for years.

"There ought to be a way for a man to earn his pardon without being beholden to anyone," he said, and out of this conference came a bill setting up a procedure by which an ex-convict could go about achieving a pardon in much the same way an alien acquires citizenship.[42]

Warren had made the proposal in 1939, when he had addressed a National Parole Conference in Washington in the spring and a California convention of peace officers in the fall:

"We could provide by law that every man who has been convicted of a felony, thereby losing some or all of his citizenship, could file in the county court of his residence a notice of intention to work for a restoration of his citizenship and for a full and complete pardon. We could further provide that at the end of a given number of years if his conduct proved satisfactory under the general supervision of appropriate law officials, he might, with the approval of the court, be restored to all the rights and privileges of American citizenship and be granted by the court a full and complete pardon for his offense."[43]

In California, where prodigious growth is as commonplace in political movements as in patio plants, the fears and frustrations of the Depression gave rise to two pension plans considerably larger than life. In 1934 a retired Long Beach physician, Dr. Francis E. Townsend, proposed a monthly pension of two hundred dollars be paid to every citizen who had reached the age of sixty. From the Townsend Plan sprang an even more preposterous proposal, "Thirty Dollars Every Thursday."

"Since it was obviously out of the question to conduct a campaign under the impossible slogan of 'Thirty-Dollars-Every-Thursday Plan,'" writes Robert Glass Cleland, "the promoters sought a name that would appeal in brevity and everyday familiarity to the mass of voters. One day, in addressing a group of campaign workers, a speaker promised that before the ensuing election the pension movement would become as familiar to the California voters as ham and eggs. The phrase was immediately seized upon as an answer to the quest for an inspired catchword, and the campaign for the millennium was conducted under that incongruous slogan."[44]

California voters turned down "Ham and Eggs" when it appeared on the ballot in 1938 and again the following year, but in the 1942 gubernatorial campaign the fantasy still held such a strong grip on the hopes of elderly residents that both candidates had to deal with it. Convinced that Governor Olson had betrayed them, "Ham and Eggs" leaders came out for Warren.

"The senior citizens of California have been deceived and misled long enough," he said on October 4th. "They are entitled to pensions, not as a charity or a dole, but as a matter of right — as something they have earned in their productive years by their contributions to the upbuilding of the community. I do not believe a senior citizen should have to be in need in order to secure a pension. I do not believe he should be forced to relinquish any outside income he may have or any property he may have acquired. I don't believe he should be forced to look to his children for support. I do not believe that a pension should be longer considered or called 'Old Age Charitable Relief.'

"It is not just the number of years people have lived that should determine their right to a pension, because many people are efficient and able to work to very advanced ages, but rather the limit beyond which they are not permitted to obtain productive employment because of the stern dictates of a machine age. In order to be both realistic and humane, therefore, we must proceed upon the theory that a system which arbitrarily freezes people out of industry and declares them to be obsolete, merely because they have lived a fixed number of years, must make honorable provision for their support during the years of their enforced idleness."[45]

Under a state law which struck him as cruel and absurd, pensioners were not permitted to keep the pittance they might be able to earn in an effort to supplement the forty dollars they received from the state each month.

"If an old man, anxious to feel that he is playing some small part in the war effort, raises a 'Victory garden' and sells five dollars' worth of vegetables to his neighbors, that amount is deducted from his pension check, and he is discouraged from performing a useful service for himself and his government," Warren said, and denounced as "reprehensible," the custom of "playing politics with the hopes and security of the tens of thousands of deserving old people who must look to the government for aid in their latter years."[46]

In the same speech he declared: "I believe that we should stop thinking of an old age pension as a dole which we grant to the needy. I believe that every elder citizen, when he reaches the age fixed in the statute, should have the right to retire on an annuity, or a pension."

As governor, Warren proceeded at once to work out a nonpartisan pension plan. He asked the "Ham and Eggers" and the Townsendites to come sit down at his conference table with the Bankers Association and the Chamber of Commerce. The AFL and the CIO received the same invitations which were sent to the Farm Bureau Federation and the Grangers. This improbable assemblage elected a banker, Ralph T. Fisher, as its chairman. A month later, when eleven of the seventeen members reached an agreement that pensions should be raised to fifty dollars a month, the Governor took the proposal to the legislature, where it was promptly adopted.[47]

"We have had our differences of opinion," Warren told the departing legislators just before they left town in early May. "That is only natural and very human, but we have shown that we can disagree at times and still work together with good feeling and goodwill."[48]

He had redeemed his campaign pledge to work with the legislature as a coequal partner in state government, and in the process had not only liberalized the pension laws, as he had promised, but had also achieved a substantial tax reduction. He had elevated the standards of public service by statute and had enriched it by his appointments. He had also established a new state guard staffed with volunteers and had created a War Council to replace the Council of Defense which had caused so much friction between Governor Olson and Attorney General Warren. Under the new arrangement, Governor Warren had acquired considerably more power than he had been willing to concede, as attorney general, to his predecessor.

Disgruntled Democrats, sniping at the record of the first one hundred days, attributed Warren's success to California's healthy economic glow. The Governor's only problem, they contended, was figuring out what to do with the surplus piling up in the treasury as a result of the state's booming war industries.

"Under such circumstances," Carey McWilliams wrote, "Miss Shirley Temple, aided by the same advisers and with the same newspaper support, could make a fairly popular governor of California."[49]

"Perhaps it should make a new governor feel good," Warren said, but explained that the word "surplus" was something of a misnomer. The state, he pointed out to the California Taxpayers' Association a few weeks after his inauguration, had a bonded indebtedness of almost $140,000,000, against which the surplus had to be measured. It was like a man getting his first paycheck after a long period of unemployment. It looked large and comforting until it showed up on the family budget alongside a list of unpaid bills.[50]

"We can always find legitimate use for more money than we ever had to spend before, but we must keep in mind that the standards we set through expenditures now may add to our disappointments later on," he warned, and put through a postwar planning act which not only set aside a chunk of the state's wartime wealth to be used for the peacetime adjustments of closed munitions plants and returning servicemen, but also set up a commission to project the need for new homes, highways, schools, bridges and airports.

When the legislature met in special session in January, 1944, it took only five days to adopt the program the Governor put before it.

"Reason for the speed," readers of *Time* learned when they picked up an issue with the Governor's picture on the cover, "is Earl Warren's established practice of thoroughly thrashing out bills in citizens' committees and informal groups of legislators before they are even submitted to the legislature."[51]

Complaining of the Governor's "safe, dull political prose," *Time* could find little in the record of his twenty-five years in public service "to reveal much promise that he is a potential giant in U.S. history." He was described as "an able, hardworking, personally attractive public servant who, with the westering sun of California behind him, is casting a longer and longer shadow across the land."[52]

Republican matchmakers paired him with Thomas E. Dewey of New York, uniting two ex-prosecutors who had gone on to become governors of two heavily populated, politically strategic states at opposite ends of the continent. When asked if he would take second place on the ticket, Warren was noncommittal, insisting only that he hoped to conclude his term as governor, then serve another four years. Meanwhile, he had been picked to deliver the keynote address at the 1944 Republican National Convention in June.

"The only good reason I was chosen was because I come from the great, hopeful, energetic West," he said, and spoke of growth and change as a daily adventure in this young land where "there is little fear of failure and no fear of trying."[53]

"Governor," he was asked on his arrival in Chicago, "have you ever told anyone that you would refuse the nomination if you were drafted for Vice-President?"[54]

"No, I have not," he said, and nimbly prevented the press from pinning him down on the subject of whether he would accept the nomination or stick with his disclaimer ("God and the people willing, I hope to be Governor for a second four years.") Despite the long-distance urging of Governor Dewey and the arm-twisting of his own delegation, he stuck with the disclaimer.

". . . I could not accept a nomination for a place on the national ticket if it were offered," he wrote the Oregon delegates when they asked permission to place his name before the convention.[55]

Making his first major appearance in national politics, Warren departed from the fire-snorting, devil-exorcising tradition of keynote oratory, delivering a friendly, earnest exposition of his belief that there was a war to be won, a peace to be made, and jobs to be assured for displaced war-plant workers and homecoming servicemen. On a partisan note of hope, he suggested that the country was returning to the Republican faith. Three out of every four Americans, living in twenty-six different states, were already the beneficiaries of "progressive, enlightened" Republican administrations:

"In those states you will find increased emphasis upon the public health, upon free education, upon care for orphaned and neglected children, upon support for the aged, for the victims of industrial accidents, for those handicapped by physical disabilities and for the victims of economic misfortune."

"The frankness, the tolerance, the reasonableness that permeated the Governor's address are indicative of the new leadership that has come up within the Republican party in recent years," the Kansas City *Star* commented editorially.[56]

Governor Dewey was left to make his futile race for the Presidency in the conservative company of Governor John W. Bricker of Ohio. In the post-Christmas lull following their defeat, Governor Warren announced his intention of getting the New Year off to a lively start when the 1945 legislature assembled on January 8th. In his biennial message, he was proposing a bill to provide "prepaid medical care through a system of compulsory health insurance."

"Enactment of this program would put California in the forefront among the states; none has such a plan," Earl C. (Squire) Behrens reported from Sacramento.[57]

The Governor had become convinced that voluntary health insurance plans would not work. The California Medical Association, frantically trying to hold back what it called "socialized medicine," had set up a program of its own, the California Physicians' Service, but in six years it had attracted only 100,000 members out of a population of 8,500,000, of whom 1,500,000 were "medically substandard." To illustrate "the sordid results of neglected health," Warren cited selective service statistics. Out of every one hundred Californians called up by their local draft boards, thirty-eight had been rejected because of some physical or mental defect.[58]

"The fact is that most of these defects could have been prevented or cured by adequate and timely medical care," he told a joint session of the legislature, and proceeded to jolt both sides of the aisle with the most liberal, far-reaching program any governor had laid out since Hiram Johnson's first inaugural.

Warren's proposals were based on his conception of the kind of California to which some 850,000 men and women in uniform hoped to return. They would want "elimination of racial prejudices, religious bigotry, and political intolerance," he said, and went on to add protection "against the ravages of mass unemployment," "strong and vigorous health programs," and "safety at their work and in their homes and justice in all their relations with government."

He recommended the creation of a Commission on Political and Economic Equality as a start toward building "a foundation for real political and economic equality for every citizen in the state." He urged reorganization of the Department of Industrial Relations, with a view to reducing the number of industrial accidents and, when accidents did occur, to speeding up the payment of compensation to the injured workers. To bring about better relations between labor and management, he proposed the establishment of a School of Industrial Relations at the University of California.

Sickened by the dismal, Hogarthian firetraps to which the mentally ill had been consigned, he called for a twentieth-century Department of Mental Hygiene to get California out of the asylum age, place its thirty thousand mental patients in modern hospitals and set up clinics throughout the state "where people undergoing mental strain can be treated and prevented, whenever possible, from mental crackups . . ." Broader coverage of unemployment insurance was recommended, along with appropriations for crippled children and new legislation to meet new demands for parks and recreational facilities, as well as for housing, highways and schools.

"It is my recommendation that you take action at this session of the legislature on a program which will bring adequate medical care to the people of our state on a prepaid basis," he said, supplying the headlines for next morning's newspapers.

He had no intention of putting California physicians on the state payroll or of denying their patients the right to select their own doctors, he explained. The idea was simply to spread the cost of medical care among all the people of the state. He had been assured that the program could be financed by a payroll tax of 3 per cent, evenly divided between employee and employer.

As usual, he had proceeded cautiously with the proposal. In early December, after mulling it over for about a year, he had called in a prominent physician and put the problem to him, then expressed the hope that it could be worked out with the cooperation of the California Medical Association. A luncheon meeting was arranged in San Francisco on December 17. After breaking bread with CMA leaders, Warren outlined his plan and, as his executive secretary recalled later, "The first response from the doctors was one of appreciation of the Governor's readiness to come first of all to the medical profession."[59]

But a week or so later, the CMA house of delegates met in Los Angeles, then announced its intention of fighting the proposal. "Socialized medicine!" the medical politicians chanted ritualistically, and to defeat the plan they hired Clem Whitaker, the same public relations specialist who had helped put Warren in office.[*]

"The doctors thought he'd double-crossed them, and he thought they'd double-crossed him," says a former member of Warren's staff. "I believe he thought at first that he could win them over, but we couldn't even get a doctor to come help us draw up a bill. I remember him telling a prominent doctor, 'If you don't do something like this yourself, it's going to come in the back door, either through the Veterans Administration or the labor unions.'"

The CIO, without waiting for Warren's bill to reach the legislature, introduced its own health insurance plan. Like the Administration's, it provided for a 3 per cent tax, but left all administrative costs of the program to the state. Also, it proposed that a physician be paid a fixed amount for each patient he looked after, no matter what maladies or misfortunes might be involved. Warren preferred a fee system, which would vary with different ailments and the different medical specialties called into play.

"It's a good thing we were a pretty healthy lot; we couldn't even get a doctor to look at our tonsils," says William T. Sweigert, who was Warren's executive secretary during the health insurance battle.

Sweigert, a Democrat, was appointed to the Municipal Court of San Francisco in January, 1949, and five months later Governor

---

[*] "Whitaker's part in the campaign has been overplayed," says one of Warren's old associates. "Actually, the two men never hit it off. The Chief just isn't the kind of man who takes direction."[60]

Warren elevated him to the Superior Court. In 1959 he was appointed to the United States District Court by President Eisenhower. In the Federal Building in San Francisco he is now a neighbor of his old friend, Albert Wollenberg, who sits on the same bench. It was Judge Wollenberg who, as a Republican legislator, led the fight in the Assembly for passage of Warren's health insurance bill.

"It was the first time I had the pleasure of being called a Communist," Judge Wollenberg says wryly, and enjoys recalling the effect of his sponsorship of A.B. 800 on his relations with his family doctor. "He was a member of the house of delegates of the American Medical Association. When he came in the house, he'd call out to us, 'Governor Warren's Medical Service!' and if he gave us a shot for something, he'd say he was sorry he had to use such a blunt needle but he couldn't afford new ones at government prices."

The California Medical Association, determined "to keep the hands of politicians from controlling the practice of medicine in California,"[61] spent a quarter of a million dollars to defeat the Governor's bill. When a CMA spokesman urged him to give up his impractical scheme, Warren said, "I'd like to inquire: 'Abandon it for what?' "[62]

"No," Judge Wollenberg said when asked if he felt that Warren's celebrated sense of timing happened to be off in 1945, when he launched his losing fight for prepaid medical care. "It had a great effect on what has happened since then. Most of its objectives were later achieved in different forms. It smoked the medical people out."

"It seemed to many of us at the time of the fight against the Warren bill that the doctors were in danger of drowning in the flood of their own invective," one of President Truman's health advisers told Richard Harris. "The people wanted the best that medicine had to offer. If it was too expensive for most of them — well, then, they were bound to demand help in paying for it. All the bombast in the world couldn't stop them from getting what they felt they had a right to."[63]

President Truman, like Governor Warren, had been shocked to learn that selective service doctors were rejecting one-third of the men they thumped, questioned and asked to cough. In November, 1945, five months after the California legislature turned down the bills drafted by the Governor and the CIO, Truman called on Congress to enact a national compulsory health insurance program. He renewed the proposal in 1947, when Warren was again pressing for the same thing in California.[64]

"To me it is just as certain we're going to have a health program for the American people, sometime, as it is that the sun is going to set tonight," the Governor told Sacramento reporters after spending more than two years trying to convince California doctors that they could either cooperate with their state government in working out a practical program of prepaid medical care or they could wait until they were forced to accept a federal plan.*[65]

"Public health has always been considered the responsibility of the community and state," he said. "Under state sponsorship, the program can be kept close to the people, can be adapted to local conditions, and can be more readily modified in accordance with experience. But, if state sponsorship is preferable, each state must accept the responsibility. If we neglect to bring about a solution of the pressing problem of medical and hospital care for typical families, the Federal Government will undoubtedly adopt some highly centralized program that will dominate the whole field of medical care in the United States."[66]

As Warren kept warning the CMA, the American people would not endure forever a system of medical care which was adequate only for the rich, who could pay for it, and for the poor, who got it free. Most Americans, as the Governor knew from his own experience, lived from one paycheck to the next. They could afford to die (for this they had insurance), but they couldn't afford to be sick.

"He was laid up for a month in the fall of 1944, kidney trouble, I think," says a state official, "and when he got back to his desk, he told me he'd done a lot of thinking while he was flat on his back. 'What does a fellow on a fixed income do when he has to go to the hospital?' he said, and then he told me what had happened to him once when he was attorney general and having trouble stretching his salary from payday to payday. His check was late one month

---

* The states got the federal plan on July 30, 1965, when President Johnson visited former President Truman at the Harry S. Truman Library in Independence, Missouri, where friends and neighbors had gathered to witness the signing of Public Law 89-97, the so-called "Medicare Bill."

and he missed a payment on his health insurance, so it was canceled. He called the company and got it reinstated right away, but he couldn't help wondering what an ordinary working man would have done in a case like that."

"I don't see how people kill bills of this kind and live with their own consciences," Warren said in the spring of 1949, when his health insurance bill went down to defeat in the legislature for the third time. "I am very disappointed. I believe all I can say is the medical lobby was too strong for us."[67]

Lobbyists have never been inconspicuous in California. The state's first legislature assembled in what came to be called "the session of a thousand drinks."[68] In 1907, four years before Hiram Johnson took office, a Republican state senator wrote of the current legislative session: "Scarcely a vote was cast in either house that did not show some aspect of Southern Pacific ownership, petty vengeance, or legislative blackmail."[69] Governor Johnson disposed of one political evil and in the process made way for another.

"He disturbed the political ecology of California," says Judge Kenny. "He did away with the bosses and opened the door to the lobbyists. When you get rid of the owls, the rat population increases."

Political machines built to Hague-Pendergast specifications were unknown in California a generation after the Progressives had come and gone, but lobbying in Sacramento had achieved the dimensions of a major scandal. A towering, three-hundred-pound manipulator named Artie Samish dominated this shadowy fourth branch of state government.

"I've got the damnedest Gestapo you ever saw," he told Lester Velie, who helped bring about his downfall with a pair of provocative articles in *Collier's* in the summer of 1949. They were given the title, "The Secret Boss of California."[70]

Samish, as Velie pointed out, was "a creative political genius who had fashioned something new in American politics — an original political machine without a party, without club houses, without precinct organizations." In the Johnson tradition of nonpartisanship, this newfangled political boss controlled lawmakers of both major parties. Instead of using the old-fashioned bribe, he bought legislators with billboards, radio time and newspaper space. He could elect or defeat a candidate by granting or withholding the support of the varied interests he represented (beer, liquor, trucking, race tracks).

"Who has more influence with the legislature," Velie asked Governor Warren, "you or Artie Samish?"

"On matters that affect his clients," Warren replied, "Artie unquestionably has more power than the governor."[71]

When Assemblyman Wollenberg was trying to steer the Governor's highway development bill through the 1947 legislature, the oil lobby showed itself to be so much at home in the Capitol that during an assembly roll call it directed its operations from phones in the speaker's office.[72] Warren had inflamed the oil interests by recommending that an additional tax of two cents a gallon be placed on gasoline to help improve and expand California's dangerously congested highways.

"Thousands of lives are being lost, thousands of people are being injured, and the development of our state is being retarded because we are trying to take care of our automotive transportation needs of nine million people on an outgrown highway system," Warren said, and was outraged by the cynical response of the petroleum industry.[73]

"I wish the public could actually be here to witness the power that these oil lobbyists are exercising over our legislative processes," he said in June, when his highway development program seemed to have died the death in a senate-assembly conference committee.[74]

The public was spared a spectacular demonstration of legislative irresponsibility and industrial arrogance. While the lawmakers kept adding miles and miles of new highways to the Governor's bill without providing the revenue to build them, the oil industry twice raised the price of gasoline. In their propaganda, the petroleum companies pictured themselves as the motorist's friend, fighting to protect him from an additional state tax of two cents a gallon. Their two price increases totaled 2.3 cents a gallon.

"This is a plain steal and an insolent disregard for the welfare of the people," Warren snapped. "While the slick lobbyists of the oil companies are overwhelming the capital with false propaganda and presumably are sobbing for the motorist, who is being asked to pay only his fair share for decent highways which will protect the lives of our people, the oil companies have connived to siphon off all the loose change of the people before the legislature arrives at a conclusion."[75]

Warren finally got a highway development bill through the legislature (he also got legislation regulating lobbyists), but not without alienating one of the Republican party's wealthiest and most influential sources of support. The oilmen would never forgive him for whipping them in public. For his part, Warren would never forget their callousness in putting corporate profit ahead of the clear-cut necessity of reducing the number of deaths on California's crowded highways. The petroleum industry, he felt, had been as selfish as the medical politicians, and equally as ruthless in its manipulation of the legislative processes to serve private ends at public expense.

11

The Road to Washington: Detour

Mr. Truman just got too many votes.
— EARL WARREN, *explaining what
happened on November 2, 1948*[1]

O N a visit to Washington in February, 1945, Warren was asked
at a National Press Club luncheon, "Will you be a candidate
for President in 1948?" "The answer is no. Period," he said. As for
running for a second term as governor, he grinned and quoted
Jefferson, "Few die and none resign."* Then he spoke of the jinx
placed on his job by time and circumstance. "Governors in California don't last long — only one has been reelected in the last
ninety-nine years."[2]

Warren was the second. His victory in the primary campaigns of
both major parties in 1946 put him in such serious contention for the
Republican nomination for President in 1948 that his prospects had
to be reexamined. When political reporters and feature writers
descended on Sacramento, they found the Governor listed in the
phone book simply as "Warren, Earl r. 1526 H St. GI 2-3636." While
the political reporters filed explanations of how a Republican candidate for governor of California had managed to appear on the
November ballot as the Democratic nominee, feature writers were
trying to catch up with the young Warrens.

Jim had married an attractive tennis champion, Margaret Jessee,
who had given the Governor one grandson in March, 1944, and in

---

* The actual quotation as given by Bartlett: "If a due participation of office
is a matter of right, how are vacancies to be obtained? Those by death are
few; by resignation, none."

the winter of 1947–1948 was about to produce a second. Virginia, at eighteen, was such a celebrity that at times her father had to stand off to one side while she signed autograph books. Earl, Jr., was diving for abalone. Bobby was playing cornet in the town band. Honey Bear was taking the hurdles at horseshows on a jumper named Billy Sunday. Dottie, a tall, slender beauty of fifteen, was papering the walls of her room with photographs of movie stars.

"Earl Warren is paternalistic and political," Farnsworth Crowder informed readers of *Better Homes & Gardens.* "He likes people as he likes children and wants them to have a good life. His definition of a good life would be more or less after the pattern of his own. He once spoke in an address of 'the dream of every man and woman — the desire to have a home and a fireside, to have happy, healthy children, taught by a good mother.' This is no dazzling or original pronouncement. But it is just as honest as it is trite."[3]

"A man's man," an Easterner said after meeting him for the first time. "You feel that if he has a direct answer to a question, he will give it; if not, he'll say so."[4]

In California to gather material for *Inside U.S.A.,* John Gunther summed up the Governor in terms of "decency, stability, sincerity and lack of genuine intellectual distinction,"[5] and then turned happily to Attorney General Kenny, who had suffered a politically mortal defeat when he challenged Warren's hold on the electorate in the spring of 1946. "Kenny's humor, vivacity, sense of phrase, bright brains, and outrageousness are a joy," Gunther reported, still amused by his introduction to the Democratic leader. "The first time I met him he was drinking amiably with two companions; one was a Jesuit priest, the other was Harry Bridges."[6]

Kenny had done well in the attorney general's office. He liked the job and could look forward to getting himself reelected in 1946 with ease, so he was understandably reluctant to trade his political comfort and security for the risks involved in running against Governor Warren.

"He virtually had to be 'pushed' into the race," says Rollin McNitt, former chairman of the Los Angeles County Democratic Central Committee. "There was a general feeling on the part of most Democratic leaders that unless the strongest possible Democrat ran for governor, the chances of the party in the 1948 Presidential election would be impaired."[7]

When he was congratulated on becoming the Democratic candidate for governor, Kenny said, "I guess I should accept congratulations in about the way that a pregnant woman does. She didn't want to get in that condition, but as long as she is — "8 Having agreed to make the race, he promptly left for Europe, where he was eager to take in the Nuremberg trials.

"The visit to Nuremberg was important to me as a lawyer interested in international cooperation," he explains in an unpublished autobiography. "The prosecution and judges represented four different legal systems — British, American, French and Russian. The lawyers of these four nations were able to work out understandings so that all four legal systems were welded harmoniously together. Ever since the U.N. meeting in San Francisco, I had been working on the formation of an international association of lawyers. The Nuremberg trials demonstrated to me that the legal profession easily adapted itself to international cooperation. Lawyers are trained in the settlement of controversy."9

"What beat him when he returned was not his wisecracking or insouciance," Gunther wrote in *Inside U.S.A.*, "but Warren's unassailable popularity and the fact that he himself was pushed into a position where he had to carry water on both shoulders. The Democratic party is a crazy hodgepodge in California; he had to hold the balance on both wings."10

Kenny had accepted the Democratic draft at a meeting in his San Francisco office in late February, when he let himself be taken in by the persuasive arguments of what he regarded as the "harmony forces" within the party.11 He soon came to realize that harmony among California Democrats was an unattainable dream that spring. He has given his explanation of the disaster in his autobiography:

"The Democrats could only win in California in 1946 if a coalition was preserved, embracing the entire political spectrum. This had been the essential ingredient of the 1944 victory. But, in 1945, the Communists decided to end their wartime collaboration. They overthrew Earl Browder, who long had advocated a coalition of all progressive forces. 'Independent' political action became their watchword. I called it 'misplaced militancy.' At the same time, many organization Democrats were also anxious to see the end of this uneasy partnership. They suspected, with considerable justification, that the eggheads and radicals wanted to supplant their leadership."[12]

Early in the campaign, when some of Kenny's CIO supporters accused Warren of being "insincere" in advocating a liberal legislative program, the Democratic challenger voiced his disagreement: "I believe he had his heart in it. His weakness was not ascribable to anything other than the system."[13] As Kenny saw the situation, the Governor had been unable to get Republican legislators to support what was essentially a Democratic program.

"Governor Warren was born on the wrong side of the political tracks," the Attorney General said, depicting his opponent as "a poor little rich boy who wants to get out and play with the Democratic urchins, but his elderly legislative chaperones won't let him."

"There will be no wisecracking contest of cheap buffoonery in this campaign as far as I am concerned," Warren said when Kenny suggested they debate the issues on radio.[14]

The Attorney General got under the Governor's skin on at least one issue. Warren was charged with being lax in pushing the Central Valley Project, a vast, multipurpose undertaking designed in the early 1930's to provide California with water and power. It had been fought at every turn by private utility interests, and championed just as vigorously by the Sacramento *Bee*.

"I have been an open and avowed advocate of the Central Valley Project in all its phases from its inception — dams, power houses, transmission lines, steam plant, canals and all," Warren said,[15] and if he had been less than sound on the issue, he would never have received the editorial blessing of the *Bee*, which had remained neutral in 1942.

Warren had forced the private power lobbyists out into the open in 1945, when he called a State Water Conference at the Capitol. In 1947, when Central Valley appropriations were before the Congress, he reiterated his stand in favor of the project:

"The great power company which serves the people of the Central Valley will of course not agree. It has always been opposed to the project, not because it objects to the solution of our irrigation and domestic water problems, but because the project includes the incidental development and transmission of hydroelectric energy, and the company desires to develop and distribute all the power in that great portion of our state.

"The hydroelectric energy to be developed by the Central Valley Project is only one of the many purposes for which it is designed, but it is an important part of it because the power must pay a large portion of the cost of the project and not leave the entire burden on the water users. The power must therefore be fully developed as an integral part of the project.

"When it is developed, it belongs to the public. It must be sold by the public. Under both the Reclamation law and our Central Valley Project Act, preference must be given to public agencies that desire to purchase it. In order to fulfill the letter and the spirit of these laws, it is essential not only that the power be generated at the dam site, but also that it be transmitted to the load center where it can be purchased by those public agencies and private operators that desire to compete for it. Otherwise, the government would have but one customer, the power company, that is in a position to build the transmission line when and where and only if it will.

"It may well be that some of this power should and will be sold to the private utility, but it should not be the only customer, because if such were the fact, the development of water resources – in fact, the development of our entire economy – would be geared to the program of a private utility whose financial interests might or might not be entirely consistent with the variety of programs essential for the development of a great state."[16]

Warren ran for a second term on the record he had made in his first four years. The state was free of debt, taxes had been reduced about 15 per cent, and the legislature had made more liberal and enlightened provisions for the unemployed, the disabled, the handicapped, the elderly and the mentally ill. At the same time the state's population had continued its relentless growth, rising from seven million in 1940 to more than nine million in 1946.

"Gentlemen, we have to plan for a whole new city of ten thousand people every Monday morning," he used to tell his Governor's Council, and then remind them that the newcomers brought no schools with them, no roads or hospitals, and, most serious of all, no water.

He enjoyed pointing out to fellow-Westerners that they occupied an area comparable in size to the continent of Europe. This Western Empire, as he thought of it, was rich in potential hydroelectric power, as well as in coal, iron and oil; gold, silver and copper. Its soil and climate could produce any crop, from desert dates to mountain apples, and its harbors looked out across the Pacific to the riches of the Orient.

"We must come to realize that we in these eleven Western states have the youngest civilization on earth," he said. "We have had brought to us the accumulated culture and experience of the world without ourselves having to experience the terrible ordeals which have produced them. The world has poured into these Western states during the lives of people still living all the wisdom and culture of the ages. It has given us the opportunity to take the best that is available and use it in the development of an area which would be a great empire if located anywhere else on earth."[17]

Campaigning on a lofty, nonpartisan level, Warren easily overshadowed Kenny who, in Kyle Palmer's opinion, "conducted an unimpressive, scolding, surprisingly dull campaign."[18] Editorially, the Los Angeles *Times* declared that the Attorney General "has developed no genuine or persuasive arguments against Warren's administration and has failed to supply any tangible reasons why he should be elected governor."[19]

"We swung and we missed," Kenny said when the final returns showed that Warren had become the first candidate for governor of California to win the nomination of both major parties. "It is a hell of a job being governor anyway."[20]

The official tabulation released by the secretary of state some weeks later put the total number of votes cast for Warren at 1,367,682, of which 774,502 were Republican, 593,180 Democratic. Kenny received 530,968 Democratic votes, 70,331 Republican.[21] A few days after his humiliating defeat, Kenny ran into Warren at a convention of district attorneys on Santa Catalina Island, where both men were to speak. The lame-duck attorney general was taking his leave of the prosecutors with whom he had worked for the last three and one-half years. He left with dignity and good humor, paying a graceful tribute to the governor who had preceded him as attorney general.

". . . I have come to feel that I, too, am a law-enforcement officer, not merely by virtue of holding office but actually through my understanding of and admiration for the profession. Those things that I was to learn, Earl Warren knew. Since his days as district attorney of Alameda County and throughout his term as attorney general, he had been one of you, crusading for improved conditions and fighting lethargy and the forces of corruption."[22]

Lunching with a friend twenty years after this farewell address, Kenny got to reminiscing about his friendly rivalry with Warren. "I saved him from oblivion in 1938, and then had the bad judgment to run against him and end in oblivion myself," he said, and then, with tongue in cheek as usual, he added, "You've got to be careful whom you help in politics."

Governor Warren, after 1946, was a dominant figure in the politics of the West. He would go to the Republican National Convention in 1948 with California's fifty-three votes in the pocket of his double-breasted suit, and he could count on another twenty-five to fifty votes from neighboring states in the Western Empire sprawled between the Rocky Mountains and the Pacific Ocean. He was the man out West that politicians back East had to reckon with in jockeying for power in what looked to be the best Republican year since 1928.

"I have a job now that keeps me busy," he kept saying in reply to questions about his political ambitions. "If I ever decide to seek another, I will come out and ask for it."[23]

He asked for it in mid-November, 1947, when the Republican State Central Committee adopted a resolution requesting his permission to place a Warren-for-President slate of delegates on the 1948 primary ballot in California.

"In response to the resolution," he wrote the state chairman, "I can only say that if such a delegation is formed and it receives the approval of the people of our state, I shall be proud to have it present my name to the convention for that purpose. I will not, however, seek delegates in other states."[24]

"I will be available for the Presidential nomination if there is any interest in my candidacy in the Republican convention," he told Washington reporters some weeks later, "but I choose to make the distinction between that availability and a burning desire for the nomination. If I should say I wouldn't take it, I would not be honest."[25]

By entering his name in the California primary, Warren made sure that no other Republican would challenge his control of the delegation. He stayed home while Harold Stassen invaded Wisconsin, scored an unexpected victory, then went on to pick up Nebraska and the Dakotas. Stassen was checked by Senator Taft in Ohio, and virtually destroyed in Oregon by Governor Dewey. Meanwhile, no one had laid a glove on Warren.

In March, 1948, when asked by Cabell Phillips of the New York *Times* Washington bureau to define "liberalism," Warren replied that, as he understood the term, it "is the political belief, and the political movement arising out of the belief, that the individual should be the all-important, precious object of consideration in every phase of social relationship . . . Civil rights, representative government, and equality of opportunity are all part and parcel of the liberal tradition.

"These institutions have been building slowly but steadily and they are still unfinished. All of them are designed to protect the individual from domination either by government or by any privileged group. Unfortunately, this great term has been abused and distorted in recent years. It has become the disguise of Communists and Communist sympathizers who are interested neither in the freedom of the individual nor in liberal institutions. It is for this reason that many people suggest a realignment of politics in our own country in two groups — conservatives and liberals.

"This would be a mistake because the term conservative, like the term liberal, has also been distorted. Many people style themselves conservative when they are in fact reactionaries opposed to every effort to solve the problems of the day.

"If I had the choice of classification, I would divide people politically into three groups — reactionary, progressive and radical. I particularly like the term 'progressive,' not necessarily as a party label, but as a conception. To me it represents true liberalism and the best attitude that we could possibly have in American life. It is distinguishable from both reaction and radicalism, because neither of these philosophies make for real progress.

"The reactionary, concerned only with his own position, and indifferent to the welfare of others, would resist progress regardless of changed conditions or human needs. The radical does not want to see any progress at all because he hopes that our democratic institutions will fail and that in the collapse he will be able to take over with some form of alien tyranny. The progressive, however, realizes that democracy is a growing institution and that, if it is to succeed, we must make steady advances from day to day to constantly improve it and adapt it to human requirements on an ever widening base . . ."[26]

On his way to the 1948 Governors' Conference in Portsmouth, New Hampshire, he stopped off in New York City where he was interviewed on a CBS television program, "Presidential Timber." He struck the editors of *Time* as "the best campaigner yet on the newest communications medium to reach into the U.S. home. His big, square-cut Scandinavian face was etched handsomely on the screen; he was relaxed, direct and confident."[27]

He deplored a recent House cut in European aid appropriations, favored a three-year extension of the reciprocal trade act, called for universal military training ("I'm for it and I'm willing that my boys should take their place"), advocated federal aid to education, and proposed a national health insurance program to protect middle-income families. The system, as he envisioned it, would be operated by the individual states.

Arriving at the conference, Warren refused to discuss his chances for the Presidential nomination when Republican delegates assembled in Philadelphia later in the month. Partisan politics, he insisted, was inappropriate at such a nonpartisan gathering. But the press quickly got wind of a story with a partisan spoor. At an executive session which dragged on all afternoon and far into the night, it was reported, Governors Warren and Dewey had tangled in an argument over lobbyists, with Warren objecting to Dewey's singling out the school lobby for criticism, when, in his opinion, the oil and trucking interests were "more venal."

"Dewey was grandstanding in front of all the governors and Warren was needling him and blocking him," Chester G. Hanson wrote in the Los Angeles *Times*.[28]

Around midnight, after the evening session had been adjourned, Hanson spotted the two governors seated on a couch in a dimly lighted anteroom of the Wentworth Hotel lobby, "heads together and talking in low tones." They had got acquainted years before, when each was beginning to make a reputation as a crusading prosecutor. After exchanging letters about criminals and other matters of mutual interest, they had finally met for the first time in New York. Warren had been agreeably surprised by the modesty of Dewey's office ("the walls were flimsy, the furnishings unostentatious"). Also, he had discovered that Dewey was a good listener.

"I consider that one of his most precious assets — the ability to sit down with people and get something from them," Warren wrote in 1944, describing one of his own most conspicuous gifts.*[29]

Despite Republican distaste for a loser, Dewey was the frontrunner when the party leaders headed for Philadelphia in late June. Senator Taft was the strongest challenger, with Harold Stassen and Senator Arthur Vandenberg trailing him. If the Taft forces could put together a coalition strong enough to stop Dewey and deadlock the convention, Governor Warren was the man most likely to be the nominee.

"There are no deals in the offing, and I shall not be a party to any," he told newspapermen accompanying the California delegation to Philadelphia, where it made an immediate hit with the other delegations by dispensing free orange juice on Sunday, when liquor was unobtainable except in hotels by the bottle (twelve dollars for a fifth of bourbon).[30]

Chatting with the delegation at its last caucus before his name was to be placed in nomination by Robert Gordon Sproul, president of the University of California (Class of '13), Warren poked fun at the talk of deals, double-deals, blitzes and the like. "There is no place on earth outside of the Army where you can hear more rumors than at a political convention," he said,[31] and twenty-four hours later, when it was all over, he seemed in good spirits as he gave his version of Dewey's victory.

"We expected that Connecticut would make the first break in our direction, thus starting a bandwagon movement. But it didn't happen that way. We thought that Senator Vandenberg would make a

* "He's a great fellow to get facts, to get information from other people," says a former member of Warren's staff. "He'd get everything they knew." A state official agrees, and stresses a trait which becomes immediately apparent to anyone calling on the Chief Justice: "He has the ability to make you think that what you're saying to him is the most important thing in the world at that moment."

better showing than he did and that the opposition would start to crack if we could get half of Michigan's vote and half of Connecticut's.

"But after Governor Dewey polled 515 votes, nobody came to our rescue. All Governor Dewey needed was thirty-three more votes. We knew we couldn't head him off. It would have served no useful purpose to continue the debate and prolong the balloting. We didn't want to do anything that would interfere with the Republican party's success at the polls. So we just accepted the verdict of our constituents and threw our vote to Governor Dewey."[32]

When rumors began to circulate that he would like to serve as attorney general in the Dewey administration, he shook his head, explaining to reporters: "The Attorney Generalship pays $15,000 a year. Period. I am not a man of means. I live only by my salary and as Governor of California I get $25,000 a year, a contingent fund and am supplied with an executive mansion. I just couldn't afford to take the Attorney Generalship, even if I wanted it."[33]

He had already made it quite clear that he was not interested in the Vice-Presidency, which paid $20,000 a year, with $5,000 for a car and $32,385 for office expenses. He thought the nomination would probably go to Charlie Halleck, the Indiana Congressman. He went to bed that Thursday night a free man. He was awakened around four o'clock next morning by a phone call from the Dewey suite.

"They put a pistol to his head," says a Sacramento political reporter.

"He didn't want the Vice-Presidential nomination in 1948 any more than he'd wanted it in 1944," says a former member of Warren's staff, "but he told me he had to take it, or the party would never consider him for national office again."

For five hours, as dawn broke over the city and its sweltering millions got ready for whatever the day might bring, Warren conferred with Dewey and his top advisers. He was assured he would be a full partner in the new administration, sitting in on Cabinet meetings, putting his executive abilities to work in reorganizing the federal bureaucracy. When he left the nominee's suite around nine-thirty, he was still undecided, but about two hours later he agreed to run and word went out to the delegates, "It's Warren."[34] He was nominated at once by acclamation.

Mrs. Warren didn't realize what had happened until a California delegate signaled to her from the floor. She hadn't dressed for a formal appearance. Honey Bear, she noticed, was wearing a cotton dress. "None of us was in our Sunday best," she said later,[35] but when they appeared with the Governor on the convention platform, one of the reporters in the press section thought the Republicans would do well "to leave Dewey and Warren at home and send those three girls out on the road . . ."[36]

"For the first time in my life," Warren said in an extemporaneous acceptance speech, "I know what it feels like to get hit by a street-car. You know, yesterday I received something of a jolt through the balloting of this convention, but I had no idea, I assure you, that there was any such shock as this awaiting me today, and before I forget it, and before you change your mind, I want to say that I accept the nomination."[37]

Jim Warren, who knew how his father fiddled endlessly with the drafts supplied by Bill Sweigert, heard the speech over the radio in San Francisco and thought it "sounded like he made it up on the way from the hotel to the hall."[38] Earl, Jr., was in Montana fishing. Bobby got the news on a car radio, en route to the office of a Sacramento dentist. When his father called him later in the day to tell him what had happened, Bobby asked, "Daddy, was that good?"

"I think it is," Warren said.[39]

"His acceptance meant a real sacrifice of ambition to loyalty to his party which strengthened itself by choosing him," Norman Thomas wrote.[40]

The following Tuesday the Warrens visited the Deweys at their farm near Pawling, New York. The two governors, trailed by reporters and photographers, inspected Dewey's cows, his new trench silo and his view of the Harlem Valley. When photographers brought the two families together, fifteen-year-old Tom, Jr., was unable to take his eyes off Dorothy. "Look at the camera please, Tom," his father called to him. Afterwards the two Dewey boys and the three Warren girls darted off together, running down the grassy slope slanting away from the main house. The girls tripped and fell, got up and shucked off their high heels, then ran in their stockinged feet.[41]

The friendly, unorthodox tone of Warren's campaign had been set in June when he replied to Truman's off-the-cuff comment about his being a Democrat and not knowing it. "I appreciate the President's generous remarks in regard to my being a Democrat because I am sure that if he were writing it, he would spell Democrat with a small 'D.' "[42] As a lower-case democrat, Warren hit the campaign trail with an upper-case Democrat, Bill Sweigert, drafting his formal speeches.

The Warren Special left Sacramento shortly before noon, September 15th, with only one of the Warren children aboard. Twenty-year-old Virginia proved invaluable, standing in for her mother in reception lines and doing whatever seemed needful in the controlled chaos of Miss MacGregor's office. Riding with the family in their private car, the *Aleutian,* was the candidate's guest, Johnny Mullins, who had started him on his political career in 1925.[43]

"In the course of seven Presidential elections I have traveled with a good many candidates, but never before on a campaign train quite like this," Ernest K. Lindley wrote in *Newsweek.*[44]

Aside from its size (fifteen cars) and its services ("down to the arrangements for laundry and pressing"), Lindley was captivated by its relaxed atmosphere. He found "strikingly little tension," a phenomenon he attributed to Warren's even temper, his staff's efficiency and to "the well-justified confidence of everyone aboard about the electoral result on November 2."

Earl Warren was doing what had always come naturally, meeting the people, shaking their hands, displaying his handsome women-folk and riding his luck. After looking at the parched wastes of Utah, he told a trainside crowd at Ogden that Utah needed rain. It rained. "I thought I might have been a pretty good railroader," he said at another stop, "but my father saw I was a failure and had no choice but to make a lawyer out of me."[45] Good Americans, progressive and conservative alike, were to be found in both parties, he said in his prepared talks, and asked only whether the time had come "for better housekeeping methods that can only be supplied by new leadership and a new broom."[46]

When the Warren Special crossed into Missouri, Tony Moitoret warned the working press in his daily travel notes: "No booze can be served today whenever the train is stopped. Missouri wants all of its drunks to be rolling."[47] Getting their first look at the California Governor, Missourians were puzzled by his lack of partisan fervor. As Ira B. McCarty reported in the Kansas City *Times*, the candidate discussed the Constitution and the operation of government. Only once, when he committed the Dewey administration to the elimination of Communists in government, did he give his audience a chance to vent the righteous wrath that wells up in the breasts of a party long out of power.[48]

Warren had raised the same subject in Pueblo, Colorado, on September 17, as the Kansas City *Star* reported next day: "I want to say that in these critical days the watchword of our government should be — 'None but Americans should be placed on guard,' and that is exactly what Tom Dewey will do. Tom Dewey will never have any trouble getting Communists out of government. He will never take them in."

As the tour was drawing to a close in central Washington on October 14, the Warrens' twenty-third wedding anniversary, Miss MacGregor wrote a friend: "For several days the Governor and I have been in a conspiracy to surprise Mrs. Warren with the arrival of Honey Bear, Dottie and Bobbie last night. They flew up and arrived at eleven o'clock. We stalled with this and that after the meeting, but Mrs. Warren insisted on coming back to the train. The plane was a little late, and in spite of everything Mrs. Warren insisted on getting ready for bed. To her great annoyance the Governor asked her to get dressed to greet some distinguished guests who were boarding the train. She found all kinds of objections — she had met them at the meeting; she would see them in the morning. The children and a group of us were on the platform. And then she saw them. How beautiful people are when they are happy."[49]

"Governor Dewey will win the Presidential election with a substantial majority of electoral votes," George Gallup reported at the end of the campaign,[50] and on Election Day Warren's old friend and admirer, Raymond Moley, concurred: "There can be no doubt about the outcome."[51] Herbert Brownell, Jr., Dewey's campaign manager, predicted a popular majority of three million. "It will be nearer five million," Moley declared. Readers of the Los Angeles

Times could skip over the headline above Frank R. Kent's column (TODAY A MIRACLE COULD HAPPEN, BUT —) and enjoy the third installment of "Eisenhower Was My Boss," by Kay Summersby, which was illustrated that Tuesday morning by a photograph of the author in a two-piece sunsuit.

Governor and Mrs. Warren made their way to their old Oakland polling place in an early morning drizzle. They were eleventh and twelfth in line. When Warren emerged from the voting booth at 7:35 A.M. his face flushed with anger at the sight of a picture-magazine photographer with camera at the ready. "Don't you know it is an invasion of privacy and illegal to photograph a person while he is voting?" the Governor demanded, and insisted on the destruction of the film. The photographer agreed and apologized. After chatting with their former neighbors for a few minutes, the Warrens left to spend the day with friends.[52]

Campaign workers assembled early in the evening at the candidate's San Francisco headquarters on the eleventh floor of the St. Francis Hotel, where a suite had been reserved for the Warren family. The three girls were already on hand when Jim arrived with his wife, who was worried about how long the victory celebration might last. She was afraid it would run up the cost of their babysitter.

"This is definitely a Republican year," Brownell said at five-thirty o'clock, San Francisco time.[53]

Cabell Phillips, summoned from the Washington bureau to help out in the New York *Times* city room, was unable to find anything useful to do (". . . there weren't any surprises in prospect"). He drifted out of the office and into a theater on Forty-seventh Street. About ten-thirty, during the second intermission, he visited a nearby bar and nearly strangled on his Scotch when he heard a voice coming over the radio: "Truman's lead now looks almost unassailable. If he can hold his edge in Ohio . . ." He ran back to the *Times*, leaving his new $47.50 coat at the theater.[54]

"This is just the big city vote; wait till the rural returns start coming in," apprehensive Republicans kept saying.

Governor Warren, meanwhile, had decided to turn in early. He slept through the entire Dewey administration, which lasted for only one edition of the Chicago *Tribune*.

"What happened?" reporters asked him next morning, and he grinned and explained, "Mr. Truman just got too many votes."[55]

Warren has never publicly expressed any criticism of the manner in which the campaign was conducted, but some of his old associates say he warned Dewey at the outset that it was a mistake to try to coast into the White House. The Presidency was not going to be won by default, he is said to have argued, but once the strategy had been worked out by the team responsible for Dewey's automated political career, Warren had followed orders. It was not an experience he had particularly enjoyed. He was never cut out to be the number two man.

"Two weeks before the election he told us we were going to be licked," says a former member of his staff. "He said, 'Truman's gotten through to the people.' We could have cleaned up if we'd put some bets down."

After sending the President a congratulatory telegram, Warren had breakfast with Mrs. Warren and the girls, then climbed in his car and headed back to the State Capitol. He had a budget to put together for the 1949 legislature which would assemble in Sacramento in January.

"I never felt better," he told reporters next day. "It feels as if a hundred-pound sack had been taken off my back." When he discovered that one of the capital reporters had lost his voice covering the electoral cliff-hanger in San Francisco, he said, "I didn't lose mine. I didn't have anything to holler about."[56]

12

Republicans, Racketeers
and a Roosevelt

He was head of the Warren party, and it was a damned
sight bigger and more important than the Republican
party.
— A FORMER CALIFORNIA LEGISLATOR

THE 1948 returns seem to have inflicted less pain on Warren,
who had never yearned for the indignities of the Vice-Presidency, than on Lieutenant Governor Goodwin J. (Goody) Knight,
who had looked forward to serving as governor of California during
the Dewey administration. "Goody" had already given thought to
his major appointments and was preparing to dispose of his Los
Angeles home. It was Knight's impatience to succeed him that
prompted the Governor to run for a third term in 1950, says one of
Warren's confidants.

"He is not a man to be pushed. Also, 'Goody' had been playing
footsie with the right-wingers."

"California cannot continue to exist half state socialism and half
free enterprise," Knight told a group of doctors in 1949, taking a
healthy swing at Warren's health insurance program,[1] and, in
September, he said in a Sacramento press conference that he had
received 13,000 letters from "people who are against 'the welfare
state' as opposed to 'the opportunity state.' "[2]

Encouraged by the well-heeled opposition elements within the
Republican party that had coalesced around his candidacy, Knight

had a notion to challenge Warren in the 1950 primary.[3] No other
California Republican in full possession of his faculties could have
seriously considered the possibility of stepping into the same ring
with the Governor, *mano a mano*. But Knight was a formidable
campaigner. For years no sizable number of Californians had
assembled in a public place without having "Goody" drop by to
shake their hands and bend their ears.

"Type-cast as a politician of the older, earthier American school,"
Theodore H. White wrote of him some years later, "he is one of the
most instantaneously charming men in American public life today. A
robust, broad-shouldered, barrel-chested man, whose rugged face is
plowed by a hundred friendly wrinkles, he has found in the carnival
of politics delight, joy, intellectual sustenance."[4]

"Knight is a far, far better political campaigner than Warren,"
Kyle Palmer wrote in the Los Angeles *Times* toward the end of
1949. "The party has never had a more personally popular leader, an
advantage which is not always translated into ballots . . ."[5]

Palmer predicted that Knight would get the applause, Warren the
votes. After taking his own soundings, "Goody" decided not to
contest Warren's renomination. When Republicans gathered in
Fresno for an unusual grass roots convention in the spring of 1950,
the State Central Committee Chairman, Philip Boyd, started things
off by telling the delegates that "only Warren can resist the Democratic tide which has swept the nation."[6] The Republican gubernatorial candidate would have to take on a Roosevelt — F.D.R.'s
oldest son — in a state containing one million more registered
Democrats than Republicans.*

---

* After Ronald Reagan won a landslide victory as the Republican candidate
for governor in 1966 despite a Democratic numerical edge of 4,720,000 to
3,350,000 registered voters, Gladwin Hill of the New York *Times* wrote in
Frontier: "Earl Warren will never replace George Jessel as a raconteur, but
in his less Olympian days Warren had a favorite anecdote that has a particular
aptness for the present California political situation. It was designated, in
Warren's speech texts, simply as 'frog story,' and it was about a farmer with
some marshland who figured he could make a fortune supplying restaurants
with frogs' legs. He planted a big herd of frogs in the marsh, and in anticipation of spring frog-calving, made grandiose contracts with restaurants far and
wide. But the frog crop turned out to be excruciatingly small. All he could do
was wire the restaurants apologetically: 'Judging by the noise, I thought there
were a hell of a lot more frogs than there turned out to be.' "[7]

James Roosevelt had been outspoken in his criticism of cross-filing, but when he decided to run against Warren, he entered the primaries of both major parties. "It reminded me of the politician who said, 'There are times when we must rise above principle,'" Warren said,[8] quoting one of his favorite political aphorisms (he had picked it up from Bob Kenny when they were in Washington, fighting for the state's tidelands oil). Unlike Kenny, Roosevelt managed to win the nomination of his party in the June primary, but he gave Warren little trouble in the fall campaign.

In a voice startlingly similar to his father's, Roosevelt began by broadcasting an attack on the Governor's celebrated "nonpartisanship," depicting him as "the agile political trapeze performer who floats through the air with the greatest of ease, first as a Republican, then as a nonpartisan in the hopes that he will please."[9]

"We have tried to give a progressive, humanitarian administration and still keep the state solvent," Warren said, and reddened with anger when his opponent, who, as the Governor put it, had not "contributed one iota to either the governmental or social advancement of the state,"[10] had the boldness to critize its public school policies. "James Roosevelt," Warren retorted, "has never been in a public school in his life, except to make a political speech."[11]

"My father worked with his hands as a mechanic," Warren told the Sailors' Union of the Pacific. "Both he and I have worked twelve hours a day, six days a week, at twenty-five cents an hour. I know what better wages mean to a home. I know what better hours mean to a family."[12]

He defied Roosevelt to name a state with better labor laws concerning collective bargaining, workmen's compensation, industrial safety, social security and old age assistance.

"My years in public service have been dedicated to these objectives," he said. "The record is clear and is available to every Californian, because all my life I have lived and worked and reared my family on a salary which, through most of the years, was small."[13]

Roosevelt's mother came out to California in September to lend a hand in his campaign. She said she thought James would make a good governor. In Sacramento, Warren told reporters, "I don't like to argue with a mother about her boy."[14] Mrs. Roosevelt's boy lost by more than one million votes, failing to carry one of the state's fifty-eight counties.

After winding up the 1950 campaign with a television appearance in Los Angeles, Governor and Mrs. Warren flew north in a chartered Beechcraft with their oldest daughter, Virginia. It was a rough trip, ending in a dense fog. They had to land at Travis Air Force Base, then grope their way into Oakland, but they were on hand when the polls opened at seven o'clock. An hour later they were having breakfast with friends when the housekeeper called from Sacramento.

"Honey Bear's awfully sick, Mrs. Warren," she said. "She's in pain and I've sent for the doctor. She didn't want me to call you, but I thought I'd better."[15]

The frightened parents rushed back to the Governor's Mansion. They found the seventeen-year-old girl in extreme pain, paralyzed from the hips down with spinal poliomyelitis. They did what they could to comfort her, then accompanied the ambulance that whisked her off to Sutter's Hospital. The Governor had trouble fighting back tears when Honey Bear tried to reassure them ("it's not so bad"). When she said, "Mother, take him home and make him rest," Warren quietly left the room, and in a corner of the hospital corridor, alone, he wept.

"I don't look back on it as a painful memory," Honey Bear says now.

Fully recovered, she is married to Dr. Stuart Brien, a Beverly Hills obstetrician. They are the parents of three small, lively children who are being brought up, as was their mother, with no first-hand knowledge of a spanking. "It's awfully hard sometimes," she says. "I don't have my parents' patience." Like her mother, Honey Bear has never sent a child to bed as punishment.

"I've always wanted them to think of bed as a pleasant place — a haven of comfort and safety," Mrs. Warren said in the winter of 1950, when Honey Bear was still confined to her bed in the Governor's Mansion. "When they are ill or injured — and our active youngsters have had more than their share of cuts and bruises — I want them to feel it's going to be fun to stay in bed for a while. Maybe that's why Honey Bear is so cheerful right now despite the prospect of a long confinement. I've always seen that the children have had special little treats when they go to bed. I see that they have games and their favorite books in bed with them, and I've let them take their favorite dolls and toys — even as many as a dozen — to bed with them."[16]

Above the mantel of the high-ceilinged living room of the Briens' large, rambling stucco house in Beverly Hills is a life-size portrait of the Chief Justice. The eyes are blue and penetrating, the jaw blunt and stubborn.

"No, never," Honey Bear said when asked if at any moment during her illness she had ever feared she wasn't going to make it. Instinctively, she glanced up at her father's portrait, her expression suggesting the child's certainty that he would never have permitted such a thing to happen.

Less than two weeks after Honey Bear was rushed to the hospital, her sister Dorothy was driving home from a fraternity dance with a fellow-student at the University of California at Davis. Blinded by rain, her date smashed into the back of a truck stopped at a railroad crossing. He was uninjured but Dottie was thrown against the dashboard with such force that she broke five ribs. She was in shock when California Highway Patrol officers reached the scene.

Her father had gone to bed, planning to get a full night's sleep before going hunting with Bobby early next morning. Mrs. Warren, bundled into a bathrobe, was in the kitchen filling vacuum bottles with hot chocolate and making sandwiches. When Dottie stumbled in, dazed (later, she could remember nothing of all this), Mrs. Warren ran upstairs and awakened her husband.

He told the officers to take the girl to an emergency clinic run by the city. When X rays revealed a punctured lung as well as the broken ribs, she was moved to Mercy Hospital. Next morning, checking the police report on the accident, Warren discovered that Dottie's frightened escort had given his right name but had tried to conceal her identity. The records were quickly corrected.[17]

"It's a wonderful Christmas this year," Honey Bear said when an Associated Press reporter called on her the day before Christmas Eve. She was propped up in bed, knitting, the walls of her room covered with hundreds of the nearly ten thousand cards, letters and telegrams she had received in the last six weeks.

"None of the children were ever seriously hurt or ill before," Mrs. Warren said. "Then to have first Honey Bear and then, twelve days later, Dorothy in the hospital."

The doctor had given Honey Bear permission to come downstairs for the opening of presents on Christmas Eve and again the next day for Christmas dinner. There would be eighteen for dinner, six more than the table could accommodate.

"We are going to set up card tables for some of the youngsters," Mrs. Warren said.

All six children would be home for the holidays, along with Jim's wife and their three sons (Jim, Jr., five; Jeff, two; and Johnny, six months). The Governor's widowed sister, Ethel, was also coming with her son, Warren (or Bud, as he was called) and his bride, Rose, making her first visit to the Mansion. In the old days, Mrs. Warren recalled, each child had a Christmas tree of his own height. This Christmas, in addition to two family trees, only Honey Bear was to have her own tree.

"They're growing up now," Mrs. Warren said.[18]

Shortly after Warren became the only California governor ever elected to a third term, the ungainly city of his birth was visited by a company of strolling players from Washington, starring Senator Estes Kefauver in the season's most successful television serial, the Special Committee to Investigate Organized Crime in Interstate Commerce.

"By our appearance in Los Angeles, we do not mean to imply that this beautiful city is any more crime-ridden than any other city of large population," the tall, courtly Tennessean said before getting down to business in the Federal Building. "Necessarily, a city of this size, with the communications and transactions that go on here, is the scene of criminal activity of an organized nature from time to time."[19]

One of the times had been the night of June 20, 1947. "The murder of Benjamin (Bugsy) Siegel, the only big-time gangland killing in Beverly Hills, was an event we did not deserve," Police Chief Clinton H. Anderson wrote in *Beverly Hills Is My Beat*.[20] "Bugsy" (the nickname derived from his "habit of going berserk whenever he lost his temper") had flown in that morning from Las

Vegas, where he operated the Flamingo Club. He was a guest in a Moorish mansion at 810 North Linden Drive rented by Virginia Hill, who was variously identified in the press as an "Alabama heiress" and a "thirty-year-old playgirl." Miss Hill happened to be in Paris at the time Ben (he didn't like "Bugsy") dropped by. She was reported to be sampling wines with the thought of opening an agency in Florida. It was her brother, Charles, who offered Siegel the guest room.

After dining at the beach (the trout had caught his eye), "Bugsy" returned to Miss Hill's with the early edition of next morning's newspapers and a business associate, Allen Smiley. At 10:45 P.M. they were sitting on a davenport, reading the papers, with the lights on and the heavy draperies pulled back from the front window. When Smiley heard the first shot and shattering glass, he hit the floor. He couldn't remember afterwards how many shots were fired, but when he looked up at "Bugsy," it was apparent that several bullets had struck him. He was lying on the davenport, his hands in his lap, a bloodstained newspaper between his legs.

"It came to me as a complete shock," Smiley testified at the inquest.[21]

"We have the gambling angle, the love angle, the racing news syndicate angle, the narcotics angle — you can take your choice," reporters were told by a deputy district attorney. "Everyone tells us how much they loved him, but it's a cinch somebody didn't."[22]

When the Kefauver Committee wound up its engagement in Los Angeles ("the situation is not as serious as I thought," the chairman said),[23] it had a two-day run in San Francisco. Among other witnesses, the Senators questioned the local district attorney, Edmund G. (Pat) Brown, who had just been elected attorney general, the only major Democratic candidate to survive Jimmy Roosevelt's defeat. Commenting on law-enforcement problems in the Bay Area, Brown mentioned the excellent record of neighboring Alameda County, where Warren's old office had been handed on to one of his former deputies, Frank Coakley.

"You mean that Frank Coakley and the police department have been very aggressive?" the committee's chief counsel asked, and Brown replied: "I think, very frankly, it goes back to a long line of good district attorneys in the county, where they have insisted upon full enforcement of the law, including Governor Warren."[24]

Law enforcement had given Warren little trouble in his first four years as governor, but it became a major problem in his second term when Bob Kenny was succeeded by a Republican attorney general, Fred N. Howser.* Unhappy with the way the state's chief law-enforcement officer was running things, Warren prevailed on the 1947 legislature to establish a Commission on Organized Crime to look into the underworld battle for control of slot machines and bookmaking.[25]

Attorney General Howser's office was less than cordial in extending staff support to the Commission, but other state agencies pitched in when asked and enabled it to do a job which brought warm praise from the Kefauver Committee.[26] Midway in Warren's third term, after Howser had been rejected by his own party in the Republican primary of 1950, the Governor was able to report to the legislature that Attorney General Brown's "gratifying" cooperation made it unnecessary for him to recommend prolonging the life of the second Crime Commission, which had been called to duty in the fall of 1951, after the first had operated from November, 1947, to July, 1950.[27]

As counsel for both crime commissions, Warren picked his friend and former assistant attorney general, Warren Olney III, who had seen sea duty in the battle of the gambling ships. The soft-spoken, gentlemanly investigator, a former professor of law, had led the wartime drive against California bookmakers. A few weeks after the first Crime Commission had disbanded and he had returned to his private law practice in Berkeley, Olney was asked to come to Washington to appear before the Kefauver Committee.[28]

The Senators wanted to hear about Tony Cornero and the gambling ships, which Olney treated as a passing nuisance compared to the operations of the state's bookmakers. In 1941, he testified, Attorney General Warren's office had become curious about the political situation in a rather large city. Unable to bribe the police

---

* Not to be confused with Frederick F. Houser, the Republican lieutenant governor in Warren's first term. In the printed hearings of the Kefauver Committee, Attorney General Howser is correctly listed in the index, but appears in the text at times as "Houser."

chief or members of the city council, local bookies had elected their own councilmen, who had obligingly proceeded to pick a new police chief.

"It was startling to us at that time," Olney said, "that it would be possible or feasible or economically worthwhile to go to the time and trouble of taking hold of a whole city government in that fashion just to have the opportunity to run a handbook."[29]

To round out his education in the business of bookmaking, Olney did graduate work in Las Vegas, where he learned from his field studies that the big money in horse parlors came from two-dollar bets. After picking his horse, Olney then discovered, the two-dollar bettor insists on knowing as soon as the race is over whether he has won or lost. Not until then does he place another bet. This made big-time bookmaking dependent on the fast, reliable information supplied by wire services. Run by a criminal syndicate, the wire services were getting the largest share of the loot.

"No bookmaker who does not have wire service can hope to compete with one who does any more than a stockbroker who hasn't got ticker service could hope to compete with one who has it," Olney explained to the Kefauver Committee.[30]

Thus, it was possible to control bookmaking by controlling the information on which it lived. A horse parlor had to pay whatever the gangsters asked for up-to-the-minute news on horse races, ball games and prize fights. In the summer of 1946, a year before "Bugsy" Siegel's untimely end, two rival wire services worked out their differences. Continental Press, an old-line company descended from Nation-Wide News Service, persuaded Trans-America Publishing & News Service to go out of business. The most persuasive argument seems to have been murder, notably the death of a Trans-America executive named Ragen.

However, branch offices in Arizona, Nevada and California continued to operate, reportedly under the management of "Bugsy" Siegel. In mid-June, 1947, two field men from Continental's Chicago office called on Jack Dragna in Los Angeles and may also have checked in with Mickey Cohen. In any event, both Californians abruptly severed relations with Trans-America. Two weeks later "Bugsy" was killed.[31]

The first California Crime Commission, headed by Admiral William H. Standley, began its deliberations that fall. It was a study group, administratively assigned to the Department of Corrections. Ordinarily it would have worked closely with the attorney general. Instead, it turned to the Public Utilities Commission, which had a subpoena power not granted to Admiral Standley's seminar. The PUC, at the Crime Commission's suggestion, used its sweeping authority to conduct an investigation of the connection between communications and crime. Obviously, bookmaking could not exist without telephone and telegraph service.

The PUC came across much the same story of corporate hospitality to lawlessness as the Federal Communications Commission had uncovered in its investigation of wartime conditions in the communications field, when bookies had tied up at least one hundred thousand telephones. In 1942, after an airplane crash knocked out telegraph wires near Bakersfield, Western Union had taken from two to three hours to restore service to the Fourth Army defending the West Coast. It had required "something like fifteen minutes" to oblige the mobsters feeding race results and ball scores to the state's bookmakers.[32]

"Take away the money and organized crime will shrivel up to nothing," Warren kept saying.[33]

Continental Press Service was put out of business in California when the Public Utilities Commission ordered the communications industry to refuse or to discontinue service whenever it was clearly being used for an unlawful purpose. In 1940, Olney testified, Attorney General Warren's office had a list of more than eight hundred horse parlors in various parts of California. In 1950, it would be difficult to find as many as half a dozen. In fact, for a while the Crime Commission had been unable to find even one, but early in the year a couple had suddenly sprung up in San Bernardino.

"We couldn't figure out how that could be done," Olney said, "because the operation was similar to what had been going on before. They were getting a quick, fast, complete service — rundowns and everything else. Nobody else was getting it. It baffled us for a long time. We spent a lot of time trying to run that down.

We thought we must be up against something new. We found out what it was. It was a wire-tap."[34]

After discovering that Continental's leased wire still physically crossed California, servicing other states and Mexico, some enterprising crooks had tapped the line. They had succeeded in getting free wire service for San Bernardino bookies and bettors, but in the process had also short-circuited the Santa Fe signal system. This led to their undoing.

While Warren was campaigning for the Vice-Presidency in the fall of 1948, Olney got caught in a crossfire between the Governor and the Attorney General. Howser had never exerted himself in helping the Crime Commission during its first productive year. Now he set out to hobble it. He ruled that Olney's name should be dropped from the state payroll because no state agency could hire legal counsel without the approval of the attorney general's office, a step the Governor had not bothered to take in selecting the Commission's counsel.

Warren offered to pay Olney's salary out of his own pocket rather than lose his services. "The public is entitled to have this job done as efficiently as possible," he said.[35] Meanwhile, State Controller Kuchel had been forced to hold up Olney's pay, but later he reminded the Attorney General that twenty-eight other lawyers serving the state in various capacities were in a similar situation.[36] Some weeks later, Howser backed down and signed a letter of consent, enabling Kuchel to pay Olney his $625 a month.[37]

As part of its investigation of punchboards and slot machines, the Crime Commission sent unofficial delegates to the 1949 convention of the Coin Machine Institute, the leading trade association in the slot-machine business. The president of the organization warned his audience that "we who have invested our time, money, and many of us the best years of our lives in this industry must get together to prevent unfavorable happenings."[38]

One of the unfavorable happenings in California proved to be most embarrassing for the Attorney General. A member of his staff, listed as "Coordinator of Law Enforcement," was arrested and convicted for conspiring to violate the gambling laws and to bribe a sheriff. The coordinator, working with a retired Los Angeles police officer, had not only helped set up the slot-machine operation in a northern county, but had also held onto a piece of the action. Once the men were indicted, Howser's chief investigator arrived on the scene with his staff and proceeded to take statements from as many witnesses as could be tracked down.

"None of those statements were ever made available to the prosecution," Olney told the Kefauver Committee, "and at the trial they showed up in the hands of defense counsel."[39]

Warren was quick to pass along to the legislature the Crime Commission's recommendation that a new law be passed making slot machines subject to seizure on sight. Before the 1949 legislature enacted the statute, it was necessary to produce evidence that the machine had actually been played and had paid off before a conviction could be obtained. The law doomed the slot machine to extinction in California, where it had been invented in 1895.[40]

The gross annual take of the slot-machine racket was estimated by the Crime Commission at $2 billion, with something like 20 per cent being paid out for protection and graft. This made $400,000 available for the racket's continued survival.[41] Some of the money went directly into the pockets of policemen and local officials, and some went into the campaign funds of candidates for public office. Slot-machine hustlers, like Artie Samish's clients, had found the Achilles' heel of popular government.

"In California," Samish explained to the Kefauver Committee, "we have eighty members of the Assembly, we have forty in the Senate. Twenty in the Senate come up for reelection every two years. You have your constitutional officers and you have a great many local councilmen and other things throughout the state of California. And we take a look at the overall picture from the Oregon line to the Mexican border, and we decide just in the interest of our industry a survey should be made to determine the candidates who are aspiring for these offices, and we go out and we make a pretty thorough check on the thing, after which we decide to probably send money, within our industry or otherwise, billboards and channels, to see that they are elected . . ."[42]

In six years, as the Internal Revenue Service was interested to learn from the Kefauver hearings, the Brewers' Institute had given Samish something like $1,000,000 to keep beer flowing freely in California.[43]

By the spring of 1953, the Treasury's tax fraud investigators had gathered enough evidence on Samish to warrant prosecution on charges of income tax evasion. A federal court jury found him guilty of cheating the government out of $71,878 in income taxes. He was tried in the court of Judge Oliver D. Hamlin, an old family friend of Warren's.*[44] Samish paid a $40,000 fine, made his financial peace with Washington (rumored to be a settlement of $750,000) and served twenty-six months of a three-year sentence (he could have got forty years).

"I feel fine," he said when he got out of the federal penitentiary on McNeil Island, March 16, 1958.[45]

The former "Governor of the Legislature," as he had identified himself in contemptuous distinction to the "Governor of California," cheerfully posed for news photographers, then sank back into the obscurity from which he'd sprung.

After scuffling with the medical and oil lobbies, Warren had taken on the power trust in the spring of 1949, a few weeks before the *Collier's* articles exploded in Artie Samish's face. Never a political pin-up of the private utility interests (for one thing, he was much too chummy with the McClatchy newspapers), Warren reiterated his stand on public power in a speech delivered in May at the annual convention of the American Public Power Association. Some three hundred delegates from the nation's publicly owned utilities had gathered in Los Angeles.

California, the Governor explained to them, lacked great coal fields. To meet the power demands of its rapidly increasing population (an additional three million in the last eight years), the state had been relying on oil and gas, but at the rate of present use known reserves would be exhausted in about twenty years. New sources of power would have to be developed, and developed quickly.

"Most of this power development must be hydroelectric power and it must be developed by public agencies," he said, and went on to point out, "Most of our power potential is inseparably connected with water conservation for all purposes: Irrigation, flood control,

---

* The judge's father, a prominent Oakland physician, performed the autopsy on the *Point Lobos* murder victim.

navigation, salinity control, municipal purposes, recreation and conservation of wildlife. It must therefore be developed in projects that
serve all of these purposes."[46]

No private interests had the money, the authority or the desire to
achieve all of these socially useful objectives. Only public agencies,
crossing jurisdictional lines to work together, could do the job. As an
outstanding example of federal-state cooperation, he mentioned the
Central Valley Project which was developing the Sacramento and
San Joaquin River basins. On that project, he said, rested the future
not only of the valley but of the state as well.

"Our oil and gas will not be depleted in the foreseeable future,"
the president of Southern California Edison Company said next
morning, "but if they ever are, there still will be five hundred or a
thousand years' of coal supply in nearby Utah. . . .

"It is not true that the government alone can develop hydroelectric power, as is evidenced by the fact that some of the greatest
and most costly hydroelectric developments in the world have been
made in California by private capital."[47]

The reply to the Governor concluded with a chant that has come
to be a sort of pledge of allegiance to the private utility flag: "We
need freedom from governmental interference, discriminatory governmental taxation, and unfair governmental competition, among
other things, to make jobs and to increase productivity."

During a round-table discussion of water resources at the 1950
Governors' Conference, Warren bristled at the suggestion that the
vast federal-state power projects so vital to the development of the
West were making the states wards of Washington.

"It is not a gift, because we are paying it back, over a period of
years — every dollar of it," he said. "You say you don't want any of
these things in your state, but I'll wager there has been a lot of
money spent by the Federal Government on flood control in your
state, and you don't have to pay a dollar of it back. We do make
repayment on our reclamation projects. We pay back every dollar
that is expended on irrigation. We pay back every dollar that goes
for power, with interest."[48]

In the West, Warren explained, no state problem was more
complicated and more controversial than water. Western lawyers
had filled volumes of United States Supreme Court Reports with

arguments over water rights. The need for water was so great that one drop of it could touch off an argument.

"My state was a gold state," Warren said. "It was the rush for gold that populated California in the first instance, and during the first hundred years they mined about $2 billion worth of gold, but at the present time our agricultural products, which are almost entirely dependent upon irrigation, are valued at $2 billion each year. It is obvious, therefore, that water is more valuable to us than gold in the Southwest, and we are always conscious of the necessity for water conservation in all its forms."[49]

"Well," said Governor Alfred E. Driscoll of New Jersey, "I think we have taken the easy way out, and that has been to go to Washington and engage in deficit financing and federal loans."

"Al," Warren replied, "I don't think we have taken the easy way out in the West. It hasn't all been a joyride to develop that great Western country. It has taken a lot of courage, and it has taken a lot of hard work and vision to develop it."[50]

In January, 1951, when he took the oath as governor for the third time, Warren was in a solemn, prayerful mood as he addressed a joint convention of the legislature. More than fifty thousand Americans had been reported killed, wounded or missing in action in Korea. Should World War III explode, "no human being on the face of this earth will be safe from its repercussions." "Only divine guidance can supply the strength and the vision for those of us who have been elected to act for the people. Human capabilities will not suffice."[51]

After proposing a broadened civil defense program, Warren ranged over the state's immediate problems (provide benefits for Korean war veterans, continue the child care centers set up during World War II, take a fresh look at workmen's compensation and unemployment insurance, include farm workers covered by federal social security legislation in the State Unemployment Insurance System, appropriate $2,000,000 to help local communities with flood control projects, subsidize a study of smog's effect on health, attack crime by way of the state's income tax law, create a more modern and humane program for the senile and do something about the schoolchildren in new communities springing up overnight in what were once bean fields and citrus groves). And, as he had done six years earlier, he again proposed a Commission on Political and Economic Equality.

"The population of our state represents every ancestral heritage on earth," he said. "Each contributes to the economic and cultural life of California. None should be subjected to differences of treatment — either thoughtless or deliberate — that might diminish its ability to make the fullest contribution of which it is capable."[52]

Although the Governor and both United States Senators (Knowland and Nixon) were native sons, two out of every five Californians in 1951 had come from some other state during the preceding ten years.

"If you want to see modern America in one state," Warren liked to say, "come to California. We have people here from everywhere. They are progressive, interested in solving the problems of today and getting ready for those of tomorrow. I think this is true of the country as a whole, too."[53]

"I am convinced that social progress is the only way under freedom to avoid periodic excesses," he told James C. Derieux of *Collier's*. "A free society is dynamic. It will not tolerate stagnation. It demands progressive change."[54]

Derieux found Warren "the very impersonation of political California. He wins every time he runs for office within the state by a bigger margin than the time before, yet he has no organization in the conventional sense, and is disliked by many of the figures in his own party, especially the conservatives."[55]

Warren's power at the polls rested on a broad base of liberal and moderate Republicans, satisfied Democrats who liked his combination of progressive politics and fiscal prudence, independent voters who had never had it so good back in Des Moines or Minneapolis, and hidebound Herbert Hoover conservatives who had no choice but to vote a Republican ticket, even when they felt it had been highjacked by a Socialist New Dealer who kept raising pensions for the old people but refused to lift a hand to help such up-and-coming young Republicans as Dick Nixon.

Warren and Nixon had never hit it off. They are cut from different cloth, their political careers formed from different patterns, but both are products of the Progressive reformation. In extirpating the political boss by virtually eliminating patronage, outlawing nominating conventions and opening primaries to all comers, the Hiram Johnson reformers did away with party discipline and party responsibility, bequeathing California a kind of factional anarchy which Warren and Nixon had successfully exploited, each in his own fashion.

Both were members of a minority party, dependent on the votes of Democrats and independents. Warren had won them over by demonstrating that good government is good politics. Nixon had scared hell out of them by crying Communism and corruption. Warren had followed the course laid out by Governor Johnson in 1911: "There can be no partisan approach to state government." Nixon is instinctively, savagely partisan.*

When Teddy White was prowling about California in 1955, trying to figure out how Republican candidates contrived to win elections in a Democratic state without bosses, an organization or the machinery for discipline, a Democratic chieftain gave his view of the Republican party:"What they've got isn't a party. It's a star system, it's a studio lot. They don't run candidates — they produce them like movie heroes, every one cast in just the right part. But sometimes you get swell fights on a studio lot."[57]

As governor, Warren was cast as the chief executive of what is in reality two states, with two capitals, San Francisco in the north, Los Angeles in the south. Although born in the southern capital, Warren had come into political prominence as a northerner. During his years in public life, the state's population had almost tripled, but while people were crowding into the south, political power had remained in the north. Nixon, a southerner, represented a threat to that supremacy. The Senator and the Governor were like the heads of two rival republics sharing a common, quarrelsome border along the Tehachapi Mountains.

". . . when I crossed the Tehachapi into Southern California," George Creel wrote in his autobiography, recalling the beating he

---

* Eisenhower dressed him down for referring to Warren in a 1956 Labor Day speech as a great "Republican" Chief Justice, who had spoken for a unanimous Court in ending racial segregation. Walter Lippmann wrote, "A man who will exploit for partisan purposes such a decision of the Supreme Court does not have within his conscience those scruples which the country has the right to expect in a President of the United States."[56]

had taken in 1934 from Upton Sinclair's disciples, "it was like plunging into darkest Africa without gun bearers."[58]

Senator Nixon and his entourage would never forget Warren's refusal to help out in 1946, when Nixon made his aggressive, brass-knuckles debut in California politics, and again in 1950, when he ran for the Senate against Mrs. Helen Gahagan Douglas. In both campaigns, as was his custom, Warren issued no statements supporting Republican candidates, including Nixon. The young man from Whittier was left out in the cold, while Warren luxuriated in nonpartisan warmth.

"People now forget that Helen Douglas had Nixon nailed to the mast," a California political leader is quoted as saying in *U.S. News & World Report*. "Every poll showed she had Nixon licked. Nixon's people were on their knees to Earl Warren, asking, 'For God's sake, endorse this boy.' But Warren wouldn't endorse his mother for Queen of the May if it would hurt a hair of his own head."[59]

"That always gives us a good laugh," says one of Warren's intimates. "The truth is that he never got any real help from the Republican party. When he ran for attorney general, they told him they were sorry but they had no money for minor races, it was all going into the campaign for governor. Four years later, when he ran for governor, they said he didn't have a chance, so they didn't want to waste money on him, they were going to spend it on the minor races."

"The Republicans did not carry Warren to power in 1942 and 1946," Herbert L. Phillips, the veteran political reporter for the McClatchy newspapers, wrote in 1949. "Rather Warren carried the GOP to power."[60]

As Kyle Palmer pointed out in the Los Angeles *Times* a few months later, Warren had put in seven years as governor and was about to undertake his third-term campaign "with no state machine to back his candidacy, with no payroll brigade to fight both for its own and his retention, no election fund to get him started."[61]

Willard W. Shea, who served as Alameda County's public defender when Warren was its prosecutor, found himself stumped in 1966 when a graduate student wrote him a letter, asking about the structure of "the Warren machine."

"I don't remember any Warren machine," he later remarked in a private conversation. "He was his own machine."

"That's what galled organization Republicans," says a former California legislator. "He was head of the Warren party, and it was a damned sight bigger and more important than the Republican party."

13

The Road to Washington: Alternate Route

Court observers voiced doubt that Warren's ascent to the bench will change the balance on that body — now considered largely conservative.

— ASSOCIATED PRESS DISPATCH, SACRAMENTO *Bee*, OCTOBER 1, 1953

O N November 14, 1951, Governor Warren informed Sacramento reporters gathered in the cabinet room of the Capitol that he would actively seek the Republican Presidential nomination. "I have no intention of making it a divisive campaign," he added.[1] In Washington, Senator Nixon expressed the opinion that "many good men" were being mentioned as possible candidates, and "certainly Earl Warren is one of them." A Los Angeles *Times* correspondent reported: "The junior California Senator, who did not receive any help from the Governor in his successful race last year, was somewhat cautious in his remarks. . . ."[2]

"I would say Senator Taft and General Eisenhower are the front-runners, with Governor Warren the strongest dark horse," Nixon said next day at a Los Angeles press conference.[*3]

Warren, he continued, had a reputation for running an honest state government, and was "considered electable by virtue of his warmth, his personality and his family." But "the country does not know too much of where he stands . . ." "Furthermore he lacks

* A Gallup Poll published in the Los Angeles *Times* July 18, 1951, had shown Warren running well ahead of Truman, with 52 per cent of the vote against the President's 29 per cent. The rest were undecided.

strength among the people who nominate outside of California. This may be partly because of his reputation for liberalism — which certainly would help him if he is nominated — and partly because the Republicans want a fighting drive. They want someone who will hit and hit hard on major issues."

Once Warren had declared his candidacy, the American Medical Association sent out an all-points bulletin to its members, warning them that the Governor, like President Truman, "repudiates the term 'socialized medicine' while warmly embracing the substance." Objection was raised to two of Warren's recent statements:

"We must make it possible for every one of our people to protect himself and his family from the economic disaster of back-breaking hospital and medical bills."

"The well-to-do can pay for good medical care. The indigent receive it from public agencies. But the self-reliant workman who contributes so much to the building of our country . . . cannot bear the financial catastrophe of serious illness."[4]

To protect the medical profession from such insidious notions, the AMA urged each of its members to contribute ten dollars to its Taft-for-President Committee.

At the same time, right-wing California Republicans were getting together to see what they could do to help keep Earl Warren out of the White House.

"We are here to bury, not to praise Governor Warren," an Associated Farmers official said at a San Francisco dinner for dissidents in mid-January, 1952,[5] and a few weeks later a spokesman for the independent oil companies roared at Warren: "We oppose you today, because you have abandoned Republicanism and embraced the objectives of the New Deal."[6]

"As I see it, they are just beating the bushes to see whom they can scare out — and they are not scaring anybody," Warren said when the opposition forces drew up what they called a "Free Republican Delegation" to challenge the slate of convention delegates pledged to his candidacy in the California primary. Asked if the oil interests were backing the campaign against him, he nodded. "Yes, I have information that they are pouring a lot of money into the movement."[7]

Despite the money and the bitterness that went into it, the

movement got nowhere. On June 3, when California's registered Republicans went to the polls to decide which delegation should represent them at the party's national convention the following month, they voted overwhelmingly for the one committed to Warren. With six Wisconsin delegates pledged to his candidacy, he was thus assured of at least seventy-six votes on the first roll call.

"I think I'll have a few more than seventy-six," he told reporters in late June, and when asked to comment on the rumor that he might make a deal with Taft or Eisenhower to trade his votes for a Cabinet post or a Supreme Court appointment, he said, "There is nothing I hope that I have ever said or done that would indicate anything of the kind. There is no basis in fact for those assumptions."[8]

The California delegation assembled in Sacramento on July 3 and at their first caucus heard the Governor voice his hope that the Republican platform would be "forward-looking," with "no weasel-words."[9] Before piling aboard the eighteen-car Warren Special, where they were joined by the Governor, Mrs. Warren and their three sun-tanned daughters, the delegates picked Senator Knowland as their chairman.

Unlike Nixon, who served no apprenticeship in California politics, starting his career by running for Congress, Knowland had worked his way up. At twelve he was campaigning for the Harding-Coolidge ticket; at sixteen he was head of the finance committee of his local Coolidge-Dawes Republican Club; at twenty-four he was the state's youngest assemblyman, and two years later its youngest state senator. Two months after his thirty-seventh birthday, when he was a major in France, he was astonished to read in *Stars and Stripes* that Governor Warren had appointed him to the Senate seat left vacant by the death of Hiram Johnson.*

Warren's critics might characterize Knowland's appointment as the squaring of a political debt he owed the Senator's father and the family's influential Oakland *Tribune*, but it could be as easily argued that the young man had earned his Senate seat. In any event, he

* This is how Knowland remembers it. According to Hollis Alpert's eye-witness account of Knowland's overnight transformation from major to Senator, the news came by telegram from the Governor. — *The New Yorker*, July 7, 1956, p. 70.

won clear title to it when he ran for a full term in 1946. At that period of his career, Knowland was generally identified with the liberal anti-Taft forces within the party. Gradually he veered further and further to the right, until his political fortunes came to be linked with Senator McCarthy at home and Chiang Kai-shek abroad. A 1949 visit to the Orient convinced him the Republic was in mortal peril unless it gave wholehearted support to the Generalissimo. This obsession had earned him the title, "The Senator from Formosa," by the summer of 1952 when he was selected to head the California delegation.

Senator Nixon, officially a member of the delegation, was bustling about convention headquarters in Chicago the Thursday afternoon the Warren Special pulled away from the Western Pacific Station in Sacramento. Before his name had been placed on the list submitted to Republican voters in the primary, Nixon — like all the other delegates — had taken an oath to support the Governor. On March 22, as required by state law, he had signed the delegate's statement of preference:

"I (Richard Nixon) personally prefer Earl Warren as nominee of my political party for President of the United States, and hereby declare to the voters of my party in the State of California that if elected as delegate to their national party convention, I shall, to the best of my judgment and ability, support Earl Warren as nominee of my party for President of the United States."[10]

A few weeks after swearing fealty to Warren, Nixon turned up in Manhattan to deliver a Republican fund-raising speech at the Waldorf-Astoria. Afterwards Governor Dewey sought him out, pumped his hand, and told him: "Make me a promise: don't get fat; don't lose your zeal. And you can be President some day." It was on this epochal evening — May 8 — that Nixon says he first gave serious thought to becoming "a possible candidate for national office."[11]

Now, two months after Dewey had taken him up to the mountaintop, Nixon found himself in Chicago as a member of the platform-writing resolutions committee. He had been legally and morally bound to Warren for more than three months, but, as he has cheerfully admitted, he was for Eisenhower "long before I met Dewey at the New York dinner in May."[12] In short, his heart had belonged to the General at the time he pledged his hand to the Governor.

On the night of July 4, Nixon flew to Denver to join the California delegation on the Warren Special. It was nine-thirty when he climbed aboard. The delegates, sporting orange-colored baseball caps with the letter *W*, had been observing Independence Day by shooting off a few firecrackers, horsing around with the working press, gathering about a piano in the lounge car, and dancing with the Warren girls. Almost at once, word spread through the train from the Nixon camp that Eisenhower couldn't be stopped and California should jump on his bandwagon.

Warren's supporters were indignant. They suspected a double-cross. "I remember Nixon going up and down the train, beaming and shaking hands with everybody," a veteran Sacramento political writer recalls. "You'd have thought *he* was the candidate, not Warren." Distrust of Nixon came easily to the Governor's associates. They felt they had been stabbed in the back earlier in the year when Nixon had polled some twenty-three thousand of his 1950 precinct workers, asking them to name "the strongest candidate the Republicans could nominate for President."* One of Warren's campaign managers had flown to Washington and persuaded the Senator not to release the results, but word had already leaked out that Warren had trailed Eisenhower.

When reporters on the Warren Special asked Nixon about his prospects of getting second place on an Eisenhower ticket, he dismissed such talk as "ridiculous." Next day, when the train reached Chicago, the delegates scrambled off, staged an impromptu demonstration for Warren, and posed for newspaper photographers. Nixon's face was missing from the group photographs. He had slipped off the train at a suburban stop.[13]

"A delegate cannot break his pledge and still be a man of honor," Warren was quoted as saying that day. "People of honor keep their word; people of dishonor don't."[14]

Warren could get the nomination only by waiting in the wings until the Eisenhower and Taft forces deadlocked the convention. At

---

* In his celebrated "Checkers" speech, Nixon took pride in "the fact that the taxpayers have never paid one dime for expenses which I thought were political," but it developed later that he had used his franking privilege to conduct this partisan poll.

the outset, on the crucial question of seating a gaggle of delegates whose credentials had been contested, it was to Warren's tactical advantage to support Taft. Instead, voting his principles, he went along with Eisenhower. Thus, the General's convention strategists succeeded in getting California's votes when they were most needed, before the delegates took their seats.

The Governor and the General met for the first time on the opening day of the convention, when Warren called on Eisenhower at his hotel suite. They spent forty minutes together, charming each other at once.[15] Eisenhower could find much to admire in Warren's record. He had denounced F.D.R.'s 1937 "Court-packing" proposal, approved the Supreme Court's decision that Truman had exceeded his Presidential powers in seizing the nation's steel mills on the eve of a strike, and had consistently fought for state control of tidelands oil. The Governor, like the General, was a strong defender of state and local governments in their struggle to survive federal encroachments.

"Reverse the trend of centralization in government and restore to the states and local government the strong position they once had in the life of the nation," Warren had said in a Boston speech on Lincoln's birthday,[16] expounding the same Republican dogma embraced by Eisenhower: "Balance the budget. Reduce the national debt. Keep our government on the road to solvency."

Subsequently, when Warren's appointment to the Court was represented in the press as the payment of a political debt incurred at the Republican convention, Eisenhower was deeply offended. Like a pregnant spinster decrying the notion that sex might have had something to do with her condition, the General seemed to resent any carnal suggestion that politics had played a part in placing him in the White House.

"The truth was that I owed Governor Warren nothing," he declared in his memoirs, and then reminded his readers that at the convention Warren had refused to give him California's seventy votes until after the presiding officer had entertained a motion from the floor to make his nomination unanimous.[17] Eisenhower neglected to call attention to the Governor's earlier support on the key procedural vote which seated his delegates, effectively ending Taft's chances for the nomination and Warren's as well.

When the tumult and the shouting died away, the only California winner at Chicago turned out to be Senator Nixon. "It came as a great surprise to me," he said after he got the Vice-Presidential nomination, and when reporters called on his happy mother in East Whittier, she told them how Dick had come to her at the age of nine and said, "Mom, do you know what I'm going to be when I get big — I'm going to be a lawyer they can't bribe."[18]

Nixon likes to remind his detractors that, along with the rest of the California delegation, he stayed with Warren "to the finish"[19] — "the finish" being a single ballot in which Nixon could not have voted otherwise, because California's seventy votes were pledged as a bloc to Warren. Nixon was suspected by the Governor's political tacticians of having made a deal to deliver to the General the secondary strength he would have had to demonstrate if he had failed to get the nomination on the first ballot.

"We are not unfriendly," Nixon later explained when the subject of his relationship with Warren came up. "We are two individuals going our own way."[20]

Nixon's friends are still convinced that it was vengeful Warren loyalists who tipped off the press to the existence of the Nixon Fund dispensed by Dana Smith, a Pasadena lawyer who complained to reporters that Governor Warren had never done a satisfactory sales job on the free enterprise system.

"But," he said, "Dick did just what we wanted him to."[21]

In the closing days of the campaign, Warren was flown to Chicago to appear with Eisenhower in a radio-television interview beamed directly at the voters of California, Oregon and Washington. The Governor was brought in to calm western apprehensions about the General's views on social welfare programs and public power projects. Eisenhower insisted he believed in "a warm-hearted government" operated with "hard-headed efficiency." As for water and power, he felt the Federal Government should be kept out of "whole hog bossing" of western reclamation and development, leaving control in local hands.

"In the far West," Warren had said earlier in reply to Democratic Cassandras, "they tell our people that the development of the West will come to a halt; that there will be no more river development, no more hydroelectric energy, no more soil conservation or rural electrification.

"Out here, Eisenhower stands for the development of our great river basins, the development of hydroelectric power, irrigation and all the other multiple purposes that water can be used for, the intelligent utilization of our forests and grazing lands and the great mineral wealth of the West."[22]

In still another recorded address, the Governor assured California voters that he had talked with the General about present and proposed plans for developing the West, and Eisenhower had said, "You know, Governor, I believe that those things represent the unfinished business of America."[23] The General carried California, along with Washington and Oregon. His gratitude to the Governor, it was widely reported, would be expressed by appointing him Attorney General. However, the Cabinet post he seems to have offered Warren was not the Department of Justice but the Department of Labor. The Governor turned it down. He let it be known, though, that he would not be unhappy with a seat on the Supreme Court.

Rumor had placed him on the bench even before the 1948 campaign, when Washington reports insisted Truman not only wanted to give the Court another liberal vote but also give California Democrats a shot at the Governor's Mansion in 1950. "Nothing to it," Warren said in the summer of 1949, when he was listed high among the possible successors to the late Justice Murphy.[24] The appointment went to Truman's Attorney General, Tom Clark.

Accounts vary as to when the subject of a Supreme Court appointment first came up in talks between Eisenhower and Warren, but a former member of the Governor's staff fixes the date as mid-September, 1952, early in the General's campaign. "Mrs. Warren always screened the Governor's calls at the Mansion. One day she answered the phone, then turned it over to him. It was John Foster Dulles. He said, 'Earl, the General wants to talk to you.' Eisenhower got on the phone, and during the course of their conversation, he said, 'The first time we get a vacancy on the Court, I want to talk to you about it,' and Warren said, 'That's something I'd like to talk about.'"

Two weeks after the election, on November 21, just before he announced the appointment of Herbert Brownell, Jr., as Attorney General, President-elect Eisenhower called Warren at the Executive Mansion. Afterwards, at his regular press conference, the Governor seemed in unusually high spirits.

"He tells me he's working eighteen hours a day and enjoying it," Warren said when asked about the Eisenhower call, and then made the point that it had not had anything to do with recent Cabinet appointments, including Brownell's. The Associated Press inferred that "the Republican Governor may be in line for the first vacancy on the Supreme Court."[25]

Early in January, a couple of weeks before he flew to Washington with Mrs. Warren and the three girls to take in Eisenhower's inaugural, the Governor called on the 1953 legislature to help "make life better for all our people, with particular concern for those who have been afflicted by misfortune or who, because of youth or age, are entitled to our special solicitude."[26] As he had done when he first settled down in "the corner pocket" ten years earlier (he had reluctantly left it in the fall of 1951 for larger quarters in the Capitol), he invited the lawmakers to drop by any time, the door was always open.

"Every facility of my office and my own personal time are available to your committees and to the individual members of both houses — new and old — for the asking," he told the heavily Republican legislature[27] (an edge of 53–26 in the assembly, 29–11 in the senate), and then delivered his annual report on the state of the State.

In the first two years of his third term, California had acquired 720,000 new residents. There were 275,000 more children, filling 9,000 classrooms. The problems of aging, still unsolved, had to be faced by 73,000 more men and women over the age of sixty-five. Overcrowded state hospitals had to take care of 3,120 more patients; correctional institutions another 1,856 residents. Along with a broadened highway development program to accommodate the state's 5,600,000 motor vehicles (an increase of 556,000 in the last two years), Warren urged the legislators to help "bring the cost of medical care within the means of people in the low and modest income brackets."[28]

Two months after the legislature buckled down to work (bypassing health insurance), Mrs. Warren was rummaging around the basement of the Governor's Mansion and innocently sparked fresh speculation that her husband was about to be appointed to the Supreme Court, a rumor which was being fed into the capital's gossip mills by "Goody" Knight's impatient supporters. A newspaperman, checking the story out, called the Governor's executive secretary and asked whether Mrs. Warren was redecorating the Mansion or packing to move out.

"Mrs. Warren," the secretary said, "reported that the only thing in the line of packing going on was she was in the basement unpacking some things she brought up from Santa Monica where the Warrens spent the summer. This is the first real opportunity since they took the cast off her foot, which was broken in Santa Monica."[29]

The Warrens made their first trip to Europe in the late spring, when they took the three girls to London for the coronation of Elizabeth II. The Governor was one of the four members of President Eisenhower's delegation, headed by General George C. Marshall. As official representatives, the family was seated in Westminster Abbey with England's peerage and Europe's royalty. They also had good seats for the royal procession through London. Never one to waste time, Mrs. Warren took advantage of the long wait in the stands to address postcards to old friends back home.

Before going to London, Warren had accompanied California's Democratic Attorney General Brown to Washington to discuss the future of the Central Valley Project and to celebrate passage of the Submerged Lands Act, one of the first major pieces of legislation put through Congress by the new administration. It turned a large part of the nation's vast offshore oil resources over to the coastal states. Just a year earlier, President Truman had vetoed a similar act of Congressional generosity, insisting that the wealth of the tidelands should be exploited for the benefit of the entire country, not just a few favored states, notably Texas, Louisiana and California.

As attorney general, Warren had appeared before the Senate Judiciary Committee to speak in opposition to federal dominion over California's tidelands. "Our coastline is one of our greatest natural resources," he said in February, 1948, when he returned to Washington as governor and testified before a joint meeting of the House and Senate Judiciary Committees.[30] Hearings were being held on a proposal to overturn a 1947 Supreme Court decision declaring that California had no title to its tidelands wealth.[31]

During his Vice-Presidential campaign that fall, Warren had told cheering Texans in Fort Worth that offshore oil was "the heritage of every schoolchild in Texas."[32] Four years later, after Truman's veto had denied the youngsters their inheritance, wealthy Texans chipped in to help send Eisenhower to the White House. It took less than four months to get their tidelands bill passed.*

After returning from a seven-week vacation trip in Europe (he had received the highest possible honor in Sweden, the Grand Cross of the Order of North Star), Warren met with Sacramento reporters on September 3, 1953. They were given an announcement they had been expecting for some weeks: "I will not be a candidate for the governorship next year and the people of California should be the first to know that fact in order to have ample time for the selection of my successor."[34]

The phrase, "the first to know," was interpreted in some quarters as an indication that the Warren Era in California was about to end abruptly with the announcement in Washington of a federal appointment for the Governor.

"I do not know of any post for which he is under consideration," Murray Snyder, the President's assistant press secretary, told White House correspondents who had traipsed out to Denver to watch Eisenhower play golf and fish for trout.

In Washington, however, "a White House source" was quoted as saying the California Governor could have the first vacant seat on the Supreme Court if he wanted it.[35]

"I do not propose to answer rumors, surmises and conjectures," Warren said when asked to comment on the speculation that he might be appointed to fill the Supreme Court vacancy expected to be created by Justice Frankfurter's resignation.[36]

---

* California and the United States Government, however, continued to dispute dominion over about six million acres of oil-rich submerged lands. In May, 1965, the Supreme Court awarded almost all of the acreage to the Federal Government. Chief Justice Warren took no part in the case, nor did Justice Clark who, as Truman's Attorney General, had participated in earlier tidelands litigation.[33]

The seventy-year-old jurist had been caught up in what *The Nation* referred to as "a curious war of nerves" intended to dislodge him from the bench. "It has taken the form of inspired stories that his letter of resignation is on the President's desk, pointed inquiries about his health, a drumbeat insistence in the gossip columns that he is about to retire, and more recently direct questions from California political writers about when he intends to retire. Governor Warren would quickly relieve his own, and by this time nearly everyone else's embarrassment, if he would publicly repudiate this unseemly campaign."[37]

In his press release announcing his decision not to run for a fourth term in 1954, Warren said he was acting on his "firm and long-standing belief that periodic change of administration is essential to the continued health of our representative system of government. It sharpens the interests of our people in the election process; it kindles new ambitions; it releases new energy, and opens doors of opportunity for others to serve."

"Yes, I am happy," Lieutenant Governor Knight said when he heard the news.[38]

His interest in the election process already sharpened (he had been lieutenant governor since 1947), his ambitions kindled, his energies waiting to be released, "Goody" was tired of staring at the closed doors of opportunity, like a poor relation whose patience and clothing had grown thin while waiting for his legacy. In the five years since Warren had returned to Sacramento as governor instead of moving to Washington as Vice-President, Knight had become increasingly restive. Relations between the two men were such that Warren had not consulted the Lieutenant Governor on his no-fourth-term announcement, nor had he tipped him off in advance that he would make it at his regular Thursday press conference preceding the Labor Day weekend.

Warren acted just two weeks before Knight was to declare himself officially a candidate for the Republican nomination for governor. As he had already indicated to friends, including newspaper reporters, he intended to run in 1954 even if it meant opposing Warren in the primary. He had good reason to be happy when the contest was canceled by the Governor's announcement.

"No," Knight said when asked if he would conduct a nonpartisan campaign in the Hiram Johnson–Earl Warren tradition. Like Warren, he would cross-file as a Democrat, but he would present himself to the electorate as an unabashed Republican. Precinct workers would be able to count on him to support the party, endorse its candidates and carry its banner in the unending struggle against the Communist conspiracy and creeping Socialism.

After announcing his decision, Governor Warren opened the state fair, posed for photographers with a pretty girl wearing a crown and a white swimsuit, and then went on with the day's work. At the Governor's Mansion that evening the main topic of conversation was the marriage of Earl Warren, Jr., which was to take place in Sacramento the following day at the First Baptist Church. Patricia Kent, the bride-to-be, was a fashion coordinator, a lovely addition to a strikingly handsome family.

"How in the hell can you beat that family?" California Democrats had groaned for years.

The family was accustomed to Papa Warren's habit of sitting up in bed reading, at times until two or three o'clock in the morning. That Labor Day weekend no one paid much attention to the books on his nightstand. He was reading Beveridge's four-volume biography of John Marshall, the Great Chief Justice.[39]

Vice-President Nixon was spending the holiday with Tom Dewey at his Pawling farm. Senator Knowland, who had succeeded the late Senator Taft as Senate majority leader, was on his way to Formosa for a week's visit with his friend Chiang Kai-shek. Former President Truman was in Detroit to address a labor rally. Chief Justice Fred Vinson was attending a Boston meeting of the American Bar Association. When he returned to his Washington hotel apartment Monday evening, Vinson complained of indigestion. At one-thirty o'clock Tuesday morning Mrs. Vinson called the family doctor. Forty-five minutes later the Chief Justice was dead of a massive heart attack.

When the news reached Eisenhower in Denver, he called off his afternoon golf date. Warren canceled his regular Tuesday press conference. He usually met with Sacramento reporters twice a week, Tuesday and Thursday, but on this particular day he preferred to avoid their questions. They were bound to ask about the possibility of his being named to succeed Vinson. Delicacy demanded that the Chief Justice be decently buried before he was replaced.

Eisenhower flew east for the funeral of his old bridge-playing friend. With the Supreme Court scheduled to begin its 1953 term in less than a month, the President was eager to fill the vacancy even though his choice would be caught in a constitutional bind. Congress was not in session. A recess appointment would place the newly designated Chief Justice in the embarrassing position of having to serve for some months before he could be confirmed by the Senate. The necessity of participating in decisions likely to stir the passions of Senators who had not yet voted on the appointment would threaten the delicate balance of power between the judicial and legislative branches. The situation was viewed with such gravity by a group of Harvard professors that they urged the President to call the Senate back to Washington to act on the nomination at once.*

In the early years of the Republic, as was well known to students of Constitutional history, a distressing precedent had been set when John Rutledge was given a recess appointment as Chief Justice by President Washington. After inflaming Federalist Senators with an intemperate attack on John Jay's treaty with England, the South Carolina jurist had taken the oath of office at the start of the Court's 1795 term. Four months later, when the Senate met, it lost no time in rejecting the nomination. Aside from the Chief Justice's politics, some doubt had arisen as to his sanity.[41]

Eisenhower, early on, had decided to have the FBI run a make on any prospective appointee to a federal job. In the case of judges, he had also made up his mind to require the approval of the American Bar Association and to fix sixty-two as the maximum age.[42] This ruled out a great many Republican judges in federal courts, because twenty years had passed since a Republican President had been able to make a judicial appointment. Incumbents, by the fall of 1953, had

---

* Warren's nomination, as it turned out, ran into a tug-of-war between the legislative and executive branches, which in the end proved to be more of an embarrassment to the Senate than to the Chief Justice. As a protest against North Dakota's lack of patronage, Senator William Langer used his position as chairman of the Judiciary Committee to hold up Warren's appointment for seven weeks, while a succession of irresponsible witnesses took turns vilifying the Chief Justice.[40]

got a bit long in the tooth. Governor Warren, only fourteen months younger than the deceased Chief Justice, was barely able to crowd in under the age ceiling.

Although John Foster Dulles was three years over the limit, he seemed so sound of wind and limb that Eisenhower tentatively offered him the appointment. He was highly complimented, he said, but would rather stay in Foggy Bottom as Secretary of State. Age disqualified another contender whose name had somehow appeared on the President's list of potential Chief Justices. John W. Davis, the 1924 Democratic candidate for President, was well into his eighty-first year. He was still a handsome and commanding figure at the bar, however, and had been retained by South Carolina to defend the constitutionality of its segregated school system. Of all the issues left unsettled by the Vinson Court, this was the most immediate and the most explosive. It would have to be faced in the new term.

In the meantime, Warren and two of his sons, Earl, Jr., and Bobby, had gone hunting with an old Ventura County friend, Edwin L. McCarty. They were looking for deer and wild pig on Santa Rosa Island on Thursday, September 24, beyond reach of a phone, when the Coast Guard got through with a message from Washington. Later, reporters reached McCarty and asked whether it were true the Governor was about to be appointed Chief Justice. They were told that if such an announcement were to be made, it should come from the President.[43]

At eight o'clock Sunday morning, the 27th, Warren met Attorney General Brownell at an Air Force base near Sacramento. They talked in private for some time (three hours, according to newspaper accounts; a little over an hour, according to Warren). Details of this conversation have never been made public by either of the principals (Eisenhower declared in his memoirs that he simply wanted a qualified lawyer to pass on the Governor's record),[44] but a former associate of Warren's confirms the rumor that Brownell was sent west to urge the Governor to accept an appointment as Associate Justice, not Chief Justice.

Eisenhower, according to this source, had promised to appoint the Governor to the Court and had no intention of reneging, but apparently it had never occurred to him that the first vacancy might be the center chair. Because Warren had no prior judicial experience, Eisenhower proposed to elevate an incumbent to Chief Justice and appoint the Governor to the new vacancy, as F.D.R. had done with Attorney General Jackson in 1941, when Associate Justice Stone was moved up to Chief Justice.

"But," says the former Warren aide, "the Governor said no, it was to be Chief Justice or nothing."

"He was smiling when he came out," says the former member of the California Highway Patrol who drove the Governor back to the Mansion at the end of the Sunday morning conference.

Tuesday night Brownell called from Washington to tell Warren to start packing. Later, when reporters asked why the Attorney General had flown out to see him, the Governor said it was to tell him he was under consideration for a Supreme Court appointment and to ask if he could be in Washington for the opening of the new term on Monday, October 5th.[45] It would hardly require a transcontinental flight and a private conference of from one to three hours to carry on a conversation that could easily have been fitted into a three-minute long distance call.

On September 30th, the morning after Warren got the official word from Brownell, who had already leaked the story to a few of his friends in the Washington press corps, "Goody" Knight boarded a plane in San Francisco bound for Los Angeles. "Tell the pilot I'd like to listen to the ten o'clock news broadcast," he told the stewardess, and when she asked why, he explained, "Tell him I may be governor." The pilot ignored the message, attributing it to a crank or a practical joker, but once the Convair transport was safely aloft, "Goody" went forward, established his identity, and listened to the broadcast. When he got off the plane in Los Angeles, he was chewing gum and beaming.[46]

He was like a bridesmaid who, after many years, had finally caught the bouquet, the irreverent Los Angeles *Daily News* reported. "Rarely has one politician been so delighted at the advancement of another," an anonymous newspaperman wrote in *Frontier*, a liberal California monthly magazine, which grudgingly admitted that Warren's appointment was better than might have been expected from the Eisenhower administration. The editors predicted that he "may become, if not a great Chief Justice, a good Chief Justice who will serve as a moderating influence on the rampant reactionary trend of the times."[47]

In his formal statement accepting the appointment, Warren fell into a common error by referring to his new title as "Chief Justice of the Supreme Court," but by the time he had cleared out his desk the following Saturday night and left a letter of resignation on it, he had the title straight. He was to be "Chief Justice of the United States." As such, he would not only preside over the Supreme Court but also serve as head of the nation's judicial system. For these additional duties he would be paid approximately ten dollars a week more than the eight Associate Justices.

Warren seemed unusually quiet and thoughtful one day during his last week in Sacramento, when he was on his way to luncheon with Beach Vasey, his legislative secretary. Vasey was about to go back home to Long Beach as a Superior Court judge, his reward for putting in nine years riding herd on California legislators.

"You know, Beach," Warren said, "you've got a better assignment. You'll be in a courtroom, with jurors, attorneys, witnesses. You'll be working with people. I'll be in an office with briefs and transcripts."

As governor, Warren had assembled a remarkable staff. Its members were clannish, closely linked to one another and united in their loyalty to the Chief, as some of the oldest among them continued to think of him. They were like a big family, inclined at times to quarrel among themselves but quick to close ranks against any outsider who threatened to make mischief for the Governor or his family. The inner circle, indeed, was an extension of the Warren family. When the Chief Justice flew to Oakland in June, 1966, for his sister's funeral, his children were waiting for him with Helen MacGregor, Oscar Jahnsen and other members of his staff who had helped rear them.

Miss MacGregor had known Oscar as a child, when he used to play in her backyard in Oakland. She had gone to high school with James H. Oakley, the gently humorous lawyer who took over as the Governor's executive secretary in January, 1949, when Bill Sweigert was appointed to the bench. Oakley had first gone to work in the office of the Alameda County district attorney in 1924, when Warren was one of Ezra Decoto's two chief deputies. After Jim moved to Sacramento with his wife and two daughters, Miss MacGregor says, "their house was my second home."

She also remembers the many evenings she came back to her own apartment after a long, trying day at the Capitol and found that Mrs. Warren had stopped by to leave a pot of baked beans and Swedish meatballs (a house specialty) or a wedge of homemade cake from one of the children's birthday parties.

"Those lovely children," Miss MacGregor says, recalling the rumpus they used to kick up in the big old Vernon Street house in Oakland, when their father was district attorney. "Sometimes we'd take files from the office and work on them in the library on the third floor. The children weren't supposed to go near the library, but every now and then a blonde head would show up, and he'd say, 'Well, honey, what is it? I'm working with Miss MacGregor now. You come back at five and we'll see what we can do.'"

"In all the years she worked for him," says a member of the inner circle, "I never heard him call her 'Helen.' It was always 'Miss MacGregor.'"

While Beach Vasey manned the bridge between the Governor and the legislature, Verne Scoggins handled his relations with the press and helped draft his formal talks. Miss MacGregor gives him much of the credit for the smooth operation of the Warren Special in the 1948 campaign. "Verne was in charge of the train and did a beautiful job of organizing it," she says. "He had a sixth sense of impending trouble and the source motivating it."

Merrell F. (Pop) Small was brought in as a campaign assistant in 1945, and Warren found him so agreeable and useful that he kept him around to help assemble factual material for speeches and legislative proposals. Eventually "Pop" became the Governor's liaison with the various department heads. A warm, likeable ex-newspaperman (oddly enough, he bears a strong physical resemblance to Warren), "Pop" was an ideal ambassador to the bureaucracy. Before each meeting of the Governor's Council, he would send Warren a memorandum on current conditions in the different departments.

"'Pop' not only looks a lot like Warren," says a veteran Sacramento official, "but he also has Warren's uncanny ability as a judge of character. It's an instinct with both of them. As for those memos 'Pop' used to write, I think Warren not only read 'em, I think he memorized 'em. He used to ask the damnedest questions, and he expected you to know everything that was going on in your department."

"After our regular meetings," says another official, "he liked to get a small group together, three or four men in related fields, so everybody knew how his work fitted in with what the other departments were doing."

"Something else he used to do," says one of Warren's political appointees (a Democratic friend of Sweigert's). "He used to have lunch at a private room at the Sacramento Hotel with small local groups, maybe five or six men from some little county seat. That's one way he kept in touch with the grass roots."

Before he left the Capitol, Warren appointed Miss MacGregor to the Youth Authority Board and placed both Jim Oakley and Beach Vasey on the Superior Court bench. "Pop" Small had already preceded him to Washington, where he was serving as administrative assistant to Senator Kuchel, whom Warren had picked to fill the vacancy created by Senator Nixon's elevation to the Vice-Presidency. Oscar Jahnsen served both "Goody" Knight and his successor, Governor Brown, as assistant adjutant general, a member of the Adult Authority, and deputy state director of motor vehicles.

Despite his friendliness, Warren has always been a loner, personally and politically. He has few intimate friends and, with the possible exception of Warren Olney, III, no one has ever served him in quite the same capacity that Colonel House, Harry Hopkins and Ted Sorensen served Wilson, Roosevelt and Kennedy. In 1958, after spending nearly four years in Washington running the criminal division of the Department of Justice, Olney thought he had finally managed to get back to private life in California, but Warren persuaded him to accept the highest office a Chief Justice can offer — the position of director of the Administrative Office of the United States Courts.

As the Warrens started clearing the Governor's Mansion of the ten-year clutter of a large family of varied interests, they had no home to go to in Washington or to return to in California once the Court recessed for the summer. The Governor told Sacramento reporters he intended to put up at a hotel, while Mrs. Warren stayed behind to get things "boxed, crated and stored." Later that Friday afternoon he drove to San Francisco with two members of his staff, scribbling revisions of the text of his farewell address. He spoke over a statewide radio hookup, reading from a heavily blue-penciled typescript.

Reviewing his years as governor, he took pride in the state's assimilation of four million new Californians "without any confusion or discord whatsoever." He saluted his successor ("worthy of the finest instincts of a progressive people") and, for the last time, squared off against the obstructionists who had opposed his efforts to keep pace with the state's prodigious growth by building new highways, schools and hospitals.

"We pay for highways we don't have in congestion, accidents, in injuries and death.

"We pay for schools we don't have in retarded young lives.

"We pay for hospitals we don't have in misery."

Finally, in an emotional passage reminiscent of Lincoln's parting words to his Springfield neighbors in 1861, he said, "Here I was born, here Mrs. Warren and I have reared our family, here our children have attended public schools . . . Here our fondest memories and greatest hopes are. Here my home will always be."[48]

Saturday, taking his leave of old friends around the Capitol, the Governor "seemed near the point of tears," the United Press reported. "So many things are passing through my mind I can hardly express them," he told members of his cabinet, his eyes blinking rapidly. "You people have worked diligently trying to give the people of this state an efficient administration." When newsmen caught up with him for the last time, one of them asked if he had any final word about state politics before slipping on his judicial robe.

"Oh, no!" Warren laughed. "I think now you'll have to excuse me."[49]

In his office that night he wrote a brief note to the secretary of state ("In order to accept the office of Chief Justice of the United States, I hereby resign as Governor of the State of California, effective at 12 o'clock midnight, Sunday, Oct. 4") and signed nineteen clemencies. One of the pardons, recommended by the Alameda County Superior Court, restored full civil rights to Ernest G. Ramsay, who had been paroled during the Olson administration along with two other *Point Lobos* co-defendants, Earl King and

Frank Conner. Thus, Warren's political career in California ended, as it had begun, with the murder of George Alberts.[50]

Sunday night, when Warren's plane touched down in Washington shortly before ten o'clock, Vice-President Nixon, sniffing with hay fever, was waiting at National Airport. Also on hand to welcome the Warrens (at the last minute Mrs. Warren had been talked into accompanying her husband) were two old friends, Assistant Attorney General Olney and Senator Knowland.

"In school," Mrs. Warren said when the reporters asked where the girls were.[51]

Senator Knowland dropped the Warrens off at their hotel, where Attorney General Brownell picked them up next morning and took them to the Court. Coming directly from the bustle of his Sacramento office, Warren found his new quarters strangely quiet, his staff absurdly small and his brethren — the Justices traditionally refer to one another as "my brother" — exceedingly hospitable and helpful. Despite its power, the Court at peak strength could hardly muster as many as two hundred employees, most of whom guard the doors, deliver messages, scrub floors, and direct tourists to the rest rooms and the cafeteria. By Washington standards such a modest table of organization would embarrass a new bureau set up to minister to the needs of migratory waterfowl.

"I walked into the Supreme Court Building," Warren says of his introduction to the Court, "and was ushered into the chambers of the Chief Justice by the marshal. There I was met by Mrs. McHugh, who had been the secretary of my predecessor, Chief Justice Vinson, and who incidentally is still there in the same capacity with me. There were also there awaiting me two very elderly messengers, one of whom soon passed away, and the other retired because of old age; and there were three young law clerks recently out of law school, two of whom the Chief Justice had appointed but had not yet seen.

"That was my staff. Can you imagine the shock after the multiple secretariat and staff I had been accustomed to? And particularly when I had not been in active legal practice for almost eleven years. I made straightaway for the chambers of Mr. Justice Black, the senior Justice. He welcomed me to the Court and offered his assistance in every possible way. He then took me to the chambers of the other members of the Court, who were also cordial in their welcome and generous in their offers of assistance. By that time, it was almost twelve o'clock noon. We robed and filed into the courtroom . . ."[52]

As senior Justice, Black presided. While Warren, in a borrowed robe, sat at the desk of the Court Clerk, Justice Black made a formal announcement of Chief Justice Vinson's death ("We join the Nation in lamenting the death of this capable and loyal public servant. We, his brethren of the Court, also mourn the loss of a congenial and treasured friend"). Then Warren's commission was read ("Know ye: That reposing special trust and confidence in the Wisdom, Uprightness, and Learning of Earl Warren, of California, I do appoint him Chief Justice of the United States . . ."). Warren stood up, placed his hand on a Bible, and took the judicial oath. He had already taken the Constitutional oath in a private ceremony in the conference room.

"I do solemnly swear," he said, as tears came to his wife's eyes, "that I will administer justice without respect to persons and do equal right to the poor and to the rich. . . ."

Beaming, he shook the Court Clerk's hand, then moved up to the high-back center chair, where he shook hands with the two senior Justices, Black on his right, Stanley Reed on his left. Taking his seat, he nodded at President and Mrs. Eisenhower. Forty lawyers, including Olney, were admitted to practice before the Court, each of them receiving a warm, individual welcome from the new Chief Justice. The day's public business concluded, Court adjourned; and while his wife was taken on a tour of the building before being driven back to her hotel, Warren worked with his brethren of the Court in their handsomely paneled conference room, getting his first look at the formidable docket of the 1953 term.[53]

Along with the constitutionality of segregated public schools, the Court would have to rule on such matters as the validity of the Federal Lobbying Act and an appeal by three baseball players seeking to apply antitrust laws to the game's "reserve clause," the device by which a ballplayer is bound to his club for as long as its management chooses to keep him. Other cases involved a fifty-dollar federal gambling tax stamp, a segregated swimming pool in Kansas City and a golf course in Houston, contempt sentences imposed on witnesses who had refused to answer certain questions put to them by the House Un-American Activities Committee, and the use in state courts of evidence obtained by means of illegal searches and seizures.

It was five o'clock before the Chief Justice could break away long enough to pose for the photographers who had been waiting for him all afternoon. He put on his robe again, explaining that he had brought one with him from California — the one he used at academic ceremonies — but had decided to wear the robe lent him by George Tudor, the Washington tailor who catered to the Court. His permanent robe was to be a gift from California's two Senators, Knowland and Kuchel.

"Fine," the Chief Justice said when reporters came on him in the corridor and asked how he felt. "We have put in a full day's work and will again tomorrow." After a pause, he added, "I'm here to work — I hope permanently."[54]

14

The Great Rights Robbery

> As Hamlet is to one generation a play of revenge, to
> another a conflict between will and conscience, and to
> another a study in mother-fixation, so the Constitution
> has been to one generation a means of cementing the
> Union, to another a protectorate of burgeoning property,
> and to another a safeguard of basic human rights and
> equality before the law.
>
> — PAUL A. FREUND[1]

THE Warren Court was convened at a time when Negroes were
voting in jungle villages of Africa but not in county seats of
Alabama and Mississippi. No Congress had passed a civil rights bill
since Reconstruction days and no President had denounced racial
discrimination as morally wrong and indefensible. The Supreme
Court, in 1917, had stepped gingerly into this moral vacuum, but
not until the 1930's had it begun to insist that "separate but equal"
facilities must be equal as well as separate.[2] Still unanswered
in the fall of 1953 was the question of whether the Negro, by the
very act of enforced segregation, was being denied equal protection
of the laws.

"The law, in its majestic equality," as Anatole France once wrote,
"forbids the rich as well as the poor to sleep under bridges, to beg in
the streets, and to steal bread."[3]

In the United States, for a hundred years, the law had permitted
the Negro as well as the Caucasian to live among his own people.
He was free to send his children to his own schools, to eat at his own
restaurants, ride in his own part of the bus, worship at his own
church, and bury his dead in his own separate but equal plot of

earth. In the South the races were segregated by potbellied deputy sheriffs enforcing local ordinances. In the North poverty segregated Negroes in rat-infested slums from which there was little hope of escape.

"All I ask for the Negro is that, if you do not like him, let him alone," Abraham Lincoln told his Springfield neighbors in 1858. "If God gave him but little, that little let him enjoy."[4]

On New Year's Day, 1863, his Emancipation Proclamation freed all slaves held in rebellious areas. Nearly three years later, when Lincoln was dead and the war ended, the Thirteenth Amendment put an end to slavery. Negroes ceased to be chattels in the United States. Congress then passed a civil rights bill asserting their citizenship. This was followed by the submission to the states of the Fourteenth Amendment.

All citizens of the United States were declared to be citizens of the states in which they resided. As such, they were to enjoy "equal protection of the laws" and — borrowing from the Fifth Amendment — they were not to be deprived of "life, liberty, or property, without due process of law." Although the amendment became the law of the land upon its ratification in 1868, it lost something in the translation. Protections given the newly liberated Negro by Congress were withheld from him by the Court.

"It establishes equality before the law," Senator Howard of Michigan said in arguing for passage of the Fourteenth Amendment, "and it gives to the humblest, the poorest, the most despised of the race the same rights and the same protection before the law as it gives to the most powerful, the most wealthy, or the most haughty."[5]

The Supreme Court, however, accepted the argument put forth in 1882 by Roscoe Conkling, one of the authors of the amendment, who insisted that Congress had meant to include corporations in its definition of a "person."[6] As a consequence, "due process" came to be used as a shield to protect corporate giants from government interference, while Negroes were semantically swindled of their right to "equal protection of the laws." Variations on this cynical theme were solemnly rung by the Court until the early 1940's. By this time the "Nine Old Men" who had used nineteenth-century precedents to block the twentieth-century innovations of the New Deal had begun to give way to Roosevelt appointees. It was a triumph of justice over geriatrics.

The first Roosevelt appointee was Senator Hugo L. Black, who took his seat in 1937, and the following year let it be known in a dissenting opinion that he did not believe "the word 'person' in the Fourteenth Amendment includes corporations."[7] Eleven years later Justice William O. Douglas, another F.D.R. selection, developed the same thesis, again in dissent.[8] By this time the question of the government's power to regulate business had been settled and the Court was making a glacial shift of emphasis from property rights to human rights. The seeds of the Warren Revolution had been sown.

The Court, in the words of Professor Robert G. McCloskey of Harvard, "has seldom lagged far behind or forged far ahead of America."[9] Before the Civil War, when slavery gnawed at the national conscience, the overriding concern of the Court was the relationship between the central government and the states. From the Reconstruction period to the judicial face-lifting of 1937, when crusaders had turned from the abolition movement to trust-busting, the Court focused its attention primarily on the relationship between government and business.

In the present day, led first by Black and Douglas, later joined for a tragically short time by Murphy and Rutledge, and then espoused by the humanitarian majority of the Warren Court, the central question before the country and the Court has been the relationship between the state and the individual, whether he be a radical, a suspected felon, a Negro, a naturalized citizen, an urban voter, an atheist, or simply an independent cuss who wants to be let alone.

"The need for vigilance to prevent government from whittling away the rights of the individual was never greater," says Justice Brennan. "Today, as rarely before, case after case comes to the Court which finds the individual battling to vindicate a claim under the Bill of Rights against the powers of government, federal and state."[10]

The first ten amendments to the Constitution (the guarantees of what is popularly known as the Bill of Rights are contained in the first eight) were designed to protect the individual from the Federal Government, not from the states, or so the Supreme Court ruled in 1833 (*Barron v. Baltimore*).[11] The decision caused little trouble until a generation later, when the Fourteenth Amendment applied "due process" and "equal protection" to the states. The Court divided sharply on the question of whether the amendment "incorporated" the Bill of Rights in its entirety as a limitation on the power of the states.

"Yes," Justice Black has argued without ever winning a clear-cut victory.*

The Court has been in general agreement that the guarantees of the First Amendment (freedom of speech, press and religion) are equally binding on the Federal Government and the states. The states have also been obliged by the Court to respect other rights which, in Justice Cardozo's often-cited words are "of the very essence of a scheme of ordered liberty,"[16] representing some "principle of justice so rooted in the traditions and conscience of our people as to be ranked as fundamental."[17] These basic rights have been considered a body of "natural law," the heritage of every freeborn child.

"To hold that this Court can determine what, if any, provisions of the Bill of Rights will be enforced, and if so to what degree, is to frustrate the great design of a written Constitution," Black argued in a classic dissent (*Adamson v. California*).[18]

Under a written constitution, Black likes to point out, courts are confined to clearly marked boundaries. Under "natural law," they operate within the framework of their own beliefs and bias. As Justice Iredell wrote in 1798: "The ideas of natural justice are regulated by no fixed standard: the ablest and the purest men have differed upon the subject . . ."[19] There was no doubt in Iredell's mind that the Supreme Court had the power to strike down any federal or state law that violated constitutional provisions, but it was quite another matter for the justices to "pronounce it to be void, merely because it is, in their judgment, contrary to the principles of natural justice."

By the process of "absorption" some but not all of the rights

---

* At the start of the October, 1956, term, only the guarantees of the First and Fourth Amendments and the Just Compensation Clause of the Fifth Amendment had been made applicable to the states by the Fourteenth Amendment. Ten years later, a series of rulings had extended the Fifth Amendment's privilege against self-incrimination,[12] the Eighth Amendment's prohibition of cruel and unusual punishments,[13] and the Sixth Amendment's guarantee of the assistance of counsel for a defendant in a criminal prosecution.[14] It had also held that the states were not to make use of the fruits of an illegal search and seizure.[15]

protected by the first eight amendments were made applicable to the states. In many states this denied the poor their right to counsel, it robbed the ignorant of their right to silence, and in the South it left the Negro at the mercy of state legislatures which were, of course, all-white. A Negro arrested by a white sheriff on a charge brought by a white man (or, worse, a white woman) was brought to trial before a white judge in a segregated courtroom where a white prosecutor could count on the sympathy of a white jury.

The Negro was a prisoner in a world he never made and could find no lawful means of changing. He was not permitted to participate in writing or interpreting the laws that governed him. Born to suffer taxation without representation, he was forced to support public schools and parks from which he and his family were barred by law. As a "person," the Southern Pacific Railroad could get relief from the courts, but not a Negro who had to put up with the indignity of its Jim Crow coaches.

The Negro was brought to the New World in chains, like a caged animal. The Marshall Court, in its 1829 term, was called on to decide whether a slave drowned in a steamboat accident should be legally classed as a passenger or as freight. To the annoyance of slaveowners, the Chief Justice ruled that "he resembles a passenger, not a package of goods."[20]

In 1857, long after Marshall's death, his frail, wizened successor wrecked a distinguished career by holding in Dred Scott's suit for liberty that no Negro of slave origins could be entitled to citizenship. Consequently, Chief Justice Taney ruled, Scott had no right to sue in a federal court. It was also agreed by a majority of the bitterly divided Court that, under the due process clause of the Fifth Amendment, Congress could not interfere with the property rights of slaveowners by forbidding slavery in the territories.[21]

It was years before the Court recovered from the almost mortal wounds it inflicted on itself by Taney's decision. It was overruled by the Civil War. Congress made it official when it declared the Negro to be a citizen. Under the Reconstruction amendments, he could not be enslaved (XIII), and no state government could deny him "due process" or "equal protection of the laws" (XIV) or deprive him of his right to vote (XV).

If the Negro remained little better off than a slave, if he was denied equal justice under law, if he was barred from polling places, much of the blame must be borne by the Supreme Court. A form of judicial larceny had been visited on the freedmen. It began with the first court test of the Fourteenth Amendment. The action was brought not by newly liberated Negroes contending for their civil rights, but by a parcel of indignant butchers, demanding the right to slaughter cattle in New Orleans.

The Louisiana legislature, in 1869, granted a monopoly to a favored company to land, keep and slaughter cattle in the New Orleans area. Rival butchers brought suit under the Fourteenth Amendment, attacking the state charter on the ground that it denied them equal protection of the laws and deprived them of property without due process of law. The Court, by a five-to-four vote, upheld the monopolistic grant and, at the same time, so interpreted the new amendment as to place virtually all civil rights under the protection of state governments.

"But," as Irving Brant points out in *The Bill of Rights,* "if a state systematically violated the privileges and immunities of one class of its citizens, or of all of its citizens, what remedy did the victims have under this clause of the Constitution? They could walk into a federal courthouse and walk out again, enjoying the full protection of the Fourteenth Amendment until they reached the sidewalk."[22]

Appropriately enough, this 1873 evisceration of the Fourteenth Amendment is known as *Slaughter-House Cases*.[23] The bloody business it began was carried forward ten years later in *Civil Rights Cases*.[24] These five cases tested the constitutionality of a civil rights bill passed by Congress in 1875. Based on the Fourteenth Amendment, "an Act to protect all citizens in their civil and legal rights" outlawed racial discrimination in inns, public conveyances, theaters and other places of public amusement.

The law was struck down by a majority of the Court on the ground that the Fourteenth Amendment left individuals free to discriminate against one another. Only the states, not their inhabitants, were forbidden to engage in discriminatory practices. The Civil Rights Act, the Court held, "steps into the domain of local jurisprudence, and lays down rules for the conduct of individuals in society towards each other, and imposes sanctions for the enforcement of those rules, without referring in any manner to any supposed action of the State or its authorities."[25]

Justice John Marshall Harlan dissented. The tall, red-headed Kentuckian (Holmes once referred to him as "the last of the tobacco-spitting justices")[26] contended that corporations and individuals engaged in the business of running railroads, keeping inns or managing places of public amusement were subject to government regulation because of the public character of their duties and functions. They were, in effect, "instrumentalities of the State." If they denied any citizen equality of civil rights, it was a denial by the State, and thus a violation of the postwar amendments.

"Today," Harlan warned, "it is the colored race which is denied, by corporations and individuals wielding public authority, rights fundamental in their freedom and citizenship. At some future time, it may be that some other race will fall under the ban of race discrimination. If the constitutional amendments be enforced, according to the intent with which, as I conceive, they were adopted, there cannot be in this republic, any class of human beings in practical subjection to another class, with power in the latter to dole out to the former just such privileges as they may choose to grant."[27]

Discrimination, as had already been established, could be biological as well as racial. In the same 1873 term in which the Court decided *Slaughter-House Cases,* it also ruled on *Bradwell v. The State,* which had challenged the right of the Supreme Court of Illinois to refuse to license a woman to practice law in a state court. When she sued under the Fourteenth Amendment, she lost, causing "no little amusement upon the Bench and on the Bar," the *Boston Daily Advertiser* reported, and *The Nation* fell into a most ungentlemanly rage:

"It is a rather ludicrous illustration of the character of the woman movement that a prominent female agitator should have seized the opportunity to prove the fitness of her sex for professional life, by taking for her first important case one which she must have known the Court would decide against her, unless she supposed that they were likely to be influenced by personal solicitation and clamor, or else that they were all gone crazy."[28]

The Fourteenth Amendment had been robbed of most of its virility by June 7, 1892, when Homer Adolph Plessy boarded a train in New Orleans bound for Covington, Louisiana, and seated himself in the coach reserved for Caucasians.[29] Plessy looked like a white man, but as he later described himself, he had "one-eighth African blood." The conductor ordered him to move to the Jim Crow car, as was required by an 1890 state law directing railroads "to provide equal but separate accommodations for the white and colored races." Plessy refused to budge. He was arrested and brought to trial before Judge John H. Ferguson.

When *Plessy v. Ferguson* was decided by the Supreme Court in the spring of 1896,[30] Justice Henry Billings Brown spoke for a majority that had found no violation of the Thirteenth and Fourteenth Amendments. Brown relied largely on *Roberts v. Boston*,[31] an opinion by the Massachusetts Supreme Court upholding Boston's segregated schools. This decision had been handed down nearly twenty years before ratification of the Fourteenth Amendment, Plessy's counsel pointed out, but his argument was weakened by the fact that Congress had subsequently established a segregated school system in the District of Columbia.

"We consider the underlying fallacy of the plaintiff's argument to consist in the assumption that the enforced separation of the two races stamps the colored race with a badge of inferiority," Justice Brown declared for the Court. "If this be so, it is not by reason of anything found in the act, but solely because the colored race chooses to put that construction upon it."[32]

"Our Constitution is color-blind, and neither knows nor tolerates classes among citizens," Justice Harlan stated in his dissent,[33] echoing the felicitous phrase used by Albion Tourgée in the brief he had filed on behalf of Plessy ("Justice is pictured blind and her daughter, the Law, ought at least to be color-blind").[34]

"The present decision, it may well be apprehended, will not only stimulate aggressions, more or less brutal and irritating, upon the admitted rights of colored citizens," Harlan wrote, "but will encourage the belief that it is possible, by means of state enactments, to defeat the beneficent purposes which the people of the United States had in view when they adopted the recent amendments of the Constitution, by one of which the blacks of this country were made citizens of the United States and of the states in which they respectively reside, and whose privileges and immunities, as citizens, the states are forbidden to abridge. Sixty millions of whites are in no danger from the presence here of eight millions of blacks. The destinies of the two races, in this country, are indissolubly linked together, and the interests of both require that the common government of all shall not permit the seeds of race hate to be planted under the sanction of law."[35]

"God Almighty drew the color line and it cannot be obliterated," the editor of the Richmond (Virginia) *Times* declared in 1900,[36] and sixty-odd years later, James Jackson Kilpatrick, editor of the Richmond *News-Leader*, heartily agreed: "The Negro is fundamentally and perhaps unalterably inferior; he is also immoral, indolent, inept, incapable of learning, and uninterested in full racial equality. The segregationist South feels no guilt about keeping the Negro in his proper place — that is to say, in separate schools."[37]

In 1936, after completing his undergraduate work at Lincoln University, an all-Negro institution which had no facilities for the study of law, Lloyd Gaines applied for admission to the Law School of the University of Missouri. His application was denied, but, as state law provided, he was offered an opportunity to attend any out-of-state law school he chose, and Missouri would pick up the tab for his tuition. This raised the question of whether Gaines had been denied equal protection of the laws. The Supreme Court, in 1938, decided that he had been deprived of an advantage extended to white students. To comply with the Fourteenth Amendment, Missouri must either admit Negroes to the state university law school or provide substantially equal facilities within its borders.[38]

Ten years after Gaines was first turned away from the University of Missouri, Ada Sipuel applied for admission to the School of Law of the University of Oklahoma, the only institution of its kind supported by the state's taxpayers. Although fully qualified, she was denied admittance because of her race. Speaking with one voice in a *per curiam* opinion, the Court insisted that Miss Sipuel was "entitled to secure legal education afforded by a state institution."[39]

In neither *Gaines* nor *Sipuel* did the Court disturb the constitutional footing of the "separate but equal" doctrine sanctified by

Plessy in 1896.* The Justices simply took a closer look at the equality of the separate facilities provided Negro graduate students in segregated states. In 1950, two years after *Sipuel,* the Court went a step further in deciding the case of a Texas postman named Sweatt who had refused to attend the state's Jim Crow law school after being rejected by the University of Texas Law School. The school set aside for Negroes, Sweatt argued, was not on a par with the one provided Caucasians. The Court agreed.

"What is more important," Chief Justice Vinson wrote, "the University of Texas Law School possesses to a far greater degree those qualities which are incapable of objective measurement but which make for greatness in a law school. Such qualities, to name but a few, include reputation of the faculty, experience of the administration, position and influence of the alumni, standing in the community, traditions and prestige. It is difficult to believe that one who had a free choice between these law schools would consider the question close."[41]

Obviously no separate facilities established for Negro students of such professions as law, medicine and engineering could ever be made equal to white graduate schools.

"You can't build a cyclotron for one student," the president of the University of Oklahoma was quoted as saying in 1948 after segregationists were hit by *Sipuel.*[42]

Although university doors had begun to open for Negroes by the start of the 1950's, the Court still had done nothing about separate elementary and high schools.

"Those racial supremacy boys somehow think that little kids of six or seven are going to get funny ideas about sex and marriage just from going to school together, but for some equally funny reason youngsters in law schools aren't supposed to feel that way," Thurgood Marshall remarked during the period he was directing the legal attack of the NAACP on segregated schools.[43]

For two years before Chief Justice Vinson's death, under one

* In 1927, in *Gong Lum v. Rice,* the Court was unanimous in agreeing that a Chinese-American girl was not entitled to attend a "white" school in Mississippi.[40] This was the last decision to be justified by the *Plessy* doctrine.

pretext or another, the Court tiptoed around the heavily mined political battleground staked out by civil libertarians who, like Marshall, contended that the mere act of separating one group of children from another because of race constituted a denial of equal protection of the laws.

In the spring of 1951, when Linda Brown was nine going on ten, she was in the fourth grade at Monroe School in Topeka, Kansas. She had to travel nearly five miles a day to and from Monroe, although she lived only four and a half blocks from Sumner School. In fact, in order to reach Monroe, she had to pass Sumner.

"I used to think, 'Why can't I go in there?'" she later recalled. "I used to ask my daddy why I couldn't go."[44]

Her father, the Reverend Oliver Brown, knew why she couldn't go. An 1867 Kansas statute permitted cities with a population of more than fifteen thousand to maintain separate elementary schools, if they so desired. Seven cities in the historically free state of Kansas had some form of segregation at the time Linda Brown was a student at Monroe, which was one of Topeka's four Negro grade schools. There were eighteen for the city's white children, who outnumbered the colored youngsters, 6,019 to 658. Once the children got past the sixth grade and went to junior high school and then high school, there was no segregation of the races.

"Somebody had to start it," Linda's father told a Kansas City *Star* reporter in 1961, a few months before he died of a heart attack at the age of forty-two, his name committed to history as the Brown of *Brown v. Board of Education.*

"I remember that my father took me by the hand and we walked together to the Sumner School," Linda says. "We went into the school and into a room that I remember was filled with other children and their parents. My father tried to enroll me in the school for the next year and they told him that I couldn't go there because I was a Negro. Then he asked to see the principal. I waited in the hallway."

"When he got home," his widow recalls, "he was sort of angry and hurt that Linda had not been admitted. We had discussed it before. We knew we would likely be refused, but he was hurt anyhow."

"I just thought that if the schools are being paid for by the taxpayers," Mr. Brown said, "we should have equal rights, and I knew if there was any way to obtain justice, it would be through the United States Supreme Court."

"It's no accident that this case is the one on which the Supreme Court based its historic decision," says Charles S. Scott, one of the three Negro attorneys who prepared the original suit. "We planned it that way. This was the first case in which we were attacking segregation *per se*. In other places we sought relief through the courts on the principle of inadequate facilities. That was never a factor here."[45]

Scott filed suit in Topeka on behalf of several Negro parents, including Oliver and Leola Brown. The names were alphabetically arranged. Brown came first on the list.

"Segregation of white and colored children in public schools has a detrimental effect upon the colored children," it was decided by a three-man federal court. "The impact is greater when it has the sanction of the law; for the policy of separating the races is usually interpreted as denoting the inferiority of the Negro group. A sense of inferiority affects the motivation of a child to learn. Segregation with the sanction of law, therefore, has a tendency to [retard] the educational and mental development of Negro children and to deprive them of some of the benefits they would receive in a racial [ly] integrated school system."[46]

However, having concluded that Linda Brown and her young neighbors were being adversely affected by a legally sanctioned system which made the children feel inferior, retarded their development and did them out of benefits they would receive in an integrated school, the court then declared that *Plessy* was still the law of the land. Thus, the school board of Topeka was held to be within its constitutional rights in providing — as Kansas law permitted — "separate but equal" elementary schools for white and colored children.

"We wanted them to rule against us," Scott says. "We wanted to fight this thing all the way through. If they had ruled for us I'm satisfied the board would not have appealed."

"I entered the Brown case reluctantly," says Harold R. Fatzer, an associate justice of the Supreme Court of Kansas, who was the state's attorney general at the time the suit was filed. "I always felt that colored children ought to have the same opportunity in school that any other child had. But it was my duty as attorney general to support the laws of the state as they were constituted."[47]

Paul E. Wilson, then assistant attorney general, now a law professor at the University of Kansas, prepared the brief defending the state law and made the oral argument before the Supreme Court, where *Brown* was one of five school segregation cases. Three were from other states (South Carolina, Virginia, and Delaware) and one from the District of Columbia.

"The arguments advanced by all states were similar," says Professor Wilson, "that segregation in the public schools had been regarded as a state policy and that court decisions seemed to approve of classification of people according to race for purposes of the public schools . . . We were not defending segregation. We were upholding the right of the state of Kansas to direct its school boards."[48]

"Here we abandon any claim of constitutional inequality that comes from anything but segregation itself," said Robert Carter, arguing *Brown* in the lower courts on behalf of the National Association for the Advancement of Colored People. "We say that on the basis of separation, Negroes do not have equal protection before the law and equality of opportunity."[49]

In early July, 1953, nearly two years after the stifling summer night in Topeka when a group of Negro parents had first got together in the Seventh-day Adventist Church and agreed to go to court to end racial segregation in the local grammar schools, Thurgood Marshall began to round up expert help in preparing the line of argument to be taken when the school segregation cases came up for reargument the following fall. One of the experts approached by the amiable, persuasive general counsel of the NAACP Legal Defense and Educational Fund was Alfred H. Kelly, professor of history at Wayne State University in Detroit.

"The five cases came up to the Supreme Court early in 1953 and were argued there by counsel along much the same lines as in the lower courts," Dr. Kelly later told members of the American Historical Association. "Instead of handing down a decision, however, the Supreme Court handed them back to opposing counsel with a request for reargument on the question of the historical intent of the framers of the Fourteenth Amendment."[50]

The Court, in effect, seemed to be asking the desegregationist lawyers to come up with a plausible historical basis for overturning the hoary "separate but equal" doctrine laid down in *Plessy*. That summer, while Governor Warren of California paid a holiday visit to the Scandinavian towns of his forebears, Dr. Kelly plowed through the 1866 volumes of the *Congressional Globe*, reexamining the arguments put forth in the House and Senate debates on the Civil Rights Act and the Fourteenth Amendment which evolved from it.

"The conclusion for any reasonably objective historian was painfully clear: The Civil Rights Act as it passed Congress was specifically rewritten to avoid the embarrassing question of a congressional attack upon State racial-segregation laws, including school segregation. . . ."[51]

It was obvious to the NAACP's scholarly consultants that the other side would also dig into the Congressional debates recorded in the *Globe*. John A. Bingham of Ohio, the segregationists would be happy to learn, had argued that Congress lacked the power to legislate against state segregation laws. He had led a successful fight on the floor of the House to send the Civil Rights Bill back to the Judiciary Committee to straighten out the wording on this particular point.

But Howard J. Graham of Los Angeles, a constitutional historian, called the attention of the NAACP strategists to another argument the same Congressman had made later, when he was defending the Fourteenth Amendment. Bingham had illuminated the difference between writing a new statute, such as the Civil Rights Act, and drafting a new constitutional provision. Statutes were necessarily narrow and specific, but an amendment to the Constitution had to be written in broader terms, designed to meet the needs of generations yet unborn.

"In our mind's eye," Dr. Kelly told his fellow-historians, "Bingham almost seemed to be speaking for our purposes, saying to the Court in the twentieth century that if your age, far beyond our span of time, sees in this Amendment a new birth of liberty it will be altogether legitimate for you to use it for that purpose."[52]

On the morning of May 17, 1954, while the Army-McCarthy hearings were shambling into their eighteenth day, the reporters who normally cover the Supreme Court were dawdling over coffee in the pressroom, looking forward to a light day. It was Monday, decision day, but no rulings of stop-the-presses significance were expected. Shortly after noon, however, Banning E. Whittington, the Court's friendly, low-key press officer, suggested they had better get upstairs. They darted up the marble steps and took their places on the old-fashioned ice-cream-parlor chairs set aside for the working press. The Chief Justice had begun to read the Court's ruling in *Brown et al. v. Board of Education of Topeka et al.**[53]

The decision was widely regarded as the most important ruling to be handed down by the Court since *Dred Scott*. In that unhappy case, there had been nine separate opinions read on two different days. In *Brown*, there were no dissents, no separate but equal concurrences. The new Chief Justice spoke simply, bluntly and briefly (twenty-eight minutes) for a unanimous Court, echoing the sentiments expressed by Justice Harlan in his *Plessy* dissent. It was an idea whose time had come.

"In approaching this problem, we cannot turn the clock back to 1868 when the Amendment was adopted, or even to 1896 when *Plessy v. Ferguson* was written. We must consider public education in the light of its full development and its present place in American life throughout the nation. Only in this way can it be determined if segregation in public schools deprives these plaintiffs of the equal protection of the laws.

"Today, education is perhaps the most important function of state and local governments. Compulsory school attendance laws and the great expenditures for education both demonstrate our recognition of the importance of education to our democratic society. It is required in the performance of our most basic public responsibilities, even service in the armed forces. It is the very foundation of good citizenship. Today it is a principal instrument in awakening the child to cultural values, in preparing him for later professional training, and in helping him to adjust normally to his environment. In these days, it is doubtful that any child may reasonably be expected to succeed in life if he is denied the opportunity of an education. Such an opportunity, where the state has undertaken to

---

* In Topeka, where the board of education had already started desegregating its school system, Linda Brown had graduated from Monroe and crossed the local color line into junior high.

provide it, is a right which must be made available to all on equal terms.

"We come then to the question presented: Does segregation of children in public schools solely on the basis of race, even though the physical facilities and other 'tangible' factors may be equal, deprive the children of the minority group of equal educational opportunities? We believe that it does."[54]

The Chief Justice then cited two previous cases, both of which turned on "intangible considerations." In *Sweatt v. Painter*, the Court had found that segregated law students did not have equal opportunities because the Negro law school lacked the qualities "which make for greatness in a law school." In *McLaurin v. Oklahoma State Regents*, a Negro Master of Arts seeking a Ph.D. in education had been admitted to a state university but had been required to sit apart in classes, in the library, and in the cafeteria. This enforced separation from his fellow-students, the Court had ruled, impaired his ability to study and to learn his profession.[55]

"Such considerations apply with added force to children in grade and high schools," the Chief Justice continued in *Brown*. "To separate them from others of similar age and qualifications solely because of their race generates a feeling of inferiority as to their status in the community that may affect their hearts and minds in a way unlikely ever to be undone . . .

"We conclude that in the field of public education the doctrine of 'separate but equal' has no place. Separate educational facilities are inherently unequal."[56]

Southern Congressmen attacked *Brown* as "a flagrant abuse of judicial power," which had "wiped out every vestige of States' rights and would end in the destruction of the Anglo-Saxon race." "The whites and the Negroes in my state have been, and are, happy together," said a Georgia Congressman, and the attorney general of this happy state was horrified by the possibility that *Brown* might open the door "to a constitutional attack on our laws prohibiting intermarriage of the Negroes and white people."[57]

Harvard gave *Brown* mixed notices. "The Supreme Court has finally reconciled the Constitution with the preamble of the Declaration of Independence," said Professor Arthur M. Schlesinger,

Sr.[58] But Professor McCloskey was disappointed with the opinion. It seemed to him not very well thought out. It leaned too heavily on modern psychological and sociological literature, and the "selection of citations was, to say the least, uninspired."[59]

"He wasn't writing for scholars," says a source close to the Chief Justice, "but the way he handled the case is really more important than the wording of the opinion. The decision was delivered with the weight of the entire Court behind it."

The unanimity of *Brown* surprised veteran Court-watchers. It was less surprising to Warren's old associates, who had seen him go to work on a mulish legislator, a recalcitrant department head, a conniving party official, and the most whimsical of all living creatures — the California voter. He is an arm-twister, a man who gets things done. He is also a man who moves slowly, taking his time, cautiously examining each step of the road ahead.

The Court was equally prudent in its handling of *Brown*. There were two rulings, delivered a year apart. First, the Court overturned the antiquated "separate but equal" doctrine of *Plessy*. Then, twelve months later, when Confederate oratory had begun to get a bit hoarse, the Chief Justice delivered a supplementary decision. Again speaking for a united Court, he put the *Brown* principle into practice. Local authorities were gently but firmly told to get cracking "with all deliberate speed."[60]

"You cannot change people's hearts merely by laws," Eisenhower remarked in a 1957 press conference,[61] restating the Court's opinion of 1896 ("legislation is powerless to eradicate racial instincts or to abolish distinctions based upon physical differences . . .").[62] Eisenhower refused to mobilize the vast moral resources of the Presidency in support of the decision. When blood began to stain Southern streets, he told reporters, "I think the youngsters that are indulging in violence are not counseled properly at home."[63]

"We are living in a world of ideas and are going through a world war of ideas," Warren said,[64] and Negroes began to beat a path to the Court's door, demanding their right to eat in the white man's restaurants, swim in his public pools, play golf on his public courses, and ride in the front of his local buses.

When Miss Mary Hamilton, a field secretary for the Congress of Racial Equality, was being questioned by an Alabama prosecutor in the circuit court of Etowah County, she refused to answer until he addressed her as "Miss Hamilton" instead of "Mary." She was sentenced to five days in jail and a fifty-dollar fine for contempt of court. She appealed, an action Alabama officials regarded as "frivolous." In April, 1964, the Court disagreed (with Clark, Harlan and White dissenting). Miss Hamilton, the majority held, was entitled to the same respect she would have received from the court as a Caucasian.[65]

The ruling cited an opinion delivered the year before, overturning the conviction of a man who had refused to sit in the Negro section of a Richmond, Virginia, traffic court. A Jim Crow courtroom, it was decided, could not be tolerated under the Fourteenth Amendment's guarantee of equal protection of the laws.[66] The Negro could no longer be sent around to the servant's entrance of the white man's law. American justice had been desegregated.

15

Crime and the Courts

It is a shame to think there should be one law for the poor and one for the rich.
— Earl Warren, 1925[1]

Although court appointees take an oath to "do equal right to the poor and to the rich," in practice American justice has been made available in the large, economy size for the rich and in small, bitter portions for the poor. In one of its most popular decisions, the Warren Court has given the poor a fairer shake. When they are haled into a state court on a criminal charge, they are now entitled to the services of a lawyer, thanks to a stubborn, middle-aged drifter named Clarence Earl Gideon, who took pencil in hand at the start of 1962 and wrote a letter to the Supreme Court from a Florida prison.[2]

Unable to afford a lawyer when brought to trial in the summer of 1961, Gideon had asked the judge to appoint counsel to handle his defense on a charge of breaking and entering the Bay Harbor Poolroom with larceny in mind. The judge had refused the request, explaining that under Florida law he could appoint counsel for an indigent defendant only in cases involving a capital offense.

"Imagine a state in this day and age not giving a fellow a lawyer," Warren had commented to a friend one afternoon long before Gideon got into trouble, and in a 1954 speech, seven years before the Florida judge refused Gideon's request for counsel, the Chief Justice had told members of the American bar, "Every lawyer appreciates the fact that no man accused of a serious offense is capable of representing himself."[3]

Nothing could be more repugnant to Warren's marrow-deep sense of fairness than the spectacle of a penniless prisoner standing defenseless and alone before the dreadful majesty and power of the state in a court of law, but the Supreme Court had held in 1942 in *Betts v. Brady*[4] that appointment of counsel is not a fundamental right, essential to a fair trial. Justice Black had dissented. Twenty-one years later, in *Gideon v. Wainwright,* the Court was unanimous in overruling *Betts,* and Chief Justice Warren had the pleasure of assigning his Brother Black the satisfying task of converting his dissent into the law of the land.

"The right of one charged with crime to counsel may not be deemed fundamental and essential to fair trials in some countries, but it is in ours," Black wrote,[5] and when Gideon was retried in Florida, his lawyer established his innocence of the crime for which he had been sent to jail.

Criminal justice in the United States has traditionally operated under a double standard. Federal courts have been bound by one set of rules, state courts by another. Illegally obtained evidence, for example, has been barred from federal courts since 1914, but a generation later, when the Warren Court was convened, it was still admissible in the courts of more than half the states, including those of California. The same police officers who were enforcing the law were also breaking it, and the courts were conniving in their lawlessness.

"The tendency of those who execute the criminal laws of the country to obtain conviction by means of unlawful seizures and enforced confessions, the latter often obtained after subjecting accused persons to unwarranted practices destructive of rights secured by the Federal Constitution, should find no sanction in the judgments of the courts which are charged at all times with the support of the Constitution . . ." the Supreme Court had declared in 1914.[6]

In this case (*Weeks v. United States*), state officers and later a federal marshal had entered the defendant's room without a warrant, searched it and taken away private papers which linked him with a lottery. He was convicted of illegal use of the mails. The Supreme Court reversed the conviction, citing the lucid language of the Fourth Amendment: "The right of the people to be secure in their persons, houses, papers, and effects, against unreasonable searches and seizures, shall not be violated . . ."

It was this decision that barred illegally obtained evidence from federal courts. The majority of criminal cases, however, are tried in state courts, where in many instances convictions continued to be obtained from illegal searches and coerced confessions. The Supreme Court, in 1936, spoke out against official violence.[7] The three defendants in *Brown v. Mississippi* were ill-educated Negroes accused of murder. When they were brought before the county sheriff to "confess," one was limping and unable to sit down. Along with another suspect he had been stripped, laid over a chair and whipped until his back had been cut to pieces. The third defendant had the marks of a rope on his neck. It turned out he had been hanged from the limb of a tree while being questioned by a deputy sheriff.

Their "confessions" were accepted as the basis for an indictment, and they were given what the community accepted as a fair trial. When called to the stand by the state and asked how severely one of the defendants had been beaten, a deputy sheriff testified, "Not too much for a Negro . . ."[8] Twenty-four hours after the trial began, the three men were under sentence of death. The Supreme Court reversed the convictions "for want of the essential elements of due process."[9]

Twenty-five years later, however, many state courts were still cheerfully ignoring constitutional dictates in regard to unreasonable searches and seizures, self-incrimination and the right to counsel. The Bill of Rights sheltered well-to-do suspects, including Mafia murderers, but not the poor, the uneducated, and the mentally handicapped, all of whom generally stood most in need of these ancient guarantees.

The Warren Court has freshened the chalk on the foul lines bordering the administration of criminal justice in state courts. As in the school prayer and Bible-reading decisions, the Court's rulings on police practices have been seized upon by demagogues to inflame an apprehensive public. At a time when law-abiding citizens are afraid to enter a city park at night, many find it difficult to understand why the Court has apparently made things harder for the police, easier for the criminal.

Even the Court itself has been angrily divided on these cases. In general, the five-man majority has been composed of Warren, Black, Douglas, Brennan and Goldberg (later Fortas). Clark, Harlan and White have spoken most vigorously for the minority, with Stewart concurring in their dissents. The opinions have been delivered in voices inclined at times toward harshness by Justices whose faces have often flushed with strong feeling as they expounded their differing interpretations of the Constitution.

"We should always be careful in considering whether to dispense with what may seem to be inconveniences of the democratic system," Warren said in February, 1965, when he flew to Manila to help the Filipinos celebrate the thirtieth anniversary of their Constitution Day.[10]

He took advantage of the occasion to answer charges that the Court was tipping the scales of justice in favor of the lawbreaker.

"We sometimes hear impatience expressed with the concern our courts have for the rights of a person accused of crime. The impatience may become greater than usual where the crime is an odious one and the defendant's guilt seems plain to all. When such a person is accorded a new trial, it is important to evaluate what has occurred in the larger perspective of the Constitution. Perhaps the defendant was not accorded the right to counsel, or maybe a confession was extorted from him, or evidence used to secure his conviction was illegally seized. But it must be remembered that the rights of one are the rights of all. Implicit in a democratic system is the realization that one charged with even the most serious crime must under the Constitution be tried by civilized standards of criminal justice. Impatience with this concept must inevitably yield to the principle that the Constitution can never bend to expediency; its underlying assumption of fair play can never be compromised by short cuts."

Warren, in his first term as Chief Justice, was called on to cast the tie-breaking vote in a prickly case involving Long Beach, California, police officers who had stolen into the home of one Patrick Irvine, planted a microphone in his bedroom, and recorded his conversations with his wife and with customers who liked to do business by phone.[11] Arrested for bookmaking, Irvine had been tried and convicted.

His only chance of beating the rap depended on whether a majority of the newly constituted Warren Court could be convinced that his case was controlled by *Rochin v. California* (1952) rather than by *Wolf v. Colorado* (1949).[12] In both cases law-enforcement officers had conducted a questionable search and seizure to gather evidence that had been used in a state court to obtain a conviction.

In *Wolf*, the office of a surgeon suspected of performing abortions had been entered without a warrant and a notebook carried off. In *Rochin*, three Los Angeles County deputy sheriffs had forced open the door of a room occupied by a man suspected of selling narcotics. When the suspect, Antonio Rochin, seized two capsules on his nightstand and gulped them, the officers handcuffed him, took him to a hospital and directed a doctor to force an emetic into his stomach. The two capsules were vomited up and found to contain morphine. It was chiefly on the basis of this evidence that Rochin was convicted.

Justice Frankfurter spoke for the Court in both *Wolf* and *Rochin*. In *Wolf*, after first rejecting Justice Black's contention that the Bill of Rights had been made applicable to the states by the Fourteenth Amendment ("the issue is closed"),[13] he went on to declare that the amendment's guarantee of "due process of law" did prohibit the states from infringing on the individual's right to "privacy against arbitrary intrusion by the police."[14]

The *Wolf* ruling left it up to the states to decide whether they would follow the example of the Federal Government and exclude from their courts any incriminating evidence the police might pick up in the course of an "arbitrary intrusion." *Wolf* became a classic example of a basic right for which no judicial remedy had been provided. It was like having one bookend. Appellate courts, during the next decade, had to manage without the guidance of case law handed down from on high. As Chief Justice Traynor of the California Supreme Court declared, "The most we learned was to be newly skeptical of the old adage that half a wolf is better than none."[15]

In *Rochin* where a man had been convicted on evidence coerced not from his mind but from his stomach, Frankfurter found that under the standards Cardozo had set for "a scheme of ordered liberty," the behavior of the arresting officers did "more than offend some fastidious squeamishness or private sentimentalism about combatting crime too energetically. This is conduct that shocks the conscience."[16] The conviction was reversed.

"If it makes you sick," professors of constitutional law jokingly explained to their students, "it is not due process."

Patrick Irvine's freedom rested on the hope that at least five Supreme Court consciences might be sufficiently shocked by the intrusion of a microphone on the privacy of his bedroom to declare his conviction an offense against due process of law. But in the interval between *Wolf* and *Rochin,* two liberal dissenters in the earlier case had died. Murphy and Rutledge had been replaced by a brace of conservatives, Clark and Minton. This shortened the odds against Long Beach's friendly neighborhood bookmaker.

His case was decided, as are all such matters, in the confessional privacy of the Court's weekly conference. These deliberations, at that time, were held on Saturday. Later, the conferences were switched to Friday. No outsider is admitted to these sessions. If anyone knocks at the door, the most recently appointed Associate Justice hops up and answers it. What transpires in the conference room is kept secret in a city noted for the looseness of its tongues. Gossips delight in spreading rumors of angry, table-pounding arguments, which Warren is quick to deny.

"I could count on the fingers of my hands — possibly one hand — all the times that there has been even a flare of temperament in the conference room, and those have always subsided in a matter of minutes," he says.[17]

A buzzer summons the Justices to the conference room at 10:55 A.M. They file into the handsome, oak-paneled chamber and, as has been the Court's custom for generations, they shake hands with one another before sitting down at the rectangular table in the middle of the room. The Chief Justice sits at the south end, the ranking senior Justice at the north end. Above them is a portrait of Chief Justice Marshall. In front of them is a copy of the agenda of the day's cases.

The Chief Justice begins the discussion of each case. His eight brothers speak in turn, according to seniority. The junior Justice has the last word, but to ward off the possibility of his being influenced by the votes of his seniors, he casts the first ballot. The voting continues in this pattern of ascending seniority. The Chief Justice votes last.[18]

When *Irvine* was decided — after what must have been a warm and spirited discussion — it was Warren who cast the deciding vote. His conscience was deeply troubled by the conduct of the Long Beach police officers ("that case really bothered him," says one of his intimates), but he voted to affirm the conviction, apparently in the forlorn hope that the Court's strongly worded displeasure at these obnoxious police practices might prompt California and other offending states to clean up their criminal procedures.

"A judgment so rank will not stand for long," the St. Louis *Post-Dispatch* predicted.[19]

It stood for a little more than seven years. Its downfall was brought about by the arrest in Cleveland, Ohio, of Miss Dollree Mapp.[20] Acting on information that Miss Mapp had stashed away some "policy paraphernalia," police officers called on her, pried open the outside screen door, then broke into the front hall, where they were confronted by the indignant suspect, who asked to see their search warrant. A paper of dubious authenticity was brandished. Miss Mapp grabbed it and stuffed it in her bosom. The officers retrieved it and, after a struggle, handcuffed Miss Mapp. They forced her to accompany them upstairs.

A thorough search was made of her bedroom, then of the first floor and the basement. In the course of this "arbitrary intrusion" the officers found some lewd pictures and pamphlets that Miss Mapp insisted had been left by a former boarder. At her trial the police failed to prove that a search warrant had ever been issued, but Miss Mapp was convicted under an Ohio statute for the knowing possession of obscene literature and given a prison stretch of from one to seven years.

The Supreme Court reversed her conviction. In *Wolf*, a majority of the Justices had affirmed the right of a free people to be secure in their homes against the unlawful entry of law-enforcement officers, but the remedy for such official misconduct had been left up to the states. In *Mapp v. Ohio*, the right and the remedy became inseparable. Because of the redoubtable Dolly Mapp, as children now learn in school, illegally obtained evidence can no longer be admitted in any court in the United States, federal or state.

"Decency, security and liberty alike demand that government officials shall be subjected to the same rules of conduct that are commands to the citizen," Justice Brandeis wrote in a 1928 dissenting opinion. "In a government of laws, existence of the government will be imperilled if it fails to observe the law scrupulously. Our Government is the potent, the omnipresent teacher. For good or for ill, it teaches the whole people by its example. Crime is contagious. If the Government becomes a lawbreaker, it breeds contempt for law; it invites every man to become a law unto himself; it invites anarchy."[21]

The ground rules for prosecution of federal cases were clearly restated in a 1957 decision involving a nineteen-year-old Negro in the District of Columbia who had been picked up on suspicion in a rape case and questioned for hours before being arraigned (*Mallory v. United States*): "The police may not arrest upon mere suspicion but only on 'probable cause.' The next step in the proceeding is to arraign the arrested person before a judicial officer as quickly as possible so that he may be advised of his rights and so that the issue of probable cause may be promptly determined."*[22]

The reason for this procedure, the Court had explained in a 1943 ruling (*McNabb v. United States*), is quite clear. "The awful instruments of the criminal law cannot be entrusted to a single functionary."[24] Federal courts, as Justice Frankfurter pointed out, had a constitutional obligation to establish and maintain "civilized standards of procedure and evidence."[25]

The states generally remained blind to the example set by the federal courts and deaf to the warnings of the Supreme Court. Reform has come gradually, and only under judicial pressure. In 1931 nine young Negroes accused of raping two white girls were rushed to trial in a lynch-minded Alabama courtroom and, without legal advice or assistance, sentenced to death. On appeal, the

---

* In January, 1958, while the *Mallory* rule was being hotly debated in Congress, District of Columbia police officers set out to find three "stocky young Negroes" wanted for robbing a restaurant. They rounded up ninety persons of that general description and held sixty-three of them overnight. None, it turned out, had any connection with the crime.[23]

Supreme Court invoked the Due Process Clause of the Fourteenth Amendment.

"The right to be heard would be, in many cases, of little avail if it did not comprehend the right to be heard by counsel," the Court declared in *Powell v. Alabama*.[26]

Ten years later Smith Betts, an unemployed farmhand, appealed his conviction in a Maryland court on a robbery charge. If he had been brought to trial in a federal court, the judge would have been required to provide the lawyer he could not afford. Maryland, however, happened to be one of a dozen states which had not chosen to follow this example of the Federal Government. When Betts asked for counsel, the judge refused. Like Gideon, twenty years later, he had to handle his own defense. He got eight years.

Dissenting from the six-to-three decision affirming Betts's conviction, Justice Black quoted an opinion delivered by the Supreme Court of Indiana in 1854: "It is not to be thought of, in a civilized community, for a moment, that any citizen put in jeopardy of life or liberty, should be debarred of counsel because he was too poor to employ such aid."[27] More than a hundred years later, when Abe Fortas was appointed to argue Gideon's appeal, it was estimated that from 30 to 60 per cent of the defendants convicted in state courts had been unable to afford a lawyer.[28]

Until the Supreme Court intervened in 1956, it was impossible in some states for an indigent prisoner to carry his case to an appellate court because he was required to provide a transcript of his trial. If he was unable to pay for the transcript, he was unable to file an appeal. This cruel distinction between rich and poor was struck down in 1956 by *Griffin v. Illinois*.[29] It was a split decision.

"Providing equal justice for poor and rich, weak and powerful alike is an age-old problem," Justice Black wrote for the Court's five-to-four majority. "People have never ceased to hope and strive to move closer to that goal."[30]

Constitutional law grows slowly, case by case, decayed fruit dropping to the ground while new buds form, ripen and gradually come to full maturity. Thus, *Betts* (1942) gives way to *Gideon* (1962), and the shocking excesses of *Irvine* (1954) are curbed by *Mapp* (1961).

In *Irvine*, as was not uncommon, the arresting officers had built their case against the suspect by committing a crime more repugnant than the offense charged against the defendant. Patrick Irvine was accused not of treason, murder, arson or rape, but of making book on horse races and sporting events. The police officers who arrested him were guilty of breaking and entering in order to eavesdrop on his bedroom conversations. If this could be done to a guilty bookmaker, it could also be done to an innocent dentist, insurance agent, fry cook or civic leader.

"I have long shared the view that the protection which the Constitution affords is assured to the best of men only if it is insured to the worst, however distasteful the results may be," says Chief Justice G. Joseph Tauro of the Massachusetts Superior Court.[31]

The Constitution, as the Founding Fathers intended, sometimes gets in a constable's way.

In the early hours of a cold January morning in 1960, Chicago police picked up a slight, twenty-two-year-old laborer of Mexican extraction whose ill-tempered brother-in-law had just been fatally shot in the back.* Danny Escobedo was arrested without a warrant and questioned without having been informed of his right to remain silent and consult an attorney. After being held from 2:30 A.M. to 5 P.M., he was released on a writ of habeas corpus. Ten days later he was back in custody. He had been fingered by an eighteen-year-old friend, Benedict DiGerlando, who was also in custody at the time.

"I am sorry but I would like to have advice from my lawyer," Escobedo said when detectives told him they had a tight case and he might as well confess.[32] He may also have been promised freedom in exchange for a full statement, but this is a matter of his word against that of the detective who allegedly made the offer.

When Escobedo's lawyer arrived at the detective bureau and asked to see his client, he was referred to Chief Flynn, who refused the request. "He said I couldn't see him because they hadn't completed questioning," the lawyer said later.[33] Meanwhile Escobedo had insisted that DiGerlando was lying.

"Would you care to tell DiGerlando that?" he was asked.

"Yes, I will," he said, and when he was confronted with his accuser, he said, "I didn't shoot Manuel, you did it."[34]

---

* According to FBI statistics, 80 per cent of all murders are committed by members of the victim's family or by his friends.

Thus, for the first time, Escobedo had admitted to some knowledge of the crime. He was then artfully questioned by an experienced lawyer, who said nothing to him about his constitutional rights. He subsequently recanted his signed statement, but the trial judge declared it to be voluntary and permitted it to be used against him. He was found guilty and sentenced to twenty years.

On appeal, the Illinois Supreme Court first reversed his conviction on the basis of the false promise, and then, after considering the detective's denial of the deal, the court reversed itself, citing two 1958 decisions of the United States Supreme Court, *Crooker v. California*[35] and *Cicenia v. Lagay*.[36] In both cases, the Court had sustained murder convictions based on confessions which had been given by defendants whose request for a lawyer had been refused. Vigorous dissents had been entered by the Chief Justice and Associate Justices Black, Douglas and, in *Crooker*, by Brennan as well (he took no part in *Cicenia*).

The *Crooker* and *Cicenia* dissents stated the underlying policies laid down in *Escobedo*, when the minority became the majority.* Frankfurter had been succeeded by Arthur Goldberg, who was assigned to write the opinion. A suspect, the Court now declared, was entitled to have a lawyer at his side once a police investigation had become an accusation, "when its focus is on the accused and its purpose is to elicit a confession."[37]

"What the Court is doing is akin to requiring one boxer to fight by Marquis of Queensberry rules while permitting the other to butt, gouge and bite," Michael J. Murphy, former New York City police commissioner, complained the following spring. In the presence of Chief Justice Warren and Associate Justice Brennan at a judicial conference, the crusty ex-cop explained that in New York, "it has been our experience that, if suspects are told of their rights, they will not confess."[38]

Murphy had already been answered by Justice Goldberg, who had declared for the Court in *Escobedo* that "no system of criminal justice can, or should, survive if it comes to depend for its continued effectiveness on the citizens' abdication through unawareness of their constitutional rights."[39]

* Casually, in a footnote to *Miranda v. Arizona* (384 U.S. 436, 479), the Court announced that *Crooker* and *Cicenia* "are not to be followed."

"Nobody thinks of hedging firemen about with a lot of restrictive laws that favor the fire," says a Buffalo, New York, police commissioner.

"The analogy does not hold water," says Chief Justice Traynor of California. "The firemen confront a catastrophe taking place before their very eyes and can train their hoses on obvious flames or smoke. In contrast, there are usually so many elements in the scene of a crime that no single witness can assimilate them all, and often witnesses conflict as to what happened. The police sometimes arrive on the scene only after the crime has been perpetrated, sometimes long after. Moreover, it should give caution that seemingly obvious suspects sometimes prove to be innocent just as the seemingly innocent sometimes prove guilty. Even when appearances do not seem inscrutable, they can still be deceiving.

"There is another fatal defect in the fire analogy. We can fight fire with fire, but it is intolerable to fight crime with crime. Precisely because the police do not always track down criminals in full public view the way firemen fight fires, we must have reasonable assurance that they will not resort to lawless methods. What assurance we have proceeds in the main from rules of the United States Supreme Court. By indirection these rules seek to deter activities of police or prosecutors that are inimical to constitutional or other guarantees of a fair criminal process but that are not subject to any punishment even when they disregard an express prohibition. By the forties and early fifties such rules were gathering force as the only noteworthy restraining influence on lawless police action. By the sixties they had become an influence of far-reaching consequence, though still akin to that of permissive parents who now and again announce a rule to improve behavior in the wake of particularly reprehensible behavior about which someone has complained."[40]

The California Supreme Court took *Escobedo* in stride, as it had done with *Mapp*. Indeed, the Court had anticipated *Mapp* in its celebrated *Cahan* decision of 1955, which outlawed the use of illegally obtained evidence in California six years before exclusion was declared a national doctrine.[41] Similarly, in *Dorado*, the state Supreme Court interpreted *Escobedo* to mean that a suspect's failure to ask for a lawyer did not waive his constitutional right to the assistance of counsel.

"The defendant who does not ask for counsel is the very defendant who most needs counsel," California Associate Justice Tobriner wrote. "We cannot penalize a defendant who, not understanding his constitutional rights, does not make the formal request and by such failure demonstrates his helplessness."[42]

To reconcile the differing interpretations of *Escobedo*, the Warren Court winnowed five cases from some one hundred and seventy appeals involving confessions. On June 13, 1966, in *Miranda v. Arizona*, the Chief Justice spoke for a five-to-four majority in defining constitutional limitations on the power of the police to question a suspect. His right to silence and to counsel had to be respected from the time he was taken into custody.

"Prior to any questioning," Warren wrote, "a person must be warned that he has a right to remain silent, that any statement he does make may be used as evidence against him, and that he has a right to the presence of an attorney, either retained or appointed. The defendant may waive effectuation of these rights, provided the waiver is made voluntarily, knowingly and intelligently. If, however, he indicates in any manner and at any stage of the process that he wishes to consult with an attorney before speaking there can be no questioning."[43]

Once a suspect is taken into custody, as Warren dryly noted, "he is not in the presence of persons acting solely in his interest."[44] Consequently, *Miranda* made it unmistakably clear that throughout the interrogation process a suspect must have a free, intelligent choice between silence and speech. No presumably innocent suspect was to be robbed of his rights by a show of force, by trickery or by his own ignorance of constitutional amenities. Quoting the doctrine laid down for California courts in *Dorado*, the decision made it binding on every court in the country. Failure to ask for a lawyer could not be construed as a waiver of the right to counsel. As the Chief Justice knew from his own experience as a county prosecutor, it might never occur to an uneducated, impoverished suspect to request the services of an attorney he had no means of paying.

"While authorities are not required to relieve the accused of his poverty," Warren wrote, "they have the obligation not to take advantage of indigence in the administration of justice."[45]

The Chief Justice, in the bygone days of rum-running and highjacking, had built a nationwide reputation as a crime-busting crusader for law and order. Thus, he spoke with authority when he declared that the limits imposed by *Miranda* on the interrogation of suspects "should not constitute an undue interference with a proper system of law enforcement."[46] As a matter of fact, the four cases involved in the decision served to illustrate the overemphasis placed on the need for confessions.

In each case the defendants had been subjected to interrogations ranging up to five days in duration, although routine investigating procedures had already turned up considerable evidence against them. Three had been identified by eyewitnesses. Marked bills from the bank robbed had been found in one defendant's car, and at the outset of another case police officers had found articles stolen from the victim.

As the Chief Justice pointed out, the FBI has not been held back by the constitutional restraints laid down in *Miranda* for the entire law-enforcement community. In real life, as in Televisionland, FBI agents scrupulously advise suspects at the start of an interview that they are not required to make any statement, that if they do it may be used against them in court, and that they are entitled to the services of a lawyer. Now the G-men are adding the information that counsel will be made available for those unable to pay for it.

"The civil rights movement and Government poverty programs focused the nation's attention on the underprivileged and spurred efforts to insure equal treatment for all citizens," Judge Irving R. Kaufman wrote in the *New York Times Magazine*.[47] "Inevitably, demands for equality turned to the law, and led to insistence that safeguards be established which would guarantee that the indigent and ill-educated were not deprived of advantages enjoyed by defendants sufficiently knowledgeable and financially able to claim all the protections afforded them by the Constitution."

"I believe the decision of the Court represents poor constitutional law and entails harmful consequences for the country at large," Justice Harlan wrote in his strongly worded dissent,[48] and Justice White took up the same theme in a separate dissent:

"In some unknown number of cases the Court's rule will return a killer, a rapist or other criminal to the streets and to the environment which produced him, to repeat his crime whenever it pleases him.

As a consequence, there will not be a gain, but a loss, in human dignity."[49]

Heretofore, human dignity, when left to the states without benefit of the Fourth, Fifth and Sixth Amendments, had often suffered at the hands of law-enforcement officers who had no compunctions about breaking into a man's home and rifling his desk, forcing him to testify against himself or denying him the assistance of an attorney when he was in danger of losing his liberty or his life.

At issue in *Miranda* was the question of just when and where these rights first become operative. In his dissent, Justice Harlan argued that the right to counsel has no proper bearing on police interrogation. In the prevailing view expressed by the Chief Justice, however, the Fifth Amendment right to silence melds with the Sixth Amendment right to counsel, especially in the interrogation room where for all practical purposes the eventual disposition of the case against the suspect may be determined.

The right to counsel, in other words, would be robbed of its meaning if it were invoked only to provide companionship in a courtroom for a defendant whose conviction had already been assured by a confession obtained in violation of his protection against self-incrimination. The Sixth Amendment right to a public trial would become equally meaningless if court proceedings did little more than confirm the results secured in private by what is politely referred to as "intensive questioning."*

Testifying before a Senate judiciary subcommittee in the summer of 1966, Truman Capote expressed the opinion that the two murderers whose infamous crime he had chronicled so ably in *In Cold Blood* would have gone "scot free" if the Kansas Bureau of Investigation had followed recent Supreme Court rulings. He was annoyed at those who "are wailing about the rights of the criminal suspect." "Why," he asked, "do they seem to totally ignore the rights of the victims and potential victims?"[51]

A dramatic reply was given by Professor Yale Kamisar of the University of Michigan, an authority on criminal law. Appearing

---

* "We hail this decision as a welcome sign that this great and powerful nation is still able to grow and fulfill its promise of civil maturity." — Editorial in *The Folsom Observer,* published by and for the inmates of the California State Prison.[50]

before the same pride of Senators, he played a tape recording of the last hour or so of an interrogation that had gone on for more than five hours after the suspect's request to see a lawyer had been denied. When the man finally confessed, his voice was a hoarse, almost inaudible whisper.

"He's in such a state that he'll say anything," Professor Kamisar explained as the Senators strained to hear what the suspect was saying.[52]

He had been picked up in connection with the death of a woman who had been beaten by a purse-snatcher and left to die in the snow on a Minneapolis street. His conviction on the basis of the confession wrung from him by teams of police interrogators was ruled invalid by the Minnesota Supreme Court. Tried again, this time on the basis of the evidence, without use of the confession, he was again found guilty and sentenced to from seven to twenty-five years for third-degree murder. The confession had never been a necessity. It had merely been a convenience in disposing of the case quickly.

"Fighting crime is a difficult, frustrating business," says Professor Kamisar. "When you can't handle it, the easiest and most politically attractive device is to blame it on the courts. It's more popular than raising taxes to increase the police force."[53]

In Los Angeles, where the force is half the size its late police chief, William H. Parker, felt it should be, Mayor Yorty denounced *Miranda* for putting "another set of handcuffs on the police department."[54] Percy Foreman, the celebrated Texas trial lawyer, had already registered his disagreement: "The police are having to think and work now — using something besides their boots and billies."[55]

It is ironical that Earl Warren, who first attracted national notice as a racket-busting district attorney, should end up presiding over a tribunal that has inflamed so many of his old friends in law-enforcement circles. His political base in California was originally built on his close ties with the state's peace officers and district attorneys.

"It's hard to realize how bad, how disorganized law enforcement was at the time Earl Warren first came along," says Robert Powers, the former police chief of Bakersfield, California. "In the late 1920's and early 1930's, California was generally corrupt. Law enforcement was run down at the heels. There were low standards, little training and not much integrity. Warren did things for Alameda County that hadn't been done before. Everybody in law enforcement liked him. He paid attention to them. Most lawyers were isolated from the rough, tough cops. There was a quality of friendly honesty about Warren. Everybody trusted him."

Two retired California lawmen who knew the Chief Justice in these early days speak of him now in the same friendly terms, but they seem to be talking about two different men. They see him as he is mirrored in their own prejudices, politics and philosophy. One of the peace officers is a sensitive, skeptical liberal; the other a gruff, God-fearing, American Legion conservative. While the latter praises Warren as "a 100 per cent American," who demonstrated his patriotism and his prescience in the 1930's by keeping a watchful eye on radical agitators stirring up trouble among California farm workers, the other lawman takes a more philosophical tack in trying to explain the current hostility of so many policemen to the Chief Justice.

"Earl Warren has moved on and away from his friends the cops, and they resent it," he says. "They know that they are going to have to change, and that is painful. Always there are a handful of men in any activity who realize that change is the nature of life, and that what is good enough today won't be good enough for tomorrow. When the cops get tired of screaming against the Court decisions, some few of them will say, 'Well, that's the way it's going to be.' Their attitudes will undergo a change for the better, and they'll look back with scorn on what they and their fellow-officers were doing in the '40s and '50s."

For the most part, the Alameda County prosecutor of the 1930's and the Chief Justice of the 1960's see eye to eye on the constitutional restraints imposed on police and the courts, but they came into conflict in the spring of 1965, when the Court was confronted with the appeal of Eddie Dean Griffin. He had been sentenced to death in a California court for the rape-murder of Mrs. Essie Mae Hodson. He had not taken the witness stand in his own defense, a circumstance the prosecutor had called to the attention of the jury.

"Essie Mae is dead," he had said. "She can't tell you her side of the story. The defendant won't."

If Griffin had been found guilty in a federal court, these sixteen words would have been enough to spring him. He had simply exercised his privilege under the Fifth Amendment not to be a witness against himself. At his trial in the Superior Court of California, the prosecutor had relied on a 1934 amendment to the California constitution that permitted him, as well as the judge, to comment on a defendant's failure to testify. The statute had been upheld by the Supreme Court in 1947 (*Adamson v. California*), with four dissents (Black, Douglas, Murphy, and Rutledge).[56]

Justice Reed, writing the majority opinion in *Adamson,* reaffirmed the stand taken by the Court in 1908 in *Twining v. New Jersey.*[57] The first Justice John Marshall Harlan (the incumbent's grandfather) dissented in *Twining,* denouncing the notion that a state could be permitted to compel a person accused of a crime to testify against himself. Justice Black, nearly forty years later, was no less outraged by *Adamson.* He ridiculed the conclusion that "although comment upon testimony in a federal court would violate the Fifth Amendment, identical comment in a state court does not violate today's fashion in civilized decency . . ."[58]

In ruling on Griffin's appeal, the Court finally caught up with the dissents of Harlan and Black. State judges and prosecutors were barred from commenting to juries on a defendant's use of his right to remain silent. "It is a penalty imposed by courts for exercising a constitutional privilege," Justice Douglas wrote.[59] Griffin was given a new trial and, a year later, was found guilty by another Superior Court jury in Los Angeles. Warren took no part in the decision which outlawed the California amendment. As a district attorney, he had pressed for its adoption.

"No district attorney may comment on the failure of a defendant to testify, although on the face of things he might be obviously guilty," he had said in the spring of 1934. "If a district attorney, in presenting his case, should make any inferences in this direction, his action would constitute error and the verdict of the jury could be reversed. However, defense attorneys are allowed a great deal of liberty in this connection."[60]

In such cases as *Mapp, Escobedo* and *Miranda,* however, Warren's position on police practices is not inconsistent with his past performance as a prosecutor. Then as now, he insisted that law enforcement be carried on by well-trained professionals, who had been given an opportunity to learn something about the law and criminology. Surrounded by able, resourceful investigators, Warren fought hard, but in the words of Oscar Jahnsen, his chief investigator, "He never let us sneak up on a fellow's blind side."

In 1932, twenty years before Long Beach police officers bugged Patrick Irvine's bedroom, Warren was asked to comment on a trial in which evidence obtained by a concealed Dictograph had been used in court. Asked what he would have done as prosecutor if he had come into possession of conversations recorded by a hidden device of this sort, he had replied: "I would have burned every scrap of the record and shot everybody who knew of its existence."[61]

In some cases, Warren's deputy district attorneys recall, they used skeleton keys to enter a room and plant a Dictograph in order to obtain leads in an investigation, but once a suspect appeared in court as a defendant, this material was not used against him. In preparing his cases, Warren was meticulous in respecting the rights of the accused, even when the trial was to be held in a state court where he could have cut a few constitutional corners.

"We don't break the law to enforce the law," District Attorney Warren used to tell his deputies a generation before Chief Justice Warren voted to exclude illegally obtained evidence from state courts. He had used these same words two years before *Mapp* in a case involving a young man who had been indicted for murder, then questioned for an eight-hour stretch, from 7:15 P.M. until 4:05 A.M. before signing what lower courts had accepted as a "voluntary" confession.

"The abhorrence of society to the use of involuntary confessions does not turn alone on their inherent untrustworthiness," the Chief Justice wrote in *Spano v. New York* (1959). "It also turns on the deep-rooted feeling that the police must obey the law while enforcing the law; that in the end life and liberty can be as much endangered from illegal methods used to convict those thought to be criminals as from the actual criminals themselves."[62]

The Warren Court has denied police officers a power withheld from the President of the United States, the power to suspend the Constitution when it becomes a nuisance. To resolve the crime crisis some would tear down the Bill of Rights, which shelters murderers, rapists and dope peddlers; others would tear down the slums which shelter desolation, despair and violence. The slum-clearers would search for new methods of preventing crime as well as of detecting and punishing it. They would raise the professional standards and quality of law-enforcement agencies, give more intensive training courses, and provide the finest possible equipment.

"We'll never get good law enforcement until we're willing to pay for it," says a retired California lawman, and the Chief Justice would readily agree.

Taking note of the "tendency to blame the courts and the rulings of the courts for the vast amount of crime," Warren told the American Law Institute in the summer of 1965 that "thinking persons, and especially lawyers, know this isn't the fact. They know that crime is inseparably connected with factors such as poverty, degradation, sordid social conditions, the weakening of home ties, low standards of law enforcement, and the lack of education."[63]

In each gradual step along the way from *Powell v. Alabama* (1932) to *Miranda v. Arizona* (1966), the Court first gave the states a warning and a chance to clean up their criminal procedures. Too many states continued to live too long on borrowed time. Inevitably, in the opinion of the Court's libertarian majority, there was no choice but to intervene to correct inequities which have most often been visited on Negroes, Mexican-Americans, and Puerto Ricans, who have committed a common crime against their affluent neighbors. They have been guilty of poverty.

16

The Cow Vote

A citizen, a qualified voter, is no more nor no less so because he lives in the city or on the farm.
— EARL WARREN, IN *Reynolds v. Sims* (1964)[1]

LOS ANGELES COUNTY, in the 1960 census, had six million wildly assorted human beings living within its borders. They were permitted by California law to send only one state senator to Sacramento, where his vote could be canceled by a colleague who represented 14,294 constituents. A proposal to end this disproportionate representation of rural areas by reapportioning the senate on the basis of population had been placed before the voters in 1948. It was supported by organized labor and opposed by chambers of commerce, farm associations, back-country politicians and Governor Earl Warren.

"Our state has made almost unbelievable progress under our present system of legislative representation," he said. "I believe we should keep it."[2]

The electorate agreed. The proposal was defeated by a two-to-one vote. It failed to carry a single county, not even Los Angeles County, which stood to profit most by its passage.

"The campaign for the adoption of the amendment gave meager support to the dogma that man is a rational being," wrote Thomas S. Barclay of Stanford in his study of the 1948 reapportionment struggle.[3]

When the California constitution was drafted in Monterey by the territorial delegates who assembled in Colton Hall in 1849, it adhered to the democratic doctrine of "one man, one vote," providing for equal representation in both houses of the state legislature. In the early 1920's, with the monstrous growth of Los Angeles, a legislative civil war broke out in Sacramento to keep the southern colossus from controlling both the senate and the assembly.

A truce was achieved in 1926 with the adoption of a constitutional amendment setting up a legislature drawn along the lines of the so-called "Federal Plan." The assembly's eighty districts would continue to be based on population, but the forty senate seats would be geographically divided among the fifty-eight counties in such a way as to favor the farm vote. No county — no matter how large its area or its population — was to have more than one state senator.

"Certain business interests in the state have found it easier to make their influence felt in the legislature through senators from rural areas," Dean E. McHenry wrote in 1946, when he was an associate professor of political science at UCLA. "Privately owned utilities, banks, insurance companies and other concerns with crucial legislative programs have discovered some 'cow county' legislators more responsive to their demands and less committed to contrary points of view on key social and economic questions than are urban representatives."[4]

Shortly before the opening of the Supreme Court's October, 1963, term, which was to be climaxed the following June by the decision requiring the apportionment of both houses of state legislatures on the basis of population, Chief Justice Warren addressed a University of California seminar looking into the state's chronic pains of growth. As often happens in California, the subject of smog came up. It reminded the former Governor of a story.

"For years it seemed to me that, if smog irritated the eyes and respiratory organs to the point of serious discomfiture, it might have more serious but less apparent consequences. There was some research being done at the universities and our department of public health had done what it could, but without funds appropriated for the purpose. On the advice of the department, I asked the legislature to appropriate a sufficient amount of money for it to make a comprehensive study of the problem and to consolidate the findings of the various educational institutions.*

* The recommendation is to be found on page 22 of the *Assembly Journal,* January 8, 1951.

"The legislative reaction to the proposal was violent. The Los Angeles delegation in wrath said smog was their local problem and they did not want the State to interfere with its business; that this was but another example of State interference with local self-government. Because the Los Angeles area was the one most seriously affected, nothing was done with the proposal.

"But in the following two years the situation worsened to the extent that the farmers became concerned about the effect of smog on their poultry, dairy cattle, and hogs. The State was told it had a responsibility to know how serious the problem was and then to do something about it. The legislature without objection appropriated money to the department of public health for that purpose. In fairness I should say that the bill did permit the department also to consider the effect of smog on people."[5]

A Los Angeles voter, in 1951, delivered himself of what seemed to at least one of his assemblymen an amusingly impractical opinion as to just how the state should be reapportioned following the 1950 census. An assembly committee, headed by Laughlin E. Waters of Los Angeles, was already at work on this delicate bit of political surgery. As committee consultant, Waters had engaged Dr. Ivan Hinderaker, a professor of political science. Both men got a good laugh out of the Los Angeles letter suggesting a method of determining the boundaries of the state's thirty Congressional districts:

"Put the political science professor which you have appointed into an office, put a 'Do Not Disturb' sign on the door and disconnect the phone. Equip him with the 1950 Census results, a map and a pencil. Have him start by dividing the State's population by 30. Then let him figure out Congressional Districts which are as nearly equal in population as it is humanly possible. Then fight for this fair plan and to Hell with local politicians."[6]

Assemblyman Waters and Professor Hinderaker included this blunt anticipation of the Supreme Court's "one-man, one-vote" doctrine in the Committee's official report as comic relief. Later they dismissed it in a learned publication as a foolish idea "grounded either in a lack of understanding of the reapportionment process or in wishful thinking."[7] In drawing up the boundaries of legislative districts, they explained, "population cannot be the *only* consideration." Admittedly, it was the most important factor to be weighed, but it had to be balanced against the realities of conflicting political, social and economic interests. Ideally, on the basis of the 1950 census, each assembly district should have had a population of 132,328, but when the local politicians finished the painful business of carving out new constituencies, deviation from the ideal figure ran as high as 50 per cent.

In California, as in many other states, including Tennessee, there had been a shift of population from farm to factory, from county seats to metropolitan areas. When the country people moved to the city, however, they neglected to take the machinery of their state government with them. It was left in the hands of their neighbors back home.

In Alabama the ballot of a rural voter carried ten times the statistical weight of a city dweller's vote. In Vermont, both Burlington (pop. 35,000) and Victory (pop. 46) had one state senator. Southern Californians were paying 80 per cent of the state's taxes, but in the state senate they had only 15 per cent of the votes. Colorado's legislature, in 1960, doled out $2,300,000 in school aid for Denver's 90,000 children and $2,400,000 for the 18,000 youngsters in semi-rural Jefferson County.

The inequity seemed to be frozen into the American political system, because the city voter had no place to go with his protest. Legislatures dominated by backwoods politicians were understandably cool to any suggestion that they relinquish their seats to strangers from the cities. Congressmen from safely malapportioned districts reminiscent of the "rotten boroughs" of eighteenth-century England were no less hostile to reform. Lower courts, citing Supreme Court decisions (not always accurately), refused to set foot in what Justice Frankfurter had described as a "political thicket."[8] Thus a partially disenfranchised voter could expect little help from his state legislators, his Congressional delegation, or his state and federal judges, but appeals to the courts persisted, and there were indications of an impending change in the wind.

"The whole thrust of today's legal climate is to end unconstitutional discrimination," a federal judge declared in an apportionment case in Hawaii in 1956. "It is ludicrous to preclude judicial relief when a mainspring of representative government is impaired. Legislators have no immunity from the Constitution. The legislatures of our land should be made as responsive to the Constitution of the United States as are the citizens who elect the legislators."[9]

In 1959, Charles W. Baker and other Tennessee voters filed suit in a Federal District Court against Secretary of State Joe C. Carr, claiming that their right to "equal protection of the laws" had been violated by the malapportionment of the state legislature. It had not been reapportioned since 1901. At the time of the lawsuit, the same representation in the legislature was enjoyed by Moore County (pop. 2,340) and Decatur County (pop. 25,316).

"The situation is such that if there is no judicial remedy there would appear to be no practical remedy at all," the judge declared,[10] and the case was carried to the Supreme Court.

Over the vigorous dissents of Justices Frankfurter and Harlan, it was decided on March 26, 1962, that courts could provide a remedy for partial disenfranchisement. "The right asserted is within the reach of judicial protection under the Fourteenth Amendment," Justice Brennan wrote.[11] The ruling in *Baker v. Carr* opened the doors of federal courts to similar civil action in every state where cities had remained in the legislative clutches of rural politicians.

"A landmark in the development of representative government," said Attorney General Robert F. Kennedy, and, speaking for southern Democrats in Congress, Georgia's Senator Richard Russell denounced the ruling as "another major assault on our constitutional system."[12]

"Never in American history has a single judicial decision opened the gates for such a massive change in the nation's political structure," James E. Clayton wrote in the Washington *Post* a few weeks after *Baker v. Carr* was decided.[13]

In Wisconsin a federal court had already taken complete jurisdiction of a reapportionment dispute, and in Oklahoma, Alabama and Georgia federal judges had set deadlines for the legislatures to clean house. "State by state," Clayton reported, "a pattern is developing. After years of refusing to reapportion, political leaders are moving quickly now to get the job done. The reason is clear. Political leaders can control the new district lines and protect their jobs if they do it; they lose that control if the courts do it."

In the authoritative opinion of Professor Paul A. Freund of Harvard, *Baker* was a "cautious" decision, which said "as little as possible about the development of this new doctrine."[14] It was

left to lower courts to develop the body of law establishing acceptable standards for legislative districts. In the meantime, as Professor
Freund pointed out, voting disparities would continue to exist in the
districts of members of the House of Representatives, whose influence on the everyday life of the American citizen was far greater
than that of state legislators.

The House of Representatives began to see the handwriting on its
marble walls in 1963, when the Court struck down Georgia's county-
unit system, which debased the votes of Atlanta residents.[15] In
choosing candidates in a primary election it took ninety-nine Atlanta
votes to equal one cast in Echols County. Speaking for the Court in
Gray v. Sanders, Justice Douglas raised and immediately answered
the central question:

"How then can one person be given twice or ten times the voting
power of another person in a statewide election merely because he
lives in a rural area or because he lives in the smallest rural county?
Once the geographical unit for which a representative is to be
chosen is designated, all who participate in the election are to have
an equal vote — whatever their race, whatever their sex, whatever
their occupation, whatever their income, and wherever their home
may be in that geographical unit. This is required by the Equal
Protection Clause of the Fourteenth Amendment."[16]

"As matters now stand," Professor Andrew Hacker of Cornell
wrote in a 1963 Brookings Institution study, "over 40,000,000 Americans are being deprived of their full voice at the polls and full
representation in the Congress simply because they make their
homes in communities that somehow have failed to secure political
favor."[17]

One of Georgia's ten Congressmen represented three times as
many constituents as another (823,680 in the Fifth District, 272,154
in the Ninth). To end this disparity, designed to reduce the weight
of an Atlanta ballot, a group of Fulton County voters brought suit in
a federal court to give every Georgian the same standing at the polls
in choosing the state's Congressmen. On February 17, 1964, when
the Supreme Court announced its decision on their case (*Wesberry
v. Sanders*), Justice Black spoke for the majority in declaring that
members of Congress must represent districts substantially equal in
population.[18]

"I had not expected to witness the day when the Supreme Court of the United States would render a decision which casts grave doubt on the constitutionality of the composition of the House of Representatives," Justice Harlan wrote in dissent.[19]

"We do not look on the future with such dark glasses," his Brother Black commented from the bench. "We cannot believe it will make the old ship of state slip one knot for this Court to say that, in choosing their representatives, the people should have one vote for one man as nearly as that is possible."[20]

Black quoted a distinguished predecessor, Justice James Wilson of Pennsylvania, who had taken an active part in the Constitutional Convention: "All elections ought to be equal. Elections are equal, when a given number of citizens, in one part of the state, choose as many representatives, as are chosen by the same number of citizens, in any other part of the state."[21]

The "one-man, one-vote" principle was reaffirmed on June 15, 1964, when Chief Justice Warren spoke for a majority of the Court in *Reynolds v. Sims*, which required both houses of state legislatures to be apportioned on the basis of population. Lawmakers who had grown old and often wealthy in the service of sparsely settled constituencies suddenly found themselves faced with the prospect of being cut off from the public purse.

"Legislators represent people, not trees or acres," Warren wrote. "Legislators are elected by voters, not farms or cities or economic interests."[22]

Chief Justice Warren, as his critics gleefully reminded him, had overruled Governor Warren.

"Many California counties are far more important in the life of the state than their population bears to the entire population of the state," Warren had said in 1948. "It is for this reason that I never have been in favor of restricting the representation in the senate to a strictly population basis. It is the same reason that the Founding Fathers of our country gave balanced representation to the states of the union — equal representation in one house and proportionate representation based on population in the other."[23]

"That was sound doctrine then, and it is sound doctrine now," says Senator Dirksen.[24]

But the relationship between the Federal Government and the

states is not the same as the relationship between a state and its counties. Thirteen states united to form the Federal Government; counties have been formed by the states. In a classic state-court decision, counties have been defined as "local subdivisions of the state created by the sovereign power of the state of its own will, without regard to the wishes of the people inhabiting them."[25] Counties, in short, were never independent governments that came together freely in a constitutional convention to form a state. They are the state's creatures.

In the long hot summer of 1787 the framers of the Constitution were dealing with thirteen sovereign and mutually suspicious political entities. They were like separate nations. Their union was brought about by the celebrated compromise which provided for a national legislature composed of a House of Representatives based on population and a Senate made up of two Senators from each state, regardless of its area or the number of its inhabitants. Justice Black referred to this solution of the Founding Fathers in *Wesberry*:

"It would defeat the principle solemnly embodied in the Great Compromise — equal representation in the House for equal numbers of people — for us to hold that, within the states, legislatures may draw the lines of Congressional districts in such a way as to give some voters a greater voice in choosing a Congressman than others."[26]

Under the ruling handed down by Chief Justice Warren in *Reynolds*, Los Angeles County has been compelled to accept the political equality in the California senate that its voters rejected in 1948. Professor Hacker was reminded of Jean-Jacques Rousseau's comment that citizens at times must be "forced to be free."[27]

Reapportionment, Hacker declared, "is not only long overdue but will also lay the groundwork for an updating of our fifty state legislatures." Cynicism toward state government resulting from mal-apportionment should give way to mounting popular approval, he felt, once truly representative legislatures had begun "to strengthen the states and give new life to the practice as well as the theory of federalism."

"State legislatures," Warren wrote in *Reynolds*, "are, historically, the fountainhead of representative government in this country. A number of them have their roots in colonial times, and substantially antedate the creation of our Nation and our Federal Government. In fact, the first formal stirrings of American political independence are to be found, in large part, in the views and actions of several of the colonial legislative bodies. With the birth of our National Government, and the adoption and ratification of the Federal Constitution, state legislatures retained a most important place in our Nation's governmental structure. But representative government is in essence self-government through the medium of elected representatives of the people, and each and every citizen has an inalienable right to full and effective participation in the political processes of his State's legislative bodies. Most citizens can achieve this participation only as qualified voters through the election of legislators to represent them. Full and effective participation by all citizens in state government requires, therefore, that each citizen have an equally effective voice in the election of members of his state legislature. Modern and viable state government needs, and the Constitution demands, no less."[28]

Many states appear to have given up trying to cope with the complexities of the mid-twentieth century, as is evidenced by the congestion of their cities, the pollution of their air and water, the injustices in their administration of criminal law, the inadequacy of their schools, hospitals, parks and public transportation. Corrupt and incompetent legislatures have increased the dependence of the states on the Federal Government. As Warren said in 1943, his first year as governor of California: "It's one thing to talk about states' rights, but the way to have them is for the states to get in and do their own job."[29]

No one has better credentials to discuss the rights of the states in terms of their responsibilities. Before he became Chief Justice, he had built more schools, hospitals and highways than any governor in American history. Instead of dealing a death blow to states' rights, as so many of its critics contend, the Warren Court may have given state government a chance to recover something of its old vitality and usefulness, particularly as a laboratory for experiments in social progress.

Shortly after he had signed the political death warrants of an undetermined number of rural legislators, including fourteen Northern California senators whose seats would be inherited by Los Angeles County, Warren flew west to spend part of the Court's summer recess at home, spoiling his grandchildren, getting in some hunting with his three boys and kidding his old friend, Bartley Cavanaugh, the former city manager of Sacramento.

Bart Cavanaugh is a large, rumpled, infectiously cheerful companion who shares Warren's love of sports. Neither of them can remember just when or how they first met, but Cavanaugh thinks their warm, ribbing relationship dates back to the days when the Chief Justice was a deputy district attorney. Later, as district attorney, Warren spent much of his time in Sacramento, lobbying for bills affecting law enforcement, and the two men became better acquainted. By 1946 they were such good friends that when Cavanaugh showed up for the first day on his new job as city manager, Governor Warren had already taken over the office, answering the phone and greeting startled visitors.

"We both liked sports, so I suppose that's how it started," Cavanaugh says. "One week, I remember, we took in a high school game Friday night, then went to Berkeley for another game next day and on the way home Sunday we stopped in Stockton to see the Forty-Niners."

The Cavanaughs have two children, a boy who was in high school with Earl, Jr., and a girl contemporary with Honey Bear. Both youngsters came down with poliomyelitis about the same time Honey Bear was stricken. "We were friends anyway, but that brought us closer together," Cavanaugh says, and happily adds that both of his children recovered. The son, a Sacramento lawyer, now has seven children, the daughter six.

Cavanaugh is the senior member of the group that attends the World Series every fall with "the Boss" (only in private does he ever call the Chief Justice by his first name). The others are Jack McDermott, an irrepressibly humorous businessman, and Wally Lynn, a wealthy San Franciscan who serves as treasurer for the outfit. Lynn picks up all the tabs for food, drink, lodging, transportation, and incidentals; then sends each member a bill for his share. On these outings Cavanaugh and the Boss usually room together.

"It's one of the few times he can really relax," Cavanaugh says. "We never discuss his business, but I've waked up many a time in the middle of the night and found him working over a pile of papers."

When they go duck-hunting at Wally Lynn's ranch, Cavanaugh will pour himself a drink, then put his feet on the table, and start needling the Boss. "You know, Earl," he used to say before the Reagan administration took office, "now that we've got rid of the Republicans in Sacramento and have a clean, honest Democratic government, the next thing we've got to do is to get those Commies off the Court."

On his way to meet the Boss in San Francisco one day in the summer of 1964, when California legislators were still trying to digest *Reynolds,* Cavanaugh ran into Hugh Burns, the presiding officer of the state senate. They stopped to pass the time of day and Senator Burns invited him to join a group of senators on an expedition to Merced County to shoot quail.

"Can't," Bart said. "The Boss is back home."

"Well, maybe he'd like to go with us," Senator Burns said, and Cavanaugh promised to pass the invitation along.

When he met Warren at his San Francisco hotel, Cavanaugh asked if he would like to drive down to Merced and shoot quail. "Who with?" Warren wanted to know, and Cavanaugh said, "Hugh Burns and some of the other senators."

Warren seemed incredulous. "All those *senators?*" he said. "With *guns?*"

It was Senator Burns, a veteran of twenty-three years, who introduced the redistricting plan drawn up by the senate to meet the Court's requirement of substantially equal representation.

"I present it with the greatest reluctance I have ever presented any bill to this house," he said.[30]

At first, neither the senate nor the assembly could bring itself to the indignity of granting Los Angeles County the full representation to which it was entitled. They held back a few seats, then got to fighting among themselves like heirs who had been harshly dealt with in their uncle's will. Finally, the state Supreme Court set a deadline for the legislators to finish the job or have it done for them by the judiciary. The assembly came up with a plan designed to redistrict the state in such a manner that no incumbents, regardless of party, would lose their seats.

In the senate, however, it was a different story. Corrective surgery could not be avoided. Fourteen or fifteen northerners would have to go in order to make room for newcomers from the south. Governor Brown passed the word along that judicial appointments would be used to ease the pain of departure. Finally, when they lost all hope of getting a last-minute reprieve from Washington in the form of a Constitutional amendment overturning the Court's decision, the senators took the Roman way out, opening their veins in a warm bath of self-pity. As the end neared, in a deathbed senate-assembly committee conference, they slipped a rider into the reapportionment bill giving themselves a reassuringly generous system of pensions.

"This is the biggest thing since they rolled a cannon up to the Brink's safe," one legislator said when it was discovered that a lame-duck assemblyman or senator with four years of service in Sacramento and six years of previous attachment to any public payroll in any capacity would be entitled to a lifetime pension of $250 a month, plus cost-of-living adjustments from time to time.[31]

"I feel this type of legislation would make a farce of all governmental pension programs," said Thomas M. Rees, Los Angeles County's lone state senator,[32] and Governor Brown agreed. He vetoed the measure.

"For many senators this bill represented an end to a way of life which they dearly loved," the Governor said in signing the reapportionment bill into law on October 26, 1965, and he gave a draft of the historic document to Los Angeles County Supervisor Frank G. Bonelli, who had worked for years to end rural domination of the state senate.

"I was tired of the county getting shortchanged," Bonelli said.[33]

"We now have control, complete control, of the state of California," Senator Rees told his seven million constituents,* who would now have fourteen senators and part of a fifteenth to be shared with Orange County, the capital of right-wing extremism in California.[34] Rather than be one of a dozen senators, Rees exchanged his plush Sacramento office for the more modest but satisfying quarters of a Congressman.

As for Senator Burns, he was not worried about his new Los Angeles County colleagues lending their support to the state's

---

* He had picked up another million since the 1960 census.

agricultural and educational needs, he said, but he could not forget that "all the 'funny money' ideas, all the socialistic proposals, emanate from the big cities, not the rural areas."[35] While Burns fretted about a recurrence of the "Townsend Plan" or "Ham and Eggs," liberal Northern Californians were delighted to have Negroes in the south given a chance to be represented in the senate, but they buckled at the knees when they thought of the political oddballs who had found friendly shelter in Los Angeles and Orange counties.

"We have the water, but they have the people," Miriam deFord Shipley of San Francisco wrote the editors of *The New Republic,* reminding her readers that it was the people of Southern California who kept running right-wing movie actors for public office. "The logical thing to do, of course," she continued, "would be to divide the state in two. But practically, that is impossible, because most of the voters are in Southern California and will always vote us down."[36]

If the state were divided along county lines near the *de facto* states dominated by San Francisco and Los Angeles, South California would be the nation's third most populous state (10,400,000) and North California its seventh most populous (7,900,000). With San Francisco as its financial center, North California would gobble up fifty counties, representing not only a large industrial and banking complex, but also water, lumber and agriculture. South California would have truck farms, aerospace and airplane plants, orange trees and people — especially people.

"Fun's fun, and all that, but this is plain ridiculous," the Los Angeles *Times* declared editorially when a "Statehood by '70" group of northerners banded together in the winter of 1965 to separate the state. As the editors pointed out, "California's bonded debt is far in excess of the $3 billion mark. Could the northern counties meet their share?"[37]

Knowing the larcenous history of Los Angeles in acquiring the water it needed for survival, North Californians had reason to fear raids by southern legislators on their resources. They were also afraid that once Southern California controlled the state's highway funds, it would allocate them to Los Angeles freeways rather than to the maintenance and expansion of highways in the northern valleys and mountains.

"A lot of Los Angeles assemblymen," said Senator Burns, "are more concerned with welfare handouts from the state than anything else because the cities are where the freeloaders are gathered. Social problems exist mainly in the metropolitan areas, not the rural areas."[38]

"There are howling liberals from small towns and there are city-dwelling legislators of a rustic frame of mind," Assembly Speaker Jesse M. Unruh pointed out, and assured rural interests in the California senate that they "have nothing to fear from an increased urban voice in that body."[39]

"It devolves upon us to use our immense new strength wisely and with grace," the Los Angeles *Times* asserted, sobered by the reflection that the eight Southern California counties now had forty-six of the eighty assembly seats and twenty-two of the forty senate seats.

In January, 1967, when the reapportioned legislature met for the first time, Senator Stephen P. Teale, a veteran rural legislator, was distressed by the committee preferences of his new colleagues. More than half of the forty senators listed the Education Committee as their first choice. Only eight wanted to serve on the Agricultural Committee, which represented the state's largest industry ($3 billion a year). Only two senators expressed a desire to be on the nine-member Fish and Game Committee.

"All of my fears have come true," said Senator Teale, and predicted, "I don't think that we are going to see the end of the effect of reapportionment on California for the next ten years."[40]

"Things look different from here," Warren has often said when California visitors have brought up the subject of his revised views on the democratization of state legislatures. When one of his oldest friends asked him why he had not made things easier on himself by assigning the writing of *Reynolds* to someone who had no political record of opposition to its doctrine, Warren answered with his usual directness: "I wasn't going to let anybody say I didn't have the guts to write it myself."

In taking his stand on the "one-man, one-vote" issue, Warren had to consider the effect of the decision not just on California, where he felt the old system hadn't worked too badly, but also on other legislatures, where it had got completely out of hand. As he keeps explaining to friends back home who wonder what has happened to him since he went to Washington, he has a different constituency now. It embraces not just a single county or a single state, but the entire country and, indeed, the world.

As he saw for himself in the summer of 1956, when he visited India as a guest of the government and sat on the High Courts of Bombay, Madras and Calcutta, the decisions of the United States Supreme Court are routinely cited by Indian lawyers as the country proceeds to build a body of constitutional law. Like the United States, India has a federal system, but its constitution takes the opposite stand in regard to the relationship between its twenty-six states and the central government. In the United States, under the Tenth Amendment, "The powers not delegated to the United States by the Constitution, nor prohibited by it to the states, are reserved to the states respectively, or to the people." In India, all powers not delegated to the states are reserved to the central government.

"Democracy is more of a way of life than it is a form of government," Warren said on his return. "All democracies have like objectives but of necessity different approaches. There are as many different ways of accomplishing democratic objectives as the ingenuity of the people can devise and, by devotion to purpose, implement."[41]

India's freedom, the Chief Justice had been pleased to observe, rested on an independent judiciary, an independent bar and a constitution "which compels recognition by everyone of the dignity of the individual and of equality before the law, without regard to race, color, creed or economic status." In India, as in the new nations of Africa, Warren is best known as the author of the decision ending racial segregation in public schools.

"He's very popular in Europe, too," says Thomas M. Storke, the peppery, octogenarian publisher-emeritus of the Santa Barbara News-Press, a friend of more than forty years who has often traveled abroad with the Warrens. "Wherever we'd go, people would crowd around him, wanting to shake his hand."

"I've always felt that much of his strength as Chief Justice lies in the fact that he reflects to a remarkable degree the prevailing concept of justice," says one of his former law clerks.

For nine Court terms, Warren's concept of justice rubbed abrasively against Felix Frankfurter's judicial philosophy. Their final, and probably most meaningful, confrontation came in *Baker v.*

Carr. Reapportionment posed a politically explosive question which the former Harvard professor would leave to the legislatures, where nothing would be done about it, and the former California politician would turn over to the courts, where it could be resolved.

". . . [T]here is not under our Constitution a judicial remedy for every political mischief . . ." Frankfurter wrote in his dissenting opinion.[42]

He was fond of quoting a remark made by Justice Holmes in his nineties: "About seventy-five years ago, I learned that I was not God. And so when the people want to do something I can't find anything in the Constitution expressly forbidding them to do, I say, whether I like it or not, 'Goddamit, let 'em do it.' "[43] Time and again, as an Associate Justice of the Supreme Court of the United States, Felix Frankfurter voted to uphold legislation he would most certainly have fought with all of his disputatious genius if he had been a legislator rather than a judge.

"One who belongs to the most vilified and persecuted minority in history is not likely to be insensible to the freedoms guaranteed by our Constitution," he wrote in his famous 1943 flag-salute dissent (*West Virginia State Board of Education v. Barnette*). "Were my purely personal attitude relevant I should wholeheartedly associate myself with the general libertarian views in the Court's opinion, representing as they do the thought and action of a lifetime. But as judges we are neither Jew nor Gentile, neither Catholic nor agnostic. We owe equal attachment to the Constitution and are equally bound by our judicial obligations whether we derive our citizenship from the earliest or the latest immigrants to these shores. As a member of this Court I am not justified in writing my private notions of policy into the Constitution, no matter how deeply I may cherish them or how mischievous I may deem their disregard."[44]

As a teacher at Harvard Law School, where he had graduated in 1906, he took an active role in the defense of Sacco and Vanzetti, helped found the American Civil Liberties Union, exerted an incalculable influence on a generation of lawyers and ended up with so many of his bright young men ("happy hot dogs," they were called) in New Deal agencies that he was denounced by conservative Congressmen as the administration's "Rasputin."

"I wish my mother were alive," the Vienna-born descendant of generations of rabbis and scholars told F.D.R. when he got word of his appointment to the vacancy left by the death of Justice Cardozo.[45]

Frankfurter came to the Court with an abiding reverence for the law and its gleaming white temple on Capitol Hill. A few years earlier, when his disciples had first swarmed over the bureaucracy, communicating a refreshing intellectual excitement to public service, a stubborn, self-willed majority of the Justices had done great violence to the Court, undermining the respect and confidence on which it depended for its survival. A generation later, when the temple was under attack from the right rather than the left, Frankfurter put an appropriate end to his twenty-three years on the bench by opposing the Court's decision to involve the judiciary in reapportionment disputes:

"The Court's authority — possessed of neither the purse nor the sword — ultimately rests on sustained public confidence in its moral sanction. Such feeling must be nourished by the Court's complete detachment, in fact and in appearance, from political entanglements and by abstention from injecting itself into the clash of political forces in political settlements."[46]

"Our Justices are not monks or scientists," Chief Justice Warren had written previously in *Fortune*, "but participants in the living stream of our national life, steering the law between the dangers of rigidity on the one hand and of formlessness on the other. Legal scholars may still debate whether the life of the law is reason, as Coke maintained, or experience, as Holmes claimed. I think it is both. Our system faces no theoretical dilemma but a single continuous problem: how to apply to ever changing conditions the never changing principles of freedom."[47]

Frankfurter was a short, bookish, nervously energetic man of ideas; Warren a large, hearty man of action. They differed in their personal tastes (the Chief Justice was not likely to show up on a forty-yard line with the *Times Literary Supplement* sticking out of his pocket) as well as in their legal philosophies, and both were warmly loved and hated. Inevitably, their differences erupted in public.

During a 1957 oral argument, Frankfurter interrupted a rather long, complicated question the Chief Justice was putting to a lawyer. When Frankfurter reworded the question for him, Warren flushed: "Let him answer my question. He is confused enough as it is." Frankfurter paled. "Confused by Justice Frankfurter, I presume," he retorted, and the Chief Justice resumed his question and, with it, his command of the situation.[48]

The most dramatic public exchange between the two men came on April 24, 1961, when the Court held in a five-to-four ruling that one Willie Lee Stewart should have another trial (his fourth) on a murder charge because of improper questioning by the prosecution. Dissenting, Frankfurter began to scold the majority for taking "an isolated sentence or two and making it color the whole trial." Warren's gorge rose visibly as he waited for Frankfurter to finish.

"That was not the dissenting opinion that you filed," he said, startling observers with the intensity of his anger. "That was a lecture — a closing argument by a prosecutor to a jury. It might properly have been made in the conference room but not in this courtroom. As I understand it, the purpose of reporting an opinion here is to inform the public and not for the purpose of degrading this Court. I assure you that if any [written] opinion had said those things I would have much to say myself, but unfortunately the record will not show it."

"I'll leave it to the record," Frankfurter snapped.[49]

Later that afternoon, when the Chief Justice was asked about the incident, which made front-page headlines across the country, he smiled and said that even Supreme Court Justices were human and apt to lose their tempers once in a while.

On April 5, 1962, less than two weeks after dissenting in the first of the landmark series of reapportionment decisions, Frankfurter suffered a mild stroke while working in his chambers. He never recovered his health sufficiently to return to the bench. When he resigned in August, his chair went to Arthur Goldberg. He died in Washington on February 22, 1965. In the opinion of Archibald MacLeish he had exerted "more influence on more lives than any man in his generation . . ."[50]

"His death leaves a great void in the communities of scholars and jurists . . ." Warren said in his eulogy. "We of the Supreme Court who knew him so well mourn his passing, both as our associate and friend, but we also know that his ebullient spirit would want us to get on with our always unfinished work."[51]

As the Chief Justice spoke, his old friend Senator Kuchel was working with Senator Dirksen on behalf of a constitutional amendment to overturn *Reynolds* and permit the people of a state to determine whether or not they would like to have one house of a bicameral legislature apportioned on some basis other than population. A front organization, the "Committee for Government of the People," was raising money from unidentified sources to support a nationwide campaign conducted by Whitaker & Baxter, the San Francisco husband-and-wife team of press agents who had helped defeat Governor Warren's health insurance program.

They were less successful with reapportionment. By the spring of 1966, when the proposed amendment had been defeated in the Senate for the third time, it was unmistakably dead. Meanwhile, thirty-eight states had reapportioned their legislatures and eight others had plans in litigation. The country and the courts had survived the application of judicial relief to the urban voter.

"It is hostile to a democratic system to involve the judiciary in the politics of the people," Frankfurter had contended in 1946, when malapportionment was before the Court in *Colegrove*.[52] He was answered eighteen years later when Warren spoke for the Court in *Reynolds*, declaring that "a denial of constitutionally protected rights demands judicial protection; our oath and our office require no less of us."[53]

17

Prayer and Pornography

God save the United States and this Honorable Court.
— COURT CRIER

NOTHING in the history of the Warren Court has aroused more misplaced indignation than its decision dealing with prayer and religious exercises in public schools.

"If the Supreme Court were openly in league with the cause of Communism, they could scarcely advance it more," Representative Robert L. F. Sikes of Florida said in 1962, when an official prayer for New York schoolchildren was declared unconstitutional.[1] In Los Angeles an outraged municipal judge filed the only appeal possible under the circumstances by opening court with the invocation: "God bless the Supreme Court, and in Your wisdom let it be shown the error of its ways."[2]

"They put the Negroes in the schools, and now they've driven God out," said Representative George W. Andrews of Alabama, and an Indiana colleague, William G. Bray, pointed out, "On the same day that the Court struck down this simple prayer, it asserted the rights of homosexuals to receive magazines about their common interests through the mail . . ."[3]

"I do not intend to let nine men tell 190 million Americans, including children, where and when they can say their prayers," Senator Dirksen said in 1966, when he proposed a constitutional amendment permitting prayer in public schools.[4] "Isn't it strange," he had remarked a few weeks earlier in an oleaginous aside, "that in this country as prayer goes down, crime goes up?"[5]

Although his colleagues had no doubt of the sincerity of his religious beliefs, some found it difficult not to attach worldly motives to his renewed interest in the school-prayer issue. It came at a time when he had just lost his fight for a constitutional amendment overturning the Court's one-man, one-vote rulings. Religion and reapportionment seemed to have melded in an act of political vengeance. Senators who had helped defeat the minority leader on reapportionment had the uneasy feeling he was out to punish them by forcing a roll-call vote on his new proposal. Much as they might oppose the amendment in principle, few of them cared to stand up in public and say "Nay" to prayer.[6]

Oddly enough, even without the Dirksen amendment Americans still seem to be worshiping where and when they please. Their currency still bears the motto, "In God We Trust"; they still pledge allegiance to the flag of one nation "under God," and their sons still march off to war in the company of tax-supported chaplains. Both houses of Congress still begin their workday with prayer, and before the Supreme Court gives ear to the arguments of opposing counsel, the crier still follows his traditional "Oyez! Oyez! Oyez!" with the words, "God save the United States and this Honorable Court."

The Chief Justice is one of the members of the Court who regularly bows his head at this daily reference to the Deity. "I just can't figure how Earl went along on that school-prayer business," says an old friend; and a former neighbor in East Bakersfield gets red in the face whenever the subject comes up. "He wasn't raised like that," she says. "He was brought up on the Bible." When asked if she had read any of the Court's prayer and Bible-reading decisions, she said, "No." She resented the question. She knew what she knew.

The trouble began June 25, 1962, at the close of the October, 1961, term.[7] The Court has a habit of holding back on its judicial bombshells until the start of the capital's hot weather when, with their bags packed, the Justices are ready to leave town. In this instance, it fell to the lot of Justice Black, who had taught Sunday school for twenty years, to speak for the Court.* It was a day well suited for the First Amendment's most dogged defender to brave the wrath of the righteous, because, as the Chief Justice and the Solici-

* Frankfurter and White took no part in the decision. Stewart dissented.

tor General had observed in handsome tributes, it marked the completion of his twenty-fifth Court term.

At issue in *Engel v. Vitale* was a twenty-two-word prayer: "Almighty God, we acknowledge our dependence upon Thee, and we beg Thy blessings upon us, our parents, our teachers and our Country." The prayer had been composed by the New York State Board of Regents and recommended for use in public schools at the start of each day's classes. No compulsion was to be used. Children were free to remain silent or to leave the room while the words were being spoken. Five parents of children attending schools in New Hyde Park took the prayer to court in January, 1959. The legal argument went on for three and one half years.

"Congress shall make no law respecting an establishment of religion . . ." the First Amendment begins, and as the words were interpreted in Justice Black's opinion, they "must at least mean that in this country it is no part of the business of government to compose official prayers for any group of the American people to recite as a part of a religious program carried on by government."[8]

Prayers, the Court held, should be left "to the people themselves and to those the people choose to look to for religious guidance."[9] It mattered not at all that the school prayer in question had been composed by bureaucrats skilled in the writing of placebo prose.

"To those who may subscribe to the view that because the Regents' official prayer is so brief and general there can be no danger to religious freedom in its governmental establishment, it may be appropriate to say in the words of James Madison, the author of the First Amendment, 'It is proper to take alarm at the first experiment on our liberties.' "[10]

Handed down a week before the Fourth of July, the school-prayer decision touched off a pyrotechnic display of fireworks fusing piety and patriotism. "It is like taking a star and stripe off the flag," said a Methodist bishop in Georgia,[11] and, meeting in Hershey, Pennsylvania, for their annual conference, the nation's governors passed a resolution urging Congress to propose a constitutional amendment which would "permit the free and voluntary participation in prayer in our public schools."[12] Within six weeks, God-fearing Congressmen had offered the House a choice among some forty-two different prayer bills, none of which ever made it to the White House.

"I always thought that this nation was essentially a religious one," Dwight Eisenhower said, apparently without having read the text of *Engel*. However, John F. Kennedy, the country's first Catholic President, pointed out that there is "a very easy remedy, and that is to pray ourselves, and I would think it would be a welcome reminder to every American family that we can pray a good deal more at home and attend our churches with a good deal more fidelity."[13]

"God pity our country when we can no longer appeal to God for help," thundered Billy Graham, the Protestant evangelist, and Cardinal Spellman denounced the decision as striking "at the very heart of the Godly tradition in which America's children have for so long been raised."[14]

Setting out to explain the furor to the English, Karl E. Meyer wrote in *New Statesman*: "The prayer lobby is a powerful one, and not always above a little dissembling. Once I heard a radio sermon given by the Rev. Billy Graham in which he glowingly recounted how Benjamin Franklin helped resolve a crisis at the Constitutional Convention in Philadelphia on 28 June 1787 — almost 175 years to the day before the Court ruling on prayer. Franklin did appeal for prayer, but Dr. Graham failed to add the relevant fact that the proposal was rejected because, as Franklin noted, 'the Convention, except three or four persons, thought prayer unnecessary.' "[15]

"It is an unfortunate fact of history," Black wrote in *Engel*, "that when some of the very groups which had most strenuously opposed the established Church of England found themselves sufficiently in control of colonial governments in this country to write their own prayers into law, they passed laws making their own religion the official religion of their respective colonies. Indeed, as late as the time of the Revolutionary War, there were established churches in at least eight of the thirteen former colonies and established religions in at least four of the other five. . . .

"By the time of the adoption of the Constitution, our history shows that there was a widespread awareness among many Americans of the dangers of a union of Church and State. These people knew, some of them from bitter personal experience, that one of the greatest dangers to the freedom of the individual to worship in his own way lay in the Government's placing its official stamp of approval upon one particular kind of prayer or one particular form of religious services."[16]

Confusion over just what limitations the Court had imposed on public schools was compounded by the attention given Justice Douglas's concurrence, which went beyond Justice Black's opinion and alarmed many laymen who mistakenly assumed it had the force of law. Douglas raised the question whether *any* religious exercise, including the Court's own opening invocation, could be financed by federal or state funds. "No," he decided, and after citing the Court's familiar words in a 1952 ruling (*Zorach v. Clauson*), "we are a religious people whose institutions presuppose a Supreme Being,"[17] he proceeded to reexamine the stand taken in *Everson v. Board of Education* (1947).[18]

In this landmark ruling, the Court had allowed the taxpayers' money to be spent in paying the bus fares of pupils attending parochial schools. "Public money devoted to payment of religious costs, educational or other, brings the quest for more," Justice Rutledge had written in his *Everson* dissent. "It brings too the struggle of sect against sect for the larger share or for any. Here one by numbers alone will benefit most, there another. That is precisely the history of societies which have had an established religion and dissident groups."[19]

To Douglas, this dissent was "durable First Amendment philosophy,"[20] and time had borne out Rutledge's prophecy, as private schools — mostly Catholic — continued to make larger and more varied demands on the public purse (hot lunches, scholarships, new equipment, dormitories), citing *Everson* as authority. In the uproar over the Douglas heresy, which would deny Congress its daily appeal for divine guidance,* little attention was paid in the press to a significant footnote in Black's opinion. Even the New York *Times* failed to include it, but it was picked up by *Time* and quoted in part:

"There is of course nothing in the decision reached here that is inconsistent with the fact that school children and others are offi-

---

* According to Capitol folklore, when a minister of the gospel was invited to stand in one day for the Senate chaplain, he began by praying for the Senators, but, after taking a closer look at them, decided to pray for the country.

cially encouraged to express love for our country by reciting historical documents such as the Declaration of Independence which
contain references to the Deity or by singing officially espoused
anthems which include the composer's profession of faith in a
Supreme Being, or with the fact that there are many manifestations
in our public life of belief in God."[21]

A year later, on June 17, 1963, when the Justices were again about
to get out of town, the Court ruled on a pair of cases brought by a
Unitarian family in Pennsylvania and a devout atheist in Maryland
(*Abington School District v. Schempp* and *Murray v. Curlett*).[22]
The Schempps had taken exception to a Pennsylvania law requiring
the reading, without comment, of at least ten Bible verses at the
opening of each school day. In Maryland, the atheistic beliefs of
Mrs. Madalyn Murray had been offended by the exposure of her son
to Bible reading and the Lord's Prayer at the start of the day's
classes in a Baltimore public school.

The Schempps had given testimony, supported by expert witnesses, that a literal reading of the Bible contradicted certain
doctrines of the Unitarian faith. Mrs. Murray's lack of faith was no
less outraged, she contended, by religious practices which pronounced "belief in God as the source of all moral and spiritual
values," thus rendering "sinister, alien and suspect" the beliefs and
ideals of a practicing atheist. Belief and disbelief, it was argued,
were equally secure against any law "respecting an establishment of
religion, or prohibiting the free exercise thereof . . ."

Justice Clark, with Justice Stewart again the lone dissenter,*
wrote the Court's opinion, settling both disputes in favor of the
protesting parents. The decision rested on the Establishment Clause
of the First Amendment, which had been made applicable to the
states by the Fourteenth Amendment in a 1940 decision.[24] In the
relationship between man and religion, the Court held, the state is

---

* A few days later, when Justice White was taking part in a swearing-in
ceremony at the Department of Justice, he jokingly remarked, "I had to
borrow this Bible. The only one left in the Supreme Court was Potter Stewart's." When the American Legion subsequently met in Baltimore for a district convention and approved a resolution calling for impeachment of members
of the Court for opposing religion and favoring Communism, Justice Stewart
was excepted because he was known to have the only Bible in the Supreme
Court Building.[23]

committed to absolute neutrality, forbidden to help or hinder. Clark wrote in language so clear that it could give trouble to no layman who cared to read the opinion before damning it.

"The place of religion in our society is an exalted one, achieved through a long tradition of reliance on the home, the church and the inviolable citadel of the individual heart and mind. We have come to recognize through bitter experience that it is not within the power of government to invade that citadel, whether its purpose or effect be to aid or oppose, to advance or retard."[25]

"Both cases involve provisions which explicitly permit any student who wishes, to be excused from participation in the exercises," Justice Stewart noted in his dissent.[26]

A few months earlier, in a discussion of *Engel*, Dean Erwin N. Griswold of Harvard Law School had stressed the same point, expressing regret that the Court had not given more weight to the "crucial" fact of the pupil's freedom to abstain from reciting the Regents' prayer, either by remaining silent or by leaving the room. Such abstention might even serve a useful purpose, the dean felt, in enabling a child to learn what it means to be a member of a minority group.

"Learning tolerance for other persons, no matter how different, and respect for their beliefs, may be an important part of American education, and wholly consistent with the First Amendment," he had said,[27] and had then gone on to talk about Sunday closing laws, which impose the Sabbath of the Christian majority on minorities who may regard some other day as holy, or no day at all.

Custom and the Constitution come into conflict every weekend wherever an orthodox Jewish merchant has to close his shop on Saturday because of his religious beliefs and on Sunday because of the laws enacted by his Christian neighbors. In such communities, a Christian is free to buy ham on Saturday, when the devout Jew is forbidden to shop, but on Sunday, when the Jew sets out to buy a kosher salami, he finds his delicatessen closed.

In Canada, the Supreme Court has upheld Sunday closing laws because they are religious in purpose. In the United States, the Supreme Court has upheld Sunday closing laws because they are not religious in purpose. "In Canada we are told purpose and effect must be distinguished," writes Professor Jerome A. Barron of George Washington Law School. "The purpose of the Lord's Day Act is concededly religious, but we are assured the effect is entirely secular."[28] The United States Supreme Court, disposing of four Sunday closing laws in 1961, denied the argument that the present statutes' purpose or effect is religious.

Although the laws originally reflected religious beliefs, Chief Justice Warren contended, they had come to be secular statutes providing a day of rest. "These provisions," he wrote, "along with those which permit various sports and entertainments on Sunday, seem clearly to be fashioned for the purpose of providing a Sunday atmosphere of recreation, cheerfulness, repose and enjoyment. Coupled with the general proscription against other types of work, we believe that the air of the day is one of relaxation rather than one of religion."[29]

"The special protection which Sunday laws give the dominant religious groups and the penalty they place on minorities whose holy day is Saturday constitute, in my view, state interference with the 'free exercise' of religion," Justice Douglas wrote, dissenting in all four cases, declaring that no one could constitutionally be placed at a competitive disadvantage and penalized for adherence to his religious beliefs.[30]

"By what authority can government compel one person not to work on Sunday because the majority of the populace deem Sunday to be a holy day?" Douglas wrote in another Sunday closing law dissent in 1962. "Moslems may some day control a state legislature. Could they make criminal the opening of a shop on Friday? Would not we Christians fervently believe, if that came to pass, that government had no authority to make us bow to the scruples of the Moslem majority?"[31]

"The question is a fair one," says Dean Griswold, "but I believe that the Justice implies a wrong answer. If I live in a state with a Moslem majority, and it passes such a law — not compelling me to do anything, I ask you to note, but only to refrain from work on a certain day — I would think that the law was appropriate and one which I should obey."[32]

Despite its reputation for godlessness, the Warren Court has permitted the Sabbath of the Christian majority to remain a secular day of rest for all, believer and nonbeliever. Massachusetts has revised its ancient statute, "An Act for the Observance of the Lord's Day." It is now "An Act for the Observance of a Common Day of Rest." The Orthodox Jew has ended up with two days "of recreation, cheerfulness, repose and enjoyment."

In December, 1965, perhaps prayerfully, the Court said "Amen" to the school-prayer controversy. Parents of twenty-one pupils in a Long Island public school (P.S. 184) had gone to court when the principal ordered an end to the recitation of grace by kindergarten pupils. Each morning, before they had their milk and cookies, they recited:

> *God is great, God is good*
> *And we thank Him for our food.*
> *Amen.*

In the afternoon, before leaving school, the children recited another nursery prayer:

> *Thank You for the world so sweet,*
> *Thank You for the food we eat,*
> *Thank You for the birds that sing —*
> *Thank You, God, for everything.*

The parents asked a Federal District Court for an order allowing the children to pray voluntarily to God each day. The court ruled in their favor, but was overruled by Judge Henry J. Friendly of the Court of Appeals for the Second Circuit, who suggested that the parents content themselves with having the children say their prayers before nine o'clock or after three.[33] The parents took their case to the Supreme Court, which refused to review it.[34] The Court, having laid down the constitutional principle, was leaving it up to state legislatures and city councils to see that departments of education and local school boards abided by the law of the land.

"I'm glad," said Mrs. Florence Flast, head of United Parents Association, a federation of more than four hundred parent-teacher groups. "We have always opposed prayers in the schools, including the 'voluntary' prayer because it cannot really be voluntary. The child feels under pressure by the teacher."[35]

"Saying prayers by rote, in an atmosphere that is nonreligious, detracts from the prayer itself," said Frederick C. McLaughlin, director of the Public Education Association. "People usually look to religious leaders, and a religious atmosphere, for prayers, and a teacher is not competent to provide that."[36]

"The people mean business this time," Senator Dirksen said in the summer of 1966, when he proposed a constitutional amendment overturning the Court's school-prayer decision,[37] but religious leaders joined with authorities on constitutional law to oppose this effort to tamper for the first time with the Bill of Rights.

". . . [T]he very purpose of the Bill of Rights is to put a check on the popular will," Professor Freund of Harvard testified, and tactfully suggested it was the duty of responsible lawmakers not to yield to sudden outbursts of passion, but to wait, "to clarify, to analyze rationally, to illuminate and to educate the lay public."[38]

Professor Freund was supported by the testimony of a Jesuit priest, the Reverend Robert F. Drinan, dean of the Boston College Law School.[39] Both agreed on the dangers inherent in the ambiguous wording of the Dirksen amendment. Setting out to promote religion in general, it would inevitably come to be used to the advantage of whatever sect happened to have the upper hand in a community. Prayer, in the meantime, would become jumbled in the child's mind with the recitation of the multiplication table and the dates of dead poets and Presidents.

"My fellow Americans, is this the time in our nation's history for the Federal Government to ban Almighty God from our school room?" Senator Goldwater had asked a Salt Lake City audience in his 1964 campaign for the Presidency,[40] and was answered not only by the voters that fall but also by Father Drinan two years later:

". . . [T]he banning of Bible reading and of prayer by the Supreme Court in 1963 merely stripped away the widespread illusion that the American public school somehow combined piety and learning in an eminently satisfactory way. The various constitutional amendments proposed by Congressmen and Senators to restore to the public schools the last vestiges of their piety — Bible reading and prayer — constitute an almost irrational refusal to surrender one of the most persistent myths in American life — the illusion that the public school can train future citizens in morality and piety."[41]

Senator Goldwater's conservative conscience has been sorely troubled by government meddling, but government could hardly seem to make a more offensive assault on the privacy of an individual than by subjecting his children to an official prayer written by an anonymous bureaucrat or to the reading of Bible verses which either contradict the religious teaching of his church or tend to set his child apart in embarrassing isolation because he was born to parents whose moral precepts do not happen to be founded on belief in a Supreme Being.

"The Chief still gets a kick out of a cartoon that came out a few years ago," says a member of Warren's official family. "It shows two kids on their way to school. One of them is telling the other that he always prays just before an exam, 'I don't care what Earl Warren says.'"

Warren, a quondam Methodist married to a devout Baptist whose children have drawn no line in their marriages between Catholic and Protestant, Gentile and Jew, has never been one to make a public display of piety. He lives by a strict moral code ("he's the kind of man who's honest even when he's by himself," says one of his closest friends), and keeps the Bible by his bed, along with twenty-five to thirty other books, mostly history, biography and Californiana, but no fiction.

"Novels are too exciting," he explains.[42]

No one could be a less promising customer for such contemporary works as *Raw Dames, The Whipping Chorus Girls, Stud Broad, Screaming Flesh, The Housewife's Handbook on Selective Promiscuity* and *Memoirs of a Woman of Pleasure,** which made up a large part of his reading matter in the winter of 1965 when the Court was having another go at trying to reconcile the Constitution with concupiscence. Obscenity, in the Court's unhappy experience, is like a disagreeable odor, easier to detect than to define.

---

* Commonly known as *Fanny Hill*, this is generally thought to be the first book suppressed in the United States on grounds of obscenity. It was seized in 1821, but the case never reached the Supreme Court.[43]

"There is no definition of the term," writes Leo M. Alpert. "There is no basis of identification. There is no unity in describing what is obscene literature, or in prosecuting it. There is little more than the ability to smell it."[44]

". . . I know it when I see it . . ." says Justice Stewart.[45]

The earliest reported case of obscenity, Alpert writes, is *The King v. Sir Charles Sedley* (1663). "Inebriated and nude, Sir Charles had exhibited himself on a London balcony overlooking Covent Garden and had hurled upon the populace bottles filled with an 'offensive liquor,' as the judge later delicately indicated, the while he engaged in eloquent blasphemy."[46]

The Supreme Court, before the Warren years, had never attempted a definition of obscenity. A generation of judges relied on a venerable test devised in 1868 by Lord Cockburn (*Regina v. Hicklin*), who had declared a work to be obscene if it tended "to deprave and corrupt those whose minds are open to such immoral influences and into whose hands a publication of this sort may fall."[47] Thus, a middle-aged college professor of English was to be permitted to buy only those books which might not embarrass a high school girl. The *Hicklin* formula was still in use in 1913 when obscenity charges were brought against the publisher of a novel called *Hagar Revelly*, succinctly reviewed in *United States v. Kennerley*:

"The book is a novel of manners presenting the life of a young woman in New York compelled to earn her living. She is represented as impulsive, sensuous, fond of pleasure, and restive under the monotony and squalor of her surroundings. Her virtue is unsuccessfully assailed by a man she does not love and later successfully by one whom she does. After her seduction she has several amorous misadventures and ends with a loveless marriage and the prospect of a dreary future. In order to give complete portrayal to the girl's emotional character, some of the scenes are depicted with a frankness and detail which have given rise to this prosecution."[48]

When the case came before Learned Hand in a federal court, the *Hicklin* rule was disapproved. ". . . I hope it is not improper for me to say that the rule as laid down, however consonant it may be with mid-Victorian morals, does not seem to me to answer to the understanding and morality of the present time . . ." In Judge Hand's view, twelve years after Queen Victoria's death, treatment of sex should not be reduced "to the standard of a child's library in the supposed interest of a salacious few . . ."[49]

But twenty years later, in the first months of the New Deal, mature Americans returning from Paris vacations were still risking embarrassment and arrest to sneak home a familiar blue-bound copy of *Ulysses*. Mere possession of this masterpiece of English literature had been adjudged a crime because, under the lingering ghost of *Hicklin*, some of its words and a few passages might bring a blush to the cheek of a susceptible maiden. On December 6, 1933, a more sophisticated test — the impact of the entire work on an average member of the community — was handed down in a federal court by Judge John M. Woolsey:

"The words which are criticized as dirty are old Saxon words known to almost all men and, I venture, to many women, and are such words as would be naturally and habitually used, I believe, by the types of folk whose life, physical and mental, Joyce is seeking to describe. In respect of the recurrent emergence of the theme of sex in the minds of his characters, it must always be remembered that his locale was Celtic and his season Spring."[50]

Although *Ulysses* was permitted to pass openly through customs, *Lady Chatterley's Lover* continued to be smuggled in. An unexpurgated copy in 1958, according to Ralph Ginzburg, "will fetch anywhere from $50 to $100."[51] Now it can be picked up at the corner drugstore for less than a dollar. After the cannibalism of *Naked Lunch*, the copulation of Lady Chatterley and her husband's gamekeeper has come to seem rather old-fashioned, and to Katherine Anne Porter a bore: "Sex shouldn't be that kind of hard work . . ."[52]

"The United States has moved from one of the most timid countries in dealing with sex in the arts to what many believe is now by far the most liberated in the Western world," Anthony Lewis wrote in 1963.[53]

The Court's role in the sexual revolution was foreshadowed in 1946 when it affirmed a decision blocking efforts of the Postmaster General to revoke the second-class mailing privileges of *Esquire*, because, in his view, the magazine served no lofty public purpose. The case had fascinated Judge Thurman Arnold when it came before him in the United States Court of Appeals in Washington, D.C. The

Post Office, Judge Arnold felt, had tried manfully but had failed to resolve the age-old question of "when a scantily clad lady is art, and when she is highly improper."[54] He suggested that the Postmaster General content himself with delivering rather than censoring the mail.

In the spring of 1952 movies came to the Supreme Court for the first time. The Justices viewed a Roberto Rosselini film, *The Miracle*, which had offended Cardinal Spellman. The New York Board of Regents had found the picture "sacrilegious" and banned it. The Court lifted the ban, declaring the term too vague and reminding the censors, "It is not the business of government in our nation to suppress real or imagined attacks upon a particular religious doctrine, whether they appear in publications, speeches, or motion pictures."[55] The free speech–free press sanctuary of the First Amendment was thus opened to motion pictures.

Two years later, when *La Ronde* played the Court, the Justices merely cited their decision on *The Miracle*.[56] The citation was another first for the Court. Never before had it struck down a prohibition based on obscenity. In February, 1957, nearly forty-four years after Learned Hand had gently suggested it was about time to stop judging books for grownups by standards set for children, a unanimous Court overturned a Michigan statute forbidding publication of anything "tending to incite minors to violent or depraved or immoral acts." Justice Frankfurter wrote the opinion in *Butler v. Michigan*:

"The State insists that, by thus quarantining the general reading public against books not too rugged for grown men and women in order to shield juvenile innocence, it is exercising its power to promote the general welfare. Surely, this is to burn the house to roast the pig."[57]

Throughout this period, beginning in the mid-1920's, Sam Roth had made a good living — between arrests — publishing pirated foreign works, crude pornography and ribald classics. He pushed the stuff, but claimed not to be a user. "If I had my way," he has been quoted as saying, "there wouldn't be an unraped woman on any street where I passed by, but I'm not interested in reading about it."[58] In 1956, when Roth was back in court on another obscenity rap, his appeal gave Judge Jerome N. Frank of the second circuit appellate court a chance to review the history of obscenity legislation and litigation, and to state the still unsettled central issue of censorship:

"To vest a few fallible men — prosecutors, judges, jurors — with vast powers of literary or artistic censorship, to convert them into what J. S. Mill called a 'moral police,' is to make them despotic arbiters of literary products. If one day they ban mediocre books as obscene, another day they may do likewise to a work of genius. Originality, not too plentiful, should be cherished, not stifled."[59]

Judge Frank, in effect, was politely asking the Supreme Court to shed some light on this murky area. The Court obliged in a ruling which committed Sam Roth to prison and to history. In *Roth v. United States* and a companion case, *Alberts v. California*, it was held that obscenity could constitutionally be declared a crime by federal and state laws.[60] Obscene material lay outside the protective shelter of the First and Fourteenth Amendments.

It was left to Justice Brennan to explain just what could be construed as obscenity. In his words, which immediately became the law of the land, it was "material which deals with sex in a manner appealing to prurient interest," but to be legally declared obscene, a work must be "utterly without redeeming social importance" and it must be judged in terms of "whether, to the average person, applying contemporary community standards, the dominant theme of the material taken as a whole appeals to the prurient interest."[61]

A federal judge, using the *Roth* test on a nudist magazine, made a judicious examination of each naked body, finding some innocent of stirring prurient thoughts, others guilty, and ending by declaring the publication as a whole obscene. To Judge Arnold, long since returned to private practice, "The spectacle of a judge poring over the picture of some nude, trying to ascertain the extent to which she arouses prurient interests, and then attempting to write an opinion which explains the difference between that nude and some other nude, has elements of low comedy."[62]

The conviction was summarily reversed by the Supreme Court (*Sunshine Book Co. v. Summerfield*),[63] along with two other curt, unsigned rulings dealing with a magazine tailored to the interests of homosexuals (*One, Inc. v. Oleson*)[64] and a coltish French movie, *The Game of Love* (*Times Film Corp. v. Chicago*).[65]

The Court, it seemed, had steered a statesmanlike course between prudery and prurience. It had declared obscenity a crime, but nothing brought before it had been found obscene under the *Roth-Alberts* test.

Warren's strong feelings about the smut-peddler surfaced one day when he clutched a pornographic work in his fist and blurted out to a colleague, "If anyone showed that book to my daughters, I'd have strangled him with my own hands."[66] But he is equally strong in his feelings about the freedoms guaranteed by the First and Fourteenth Amendments. He would distinguish a reputable bookseller stocking a ribald classic from a huckster who decks the same work in lurid covers and hustles it to high school students.

"It is not the book that is on trial; it is a person," he wrote in his *Alberts-Roth* concurring opinion. "The conduct of the defendant is the central issue, not the obscenity of the book or picture."[67]

Both Alberts and Roth, he took pains to point out, "were engaged in the business of purveying textural or graphic matter *openly advertised* to appeal to the erotic interest of their customers. They were plainly engaged in the *commercial exploitation* of the morbid and shameful craving for materials with prurient effect. I believe that the State and Federal Governments can constitutionally punish such conduct." (Emphasis added.)[68]

The Court, in 1959, took notice of the side effects of obscenity laws. A Los Angeles ordinance had made it a crime for a bookseller to have an obscene work for sale in his shop. With a possible fine or prison sentence riding on his ability to guess whether some local judge would find a certain work obscene, a bookseller would tend to play it safe, the Court felt. He would remove the danger by removing the book in question.

"The bookseller's self-censorship, compelled by the State, would be a censorship affecting the whole public . . ." Justice Brennan wrote.[69]

The Court, beginning with *Roth*, had developed what Professor Harry Kalven, Jr., of the University of Chicago, called "the two-level speech theory," with one level of expression shielded by the Constitution, the other lying beyond its pale.

"At one level," he writes, "there are communications which, even though odious to the majority opinion of the day, even though expressive of the thought we hate, are entitled to be measured against the clear-and-present-danger criterion. At another level are communications apparently so worthless as not to require any extensive judicial effort to determine whether they can be prohibited. There is to be freedom for the thought we hate, but not for the candor we deplore."[70]

On a spring day in 1959, eight members of the Supreme Court assembled in their paneled conference room for a private screening of the film version of *Lady Chatterley's Lover,* which had been refused a license by the New York Board of Regents because it condoned adultery under certain circumstances. Justice Black passed up the movie, but as is well known, he is opposed to all forms of censorship anyway. In this case, obscenity was not a matter of words or pictures, but an idea. The Court was unanimous in striking down the statute under which the license had been denied:

"It is contended that the state's action was justified because the motion picture attractively portrays a relationship which is contrary to the moral standards, the religious precepts, and the legal code of its citizenry," Justice Stewart wrote for the Court. "This argument misconceives what it is that the Constitution protects. Its guarantee is not confined to the expression of ideas that are conventional or shared by a majority. It protects advocacy of the opinion that adultery may sometimes be proper, no less than advocacy of socialism or the single tax."[71]

"My belief," Justice Black grumbled, "is that this Court is about the most inappropriate Supreme Board of Censors that could be found."[72]

The Supreme Board of Censors was attacked in June, 1964, by William Ferguson, the attorney general of Kansas, addressing a group of clergymen and church leaders: "In a series of decisions in recent years, the Warren-led United States Supreme Court has opened the door to a flood of filth in books, magazines and movies. The Court opened the door even wider in last Monday's ruling overturning a decision of the Geary County District Court and the Supreme Court of Kansas, which had ordered the destruction of a number of obscene publications."[73]

At issue in *A Quantity of Copies of Books v. Kansas*[74] were

1,715 paperbacks — *Original Nightstand Books* — seized from the P-K newsstand in Junction City, Kansas. Judge Albert B. Fletcher of the Geary County District Court found the books obscene and ordered them burned. The state Supreme Court affirmed the decision, and the newsstand operators appealed to the United States Supreme Court, where the case for Kansas was argued by Attorney General Ferguson, who did not seem to get on well with the Chief Justice.

"No," Ferguson said, when Warren asked if the newsstand operators had been prosecuted.

"Why not?"

"It is more important to reach the books themselves," Ferguson said.

"It's easier to burn books than to prosecute a seller of obscenity?" said the Chief Justice, who demanded to know, "Why don't you prosecute people who are indulging in obscenity? They don't like going to jail any more than anyone else. If they are prosecuted, can't we believe obscenity can be almost stamped out like perjury and robbery, and avoid all these constitutional questions of book burning? Why don't the law-enforcement officers do their job and prosecute these purveyors of obscenity instead of coming to this Court all the time?"[75]

It took the Supreme Board of Censors two and one-half months to decide *A Quantity of Books,* and even then no five Justices could agree on the same opinion, although seven voted to reverse the Kansas Supreme Court. The Chief Justice, along with Justices Goldberg, White and Brennan, reversed because the books had been seized in such a fashion as to endanger non-obscene works. Thirty-one different titles had been impounded under a warrant specifying only seven books, and no hearing had been afforded the newsstand operators before any of the books had been carted off to be read by a judge, then committed to the torch. If this could be done in one county to *Sex Circus* and *The Wife Swappers,* it could be done in another to *The Catcher in the Rye* and *Tom Jones.*

"State regulation of obscenity must 'conform to procedures that will ensure against the curtailment of constitutionally protected expression, which is often separated from obscenity only by a dim and uncertain line,'" Justice Brennan wrote in the plurality opinion.[76]

Justices Black and Douglas concurred on the ground that the Kansas statute, like all obscenity laws, was in conflict with the First Amendment, as applied to the states by the Fourteenth. Justice Stewart went along with the other six because, in his opinion, the books were not hard-core pornography and could not, therefore, be constitutionally suppressed. In dissent, Justices Harlan and Clark were less troubled by book-burning procedures in Kansas than by the Court's decision, which "straitjackets the legitimate attempt of Kansas to protect what it considers an important societal interest."[77]

"If Kansans and Americans do not begin active measures to restore our moral standards," Attorney General Ferguson said when the decision was announced, "this country may follow the path of the Romans from moral degeneration to political collapse."[78]

On the same day that the moral fibers of Junction City, Kansas, were imperiled by the return of Sex Circus and The Wife Swappers to the P-K newsstand, the Court opened Cleveland Heights, Ohio, to the possibility of degeneracy and decay by reversing the conviction of a local theater manager, Nico Jacobellis, who had been fined $2,500 for possessing and exhibiting a French movie, Les Amants (The Lovers), which had been well received by many established critics.[79]

In A Quantity of Books, four Justices had been of one mind in the plurality opinion. In Jacobellis v. Ohio, there were only two, Brennan and Goldberg. Brennan, speaking for the the Court, made a brave stab at clarifying the Roth test. In acknowledging its imperfections, he seemed to swing over to Justice Stewart's view that the only material not protected by the Constitution was hard-core pornography.

"But," the Chief Justice asked, "who can define 'hard-core pornography' with any greater clarity than obscenity?'"[80]

". . . I know it when I see it," Justice Stewart said, "and the motion picture involved in this case is not that."[81]

"Consequently," the Harvard Law Review declared in appraising the Court's October, 1963, term, "Jacobellis leaves the relevant tests so subjective and devoid of explication as to offer little guidance for determining the obscenity of a specific work."[82]

In dissent, Warren defended the *Roth* rule ("I believe that we should try to live with it — at least until a more satisfactory definition is evolved").[83] He also sided with the minority on the question of whether the "community standards" used to determine obscenity under *Roth* should be national in character or drawn up locally to meet the needs of different areas. For the Chief Justice, "there is no provable 'national standard,' and perhaps there should be none."[84] This, to the *Harvard Law Review*, was an invitation to chaos.

"Because a decision in one locality that a work was not obscene would give no assurance to booksellers or movie exhibitors in other areas, the sale or exhibition of questionable works would be inhibited. Although state courts may still disagree on the application of a national standard to a given work, such conflicts can, at least, be resolved by the Supreme Court. Even granting Chief Justice Warren's premise that different localities have different needs, the national interest in a free flow of ideas and expression should take precedence."[85]

To keep the expression of sexual ideas flowing freely in constitutional channels, the Court braced itself on December 7, 1965, for two days of oral arguments on three obscenity cases which had come up from courts in three different states. Massachusetts had lowered the boom on a reputable New York publisher, G. P. Putnam's Sons, for bringing out a trade edition of John Cleland's disreputable eighteenth-century romp, *Memoirs of a Woman of Pleasure* (*Fanny Hill*). New York had clamped down on Edward Mishkin for catering to sadistic and masochistic tastes with such specialized items as *Screaming Flesh, Dance with the Dominant Whip* and *Cult of the Spankers*. A federal judge in Pennsylvania had fined Ralph Ginzburg $28,000 and sentenced him to serve five years in prison for publishing a pretentious hardcover quarterly, *Eros* (it had been dubbed "*The American Heritage* of the bedroom"); a raunchy newsletter, *Liaison;* and a clinical series of sexual reminiscences, *The Housewife's Handbook on Selective Promiscuity.*

"Do we have to read all of them to determine if they have social importance?" Warren asked plaintively as arguments began on the three appeals. "I'm sure this Court doesn't want to read all the prurient material in the country to determine if it has social value. If the final burden depends on this Court, it looks to me as though we're in trouble."[86]

In defense of *Fanny Hill*, Charles Rembar argued that scholarly testimony about the book's literary and historical value should suffice to demonstrate its possession of the magic ingredient, RSI (Redeeming Social Importance). On behalf of Massachusetts, William I. Cowin insisted that such an approach would make it virtually impossible ever to ban a book as obscene, because some trace of RSI could always be vouched for in its defense. He urged the Court to consider the book itself, not its apologists.

"What you are saying is that the Court must look at this stuff and read it," Justice Brennan interjected, and Justice Black commented: "The problem still arises whether this Court can do all this censorship and do anything else and whether it is the one who should do the censoring — if anyone should."[87]

"We are judges, not literary experts or historians or philosophers," Justice Douglas protested the following spring when fourteen different opinions were required to dispose of the three cases.[*88]

The Court cleared *Fanny Hill* (as long as the advertising and promotion remained decorous) and affirmed the convictions of both Mishkin[89] and Ginzburg.[90] In the process, something new was added to juridical territory already beset with thorns and overcast with fog. A book could now be judged by its cover as well as by its contents, and a bookseller could be jailed for selling an otherwise innocent book if he leered at his customer. Again Justice Brennan had the bleak task of speaking for the Court:

"Where the purveyor's sole emphasis is on the sexually provocative aspects of his publications, that fact may be decisive in the determination of obscenity."[91]

In fitting out a new test-kit for the detection of obscenity, Justice Brennan went beyond *Roth's* RSI and added CEPT ("Commercial Exploitation," "Pandering" and "Titillation"), but as Justice Stewart pointed out in dissent, no federal law makes a criminal offense of "commercial exploitation," "pandering" and "titillation," nor had any

---

* In the six obscenity cases decided between 1957 and 1964, there were twenty-three separate opinions.

such charges been brought against Ginzburg at his trial.[92] He was to be sent to jail for five years on grounds he could not have known about at the time of his arrest, because no such grounds had been mapped out by the Court.

"The advertisements of our best magazines are chock-full of thighs, ankles, calves, bosoms, eyes, and hair, to draw the potential buyer's attention to lotions, tires, food, liquor, clothing, autos, and even insurance policies," Justice Douglas wrote in his *Ginzburg* dissent. "The sexy advertisement neither adds to nor detracts from the quality of the merchandise being offered for sale. And I do not see how it adds to or detracts one whit from the legality of the book being distributed. A book should stand on its own, irrespective of the reasons why it was written or the wiles used in selling it."[93]

The editors of *The Nation* feared "the banning of cleavage from advertising would instantly plunge America into a financial depression worse than that of the thirties."[94] To *The New Republic,* "It was a grim day in the temple of justice," and "this judgment is the beginning of the problem, not the end." The editors considered obscenity "much too vague a term to form an allowable part of criminal law."[95]

"What should be protected," the editors felt, "is the right of adults — consenting sado-masochists, let us say, to write and read — and do — what they like, in private." The editorial ended with a position somewhat short of the Black-Douglas stance: "A man should be entitled to have dirty pictures in his inside coat pocket, but they should stay there, and it is not beyond lawmaking ingenuity to see to that, and only to that."

Writing to the lay philosophers who edit *Playboy*, a publication which in Judge Arnold's learned opinion is designed in large measure "to prove that women are mammals,"[96] Professor Harry Elmer Barnes was particularly interested in the criminal weight the Court had assigned to Ginzburg's use of Middlesex, New Jersey, as a mailing address after failing to gain access to the limited postal facilities of Intercourse, Pennsylvania:

"I once had an impulse to mail some postcards from the century-old Adirondack town of Sodom, New York. Had I done so, I might, under the new ruling, be accused of pandering to homosexuals. This judicial aversion to facetiousness is not only silly but illogical. I would wager that any normal person, receiving a card from Middlesex, Intercourse or Sodom, would regard it as a joke, and, of course, nobody can laugh and lust at the same moment."[97]

One Saturday night, four months after the Court had ordered publishers to wipe the leer from their faces when they set out to peddle the spring line, a Nashville, Tennessee, police sergeant took his wife to the Crescent Theater to see a movie called *Who's Afraid of Virginia Woolf?* They walked out midway through the film. Next night, armed with a warrant, the sergeant returned with two fellow-officers, stopped the show and marched the manager off to jail.

"I represent the thinking of the good people of this town, and I just don't feel like they would approve of this type of film for the young people to see," the sergeant explained.[98]

A Sunday school teacher and a Baptist Church deacon, he was applying "community standards," as he understood them, to a work which, in his opinion, had no "social importance" to redeem it. The film, to him, was "a lot of trash that should be sent back to the West Coast." On the West Coast, at that very moment, a successful effort was being made to obtain nearly half a million signatures on behalf of a proposition which would remove the phrase "utterly without redeeming social importance" from the state's anti-obscenity law. It would also enable any outraged citizen to bring action to compel his local district attorney to prosecute any arrangement of words or pictures he found offensive. Put on the November ballot as the CLEAN proposal (California League Enlisting Action Now), it was rejected by the voters.

"Censorship reflects a society's lack of confidence in itself," Justice Stewart wrote in his *Ginzburg* dissent. "It is a hallmark of an authoritarian regime. Long ago those who wrote our First Amendment charted a different course. They believed a society can be truly strong only when it is truly free. In the realm of expression they put their faith, for better or for worse, in the enlightened choice of the people, free from the interference of the policeman's intrusive thumb or a judge's heavy hand."[99]

Censorship represents a subtraction from the freedoms proclaimed in the Bill of Rights. Historically, it has been justified by the courts in terms of balancing the public good against a private privilege or of warding off some clear and present danger. Modern research, however, questions the public good and discounts the danger.

"There is not any evidence that pornography instigates antisocial activities," reports Wardell Pomeroy, who has been carrying on Dr. Alfred Kinsey's work at the Institute for Sex Research, and in the same issue of *Newsweek* a Times Square peddler of "flag" (for flagellation) books suggests a socially desirable aspect of this specialized branch of pornography: "It keeps the nuts down. If a guy wants to beat a woman and he can read a magazine and be satisfied, he won't do no harm."[100]

"As I read the First Amendment," Justice Douglas wrote in his *Fanny Hill* concurrence, "judges cannot gear the literary diet of an entire nation to whatever tepid stuff is incapable of triggering the most demented mind. The First Amendment demands more than a horrible example or two of the perpetrator of a crime of sexual violence, in whose pocket is found a pornographic book, before it allows the Nation to be saddled with a regime of censorship."[101]

In a footnote, Justice Douglas quotes a law review article: "John George Haigh, the British vampire who sucked his victims' blood through soda straws and dissolved their drained bodies in acid baths, first had his murder-inciting dreams and vampire-longings from watching the 'voluptuous' procedure of — an Anglican High Church Service!"

"A dirty book is a dirty book," says Dr. Max Rafferty, California's Superintendent of Public Instruction, who needs no *Roth-Ginzburg* rules to confuse the obscenity issue. Standing on firm nineteenth-century ground with *Hicklin,* he insists: "The test for a dirty book is whether it can be read over radio and television or be printed in a newspaper. It's a simple test."[102]

The Rafferty test seemed hopelessly out of date to Learned Hand in 1913 and to Judge Curtis Bok in 1949, when he answered a familiar question:

"It will be asked whether one would care to have one's young daughter read these books. I suppose that by the time she is old enough to wish to read them she will have learned the biologic facts of life and the words that go with them. There is something seriously wrong at home if those facts have not been met and faced and sorted by then; it is not children so much as parents that should receive our concern about this. I should prefer that my own three daughters meet the facts of life and the literature of the world in my library than behind a neighbor's barn, for I can face the adversary there directly. If the young ladies are appalled by what they read, they can close the book at the bottom of page one; if they read further, they will learn what is in the world and in its people, and no parents who have been discerning with their children need fear the outcome."[103]

18

From Left to Right

FLUORIDATE EARL WARREN
— *Bumper sticker, Southern California,
ca. 1965*

THE official document certifying the appointment of Earl Warren as Chief Justice of the United States hangs on a wall of his library. Directly below it is Lorenz's *New Yorker* cartoon depicting an indignant caricature of Whistler's *Mother* frantically embroidering a sampler, IMPEACH EARL WARREN.

"It breaks him up," says one of his sons.

The Chief Justice was not amused, however, when right-wing criticism of the Court's handling of the constitutional rights of political heretics cropped up in London in the summer of 1957 while he was taking part in a joint meeting of the American Bar Association and the British Law Society. A special committee of the A.B.A. chose this occasion to issue a blistering report on the major decisions of the Warren Court in cases involving the Marxist menace. It was like engaging in a family quarrel while dining with neighbors.

Warren was subjected to additional embarrassment at a gathering in Royal Festival Hall addressed by the Prime Minister. At a preliminary meeting, not attended by the Chief Justice, the American delegates had decided to dress rather formally, but nobody had bothered to pass the word along to Warren. He turned up in a double-breasted brown suit and gray tie. He was smiling and apparently unconcerned, but as intimate friends attest, he is extremely sensitive to even the slightest reflection on the dignity of his office.

"Yes, he's very meticulous about the proprieties," says an old friend in Washington. "Mrs. Warren reads up on this sort of thing, and she sees that they go by the book. I attended a dinner party one night where he was the ranking guest, which meant that nobody was supposed to leave until after he'd gone. The host, a Congressman, had also invited the chairman of his committee. The chairman is a simple soul who likes to go out in the evening, have a few belts of bourbon, eat his dinner, then go home and go to bed. After dinner, when he started yawning and it became apparent that, Chief Justice or no Chief Justice, he was damned well going home, you should have seen Warren's footwork, maneuvering his wife across the room. He was determined to get to that door first, and he did."

When he got home from the A.B.A. meeting in London, after a side trip to Scotland and Ireland, Warren flew to San Francisco for his forty-fifth class reunion. "We had a whale of a time in Britain," he said,[1] then quietly resigned from the A.B.A. It was done so quietly, in fact, that not until a year later did the association's executive director discover that Warren, Earl, was no longer a member.[2] Meanwhile, no official action had been taken on the committee report attacking the Court, but the late Senator Styles Bridges had inserted it into the *Congressional Record*, and it is still being distributed by the John Birch Society.

Warren was serving his sixth term as Chief Justice when the eleven founding fathers of the John Birch Society assembled in Indianapolis on December 8, 1958, and spent two days listening to Robert Welch's reading of *The Blue Book*. The Massachusetts candy man called for the establishment of an authoritarian, monolithic organization which, like the American Communist party, would be composed of local cells and would function through fronts — "little fronts, big fronts, temporary fronts, permanent fronts, all kinds of fronts." Along with such fronts as "Women Against Labor Union Hoodlumism" and a "Committee to Investigate Communist Influences at Vassar College," Welch proposed "A Petition to Impeach Earl Warren."[3]

"I think we could get the names of a hundred outstanding leaders from the South and many from the North on the letterhead right now," he said, and three years later Dan Smoot reported from his command post in Dallas: "In the past few weeks I have received an astonishing volume of mail from individuals all over the United States, saying they are participating in activities intended to urge upon Congress impeachment proceedings against Earl Warren, Chief Justice of the Supreme Court."[4]

Smoot not only slipped up on Warren's title (he is Chief Justice of the United States), but also stumbled again when he declared that "Warren is the only Chief Justice in history who had absolutely no previous judicial experience." Despite his FBI background (1942–1951), Smoot apparently neglected to run a routine check on the thirteen Chief Justices who preceded Warren. Five of them lacked previous judicial experience (John Marshall, Roger B. Taney, Salmon P. Chase, Morrison Waite and Melville Fuller).

The movement to impeach Earl Warren has metastasized from cells feeding on Texas oil wealth, Bible Belt collection plates, and the checkbooks of California's proverbial old ladies in tennis shoes. Tom Storke, the feisty Santa Barbara newspaper publisher, won a Pulitzer Prize in 1962 (he was eighty–five at the time) for his editorial campaign against the Birchers. "When I fought 'em, I fought 'em to a frazzle," he says, and in his ninetieth year was impishly pleased at having been hanged in effigy alongside the Chief Justice. "They hung me twice," he told a visitor, and obviously disappointed by the oversight, he added, "They hung Earl three times."

The impeachers rest their case against the Chief Justice and the Court on a seventy-five-page brief, *Nine Men Against America,* the work of Rosalie M. Gordon. She indicts Warren for supporting, as governor, the United Nations, social security, government housing, and federal aid to farmers. He was not only "quick to take up the cry of McCarthyism" (at a Governors' Conference in 1950), she writes, but he also advocated a Federal Fair Employment Practices Commission and "opposed loyalty oaths for teachers."[5]

The loyalty-oath controversy flared up in 1950, not long after Senator McCarthy told a Wheeling, West Virginia, audience that the State Department was harboring 81 Communists (or maybe, he said, it was 57 or 205). Some troubled members of the board of regents of the University of California proposed a special vow of political chastity for faculty members, although they had already taken the traditional oath required by the state constitution. As governor, Warren was an ex officio member of the board. He voted against the oath, denouncing it as redundant and absurd ("any Communist would take the oath and laugh . . .")[6]

As Chief Justice, Warren sided with Black, Douglas, Brennan and Fortas in striking down Arizona's loyalty-oath law which had been challenged by Vernon and Barbara Elfbrandt, a young Quaker couple who taught school in Tucson.[7] Under the 1961 law, no penalty was provided for noncompliance, except that anyone who refused to take the oath could not be paid. Neither could he be fired. When the Elfbrandts were removed from the payroll for not signing the oath, they went right on teaching. For five years they lived on loans from friends and fellow-Quakers.

"I wouldn't let a child of mine go to class with either one of them," a mathematics teacher at Mrs. Elfbrandt's junior high school told Ed Meagher of the Los Angeles *Times* a few weeks before the Court's ruling was announced in April, 1966. A housewife with two daughters in the school where Elfbrandt taught geography and American history saw it somewhat differently. "I admire that woman. It takes a lot of courage to stand up the way she's done and fight for what she believes is right."[8]

Under the Arizona law, any teacher who signed the oath and belonged to an organization which had the overthrow of the government as "one of its purposes" could not only be dismissed but also prosecuted for perjury. As the Court pointed out in a majority opinion written by Justice Douglas, the law embraced the doctrine of "guilt by association." It ignored the "specific intent" of membership. For example, a teacher might join a seminar group dominated by Communists and, without subscribing to any of the organization's purposes, might still be convicted simply on the basis of membership.

"I'm speechless," Mrs. Elfbrandt said when she was called from her English class at Amphitheater Junior High and told of the decision. When she recovered, she explained, "It was never a question of loyalty but rather one of the basic freedoms of every Arizonan."[9]

As the Court had ruled in 1964,[10] loyalty oaths could not be given constitutional sanction if they were worded so vaguely as to proscribe innocent conduct, such as giving legal advice to the

Communist party, for instance. In *Elfbrandt*, the Court made it quite clear that oaths of this sort must be directed only at those who were specifically bent on carrying out the objectives of an illegal organization. Such criminal activity could best be dealt with under normal criminal law. Thus, the loyalty oath was redundant as well as ridiculous.

In January, 1967, the Justice Department spared Medicare applicants the necessity of disclaiming membership in Communist organizations,[11] and the State Department announced that passports would no longer be denied citizens who refused to swear allegiance to the United States.[12] Later in the month, the Supreme Court, with Clark, Harlan, Stewart and White again dissenting, declared unconstitutional New York's "complicated and intricate scheme" of laws and regulations designed to keep subversives off the faculties and staffs of public schools and state colleges.[13]

"Our nation is deeply committed to safeguarding academic freedom, which is of transcendent value to all of us and not merely the teachers concerned," Justice Brennan wrote for the majority. "That freedom is therefore a special concern of the First Amendment, which does not tolerate laws that cast a pall of orthodoxy over the classroom."[14]

"The decision was a historic victory for academic freedom by any standard, but it was particularly impressive in view of the fact that it was only about ten years ago that the Supreme Court recognized academic freedom as a constitutional right," Fred P. Graham wrote in the New York *Times*,[15] referring to a 1957 decision in which Warren had declared, "Scholarship cannot flourish in an atmosphere of suspicion and distrust. Teachers and students must always remain free to inquire, to study and to evaluate, to gain new maturity and understanding; otherwise our civilization will stagnate and die."[16]

In the early summer of 1940, a time of terror abroad and confusion at home, a jittery Congress passed the Smith Act, which made it unlawful to teach or advocate the forceful overthrow of any government in the United States, or to join any organization bent on such a course. Eleven Communist leaders, including Eugene Dennis, were subsequently tried and convicted, not for "treason, spying, sabotage or any such *act* of any kind," as Professor Fred Rodell of

Yale points out, but for "talking and writing . . ."[17] Chief Justice Vinson wrote the majority opinion, upholding the convictions in *Dennis et al. v. United States*.[18]

"Public opinion being what it is now," Justice Black wrote in dissent, "few will protest the conviction of these Communist petitioners. There is hope, however, that in calmer times, when present pressures, passions and fears subside, this or some later Court will restore the First Amendment liberties to the high preferred place where they belong in a free society."[19]

Times were a bit calmer by the late spring of 1957, but the passions and fears of right-wing radicals had not begun to subside when the Warren Court on June 17th staged what is now referred to in Impeach Earl Warren circles as "Red Monday." On this momentous decision day, to quote a pamphlet circulated by an outfit in New Orleans,[20] the Chief Justice tried "to stop congressional investigations" (*Watkins v. United States*) and voted "in favor of advocating treason" (*Yates v. United States*). In a third case decided the same day (*Sweezy v. New Hampshire*),[21] Warren is accused in *Nine Men Against America* of clamping down "on the rights of the states to protect their students against subversive teachers."[22]

Speaking for five members of the Court in *Watkins,* Warren started with the basic premise, "The power of the Congress to conduct investigations is inherent in the legislative process. That power is broad."[23] But, even so, there are certain constitutional margins: "No inquiry is an end in itself; it must be related to, and in furtherance of, a legitimate task of the Congress. Investigations conducted solely for the personal aggrandizement of the investigators or to 'punish' those investigated are indefensible."

John T. Watkins, a labor union official, had appeared as a witness before a subcommittee of the House Un-American Activities Committee in the spring of 1954. "I will answer any questions which this committee puts to me about myself," he had said, after first declaring that he was not going to invoke the protection of the Fifth Amendment. "I will also answer questions about those persons whom I knew to be members of the Communist Party and whom I believe still are. I will not, however, answer any questions with respect to others with whom I associated in the past. . . .

"I do not believe that such questions are relevant to the work of this committee nor do I believe that this committee has the right to undertake the public exposure of persons because of their past activities."[24]

Once the witness had raised the question of pertinency, the Chief Justice declared, it was up to the committee to give a satisfactory answer, something less vague than the chairman's explanation that the committee was investigating "subversion and subversive propaganda." Supposedly, the subcommittee was looking into Communist infiltration of labor unions, but of the thirty persons Watkins had been asked to identify, seven had nothing to do with the labor movement. One ran a beauty parlor. Another was a watchmaker. Thus, Watkins had not been given "a fair opportunity to determine whether he was within his rights in refusing to answer, and his conviction is necessarily invalid under the Due Process Clause of the Fifth Amendment."[25]

In *Yates*, the case in which Warren is charged with favoring the advocacy of treason, he concurred in the majority opinion written by Justice Harlan. The decision spelled out the difference between what a person says and what he does. When suspected Communists were brought to trial under the Smith Act, the Court held, the jury must be advised that "advocacy of abstract doctrine" — as opposed to "advocacy directed at promoting unlawful activity" — could not be accepted as ground for conviction. Ideas were to be distinguished from actions, books from bombs.

"The essential distinction is that those to whom the advocacy is addressed must be urged to *do* something, now or in the future, rather than merely to *believe* in something," Justice Harlan wrote.[26]

In *Sweezy*, the Court considered a case growing out of New Hampshire's efforts to thwart the Communist conspiracy. The legislature, in 1953, had adopted a resolution establishing the attorney general as a one-man investigating committee to track down violators of the state's 1951 Subversive Activities Act. When Professor Paul M. Sweezy was called in to answer some questions in 1954, he denied ever having joined the Communist party or having advocated overthrow of the government by force and violence. However, he refused to take the attorney general into his confidence when the inquiry turned to his wife's politics, the makeup of the Progressive party in the state, and a lecture he had given at the University of New Hampshire as the guest of the humanities faculty.

"We believe that there unquestionably was an invasion of petitioner's liberties in the areas of academic freedom and political expression — areas in which government should be extremely reticent to tread," Warren wrote for the Court.[27]

While making it quite clear that in finding Professor Sweezy's conviction for contempt a violation of his right to due process of law, the ruling did not deny New Hampshire the right to turn its attorney general loose on Kremlin agents operating within the state's sovereign borders, just so long as he limited himself to information the legislature actually sought for a legitimate purpose and so long as he kept within the boundaries of the Fourteenth Amendment.

"New Hampshire continues admirably immune to any subversion," Arthur E. Sutherland reported in the *Harvard Law Review* in November, 1957.[28]

Two years (and two new Associate Justices) later the Court inched away from the proud stand it had taken on "Red Monday." The application of the *Watkins* and *Sweezy* decisions was sharply limited to the facts in each case. By five-to-four votes, with the liberals on the short end, the Court declared in *Barenblatt v. United States*[29] and in *Uphaus v. Wyman*[30] that a suspected subversive could be compelled to answer relevant questions and produce pertinent records when a valid legislative purpose had been established and explained to the witness.*

In *Barenblatt,* as in *Watkins,* the Court was dealing with an unfriendly witness who had been found guilty of contempt after refusing to answer questions put to him by the House Un-American Activities Committee. The security of the Republic, in this instance, had been placed in peril by an unemployed, thirty-one-year-old psychology teacher whose contract at Vassar had not been renewed when it expired in the interval between the delivery of his HUAC subpoena and his appearance as a witness.

---

* In the interval between *Watkins-Sweezy* and *Barenblatt-Uphaus,* only Justice Potter Stewart had actually been appointed to the Court, but Justice Charles E. Whittaker, a conservative newcomer who had taken no part in the two earlier cases, participated in the two subsequent decisions.

"We conclude that the balance between the individual and the governmental interests here at stake must be struck in favor of the latter, and that therefore the provisions of the First Amendment have not been offended," Justice Harlan wrote for the Court in affirming Professor Barenblatt's conviction.[31]

"I do not agree that laws directly abridging First Amendment freedoms can be justified by a congressional or judicial balancing process," Black wrote in dissent, with Warren and Douglas joining him. As they saw it, "To apply the Court's balancing test under such circumstances is to read the First Amendment to say 'Congress shall pass no law abridging freedom of speech, press, assembly and petition, unless Congress and the Supreme Court reach the joint conclusion that on balance the interest of the Government in stifling these freedoms is greater than the interest of the people in having them exercised.' This is closely akin to the notion that neither the First Amendment nor any other provision of the Bill of Rights should be enforced unless the Court believes it."[32]

After losing *Sweezy* (1957) and winning *Uphaus* (1959), New Hampshire was back in Court again in the late winter and early spring of 1966, when Hugo DeGregory, a bookkeeper, appealed his conviction under the same state law. Questioned by the attorney general in 1963, he had denied any involvement with the Communist party since 1957 and had refused to answer questions concerning his political associations before that time.

New Hampshire failed to demonstrate just how such stale information could help it ward off subversion, but its publication would obviously be harmful to the witness. In protecting himself against this mischievous exposure of his dead political past, he relied not on the Fifth Amendment's protection against self-incrimination but on his First Amendment right to speak freely and assemble peaceably. He was tried, found guilty of contempt, and given a one-year prison sentence.

As had happened between *Sweezy* and *Uphaus*, the composition of the Court had changed in the seven years between *Uphaus* and *DeGregory*. Whittaker's replacement by White made little difference, but Frankfurter's chair had been surrendered to Goldberg who had given way to Fortas. This time out, New Hampshire got only three votes (Harlan, Stewart and White). Clark, the author of

Uphaus, swung over to the majority. Douglas spoke for the Court in citing the First Amendment as a shield against "the power to investigate enforced by the contempt power to probe at will and without relation to existing need."[33]

The compulsion to punish any deviation from political respectability, no matter how long ago it had taken place, was given judicial sanction in Warren's third term, when he dissented from a harsh five-to-four ruling in *Jay v. Boyd.*[34] Looking back from a healthier vantage, it is difficult to understand how McCarthyism could have produced such fevers and chills that after forty law-abiding years in the United States a sixty-five-year-old English alien should have been deported because — quite legally — he had belonged to the Communist party from 1935 to 1940. He had joined ten years before such membership had been made a ground for deportation. The man was given no trial, merely an administrative hearing which denied him the safeguards he would have enjoyed in a court of law. He was driven from home on the basis of undisclosed "confidential information."*

"In conscience, I cannot agree with the opinion of the majority," Warren wrote. "It sacrifices to form too much of the American spirit of fair play in both our judicial and administrative process."[36]

As early as 1949, when Joseph McCarthy was still an obscure Senator from Wisconsin, pollsters reported that nine out of ten Americans favored legislation compelling Communists to register with the Federal Government. To President Truman this was like ordering thieves to stop by the sheriff's office and sign in, but in 1950, with an off-year election at hand, Congress passed such a law as part of the Internal Security Act. Truman vetoed it.

"In a free country, we punish men for the crimes they commit, but never for the opinions they have," he advised the Congress.[37]

The bill was passed over his veto by whopping majorities which included the votes of Representative John F. Kennedy and Senator Lyndon B. Johnson. By the mid-1950's, the search for subversives had become such a popular pastime that forty-two states and two

---

* In dissent, Justice Black quoted a letter written by the Roman Emperor Trajan to Pliny the Younger around the end of the First Century: "Anonymous information ought not to be received in any sort of prosecution. It is introducing a very dangerous precedent, and is quite foreign to the spirit of our age."[35]

territories had adopted some sort of legislation encouraging local dowsers to get out their divining rods and hunt for the wellsprings of sedition. The Warren Court, on May 14, 1956, handed down a spoilsport ruling written by the Chief Justice.

In *Pennsylvania v. Nelson*,[38] the decision of the Supreme Court of Pennsylvania was upheld. "Sedition against the United States is not a *local* offense," the lower court had ruled. "It is a crime against the *Nation*."[39] State laws were declared to have been preempted by the Smith Act, a federal statute. Thus, a suspected seditionist could not be tried and punished by a state court for committing a federal crime, but, as *Uphaus* subsequently pointed out, the states were still free to take defensive action when seditious activity was directed against their own sovereignty.

In the summer of 1965, twenty-five years after passage of the Smith Act, fifteen foreign journalists wound up a year's stay in the United States with a pleasant visit to the Center for the Study of Democratic Institutions in Santa Barbara, California. Chatting with Robert M. Hutchins and his resident thinkers, they got to talking about the American obsession with Communism, a national affliction which, in their view, caused otherwise rational adults to believe that "all the evils of the world, including a decline in the stock market and the failure of the New York Yankees, are attributable to machinations behind the Iron Curtain."[40]

Fear of alien ideas had prompted Congress in 1962 to order the screening of mail from Communist countries. At a time when the overburdened Post Office was considering further curtailment of mail service, including the elimination of Saturday deliveries, the Postmaster General was saddled with the task of sifting through nearly three million periodicals, magazines, tracts and newsletters each month, isolating unwanted propaganda.

Under the law, a sealed letter was exempt. It was delivered routinely. Other mail from the unapproved countries was intercepted and screened by the Customs Bureau. If the addressee had filed an official request for the material, it was sent to him. Otherwise, it was detained and the addressee received POD Form 2153-X, which he had to fill out and return. At the end of twenty days, if no Form 2153-X had come in requesting the material, it was destroyed.

The mouse produced by this bureaucratic mountain in labor was described by *The Reporter* in July, 1963:

"You begin with the 8,575,367 pieces of mail that were sent to the special screening units in the three-month period of March through May of this year. More than half were immediately discovered to be exempt. 286,583 pieces were determined to be propaganda, but 261,310 of these were known to be wanted and 8,863 were known to be unwanted. In all, 8,072 POD Forms 2153-X were sent out. Of those who answered, 1,658 said they *wanted* the propaganda and 972 said they wanted some of it. Those whom the law set out to protect in the first place numbered 1,835. They said they did not want to receive the propaganda."[41]

It cost something like $230,000 a year for Customs officers to protect Americans from unwanted Marxist mail. The law was struck down by the Supreme Court in May, 1965, in an unanimous opinion in which Justice White took no part.[42] As deputy attorney general at the time the bill had passed, he had called attention to its constitutional shortcomings and had suggested it would do "substantial injury"[43] to the country's prestige abroad.

While Congress was taking unconstitutional action against Marxist magazines, the State Department was exercising questionable authority over American travelers. The director of the Passport Office was deciding which citizens should be permitted to go abroad and which should be kept at home.

For six years, between 1952 and 1958, the lower courts whittled away at this dictatorial power. Finally, in *Kent v. Dulles* (1958), after a prominent American artist had been refused a passport to attend a World Council for Peace in Helsinki, the Supreme Court declared that "the right to travel is a part of the 'liberty' of which the citizen cannot be deprived without due process of law under the Fifth Amendment . . ."[44]

Even if a citizen was denied a passport after proper legal procedures had been followed, the question arose as to whether his right to travel abroad could be restricted by an existing federal statute. Two Communist party leaders, Herbert Aptheker and Elizabeth Gurley Flynn, were granted hearings to review the revocation of their passports. This satisfied the due process requirement laid down in *Kent*. But Aptheker and Flynn went further. They attacked the constitutionality of the law under which the State Department had acted.

Section 6 of the Subversive Activities Control Act made it unlawful for any member of a Communist organization to apply for or to make use of a passport. It mattered not whether the would-be traveler had joined an organization without knowing it had been declared a Communist front, nor was any consideration given the extent of his participation in the activities of the organization. Membership alone disqualified him for foreign travel, even if he simply wished to visit a sick relative. Section 6, the Court held in *Aptheker v. Secretary of State* (1964), was clearly unconstitutional; it "sweeps too widely and too indiscriminately across the liberty guaranteed in the Fifth Amendment."[45]

It was, however, a liberty with limits, as the Court ruled in 1965 when Louis Zemel challenged the State Department's ban on travel to Cuba.[46] He wanted to visit the island, he said, to satisfy his curiosity and to make himself a better informed citizen. Over the dissents of Black, Douglas and Goldberg, the Chief Justice spoke for the Court in finding that the Secretary of State had exercised constitutionally permissible authority in refusing to endorse passports for travel to Cuba in order to avoid serious international incidents. Black dissented. The power to regulate travel lay with Congress, he argued, not with the bureaucracy:

"The Congress was created on the assumption that enactment of this free country's laws could be safely entrusted to the representatives of the people in Congress, and to no other official or government agency. The people who are called on to obey laws have a constitutional right to have them passed only in this constitutional way. This right becomes all the more essential when as here the person called on to obey may be punishable by five years' imprisonment and a $5,000 fine if he dares to travel without the consent of the Secretary or one of his subordinates."[47]

It is one thing to lift a tourist's passport, quite another to throw him in jail, as the Court made clear in January, 1967, when it decided unanimously that it was not a crime for a person with a valid passport to visit a country declared off-limits by the State Department. Without ruling on the issue of whether travel to a proscribed area could constitutionally be made a crime, the opinion written by Justice Fortas held that Congress had not enacted any such law.

"If there is a gap in the law, the right and the duty, if any, to fill it do not devolve upon the courts," Fortas wrote, and pointed out that "crimes are not to be created by inferences."[48]

Earlier, in the October, 1964, term, Warren had spoken for a divided Court in striking down a section of the Labor-Management Reporting and Disclosure Act (1959) which made it a crime for a Communist to serve as an official of a labor union. The provision was found to be a bill of attainder, a prohibition written into the Constitution to prevent "trial by legislature."

Congress might be free to "weed dangerous persons out of the labor movement," Warren wrote in *United States v. Brown*,[49] but the legislative branch was not empowered to exercise a judicial power by disqualifying all members of an organization from union activity. Punishment is to be meted out in courts of law to individuals who have been given a fair trial on specific charges.

"Americans have a great tolerance for the neighborhood radical," Herbert Aptheker told Saul Pett of the Associated Press in December, 1965.[50]

The former field artillery officer, a combat veteran of the Second World War, was described as "a man of 50, with gray, crew-cut hair, heavy-rimmed glasses, a friendly, slightly professorial manner, and the slow, deliberate diction of someone who has fought the New York accent." He spoke thoughtfully, without rancor, of the personal inconveniences he put up with as a member of the Communist party.

"People will, now and then, cross the street or turn away. It all varies with the period, and I suppose I've gotten used to it. During the McCarthy period, when I got a lot of notoriety as a witness before the Senator's committee, I, myself, would never say hello to anybody I knew casually — even to some of my relatives — for fear it might embarrass them or create difficulties for them. But, generally, people have treated me well. My neighbors show no hostility and I don't feel deprived socially."

A month before the Aptheker interview, the Court had taken another whack at the Subversive Activities Control Act, a legislative monument to McCarthyism. Adopted in haste by an uneasy Congress about to go home and face the voters, the 1950 law had long since become a national embarrassment. It had been judicially disassembled, piece by piece. In *Albertson v. Subversive Activities Control Board*,[51] eight members of the Court (Justice White did not participate) decided that the provision requiring Communists to register with the Federal Government violated the Fifth Amendment's protection against enforced self-incrimination.*

"What will our boys fighting in Vietnam say about this?" Senator Eastland roared,[53] but he seemed to be speaking a dead language in the ruins of a deserted forum. McCarthyism was one with Nineveh and Tyre. Even Barry Goldwater applauded the ruling as "a very proper injunction."[54]

"There is a moral rebellion growing among young people," Aptheker told the Associated Press, "a growing sense of the aimlessness, purposelessness and cynicism in America today, and a growing sense of injustice. The problem here is not bread, but soul. All these things don't make them join the party but they are aware of a general malaise and they are shopping around for ideas."

The generation fighting the war in Vietnam and protesting it in the streets at home were too young even for kindergarten at the time Senator McCarthy first bludgeoned his way into the news, and were in the second or third grade when he was censured by the Senate. Long before the young soldiers and demonstrators had begun to notice girls, much less subversives, the Warren Court had made its major rulings in establishing a constitutional balance between the right of a free man to be protected against the harassment of government officials and the right of a free government to protect itself against an international conspiracy scheming to overthrow it by force and violence.

T.R.B. of *The New Republic* was in the courtroom the day Justice Brennan delivered the Court's ruling in the Communist registration case. "It was so calm, so casual, you hardly realized it," he wrote. "But it was the end of an era."[55] The era had put Alger Hiss in prison and had almost put Richard Nixon in the White House. It

---

* The Fifth Amendment, however, does not appear to afford the same protection to a bookmaker. The Court has upheld a federal law requiring professional gamblers to pay an occupational tax which would appear to be self-incriminating.[52]

had hit Shirley Temple a glancing blow and paralyzed the State Department. It had slandered a great American general and saved California from subversion by the summary dismissal of a woman who played piano in the girls' gym on a Los Angeles campus. It had begun with wild, reckless charges; it ended in the calm, precise language of the law. It had taken fifteen litigious years to correct what President Truman had originally declared a "terrible mistake."

19

Forces of Hatred and Malevolence

> . . . he said that if anybody really wanted to shoot the
> President of the United States, it was not a very difficult
> job — all one had to do was get a high building some day
> with a telescopic rifle . . .
>
> — KENNETH O'DONNELL, *recalling*
> *a remark made by John F. Kennedy*
> *on the morning of November 22, 1963*[1]

ON November 22, 1963, while the President was doing a little
political fence-mending in Texas, the Chief Justice was presiding over a Friday conference of the Court. When, as happened
that day, someone knocks at the door, it is the custom for the most
recently appointed Associate Justice to answer it. Thus, it was Mr.
Justice Goldberg who took the note handed in by Mrs. Margaret
McHugh, Warren's executive secretary, informing him that the
President had been shot and taken to a Dallas hospital.

"The Chief Justice spent the time after the conference adjourned
listening to the radio until all hope was gone," Mrs. McHugh recalls.

Earlier in the week, the Warrens had attended the annual judiciary reception at the White House, where the Chief Justice had
shared the evening's honors with the President's brother, Robert,
who had celebrated his thirty-eighth birthday. The President had
made it a family evening, doing away with the reception line and
moving about informally, shaking hands and chatting with the
guests. His wife had come downstairs for a little while, making her
first appearance as a hostess since the birth and death of their son,
Patrick Bouvier, in August.

"Mrs. Kennedy had not planned to resume public appearances or
social duties until the new year," Marjorie Hunter wrote for the

New York *Times* that night. "However, her schedule was revised several weeks ago to include a trip to Texas with the President tomorrow . . ."[2]

Before the reception the Supreme Court Justices and their wives were entertained in the upstairs Oval Room, where they found the President in a mood to banter. "We were joshing and laughing," says one of the guests. "We told him to watch out for those Texans, they're a wild bunch." Three days later the Warrens returned to the White House, Mrs. Warren in tears.

"It was like losing one of my own sons," says the Chief Justice. "You know, he was just a little older than my oldest boy."

Standing beside the flag-draped casket resting on a black-covered catafalque in the rotunda of the Capitol, Warren had never been more eloquent than on the Sunday afternoon he delivered his eulogy. Sorrow, shock and anger fused in what one of his intimates called "a typical gut reaction to violence." When he spoke of "the hatred that consumes people, the false accusations that divide us, and the bitterness that begets violence,"[3] he infuriated right-wing evangelists who felt the snug fit of the shoe.

"What moved some misguided wretch to do this horrible deed may never be known to us," he said, "but we do know that such acts are commonly stimulated by forces of hatred and malevolence, such as today are eating their way into the bloodstream of American life."

The bullets that killed the President ricocheted to the political right (it had happened in Dallas, the feudal stronghold of wealthy extremists) and to the left (the alleged assassin was a self-styled Marxist, who had tried to defect to the Soviet Union). Radicals of both right and left found themselves on common ground in agreeing that it was a political murder, not the wanton, unassisted act of Lee Harvey Oswald.

"Kennedy was executed by the Communist conspiracy because he was planning to turn American," said Revilo P. Oliver, a professor of classical philology who served for years on the council of the John Birch Society.[4]

"In his last tax message to the Congress before his death, the President had proposed a serious reduction in the oil depletion allowance," wrote Thomas G. Buchanan, a left-wing American expatriate who insisted a conspiracy had been contrived and financed by right-wing multimillionaires determined not only to protect their 27½ per cent tax break but also to reduce "the danger of disarmament which would disrupt the industries on which the plotters depended . . ."[5]

"Desperate quarters are now striving to cover up the traces of the bloody crime . . ." *Pravda* reported,[6] and the Russian news agency, *Tass*, informed its clients: "All the circumstances of President Kennedy's tragic death allow one to assume that this murder was planned and carried out by the ultra-right-wing, fascist and racist circles . . ."[7]

"The year 2000 will see men still arguing and writing about the President's death," a New York *Times* editor remarked after reading the bulletin from Parkland Hospital that Kennedy was dead.[8]

As the body of the President was being flown back to Washington, the Kennedy legend sprang to life. It was the *Morte d'Arthur* of a twentieth-century Camelot-on-the-Potomac, where bold knights rode into the damp mists of Foggy Bottom to do battle with the Cuban Ogre and the Red Dragon. Stories were told without number of the dead President's courage and humor, his defeat at the Bay of Pigs, his victory in the island missile crisis. The young man's life lent itself to the making of myth. The mysterious circumstances of his death were equally hospitable to the making of mischief.

After the first shock of the whining bullets and slumping figure came a welter of conflicting accounts as to how many shots had been fired and where they had come from. Some had heard three; others two, four or six. Some thought they had come from a triple underpass or a grassy knoll ahead of the President's car, others from a seven-story orange brick building behind it. No one could say for sure whether the bullets had struck the President from front or rear, or perhaps from both directions, because suspicion arose at once — particularly in Europe — that more than one assassin had taken aim at the President as his limousine rolled slowly down Elm Street past the Texas School Book Depository.

"A piece of each of us died at that moment," said Senator Mike Mansfield,[9] and Mary McGrory of the Washington *Star* remarked to Daniel Patrick Moynihan, Assistant Secretary of Labor, "We'll never laugh again."

"Heavens, Mary," he said, "we'll laugh again. It's just that we'll never be young again."[10]

During the first stunned week following the Dallas bloodletting, two Presidential emissaries from the Department of Justice approached Warren and asked if he would preside over an investigation designed to get at the truth and end the wildly speculative stories circulating at home and abroad. He declined.

"Then," the New York *Times* reported, "President Johnson called him over to the White House and talked to him about patriotism, about the country's urgent need to settle the assassination rumors, about the special trust foreign lands would place in an inquiry he headed. Mr. Johnson said he knew Earl Warren would get back into his soldier's suit from World War I if the country were attacked and needed him. The President asked him to take on the inquiry as a similar duty."[11]

When Warren left Johnson's pleasant oval office after agreeing to moonlight as chairman of the President's Commission on the Assassination of President Kennedy, there were tears in his eyes. Once he had let himself be drafted for the job, however, he set to work with a vigor that left younger men wilting in his wake.

"I don't know where he got the energy," says a member of the Commission staff. "We'd start a hearing at nine in the morning. He'd preside until a few minutes before ten, then leave for the Court. At two-thirty he'd come back and sit there well into the evening. At times he was presiding at the Commission and the Court for stretches of eight and ten hours. During those last weeks, when we were finishing the report, he'd work till one in the morning, then be the first to show up next day."

What immediately came to be known as the Warren Commission (Warren refers to it as the "Kennedy Commission") was composed of two Senators (Richard B. Russell and John Sherman Cooper), two Representatives (Hale Boggs and Gerald R. Ford) and two prominent lawyers who had served both Republican and Democratic Presidents (Allen W. Dulles and John J. McCloy). Acting on a suggestion put forth by the chairman, the Commission chose James Lee Rankin, a former Solicitor General, as its chief counsel.

"Truth is your only client," he told his staff at its first meeting,[12] and truth seemed to have been well served in late September, 1964, when the Commission published its findings in an 888-page report which concluded that Lee Harvey Oswald, unassisted, had fired the shots that killed the President and wounded Governor John B. Connally of Texas. Within the hour, the Commission also concluded, Oswald had murdered Officer J. D. Tippit of the Dallas Police Department, and two days later had been mortally — and publicly — wounded by Jack Ruby. No evidence had been found that either Oswald or Ruby "was part of any conspiracy, domestic or foreign, to assassinate President Kennedy."[13]

"Now the hysteria ends . . ." sighed an English writer in *New Statesman*,[14] but in California a Stanford University law professor was not so sure. Although Herbert L. Packer found the *Warren Report* a "conscientious and at times brilliant job," convincingly demonstrating that "Oswald, acting alone, was the assassin of the President," he warned readers of *The Nation:* "We have not seen the end of this affair."[15]

Two years after it was published to almost universal acclaim, the *Warren Report* had come under such heavy attack from what Governor Connally called "journalistic scavengers"[16] that pressure for a new investigation was building up. And yet no new suspect had been produced, no hitherto undetected evidence of a conspiracy brought to light.* It was not the facts that had changed, but the emotional climate.

Lyndon Johnson, in the fall of 1964, was riding the high tide of his Presidency. Two years later his administration was bogged down in a remote and unpopular war. Negroes were burning and looting their ghettos. Streets were unsafe. Money was hard to come by. The cost of living was up, the stock market down.

Young and old, the emotionally aberrant and the politically dispossessed, all joined in the attacks on the Warren Commission, relieving their frustrations, their annoyances, their massive indignation. They saw the *Warren Report* as another official lie put out to hide an untidy truth which, if revealed, would embarrass the

---

* No legal test was made of the *Warren Report's* central findings until February-March, 1967, when District Attorney Jim Garrison of New Orleans went to court with widely publicized charges of a locally organized plot to kill the President.

Establishment, the White Power Structure, the Communist Conspiracy or the Texas Oil Oligarchy. Doubt and distrust, taking root in such fertile soil, caught on like crabgrass.

"Nothing is easier to create than an atmosphere of suspicion, nothing — so long as the crackpots and the credulous abound — more difficult to dispel," wrote John Sparrow of Oxford University, replying to a colleague's inaccurate and intemperate attack on the *Warren Report*.[17]

President Kennedy was shot at twelve-thirty. At one-twelve three spent rifle cartridges were found on the sixth floor of the Texas School Book Depository near the southeast corner window from which the assassin was thought to have fired. ("Look up in the window!" a television newsreel cameraman had shouted right after the third shot. "There's the rifle!")[18] Ten minutes after finding the cartridges, Dallas police officers located a bolt-action rifle with a telescopic sight near the back staircase at the northwest corner of the same floor.

The rifle was turned over to Lieutenant J. C. Day of the crime scene search section of the identification bureau. He photographed it, dusted it with black fingerprint powder, and scratched his name on the stock for future identification. Once he had examined the bolt under a magnifying glass to make sure it contained no prints, he held the stock while a live cartridge was ejected by Captain J. Will Fritz, chief of the homicide and robbery bureau. Fritz kept the cartridge, Day the rifle. Deputy Constable Seymour Weitzman, who never actually handled the weapon, mistook the 6.5-millimeter Mannlicher-Carcano for a 7.65 Mauser.

"In a glance, that's what it looked like," he said later[19] and Joseph A. Ball, one of the Commission's most distinguished attorneys, explains, "The basic patent on bolt-action rifles is a Mauser. This is an Italian rifle built on the Mauser patent. It's an Italian Mauser . . ."[20]

About the time the rifle was found, Roy S. Truly, the building superintendent, told Captain Fritz that one of the Depository's employees was missing. His name was Lee Harvey Oswald and he lived at 2515 West Fifth Street in Irving, a Dallas suburb. Fritz left the building, intending to find out whether Oswald had a police record. On the way back to headquarters, he got word of another killing. Officer J. D. Tippit, patrolling the Oak Cliff area in car number ten, had been shot. When Fritz reached his office, he learned that a suspect in the Tippit shooting had been arrested in the Texas Theater, about eight blocks from the scene of the murder. The man had been armed with a Smith & Wesson .38 Special caliber revolver. His name was Oswald. Fritz asked for his full name.

"Lee Harvey Oswald," he was told, and he said, "That is the suspect we are looking for in the President's killing."[21]

Oswald, it developed, had rented a room in Dallas at 1026 North Beckley Avenue (using the alias "O. H. Lee"), but usually spent his weekends in Irving, where his Russian-born wife, Marina, and their two little girls lived at the West Fifth Street home of a Russian-speaking friend, Mrs. Ruth Paine.

"I've been expecting you all," Guy F. Rose remembers Mrs. Paine saying when he came to her door with two other detectives from Captain Fritz's bureau and three from a county unit.[22]

"Why?" she was asked, and she said, "Just as soon as I heard where the shooting happened, I knew there would be someone out."

Mrs. Paine translated for Marina when she was questioned by Rose. He asked if her husband owned a rifle. "No," she said, and a minute later changed her story. "Yes, he does have." She led the detectives to the garage and pointed to a rolled-up blanket on the floor. It seemed to Rose to have the outlines of a rifle. It had the same appearance to Marina, who had taken an apprehensive look at the blanket earlier, after hearing the Book Depository mentioned as the suspected source of the assassin's shots.

"Well, now they will find it," Marina later remembered thinking as the detectives started to open the blanket, but the rifle was missing. "Then, of course," Marina testified, "I already knew it was Lee."[23]

Oswald was driven to and from Irving by a fellow-employee at the Book Depository, nineteen-year-old Buell Wesley Frazier, who lived with his married sister, Linnie Mae Randle, half a block from Ruth Paine. Ordinarily, the two young men drove out after work on Friday and returned together Monday morning. On Thursday, November 21, however, Oswald had asked Frazier to give him a ride home that afternoon. He wanted to pick up some curtain rods, he had explained.

"The room had curtain rods on the window when he came in there?" Oswald's landlady was later asked.

"Yes, sir; sure did."

"Also curtains?"

"Yes, sir."[24]

"On the evening of the 21st," Marina Oswald was asked, "was anything said about curtain rods or his taking curtain rods to town the following day?"

"No, I didn't have any."[25]

Friday morning, as Frazier got into his car with Oswald, he spotted a long, bulky package on the back seat wrapped in brown paper. "What's the package, Lee?" he asked.

"Curtain rods," Oswald said.[26]

Frazier's sister, Mrs. Randle, had also noticed the package ("a sort of a heavy brown bag, heavier than a grocery bag it looked to me"),[27] but she paid little attention to it because she remembered Wesley had said something the night before about curtain rods in explaining why Lee had come home on Thursday instead of Friday. Later, when asked to estimate the length of the paper bag, both Frazier and his sister said it was a little more than two feet (27 to 28 inches, they judged in demonstrations). Such a bag could not have concealed the rifle found at the Book Depository. Its stock was 34.8 inches long.

But after the assassination, a handmade paper bag of adequate length was found on the sixth floor of the building near the southeast corner window. It bore Oswald's left index fingerprint and right palmprint. Although it was long enough to accommodate the disassembled rifle, it could not have been carried into the building by Oswald in the manner described by Frazier — one end in the palm of his hand, the other stuck under his armpit. "Frazier could easily have been mistaken . . ." the Commission concluded after quoting his testimony (. . . "I didn't pay too much attention to the way he was walking . . .").[28] Brown and green fibers found inside the paper bag, the Commission reported, matched some of the fibers of the blanket in which Marina said the rifle had been stored.[29]

The rifle — serial number C2766 — was quickly traced to Klein's

Sporting Goods Company in Chicago, where records showed it had been shipped to A. Hidell, Post Office Box 2915, Dallas, on March 20, 1963, a week after an order had come in signed "A. Hidell." The signature and the return address on the envelope were both in Oswald's handwriting. The rifle had been paid for by a U.S. postal money order for $21.45, purchased in Dallas on March 12th. The handwriting on the money order (No. 2,202,130,462) was also Oswald's. The application for Post Office Box 2915, rented to Lee H. Oswald," was in the same handwriting.[30]

"Hidell," Oswald had told Detective Rose when asked his correct name after his arrest for the shooting of Officer Tippit.[31] Among the cards in his billfold, one identified him as "Lee Harvey Oswald," another as "Alek James Hidell." In a later interrogation, Oswald admitted having rented Box 2915, but denied having received any package addressed to it in the name of "A. Hidell."[32]

Saturday morning, when Rose returned to the Paine home for a more thorough search, he found two photographs of Oswald holding a rifle which appeared to be the one found at the Book Depository.

"Well, that's just a fake, because somebody has superimposed my face on that picture," Rose remembers Oswald saying when he was confronted with the photographs,[33] but Marina recalled the Sunday she had taken such a picture in the backyard of a house they had rented for a while in Dallas.

"I was hanging up diapers, and he came up to me with the rifle and I was even a little scared, and he gave me the camera and asked me to press a certain button."[34]

Both photographs were widely published, and in many instances were retouched before publication, which cast some doubt on their authenticity. However, the negative of one photograph (Commission Exhibit 133-B) was examined by an expert who compared it with a negative he produced from Oswald's camera. The original photograph was found to have been taken with this Imperial Reflex "to the exclusion of all other cameras."[35]

Saturday night, exhausted reporters, photographers and television crewmen were waiting to get a glimpse of Oswald when he was moved from the city jail to the county jail. "Are you going to transfer him tonight?" they kept asking, and Chief of Police Jesse E.

Curry said, "No, we are not going to transfer him tonight. We are tired. We are going home and get some rest." The press grumbled, "We're tired, too," and the police chief said, "If you are back here by ten o'clock in the morning, I don't think that you would miss anything that you want to see."[36]

At ten o'clock next morning, Jack Ruby (he had changed his name from Jacob Rubenstein) still had not bothered to get dressed. Sometime between eight-thirty and nine o'clock, while his roommate was in the basement doing his laundry, Ruby received a call from Mrs. Elnora Pitts, his cleaning woman. He sounded "terrible strange" to her.[37] He turned on the television, scrambled some eggs and made coffee. At 10:19 the phone rang again. This time it was Karen Bennett Carlin, a nineteen-year-old stripper who worked as Little Lynn at his night club, the Carousel. She wanted twenty-five dollars to pay her rent and lay in some groceries.

"It will take me about twenty or thirty minutes to get dressed, and then I will go down," Mrs. Carlin remembers Ruby saying after he had agreed to send the money to her by way of Western Union.[38]

It was nearly eleven o'clock when Ruby left his apartment with his dachshund, Sheba, and drove downtown to the Western Union office situated a block from the Police and Courts Buildings. Oswald was to have been transported to the county jail an hour earlier, but he was still upstairs being questioned. No precise time for the transfer had been set at the time Ruby parked his car in the lot across from the Western Union office. He apparently locked his keys and billfold in the trunk, then placed the trunk key in the glove compartment before crossing the street and waiting his turn at the Western Union counter.

Ruby filled out the necessary forms, paid for the telegram and was given a receipt. It was one of three documents stamped with the time of the transaction. The time was 11:17. At approximately 11:21 Oswald was led from the jail office into the basement where reporters and television cameras were waiting. Ruby lunged forward with a .38-caliber revolver, shooting his way into the Dallas drama and making it impossible for its central mystery ever to be solved to universal satisfaction.[39]

"It was claimed that Ruby got in there pretending to be a reporter," says Mrs. Nancy Perrin Rich, who used to mix illegal drinks at the Carousel for members of the Dallas Police Department. It was inconceivable to her that any of them would ever fail to recognize their host. "Ye gods," she said, "I don't think there is a cop in Dallas that doesn't know Jack Ruby. He practically lived at the station. They lived in his place."[40]

According to some theorists, Ruby's ability to stroll into the guarded basement of police headquarters and, in the presence of seventy to seventy-five lawmen, commit the first nationally televised murder could be explained only in terms of a conspiracy, but as Ruby pointed out, "You wouldn't have time enough to have any conspiracy . . ."[41]

As he lay dying of cancer in the same hospital where President Kennedy and Lee Oswald had died of bullet wounds, Ruby kept telling one of his lawyers he couldn't understand why it wasn't "plain to everyone that it was a million-in-one chance that he would stumble into a situation in which it was even possible that Oswald could be shot."[42]

Theorists who insist that Ruby was part of a conspiracy have yet to explain just how he could have been tipped off to the exact time of Oswald's transfer an hour and twelve minutes behind schedule. Plans were still being changed while Ruby was standing in line to be waited on at the Western Union counter. Belief that Ruby was hired to silence Oswald must also accommodate the bizarre notion that a man bent on murder would risk losing his only chance to shoot his victim in order to dispatch twenty-five dollars to a distressed stripper he didn't particularly like.

"Whatever the legal culpability of Jack Ruby for his act of November 24, the evidence is persuasive that he acted independently in shooting Oswald," says the *Warren Report*.[43]

Ruby first testified before the Commission on June 7, 1964. He was led into an austere interrogation room in the Dallas county jail, where he sat at a long, narrow table with the Chief Justice, Representative Ford, Lee Rankin and two Commission lawyers. As Ford wrote later in *Life*, Ruby "wore sandals and a white jumper with several buttons undone," and was so tense "it seemed to be touch-and-go whether we could keep his nerves from exploding."[44]

"You have a lost cause, Earl Warren," Ruby blurted out at one point. "You don't stand a chance. They feel about you like they do about me, Chief Justice Warren. I shouldn't hurt your feelings in telling you that."

"That won't hurt my feelings," Warren said, "because I have had some evidence of the feelings that some people have concerning me."[45]

Whatever form and meaning emerged from Ruby's disjointed, often incoherent testimony seems to have come as a result of Warren's calm, patient handling of the interrogation. When Ruby had trouble reading a document with borrowed glasses, the Chief Justice removed his own spectacles and handed them to him.

"Do I sound dramatic?" Ruby asked, stating a recurring fear. "Off the beam?"*[46]

Conspiracy-minded critics of the *Warren Report*, treating Ruby's testimony as the evidence of a witness in full possession of his faculties, have made much of his remark, "Well, it is too bad, Chief Warren, that you didn't get me to your headquarters six months ago." The Chief Justice's reply has been less frequently quoted, "Well, Mr. Ruby, I will tell you why we didn't. Because you were about to be tried and I didn't want to do anything that would prejudice you in your trial."[48]

Sinister conclusions have also been drawn from Warren's refusal to grant Ruby's request to be taken to Washington for further questioning, but the Chief Justice's decision can be rationally appraised only if it is placed in the full context of testimony which Professor Alexander M. Bickel of Yale has characterized as "pathetically deranged":[49]

". . . I am under a very bad mental strain here."[50] "Now if I sound screwy . . ."[51] "Gentlemen, my life is in danger here . . ."[52] "The Jewish people are being exterminated at this moment."[53] ". . . if they found out I was telling the truth, maybe they can succeed in what their motives are, but maybe my people won't be tortured and mutilated."[54]

It seems unlikely that Jack Ruby's people are in imminent danger of torture and mutilation, even in Dallas, but his testimony has been swallowed whole, without salt, by assassination cultists who have found spiritual kinship in a common skepticism about the *Warren*

---

* Sexual orientation was another of his anxieties, according to Karen (Little Lynn) Carlin, who told the Commission: "He was always asking the question, 'Do you think I am a queer? Do you think I look like a queer? Or have you ever known a queer to look like me?' Everytime I saw him he would ask it."[47]

Report. No offbeat religion could rest on a broader base. It embraces those who dislike Earl Warren, Lyndon B. Johnson, J. Edgar Hoover, the State Department, the CIA, Texas, Communism, the John Birch Society and Members of Congress.

The faithful may differ on dogma (whether Oswald was a participant in the plot or was framed, for example), but all share the same hostility toward the Warren Commission and its findings. Their devout disbelief has been sustained by the doctrinal writings of a small-town editor in Texas, a lawyer in Philadelphia, a waterfowl-breeder in Maryland, and housewives in New York, Beverly Hills and Hominy, Oklahoma.

"What did you do before you got involved in the assassination?" one of the housewives was asked, and she pointed to a collection of books on unidentified flying objects. "Oh," she said cheerfully, "I used to be in flying saucers."

Communicants pore over maps and diagrams, exchange clues, burrow into the gray cardboard boxes preserved in the National Archives, make pilgrimages to Dealey Plaza, and comb the *Warren Report* and the twenty-six volumes of *Hearings* and *Exhibits* for some fresh evidence of concealment and corruption. In a world of violence and conspiracy, where nothing is ever quite what it appears to be, they live with an abiding faith that truth crushed to earth by the Chief Justice and his fellow-conspirators on the Warren Commission will someday rise again, and they will all sit at the right hand of Mark Lane.

"Mr. Lane's erudition on this subject is enormous," Lord Devlin, one of England's foremost jurists, wrote in *The London Observer* after reading *Rush to Judgment.* "But for the general reader who prefers to approach the Commission's conclusions by a reasonably impartial route, Mr. Lane is not a safe guide."[55]

To read *Rush to Judgment* without checking each allegation and each innuendo against the material published by the Warren Commission in its *Report* and supporting documentation, is like listening to the closing argument of a defense attorney without having heard the other side of the case. "The book is wildly speculative," says Professor Bickel.[56] It has been characterized by Wesley J. Liebeler, one of the Commission lawyers, as "a tissue of distortion, a masterwork of deceit."[57]

"I've got three seniors at the UCLA Law School who have gone through Lane's book and prepared a series of memoranda describing the discrepancies they found," Professor Liebeler says. "Close to 90 per cent of Lane's footnotes don't check out. There's either a distortion involved or a flat misrepresentation. He twists evidence out of context and often uses himself as his own expert witness."[58]

Lane begins with the grassy knoll west of the Texas School Book Depository, the direction from which many eyewitnesses thought the shots were fired. He gives great weight to the testimony of a schoolteacher, Jean Hill ("I thought it was just people shooting from the knoll — I did think there was more than one person shooting").[59] Lane fails to mention that this same witness also saw a white, fuzzy dog in the back seat of the President's car ("I said, 'I could see Liz Taylor or the Gabors traveling with a bunch of dogs, but I can't see the Kennedys traveling with dogs'").[60] The white, fuzzy dog was actually a bouquet of red roses.

Mrs. Hill also saw a man she thought was Jack Ruby running past the knoll right after the shooting, when the Commission had convincingly established his presence in the second-floor advertising offices of the Dallas *Morning News*.[61] According to Lane, a man resembling Ruby appears in a photograph of the Book Depository entrance taken right after the assassination by Phillip L. Willis, a retired Air Force major.[62] It was one of a series of twelve pictures taken with a 35-millimeter camera and published by the Commission. Lane accuses the Commission of trimming this particular picture (slide No. 8) in such a way as to remove a large part of the man's face.

"Here's what happened," says Liebeler. "Thirty-five-millimeter slides come in cardboard holders, held in by inserting a portion of the edges of the slide under the cardboard. When prints are made from the slides, the edges under the cardboard do not appear on the print unless the slide is removed from the holder. In this case, the holder was not removed."[63]

Lane devotes most of two pages to this "trimmed" photograph, but makes no mention of the photographer's immediate reactions to the shooting, although Willis was standing in front of the Book Depository, ten feet from the President's car at the moment the first bullet struck him. Unlike Lane's schoolteacher, Willis happened to be familiar with high-powered rifles. He is a deer hunter.

"Three shots," he said when asked how many he had heard, and later added, "The minute the third shot was fired, I screamed, hoping the policeman would hear me, to ring that building because it had come from there."[64]

The Warren Commission visited the building, retraced Oswald's probable route after the shooting, and placed themselves in the position of a witness (Harold Norman) who had watched the Presidential motorcade from a fifth-floor window. He, too, had heard three shots (". . . and I could also hear something sounded like the shell hulls hitting the floor . . .").[65] While a Secret Service agent operated the bolt of a rifle at the southeast corner window of the sixth floor, the Commissioners on the floor below could hear the empty shells drop to the floor.

"The shots were fired smoothly and evenly," says Merriman Smith of United Press International, who was in the motorcade with a clear view of the President's car. A hunter and target marksman, Smith knows the sound of rifle fire. "There was not the slightest doubt on the front seat of our car that the shots came from a rifle to our rear (and the Book Depository at this point was directly to our rear)."[66]

As the driver of his press car raced to Parkland Hospital, Smith reported by radio-telephone that three shots had been fired at the President's motorcade. He won the Pulitzer Prize for his coverage of the assassination. Three years later, he still said, "I would swear there were three shots and only three shots . . ."

One of the most important pieces of evidence available to the Commission was the 8-millimeter motion picture film of the assassination taken by Abraham Zapruder, a dress manufacturer, whose footage has been used to prove beyond question that (1) Oswald was the assassin, (2) Oswald could not have been the assassin, (3) Oswald acted alone, and (4) Oswald could not have carried out his part in the conspiracy without an accomplice.

Zapruder's film runs at the speed of 18.3 frames per second. By numbering the frames, each of which is an individual picture, it was possible to fix the average speed of the President's car (11.2 miles per hour) and to reconstruct the crime, with a camera mounted on Oswald's rifle photographing sit-ins for the Presidential party at each moment of the actual shooting, which took place in a period of five or six seconds.

Experts established 2.3 seconds as the minimum time required to operate the Mannlicher-Carcano rifle found at the Book Depository. If Oswald were the lone assassin, using this weapon, he could have fired only two or, at most, three shots. One bullet seems to have missed the car, and two struck the President. But Governor Connally, on the jump seat in front of the President, was also wounded (back, chest, right wrist, left thigh).

After a spirited debate as to which adjective to use ("compelling" and "credible" were rejected), the Warren Commission agreed there was "persuasive" evidence to support its belief that the President and the Governor had been wounded by the same bullet (Commission Exhibit 399).[67] On this point the Governor disagrees.

"I am convinced, beyond any doubt, that I was not struck by the first bullet," he says. "I know that I heard the first shot, that I turned to see what happened, and that I was struck by a second shot. The third shot struck the President and not me."[68]

Connally made it clear to reporters that his disagreement with the Commission's single-bullet theory was not to be interpreted to mean that "I disagree with the substance of their overall findings." As Zapruder's footage indicates, no more than 1.8 seconds elapsed between the time Kennedy and Connally were hit. Oswald could not have fired two shots so quickly. If he did not wound both men with one bullet, a fourth shot must have been fired. It could have come only from the rifle of a second assassin. No such weapon or suspect has ever been found.

The two bullets that struck the President inflicted wounds in the head and neck. If Oswald fired both of these shots from a window above and behind the President's car, as the Warren Commission concluded, neither bullet could have entered the front of the President's head or neck. If one such entry wound were found, it would indicate a second assassin. If both wounds had been caused by bullets fired from in front of the car, Oswald was innocent.

In arguing for Oswald's innocence, Mark Lane bears down heavily on the discrepancies between what was observed at Parkland Hospital, where the President was given emergency treatment, and what was reported by the pathologists who performed the autopsy at the National Naval Medical Center in Bethesda, Maryland. The autopsy required about three and one-half hours. In Dallas the doctors worked over the President for exactly seventeen minutes before he was pronounced dead. No post-mortem examination was made.

In the confusion at Parkland, doctors saw a throat wound which looked as though it might be an entry wound, and they failed to notice a small, clean-edged bullet hole at the rear of the President's skull which was discovered during the autopsy that night. It proved to be the point of entry for the fatal bullet that caused the President's massive head wound.

The bullet hole in the throat, it developed, was not an entry wound, as had seemed "possible" at Parkland.* Instead, the bullet had come from behind, striking the back of the neck and emerging from the front, just below the Adam's apple. The autopsy findings were corroborated by the bullet holes in the rear of the President's jacket and shirt. The fibers of both garments were brushed inward, indicating a wound of entry rather than of exit.

In seeking to discredit the autopsy report, which concluded that both of the bullets responsible for the President's wounds had been "fired from a point behind and somewhat above the level of the deceased,"[70] Lane encourages his readers to infer that the report was adjusted to fit the Commission's preconceived theory that Oswald, acting alone, shot the President. Eight doctors in Dallas, Lane emphasizes, "did not see a bullet hole which the Commission said was there."[71] Four Parkland physicians are quoted on this point, including Dr. Kemp Clark who signed the hospital's medical report on the President's death. Lane does not quote Dr. Clark's statement that the small, undetected head wound "could have easily been hidden in the blood and hair."[72]

Neither does he bother to explain — or, indeed, even to mention — one of the most important details regarding the disparity between the observations in Dallas and in Bethesda. Lane's readers are not told that throughout the entire time the President was being

* Lane quotes Dr. Malcolm O. Perry, the physician in charge, as saying, "There was an entrance wound below his Adam's apple." According to the Washington *Post,* Perry said, "It is possible that the neck wound was the entrance wound . . ." Testifying before the Warren Commission, he said, "It could have been either."[69]

treated at Parkland Hospital, he was lying on his back. The doctors never turned him over.[73]

Thus, the Parkland physicians had not been in a position to observe the entry wound in the rear of the President's head, and the autopsy surgeons in Bethesda had been unaware of the throat wound because it had been obliterated by the hole cut in the President's windpipe in an effort to help him breathe. Once the Bethesda pathologists checked with the Dallas doctors and learned about the tracheotomy, they could see why they had failed at first to find a point of exit for this bullet. It had passed between two large strap muscles and had met with almost no resistance before it emerged from the soft tissue in front of the throat.

Before the bullet's path had been traced and the mystery of its exit cleared up, two FBI agents recorded a preliminary hypothesis that one bullet — not found in the body — had penetrated a distance less than a finger length. This tentative theory turned up as fact in an FBI summary report dated December 9 and was repeated in a supplemental report on January 13. The contradiction between the two FBI reports and the autopsy findings published by the Warren Commission figures prominently in *Inquest,* a scholarly appearing book by Edward Jay Epstein which began as a master's thesis in government at Cornell University.

"I was at first persuaded that this young man had, by dint of digging and hard analysis, come up with one of the big stories of the decade, namely, that the eminent Warren Commission had done a fantastically sloppy job and that few of its major conclusions were to be credited any longer," Fletcher Knebel wrote in *Look.* "Then, I started to check some of Epstein's statements. . . ."[74]

"If the FBI reports are accurate, as all the evidence indicates they are," Epstein writes, "then a central aspect of the autopsy was changed more than two months after the autopsy examination, and the autopsy report published in the *Warren Report* is not the original one. If this is in fact the case, the significance of this alteration of facts goes far beyond merely indicating that it was not physically possible for a lone assassin to have accomplished the assassination. It indicates that the conclusions of the *Warren Report* must be viewed as expressions of political truth."[75]

In declaring that *all* of the evidence (not *most* of it, *much* of it, or *some* of it, but *all* of it) supported the accuracy of the FBI reports, Epstein was suggesting that *no* evidence substantiated the accuracy of the autopsy report published by the Warren Commission and corroborated by the sworn testimony of the autopsy surgeons. This could only mean that the Commission's staff had (1) deceived the Chief Justice and his fellow-Commissioners with perjured evidence or (2) joined them in perpetrating a monstrous fraud.

When the autopsy surgeons testified under oath, they knew that their findings could be checked against the X rays and photographs of the President's wounds which had been turned over to the Secret Service. Thus, indisputable evidence existed to disprove any false-hoods. Finally, any conspiracy within the Commission to conceal the facts about the wounds would have had to be carried out during a time when the vast investigative resources of the Department of Justice were under the command of the dead President's brother, who as late as August, 1964, informed the Chief Justice that he was receiving periodic reports on the Commission's work from his Deputy Attorney General (Nicholas deB. Katzenbach) and the De-partment's liaison with the Commission (Howard P. Willens).[76]

The autopsy report signed on November 24 by two Navy Com-manders (J. J. Humes and "J" Thornton Boswell) and by an Army Lieutenant-Colonel (Pierre A. Finck) was published in the *Warren Report* "exactly as it was written," Dr. Boswell told Fletcher Knebel,[77] who asked Epstein whether he had made any effort to confront the autopsy surgeons with the documents he had used to impugn their integrity.

"He contended that he was not required to check statements made in his book with the person involved," Knebel wrote. "Thus, he erected for himself remarkably secure and comfortable academic ramparts from which to fire a barrage at the Warren Commission. Yet any newspaperman who assumed such a stance — that people involved in highly suspect operations need not be asked for their version of the story — would be fired in a week."[78]

"It is ridiculous to indicate that the autopsy findings were changed after November 24 . . ." says Arlen Specter, the Commission lawyer who did most of the work in this area of the investigation.[79] In an interview with *U.S. News & World Report*, he said he had seen both the longhand and typewritten versions of the autopsy report when he first went to work for the Commission in mid-January, 1964.[80] He says they were essentially identical. Both have been published by the Commission.*

"There can be no doubt that the autopsy findings were known to the FBI when it prepared the Summary Report," Epstein writes,[81] and cites as his source not someone in the FBI but a Commission lawyer, Francis W. H. Adams, who later told Jacob Cohen, author of *Honest Verdict*, that he had no knowledge of whether the FBI had seen the autopsy report before December 9 and, he added, he had no recollection of ever having talked to Epstein.[82]

In late November, 1966, J. Edgar Hoover cleared up this aspect of the controversy. The FBI, he said, had *not* seen the autopsy report at the time its summary report was completed on December 9.[83] The autopsy report was sent to the FBI and to the Warren Commission two weeks later, on December 23. Before the January 13 supplemental report was written, the FBI made a laboratory examination of the President's clothing and found "a slit characteristic of an exit hole for a projectile in the front of the shirt one inch below the collar button." Thus, the "possible" entry wound in the throat observed in Dallas was shown to be what the autopsy report had stated — an exit wound.

"These findings clearly indicated the examining physician's early observation that the bullet penetrated only a short distance into the President's back probably was in error," Hoover continued. "Since this observation had been included in the FBI report on December 9, 1963, another reference was made to it in the report of January 13, 1964, in conjunction with the laboratory findings to point up this probability."

In an effort to shore up his theory that the FBI's two lay observers were correct and the military's three experienced pathologists were wrong, Epstein devotes considerable space to a work-sketch of the President's wounds which was hastily drawn during the autopsy and published by the Commission as part of Exhibit 397.[84]

Two bullet holes appear in the drawing. One bullet was responsible for the President's fatal head wound; the other caused the controversial neck wound. The sketch places this latter wound so far

* The typewritten version is in the *Warren Report*, pp. 538 ff.; the handwritten original in Vol. XVII of the *Exhibits* (Commission Exhibit 397).

down on the President's back that it could not have been the point of entry for a bullet that penetrated his neck and emerged from his throat, as stated in the autopsy report and reaffirmed by Commander Humes when he testified before the Commission.

Epstein produces evidence to suggest that Humes's testimony may have been erroneous and the autopsy drawing correct,[85] but the drawing itself negates this theory. Instead of being the work of Commander Humes, as Epstein assumed, the drawing had been made by Dr. Boswell, who later explained that it was "strictly a work-sheet — the same as rough working notes."[86] In the margin of the sketch is a notation in Dr. Boswell's handwriting made during the autopsy, which fixes the precise location of the wound.

The bullet hole is placed at a point fourteen centimeters — five and one-half inches — from the tip of the right mastoid process (the bony tip behind the ear) and fourteen centimeters from the right acromion (the outer extremity of the shoulder blade). The wound, in short, was at the base of the President's neck, above the throat wound, as stated in the autopsy report on November 24, in the testimony of Commander Humes on March 16, and in the *Warren Report*.

"Mr. Epstein's work has had more effect than that of any other critic of the Commission, and this results from what I must call a superficial appearance of scholarship," says Wesley Liebeler, the Commission lawyer most often cited in Epstein's footnotes.[87]

The book has all the appurtenances of scholarship, but the footnotes become less impressive when the sources are asked if they were quoted accurately and fairly. "Utterly unreliable," says one of the Commission lawyers, and another told *Newsweek*, "Frankly, I am appalled by the inaccuracies of the book . . ."[88]

"Epstein, instead of getting a master's degree for his product, should go to the foot of his class," said Associate Justice Stanley Mosk of the California Supreme Court, who found the book "superficial and inaccurate."[89]

In time, when *Rush to Judgment* and *Inquest* are at one in secondhand bookstores with *The President's Daughter*, the most remarkable thing about the books may prove to be the seriousness with which they were taken. But with all their defects, the books raised such an international hue and cry about the autopsy that the

Kennedy family turned the fourteen X rays and fifty-one photographs of the President's body over to the National Archives under terms which permitted only federal investigators to view the material during the first five years. This stipulation, a family spokesman explained, had been based "on the grounds that by that time there will not be a lot of people making money out of the assassination."[90]

Called in to authenticate the autopsy material, both Dr. Humes and Dr. Boswell (Dr. Finck was in Vietnam) said the X rays and photographs corroborated their testimony before the Warren Commission that the President's wounds indicated the assassin's bullets had come from "above and behind."[91] This should have put an end to all second-assassin theories arising from a supposed entry wound in the throat and from the contradiction in the FBI reports featured in *Inquest*, but the cultists were prepared for this Establishment ploy.

"The pictures were faked," they said, making a last-ditch stand against the encroachment of reality.

In writing its report, the Warren Commission drew on the material contained in approximately 25,000 interviews conducted by the FBI and 1,550 by the Secret Service, along with the testimony of its own 552 witnesses. In the first three years following the assassination, some of the interviewees died. Among them were the diabetic manager of Oswald's rooming house (heart attack), the taxicab driver who picked him up shortly after the President was shot (killed in an automobile accident), a witness who had enjoyed a particularly good view of the celebrated grassy knoll (another automobile accident) and a lawyer friend of Ruby's (heart attack).[92]

Two reporters who met with Ruby's roommate at Ruby's apartment the night Oswald was shot have come to strange and violent ends. One, a young Dallas bachelor, was found with a broken neck, apparently the result of a karate chop. He had been working with two colleagues on a book about the assassination. The other reporter was a Californian, Bill Hunter, who was accidentally shot by a Long Beach detective.

One of the Tippit murder witnesses who identified Oswald as the man he had seen fleeing the scene of the crime (Warren Reynolds) was shot in the head as he closed his car lot for the night. He survived what has come to be known as The Kennedy Curse, but it fell on Betty (Nancy Jane Mooney) MacDonald, a stripper who allegedly had worked at Ruby's night club. About a week after she provided an alibi for a suspect arrested in the Reynolds shooting, she was picked up for fighting with a girl friend. While in the Dallas city jail, she hanged herself.[93]

Only the more extreme believers in the curse connect the death of Dorothy Kilgallen with her determination to uncover the truth about Dallas (she was convinced of a conspiracy). Officially her death was attributed to "acute barbiturate and alcohol intoxication, circumstances undetermined," but a fan magazine editor has been quoted as saying that a few hours before the columnist's body was discovered she got a phone call informing her that Miss Kilgallen had been murdered.

The dark legend of The Kennedy Curse has developed simultaneously with speculation about a "second" Oswald, whose nebulous existence is a product of some intriguing evidence gathered — and published — by the Warren Commission (and exploited by its critics), indicating that a man thought to be Oswald was seen at places where the *real* Oswald could not have been, doing things he could not have done.[94]

Oswald never learned to drive a car, but an automobile salesman swears he rode in a demonstration car with Oswald at the wheel (he drove a bit too fast for the salesman's taste). Oswald II turned up at a furniture store in Irving and a Selective Service office in Austin; he fired at targets at the Sports Drome Rifle Range in Dallas and left a rifle at the Irving Sports Shop to be drilled for a telescopic sight (the Italian carbine sent to "A. Hidell" at Oswald's post office box arrived with a telescopic sight, as ordered). In late September, 1963, when Oswald I was in New Orleans, a "Leon Oswald" called on Mrs. Sylvia Odio at her Dallas apartment with two Cubans (or Mexicans).[95]

Oswald II provides an all-purpose solution to the Dallas mystery. He can be used to fit any sort of conspiracy, support any theory. For those who believe the real Oswald was innocent, Oswald II explains how he was framed (Léo Sauvage, a French journalist, has consistently contended that racists conspired to kill Kennedy and set Oswald up as the patsy).[96] For those who believe Oswald was involved, but not the lone assassin, Oswald II explains how a marksman of relatively modest ability could shoot so accurately, then escape so quickly. One was the killer, the other a decoy.

Fifteen minutes after the assassination, Dallas police broadcast a description of a suspect resembling Oswald. It has been theorized that the plotters planted the description as part of their scheme to use the real Oswald to confuse the local constabulary (a simple assignment well within his limited capacities). It would take at least two Oswalds, say the theorists, to cover as much ground and do as many things as the Commission claims for Oswald between 12:33, when he is thought to have left the Book Depository, and 1:51, when police officers reported his arrest for the murder of Officer Tippit.

Tippit may or may not have been involved in the plot, depending on which theory is being advanced. He may have blundered into the decoy's path, or Oswald may have been afraid that Tippit had recognized him as the assassin's reasonable facsimile. Either Tippit or Oswald, or both men, may have been on their way to Jack Ruby's place. Tippit may have been hired by the plotters to assassinate Oswald after he had assassinated the President. In any event, once Oswald landed in the city jail, it was obvious that They (the Communists, the Birchers, the oil barons) were never going to let him testify in open court — Ruby was hired to see to that.

"The Commission has been unable to establish as a fact any kind of relationship between Ruby and Oswald other than that Oswald was Ruby's victim," the Warren Commission reported.[97]

"It's perfectly obvious that there was enough relationship between Rubenstein and Oswald to prove there was a conspiracy," said former Major General Edwin A. Walker, speaking for the far right,*[98] and he was echoed by a Communist writer for *The Worker*, who told a capitalist reporter, "The full story of the plotters

---

* Professor Oliver, meanwhile, had told a right-wing California audience that "the headquarters detachment of our Army under orders from McNamara's office began to rehearse for the funeral more than a week before the assassination." It is true that a Presidential funeral had been rehearsed. The professor simply neglected to explain that it had been conducted in anticipation of the death of Herbert Hoover, who was gravely ill at the time.[99]

of this crime was not told. We refuse to believe that just on his own Jack Ruby would kill Oswald to avenge the President."[100]

"As we all know," says Oswald's mother, advancing as a universal truth one of the more fanciful theories about the assassination, "President Kennedy was a dying man. So I say it is possible that my son was chosen to shoot him in a mercy killing for the security of the country."[101]

"The Commission is not engaged in determining the guilt of anybody," its general counsel said at the start of its inquiry. "It is a fact-finding body."[102]

But, as Professor Maurice Rosenberg of Columbia University has pointed out, "it soon became apparent that the whole venture was instinct with accusation, try as one might to be neutral, impartial or merely 'fact-finding.' As the inquiry went on, the Commission realized that the dividing line between fact-finding and accusation was nonexistent when the facts alone might both accuse and pronounce guilt."[103]

The Commission turned down Mark Lane's request to take part in its proceedings on behalf of Oswald's mother, who had retained him for a short while to look after her son's interests.[104] ("He strikes me less as a truth seeker than as a tireless and somewhat demagogic advocate, and I can imagine the publicity circus, the confusion, the waste of time had he been given status before the Commission . . ." says Dwight Macdonald.)[105] Instead, the Commission asked Walter E. Craig, president of the American Bar Association, to keep an eye on its proceedings to see that they "conformed to the basic principles of American justice."[106]

Critics of the Commission have suggested that Craig merely lent an air of legal respectability to an inquiry which stood more in need of rude questions than polite approval. They have also suggested that the Commission's search for truth might have been better served if one of its more imaginative and aggressive lawyers had been designated a devil's-advocate-in-residence, who could have played in private deliberations the role Mark Lane has played so profitably in public. In self-defense, the Commission reminds its critics that it was conducting an investigation, not a trial. But its inquiry was as close as Oswald is ever likely to come to a trial.

"No innocent man stands convicted," says Professor Bickel, who is convinced of Oswald's guilt but critical of what he calls "The Failure of the Warren Report."[107]

If he had been brought to trial, Bickel believes, Oswald would have been convicted, but a trial would have left even more loose ends lying about, because much of the evidence produced by the Commission could not have been admitted in a Texas courtroom. The same point had been made earlier by Alfredda Scobey, a member of the Commission's staff, writing in the *American Bar Association Journal*.[108] She had pointed out that Marina, who was the sole source of some of the Commission's most significant evidence (the rifle photograph and Oswald's alleged attempt on General Walker's life, for instance), would not have been permitted to testify against her husband. It was Marina who dredged up from Oswald's brief, wretched life the details which best explain what may have driven him to shoot the President:

". . . he liked some things in Russia, he liked some other things here, didn't like some things there, and didn't like some things here. And I am convinced that as much as he knew about Cuba, all he knew was from books and so on. He wanted to convince himself. But I am sure that if he had gone there, he would not have liked it there, either. Only on the moon, perhaps."[109]

"Many factors were undoubtedly involved in Oswald's motivation for the assassination, and the Commission does not believe that it can ascribe to him any one motive or group of motives," says the *Warren Report*. "It is apparent, however, that Oswald was moved by an overriding hostility to his environment. He does not appear to have been able to establish meaningful relationships with other people."[110]

"They lived like mice, you know," said one of Marina's Russian-colony friends, and when asked her impressions of Oswald, she replied, "Disagreeable. He was very, very disagreeable, and disappointed. He is like a puppy dog that everybody kicked."[111]

Marina was the first witness to appear before the Warren Commission. The twenty-six-volume record of its hearings begins with the Chairman's polite inquiry: "Well, Mrs. Oswald, did you have a good trip here?"[112] Later that day (February 3, 1964), when she was asked whether her late husband had owned a rifle or a shotgun at the time he lived in the Soviet Union, she said, "I don't know the difference. One and the other shoots. You men. That is your business." The Chief Justice, who happens to be fond of hunting, broke in to remark: "My wife wouldn't know the difference, so it is all right."[113]

Marina seems to have made a more favorable impression on the Commission's chairman than on the younger members of its staff, some of whom found her testimony sprinkled with contradictions and inconsistencies. When she was recalled to Washington to testify again in June, Senator Russell found her "elusive."[114] In September, when the *Report* was in its final stages, she was questioned once more (this time in Dallas) and, running true to form, she again came up with a new conjecture.

"I feel in my own mind that Lee did not have President Kennedy as a prime target when he assassinated him," she said.

"Well, who was it?" Representative Boggs asked.

"I think it was Connally."[115]

"Baffling," Senator Russell commented later, when discussing the young lady's ever changing mind.[116]

The Commission placed its trust in Oswald's wife, who said she thought he was guilty, while its critics tend to rely on the testimony of his mother, who still insists he was innocent. When Marguerite Oswald came before the Commission, she was clutching a large black handbag crammed with letters, newspaper clippings, magazine articles and documents of various sorts. A stubborn, aggressive woman (her own adjectives),[117] she kept fishing through her portable file cabinet without ever seeming to find just the right piece of paper to prove her son's innocence.[118]

When the discussion got around to money, as it often does with Mrs. Oswald ("I married Mr. Edwin Ekdahl who was an electrical engineer and a $10,000-a-year man with an expense account"),[119] she complained, "My contributions up to now are just a little over $900 — about $905. This is the money that has been given direct to me, the mother of Lee Harvey Oswald."[120] Marina, she understood, had received $35,000.[121]

Marina's ex-business manager, James Herbert Martin, testified that she had received over $132,000 in advance royalties and another $68,000 in contributions.[122] "The American people are crazy for sending me that money," he quoted her as saying, and recalled a day when "she opened a letter and there was a dollar in it and she said, 'Oh, a dollar,' and threw it on the table . . ."[123]

"Oh, when Marina went to Washington," Marguerite Oswald told Jean Stafford, "Washington fell in love with Marina Oswald, and Chief Justice Warren was her grandfather, but when I went to Washington — 'Don't listen to her. Momma hadn't seen Lee in a year, and she doesn't know anything, blah, blah, blah.' Everything was against me. Yet *I* was the mother."[124]

"Oswald's mother, Mrs. Marguerite Oswald, testified before the Commission that she believes her son went to Russia and returned as an undercover agent for the U.S. Government," says the *Warren Report,* and politely goes on to add: "Though provided the opportunity to present any material she considered pertinent, Mrs. Oswald was not able to give the Commission any reasonable basis for her speculation."[125]

On first reading the *Warren Report* (two years later, after *Inquest,* he changed his mind), Raymond Moley was favorably impressed. He found it bore "a heavy imprint of the Commission's chairman."* [126] Moley also commented on the "thoroughness of detail which is the mark of a great criminal prosecutor" and on "Warren's capacity as an administrator." He had managed to produce a document signed by all seven members of the Commission. As in *Brown v. Board of Education,* there were no dissenting opinions.

"Warren was determined he was going to have a unanimous report," Senator Russell told interviewers in the fall of 1966, explaining his refusal to go along with the original wording which had stated categorically there had been no conspiracy. "I said it wouldn't be any trouble just to put a little asterisk up here [in the text] and then down at the bottom of the page saying: 'Senator Russell dissents to this finding as follows.' But Warren wouldn't hear of it. He finally took that part and rewrote it himself."[129] (Instead of a

---

* "Warren was the Commission," Epstein quotes Liebeler as saying.[127] Other members of the staff agree. One of them told a *Newsweek* reporter that the Chief Justice "almost killed himself with exhaustion working on this."[128]

flat denial of a conspiracy, the *Warren Report* simply states that the Commission "found no evidence of conspiracy.")[130]

Hugh Trevor-Roper, the English historian who joined Bertrand Russell in launching one of the first organized efforts abroad to challenge the evidence of Oswald's guilt, regards the *Warren Report* as "an advocate's summing up."[131] "I am an advocate by nature," Warren said early in his career,[132] and, without question, the *Report* shows the influence of a prosecutor building a strong case. ("It was not ever possible," says Murray Kempton, "to read these findings without becoming at once aware of the special defects of the prosecutor's mind.")[133]

The *Report* may be faulted for playing up the testimony of two shaky witnesses who placed Oswald at the scene of the Kennedy and Tippit murders (Howard Brennan and Helen Markham), and for neglecting to quote the damaging statement of a Marine Corps contemporary of Oswald's who described his performance on the rifle range as something of a joke (Nelson Delgado).[134] The *Report* is also much too tactful in its treatment of the Dallas Police Department. It ignores the lively testimony of Nancy Rich who mixed drinks for the local lawmen, and passes no censure on the department's failure to make a record of Oswald's interrogation.

"No, sir; I have requested one several times but so far they haven't gotten me one," the head of the homicide bureau replied when asked if the Dallas Police Department owned a tape recorder[135] (he was not asked why he had not rented or borrowed one for the occasion).

Oswald's unrecorded interrogation, taking up a total of twelve hours in two days, caused Professor Trevor-Roper to tumble into an embarrassing trap of his own making. American police, he informed readers of London's *Sunday Times* in December, 1964, "automatically" make a transcript of all interrogations of suspects, no matter how trivial the case. The Dallas Police Department insisted it had made no such record of Oswald's interrogation.

"This, I do not hesitate to say, cannot possibly be true," Professor Trevor-Roper declared, and suggested it had been "destroyed by the FBI or the police, and the Commission, with culpable indifference, has not troubled to ask why."[136]

He was answered by Dwight Macdonald in his brilliant *Esquire* critique of the *Warren Report* (one of the rare pieces of good writing in the entire body of assassination literature). American police, Macdonald informed the Regius Professor of Modern History at Oxford, do not "automatically" record interrogations. They wait until the suspect has begun to make incriminating admissions. In Oswald's case, this had never happened.[137] But because a transcript *should* have been made in Dallas, it was assumed in Oxford that it *had* been made, and having disappeared, it *must* have been destroyed.

The FBI and the Secret Service agents who sat in on the questioning of Oswald have also been rebuked for not having insisted that a stenographer or recording device be brought into the interrogation room, but their critics — especially foreign journalists — have often failed to realize that the government agents had no jurisdiction in the case. Under the law at that time, it was a federal crime to threaten the President but not to shoot him. Federal jurisdiction could have been asserted only if evidence had pointed toward a conspiracy. No such evidence turned up, at least as far as the federal agencies have reported, but suspicion of a plot of some sort took hold of the public mind at once and has never been dislodged — or substantiated.

After failing to find evidence of a conspiracy in Dallas to kill the President, assassination cultists transferred their suspicions and their malice to the Warren Commission, vilifying it as a conspiracy to conceal the truth. They have played up the notoriously unreliable testimony of eyewitnesses, picking and choosing among conflicting memories and minor inconsistencies, while glossing over the hard physical evidence of Oswald's guilt. He bought the rifle found at the Book Depository and left his palmprint on it. Two bullet fragments from this rifle were retrieved from the front of the President's car, and another bullet from the hospital where he was pronounced dead.

It is difficult to believe that a young ne'er-do-well who failed at everything he set out to do could single-handedly have shot the President. For a stubborn minority, it has been no less difficult to believe that *Hamlet* was written by a Tudor dropout, but in three hundred years no acceptable substitute has been found for William Shakespeare. Dallas may have spawned a new and even noisier breed of Baconians who will go thundering through the centuries insisting Oswald was innocent or was part of a conspiracy covered up by the Warren Commission, but they have yet to produce a plausible, provable alternative to its *Report*. They have been more successful in ridiculing and reviling it than in replacing it.

"Frankly," says one of the members of the Warren Commission, "I thought that the Lane-Epstein and other attacks were so frivolous and the authors so undistinguished that it was better to ignore them. I now see that I was wrong."

Shortly after the assassination, a Gallup poll revealed that more than half of the American people (52 per cent) believed "some group or element" was involved. Three years later, following the Lane-Epstein attacks on the Commission and its conclusions, a Louis Harris survey indicated that two out of three Americans thought the *Warren Report* had not told the "full story."

"The largest lack of acceptance of the explanation by the Warren Commission persists among lower income, less well educated Americans," the Harris survey noted. "The more articulate, better informed groups tend to give more credence to the official report."[138]

Among the mass of its critics, the *Report* was immediately suspect because it was the *official* version of what happened in Dallas. In a Republic overrun with rebels who regard the District of Columbia as a foreign and unfriendly power, it is difficult for even the most eminent group of public officials to make a thoroughly convincing case for any debatable proposition. Chances of total acceptance are further reduced when the group is headed by a highly controversial figure who has aroused the wrath of bigots, right-wing extremists and back-country evangelists.

When President Johnson first set out to seek the truth about the assassination, it was natural for him to turn to public officials. He had spent most of his adult life in their company. The Kennedy family, seeking the same truth, chose a writer. In *The Death of a President*, William Manchester, like the Warren Commission, came to the conclusion that Lee Harvey Oswald, acting alone, was the assassin. Unlike Epstein, who could merely speculate about the autopsy X rays and photographs, Manchester was able to interview "three people with special qualifications," who had examined the material. It fully supported the autopsy findings in the *Warren Report*.[139]

As an official body, the Warren Commission had to deal more gingerly with political sensitivities and personal egos than Manchester. In the *Warren Report* the FBI is let off with a slap of the wrist, but even this was enough to provoke a howl of rage from the bureau's venerable director. "It is Monday morning quarterbacking," he said in one of his rare press conferences, and denounced the Commission's criticisms as "entirely unwarranted and untrue."[140]

The Commission worked within the limitations of the Chairman's courtesy and thoughtfulness. Warren broke off interrogation of the President's young widow after ten minutes. Manchester interviewed her for ten hours. Warren deleted references to her husband's wounds from her testimony. Manchester spares his reader no clinical detail.

Again in character, Warren deferred to the Kennedy family and to good taste in making sure that the autopsy photographs were never peddled and published. He may well have remembered police and newspaper photographs of his own father's battered, blood-stained body. With the advantage of hindsight, it is easy to see what difficulties could have been avoided if the Commission had called in an independent panel of pathologists to study the autopsy material and corroborate the findings contained in the official report.

Looking back, it is also apparent that the Commission was too official in its composition. It might well have been seasoned with a few citizens drawn from literature and history rather than the law (Edmund Wilson and Samuel Eliot Morison, for example), but whatever its composition, its pursuit of truth would still have taken it into the same tanglewood of myth and mystery. The Kennedy family picked an investigator who had trafficked in fiction as well as fact. Johnson chose men from public life who were more at ease with facts than fantasies. Manchester wrote an epic tale, the Commission a legal document.

"It is a monumental work," Lord Devlin wrote when he read the *Warren Report*, and went on to praise the superb organization of its material. "The structure is clear. Each fact is to be found in its proper place to sustain each conclusion. The minor conclusions support the major, and on the major the verdict rests."[141]

But it was not a popular verdict. Politically, the right still insisted the assassination was a conspiracy of the left, and the left remained equally certain it had been a right-wing plot. Emotionally, the Dallas tragedy demanded a more satisfying denouement than could be drawn from evidence that the President had met his death at the hands of an insignificant youth who, in the words of his widow, had wanted "to do something that would make him outstanding, that he would be known in history."[142] To accept Oswald's guilt, rejecting all plots, cabals and conspiracies, was to accept a murder without meaning. In a drama of such noble proportions the young prince is not to be killed by a stockroom clerk.

"My book proves how the FBI and the Secret Service framed the whole thing," says Harold (*Whitewash*) Weisberg in Richard Warren Lewis's examination of "The Scavengers,"[143] which also includes two other notable comments:

Penn (*Forgive My Grief*) Jones: "I honestly believe that Lyndon had it done."

Malcolm Kilduff, the former White House assistant press secretary who accompanied President Kennedy to Dallas: "Most of the books that have been written since the assassination can be described as garbage."

"This has been a long and depressing job," Warren said after the Commission had submitted its report to the President on September 24, 1964.[144] ("It's pretty heavy," Johnson said.)[145] The Chief Justice and Mrs. Warren then flew west for a brief vacation with the children and grandchildren before the opening of the new Court term.

"I think it was the most difficult job he ever had," says his old friend, Bart Cavanaugh. "Mrs. Warren was terribly worried about him during this period. He lost a lot of weight. I went back there, spent a week or so with him. We went up to New York to see some ball games, and before we left, Mrs. Warren took me aside and said, 'Bart, see that he eats well.'"

"You should have seen the hate mail he got," says one of his intimates, and Cavanaugh recalls his surprise at finding "The Boss" guarded by Secret Service agents. But when the Chief Justice, Cavanaugh and the three Warren sons went duck-hunting at Wally

Lynn's ranch, the Secret Service detail was excused. "We figured he didn't need any protection up there," Cavanaugh says. "Not with us. We know how to handle a gun."

In the fall of 1966, at the height of the attacks on the *Warren Report*, the Chief Justice could be found on pleasant evenings strolling the streets of Washington unguarded and, apparently, untroubled by The Kennedy Curse.

"I like to walk," he told Bill Gold of the Washington *Post*.

"Do very many people try to strike up a conversation?" Gold asked.

"No, not many. For the most part they just smile or nod or say 'hello' and keep on walking."

"Do you sometimes hear some passing comments?"

"The comment I hear most often," the Chief Justice said, "is from people who do a double take and then say, 'Y'know, you're a dead ringer for Earl Warren.' "[146]

For twelve years, it seemed that Warren's luck had followed him to Washington, where he was so fortunate in the enemies he attracted that some of the Court's learned critics hesitated to take up the cudgels against him for fear of being regarded as racists or reactionaries. Overnight his enemies changed. Attacks on the Warren Commission came from admirers who had once looked up to its chairman as the man who had taken the measure of Congressional witch-hunters and southern sheriffs.

Commercial exploitation of the President's death subjected the Chief Justice to the slander and abuse of a new form of McCarthyism. At the height of the Impeach Earl Warren furor, when his photograph was being distributed on circulars marked: WANTED — FOR TREASON, the John Birch Society had not been more vicious than some of the liberal critics of the Warren Commission. The demagogic campaign drew its vitriol from the sumps of the Far Right and the New Left.*

Publicly, Warren has made no reply to the attacks and has no intention of dragging the Court into the controversy. Privately, he has

---

*"It is sad to acknowledge one more indication that political paranoia is not a monopoly of the far right," Professor John Kaplan of Stanford writes in his microscopic examination of "The Assassins" in *The American Scholar*, Spring, 1967, p. 306.

expressed amusement at the imaginative sweep of the conspiracy-minded critics of the *Report* ("What possible set of circumstances," he muses, "could get Dick Russell and me to conspire on *anything?*"). He agrees that some questions about the assassination may never be satisfactorily answered, but, along with other members of the Commission and its staff (as well as the author of *Inquest*), he considers the evidence of Oswald's guilt to be overwhelming.

"If I were still a district attorney and the Oswald case came into my jurisdiction, given the same evidence I could have gotten a conviction in two days and never heard about the case again," Warren remarked at a Washington party, and went on about his business, outwardly unperturbed by the character assassins who had picked a target too tall to miss and too proud to duck.[147]

20

The Mountain Climber

Don't complain about growing old. There are so many
who don't have the privilege.
— A FRIEND'S ADVICE TO EARL WARREN, 1931

ORDINARILY Warren pays little attention to his birthdays, but his
seventy-fifth, on Saturday, March 19, 1966, could not go un-
observed by his family, his friends and the press. Reporters gathered on Friday in the book-lined study adjoining the Court's conference room for their first group interview with the Chief Justice
in five years. He came striding in, fit and smiling, shook hands with
everybody, and then sat down behind a long, narrow table, starting
things off with a comment on the fine spring weather.

"I want to play baseball again," he said.[1]

"Do you have any plans for retiring?" he was asked.

"I knew that would be a question," he said. "I have not given
serious thought to that at the present time."[2] A few moments
later, in response to a question regarding his general views on the
subject, he added, "For many years I have been of the opinion that
it would be a good thing to have a compulsory retirement date for
all public officials — whenever the Congress and the people come to
the conclusion that such retirement should be enforced in all
branches of government."[3]

With obvious relish, he bore down on "all branches of government." This was the catch, or as one reporter remarked, "the
klinker." It was inconceivable that members of Congress would ever
impose any limitations on the length of their own service to the
Republic. Consequently, the Chief Justice and his brethren could

look forward to continued enjoyment of the same working conditions.

Under the ground rules laid down for the press conference (no inquiries on any matters relating to court cases), reporters were pressed for questions to put to the Chief Justice. They covered his daily work schedule, his love of sports ("it's one form of relaxing I really enjoy"), his Bible reading. ("I cannot say to you I read the Bible every night. I have the Bible along with other books by my bed. I read as the spirit moves me. Sometimes it is the Bible.") He seemed especially pleased when a reporter asked about his recent weekend trip to Geneva, where high court judges from around the world had been convened under the auspices of the World Peace Through Law Center. At the conclusion of the two-day conference, Warren's fellow-jurists had elected him chairman of the World Association of Judges.

"Our purpose is to direct as far as we can, as judges and lawyers, public opinion toward world law, and then to ascertain the means of bringing that about," he said, after explaining that the judges were acting as individuals, and not as representatives of their countries.[4]

"He talked easily and undramatically," Robert Cahn wrote in the *Christian Science Monitor*. "It was hard to picture him as the controversial head of the so-called 'Warren court,' assailed by some as a traitor to his country because of his liberal opinions, and lauded by many others as a great leader in furthering equality and social justice under the Constitution."

"I happen to rate him as the greatest Chief Justice in the nation's history," Professor Fred Rodell of Yale Law School had informed readers of the *New York Times Magazine* the preceding Sunday.[5]

"Extravagance is used in all sorts of articles," Warren said when asked if he had read the piece (he hadn't).[6]

The professor's sentiments, it turned out next day, were shared by the President.

As hosts of the seventy-fifth birthday party set for Saturday night at the Columbia Country Club, John and Virginia Daly checked the guest list with Papa Warren. The question arose at once as to whether the Dalys should invite the President.

"No, that wouldn't be right," Warren told them, and went on to explain that the President was a very busy man carrying crushing burdens. If he were invited, he'd feel obligated to come, and once that sort of thing began, he'd never have another evening to himself. "I'm not going to be a party to taking that man away from his family on a Saturday night just because it's my birthday."

Saturday evening, when the Warrens were dressing for the party, the phone rang. It was the White House. The President was on his way to see the Chief Justice. Mrs. Warren darted about the living room, tidying up the litter of gift wrappings, calling to the children to please hurry, and making sure the White House bouquet of yellow, white and brown chrysanthemums was prominently displayed.

When the President arrived with his birthday presents, which included a copy of Samuel Eliot Morison's *The Oxford History of the American People* and a photograph inscribed to "the greatest Chief Justice of them all," the Warrens were in evening clothes. After shaking hands with the Chief Justice and bussing his handsome womenfolk, the President sat down to chair a spell. "Looks like you all are going out somewhere," he said rather pointedly, and all eyes turned to Papa Warren.

"Well, yes, John and Virginia are having a little party," he said, and then explained that they had wanted to invite him and Mrs. Johnson but had been overruled.

The Chief Justice cited his grounds, the President nodded, chatted for a few more minutes, and then got up to leave. When he reached the door, after again pumping the men's hands and kissing the women's cheeks, he said good-bye to the Chief Justice, taking him by the hand and wishing him well. "But next time," he said as a parting shot, "you let your daughter and her husband pick their own guests."

Four nights later the Johnsons invited the Warrens to a White House reception for the federal judiciary. They were accompanied by their three daughters, two sons-in-law, and their oldest son, Jim, and his wife, Maggie. Chatting with the family, the President recalled that when Speaker Sam Rayburn dominated the House of Representatives, he considered the head of the table to be wherever

Mr. Sam happened to be sitting. "Now," the President said, "wherever Warren sits is the head of the table."[7]

"When I turned forty, I was very much worried about old age," the Chief Justice remarked when the President's guests crowded around, commenting on how lightly the years seemed to weigh upon him. "A friend of mine — past forty, of course — told me, 'Don't complain about growing old. There are so many who don't have the privilege.' "[8]

A month before the Chief Justice celebrated his seventy-fifth birthday, his Brother Black had marked his eightieth. It came at a historically significant time in the judicial career of the Court's philosopher and prophet. The Negro's revolutionary struggle for equality had shifted from the courts to the streets, from legal briefs protesting unequal justice under law, which had Black's wholehearted support, to marches and sit-ins protesting social and economic injustices, which had caused him to vote more and more with Harlan, Stewart and White against Warren, Douglas, Brennan and Fortas (Clark tends to veer between the two poles). In the preceding term, Black had dissented twenty-eight times, more than any other member of the Court.

A few days before his birthday, he had been on the losing side of a five-to-four decision striking down breach-of-peace convictions of five Negroes who had tried to integrate a public library in Louisiana. For nearly half an hour, speaking extemporaneously much of the time, he had excoriated the three opinions setting forth the majority's reasoning.

"The psalm-singing crowds that gather to express their views can be transformed into a loud, boisterous, arrant, dangerous mob," he had warned,[9] although in this case no crowds had gathered, no psalms had been sung. Five men had simply walked into a public building and politely requested the same service available to their white neighbors.

On March 7, 1964, Henry Brown, accompanied by four other Negroes, entered the Audubon Regional Library in Clinton, Louisiana, and asked for a book. The librarian said she didn't have it, but would order it from the state library. He could then have it mailed to him or could pick it up from the blue bookmobile which served the community's Negroes. (Caucasians had a separate but presumably equal red bookmobile.)

When asked to leave the white-only library, Brown and his companions refused. Brown sat down, the others remained standing. There was no loud or offensive talk, no threats, no damage. The sheriff was called and took the men away. The entire episode lasted no more than ten or fifteen minutes. Tried and convicted, Brown was sentenced to pay $150 plus costs or serve ninety days in jail, and the others were given a choice between $35 and costs or fifteen days. The state Supreme Court refused to review the case.

"Can any provision of the United States Constitution tell any citizens — white or colored — they can march with impunity into a public library and demonstrate against some public policy!" Black demanded[10] after Fortas, speaking for Warren and Douglas (Brennan and White filed separate concurrences), had declared the convictions a violation of the Negroes' constitutional rights of free speech and assembly, and the right to petition the government for a redress of grievances.

"Mr. Justice Black, it is clear from this and several recent cases, is rendered queasy by sit-ins," I. F. Stone wrote in his weekly newsletter, labeling his dissent "A Friendly Disagreement with a Great Justice on his 80th Birthday." "It is natural for one who prizes the First Amendment above all else to be suspicious of efforts to change law and custom not by the debate and persuasion it protects but by a kind of force, however peaceful. But the First Amendment, ideal and splendid as it is, has its limitations. The Negro cannot speak freely in the South, and even if he could, he could speak from now to doomsday without ever persuading Southern white supremacists. The sit-in has done more in a few years than persuasion could do in a century."[11]

Southern demonstrations were again before the Court in the fall of 1966 in *Adderley v. Florida.*[12] Harriett Louise Adderley and thirty-one other students at the Florida A. & M. University in Tallahassee had been found guilty of "trespass with a malicious and mischievous intent" after taking part in a 1963 march on the county jail protesting the arrest of some fellow-students, seeking integration of the local theaters. When they refused to leave the jail grounds and disperse, they were arrested.

"The State, no less than a private owner of property, has power to preserve the property under its control for the use to which it is lawfully dedicated," Justice Black wrote for a majority of the Court.[13]

"We do violence to the First Amendment when we permit this 'petition for redress of grievances' to be turned into a trespass action," Justice Douglas declared in a dissent in which Warren, Brennan and Fortas joined. The dissenters went on to warn, "Today a trespass law is used to penalize people for exercising a constitutional right. Tomorrow a disorderly conduct statute, a breach of the peace statute, a vagrancy statute will be put to the same end."[14]

"The case is the first in which the Court has sustained a conviction, under Southern police laws, of peaceful demonstration for civil rights," Professor Thomas I. Emerson of the Yale Law School wrote in *The Nation*.[15]

He was not sure how far the decision reached. It could mean that the right to assemble peaceably did not extend to certain public areas, such as jails, which, in Black's words, are "built for security purposes."[16] Or it might involve repudiation of an earlier doctrine ("Wherever the title of streets and parks may rest, they have immemorially been held in trust for the use of the public and, time out of mind, have been used for purposes of assembly . . .").[17]

"The tensions between change and order cannot be totally eliminated," Professor Emerson concluded, "but they can be accommodated, among other ways, by an effective system of free expression."

"It is high time to challenge the assumption in which too many people have too long acquiesced, that groups that think they have been mistreated or that have actually been mistreated have a constitutional right to use the public's streets, buildings, and property to protest whatever, wherever, whenever they want, without regard to whom such conduct may disturb," Black contended in February, 1966.[18]

As he reads the Constitution, he finds himself unable to cite any provision empowering the Supreme Court "to sit as a supervisory agency over acts of duly constituted legislative bodies . . ."[19] Thus, he considered Connecticut's laws against contraceptives "offensive," but not unconstitutional. He dissented again when the poll tax was outlawed, criticising the Court's tendency "to use the

Equal Protection Clause, as it has today, to write into the Constitution its notions of what it thinks is good governmental policy."[20]

"Justice Black's new orientation probably indicates as well as anything that the issues before the Court are changing," Fred P. Graham wrote in the New York *Times*. "The Bill of Rights has been virtually applied to the states in toto. Congressional committees and Red-baiters give the Court a wide berth. The school prayer controversy has died."[21]

Hope sprang in the eternally conservative breast of *U.S. News & World Report* that "in the thirteenth year of what is being called the 'Warren Revolution,'" the Chief Justice and the Court might now be "inclined to slow the rapid tempo of court-directed changes in America."[22] Writing in the liberal Washington *Post*, John P. MacKenzie also detected signs of change.

"For all of Warren's fearlessness," MacKenzie wrote, "he is known to be gratified that activist Presidents, Congresses, state legislators and even Southern judges have begun to assume part of the burden of protecting civil rights and liberties after a decade when some Justices felt compelled to go it alone."[23]

The Chief Justice, only two weeks earlier, had spoken for the Court in upholding the 1965 Voting Rights Act, a piece of legislation which, like the Civil Rights Act of the year before, had been made inevitable by a series of judicial rulings beginning in 1954 with *Brown v. Board of Education.*

"Hopefully," Warren had written, "millions of non-white Americans will now be able to participate for the first time on an equal basis in this government under which they live."[24]

As Chief Justice, Warren not only presides over the Supreme Court, runs the building and administers the oath of office to the President of the United States (and, by a pleasant custom he initiated some years ago, to the president of the National Press Club as well),[25] but is also responsible for the efficient operation of the federal courts. Every district judge rules an island kingdom, his drawbridge raised against outside interference, but working with Warren Olney III, the director of the Administrative Office of the United States Courts, the Chief Justice has managed to assert his administrative authority over the judicial system, rejuvenating it, speeding up its cumbersome processes and modernizing its moss-covered rules.

"The result," writes John P. Frank in *The Warren Court*, "is that Warren is the first true 'Chief Justice of the United States,' as distinguished from being the 'Chief Justice of the Supreme Court,' that the country has ever had."[26]

Frank has been particularly impressed by what the Chief Justice has had to say at the annual meetings in Washington of the American Law Institute, composed of some fifteen hundred lawyers and judges. Warren attends the meetings regularly, makes a formal report and participates in discussions of matters involving county, state and federal courts. What strikes Frank as most remarkable is not what the Chief Justice reads from his prepared text, but what he says impromptu as he goes along.

"The topics in his planned text bring his mind to other related illustrations, and so he spontaneously speaks of problems of improving the probation system of one area of the country or of bringing down the costs of bankruptcy administration in another," Frank writes. "As one listens, the realization washes over the audience that the legal system of the United States is not simply a headless juggernaut; there is one single individual in authority who actually knows what is going on from coast to coast and is concerned about making it go better."

"The Judiciary is an intrinsic part of this fast-moving world," Warren says, "and like all of the other parts, it must be properly geared and attuned to the realities of our time."[27]

When the American Law Institute met in May, 1966, he spoke with all the enthusiasm of a young law school graduate about the possibilities of using data processing methods to facilitate the work of the courts. Toward the end of his report, coming to "Crime and the Rule of Law," he was brief and blunt:

"Some critics who apparently do not share the opinion of most of us that we can successfully combat the criminal element and live within our constitutional guarantees take the easy approach of placing the blame for our high rate of crime on our courts and our system of law enforcement. You and I know that, as the President has recognized in his message to Congress, crime is a problem the root causes of which go deep into the whole fabric of our civilization and into our moral, social and economic systems."[28]

He also expressed fear that in seeking to correct deep-seated social evils, such as discriminatory jury systems, Congress might pass some "ill-advised" legislation which "would radically change the relationship between our federal and state governments." His interest in preserving the rights of the states to run their own affairs came as an agreeable surprise to some of his critics, but old friends and associates have always known the depth of his respect for the separation of power, not only between the Federal Government and the states, but also between the White House, the Congress and the Court. What he has never tolerated is fear of using power to meet the responsibilities of public office.

He came to Washington in the fall of Eisenhower's first year in the White House. After twenty years of a social revolution and a global war, waged by two strong Presidents, it was pleasant to relax under the General's warm, paternal smile. Power concentrated in the White House in the Roosevelt-Truman years was returned to Congress, where it was chopped up and parceled out to elderly, often cantankerous committee chairmen.

It wasn't time for a change, as the slogan-writers had insisted during the 1952 campaign. It was a time for no more changes.

"In looking back over this period," Clayton Fritchey wrote in *Newsday* on the weekend of the Chief Justice's seventy-fifth birthday, "it hardly seems possible that a judicial agency could have stepped into the vacuum left by the other two branches of government, and launched a transformation of our society."[29]

In the closing years of the Eisenhower administration, rumors began to circulate in Washington that the Chief Justice and the President who had appointed him were suffering from mutual disenchantment. According to the bush telegraph of the capital's cocktail circuit, Warren was privately expressing his annoyance at Eisenhower's "wishy-washy" conduct in the desegregation crisis. At the same time, it was said, the President was grumbling to friends about his inability to understand some of the Court's decisions, particularly recent rulings dealing with the rights of American citizens suspected of past or present membership in the Communist party.

"I know of no personal rift . . ." Eisenhower said when Robert J. Donovan wrote of the chasm in the New York *Herald Tribune*. Warren snapped, "The story merits no comment. It is wholly without foundation." But Donovan, a first-rate reporter who is now head of the Los Angeles *Times* Washington bureau, stuck by his dispatch.[30]

"Their relations were always cordial and correct, but they were never close," says a Warren confidant. "Their wives got along beautifully, though."

Both Eisenhower and Warren, only five months apart in age, were born to make their way in a McKinley world where individual initiative had an opportunity to develop through hard knocks and honest toil. They spring from the pages of Horatio Alger, not from the bureaucratic loins of a welfare state. But when they discuss the great American experiment in self-government, the two men seem to be speaking from different backgrounds, even from different centuries.

"Why should the Federal Government assert and assume a priority interest in the problems of the youth and the aged, the ill and the poor, and the temporarily unemployed?" Eisenhower has been heard to wonder.[31]

"If I were a private citizen," Warren said when he was governor of California, "I'd be pretty sore at my government if it were not concerned about my welfare. That's what government is for. That's what the preamble to the Constitution says our government is framed for — to promote the general welfare."[32]

Warren, as governor, agreed with Eisenhower that "our democratic processes should be kept close to the people," but as a practicing politician rather than a military man, he was well aware of the deficiencies of local governments. "If our states are to survive as strong governmental units, they must think more and more of their responsibilities and discharge them," he said, and pointed out, "What are called federal encroachments often result from the failure of states to solve problems that should be solved by state governments."[33]

The Federal Government's inability to run California from Washington was illustrated during Warren's first year as governor when farm machinery was being allocated to meet wartime needs. "They said we were not to use machinery between December and April," he recalled later, "and that's when we plant most of our early crops. But you know for years the government planned California post offices with snow eaves, and those people in the Imperial Valley had never seen snow."[34]

As Chief Justice, Warren reiterated his position on the federal-state relationship in September, 1963, when seven of the Associate Justices made their way to San Francisco to take part in the homage paid him by the state bar on the tenth anniversary of his appointment to the bench. In taking up the heated question of whether the Warren Court had gone too far in upsetting state court decisions in criminal cases, the Chief Justice cited statistics to show that "where the supreme court of a state is vigilant concerning constitutional rights, the Supreme Court of the United States is equally vigilant in supporting its decisions."[35]

Consistently, both as governor and as Chief Justice, Warren has preferred to have local problems solved at home by local authorities, but when a city council, a legislature or a state court has failed to act, he has never hesitated to call on the Federal Government. He has no patience with the timeless cry of "States' rights" when it has been used to defend the right of a state to commit some wrong against an individual because of his race, his beliefs, or his poverty.

"Some men learn from history," Emmet John Hughes has written of Eisenhower. "Some men run from it."[36]

The Negro, in the first months of the Eisenhower administration, found himself disinherited by history, disenfranchised by law. Even if a bolder President had drafted a civil rights proposal to be tossed in the Congressional hopper, it faced certain death at the hands of Southern Democrats and rural Midwestern Republicans who bartered bigotry and farm subsidies in an exchange of votes which kept the white Iowa farmer solvent and the black Mississippi sharecropper subservient.

"It is no sign of healthy progress in our society that so many of its supposed ills should have remained to be cured by the Supreme Court, says Alexander M. Bickel.[37]

Professor Bickel writes about the Court with authority and distinction, but with a point of view more commonly associated with the Harvard Law School, where he graduated, than with the Yale Law School, where he teaches. A former Frankfurter law clerk (1952–1953), he is less sympathetic with the activist turn the Warren Court has taken than his colleague, Fred Rodell, who represents what is generally regarded as the Yale philosophy of law.

"According to the compound of cliché, caricature and quarter-truth which has survived, particularly among undergraduates trying to make up their minds about which of these elite establishments to attend, the 662-man Yale and the 1,683-man Harvard are easily distinguished on other than numerical grounds," Victor S. Navasky, a Yale graduate, writes in an amusing *New York Times Magazine* article, "The Yales vs The Harvards (Legal Division)."

The myth persists that: "Yale trains judges, Harvard trains lawyers; Yale doesn't teach you any law, Harvard teaches you nothing but; Yale turns out socially conscious policy-makers, Harvard turns out narrow legal technicians; Yale thinks that judges invent the law, Harvard thinks that judges discover the law; Yale is preoccupied with social values, Harvard is preoccupied with abstract concepts; Yale is interested in personalities, Harvard is interested in cases; Yale thinks most legal doctrine is ritual mumbo-jumbo, Harvard thinks it comprises a self-contained logical system; Yale cares about results, Harvard cares about precedents; Yale thinks the law is what the judge had for breakfast, Harvard thinks it is a brooding omnipresence in the sky."[38]

With the Yale faculty infiltrated by Harvard graduates, the philosophical differences between the two institutions have become blurred (one attorney trained in New Haven says, "Yale is the Harvard of law schools").[39] On the Warren Court, Brennan (Harvard '31) and Fortas (Yale '33) are likely to line up against two Yale men (Stewart, '41, and White, '46), but in general the libertarian majority derives more from New Haven, where Douglas taught, than Cambridge, where Frankfurter held sway.

Chief Justice Warren and the learned men who criticize him often start out in the same general direction, heading for the same desirable destination, but they part company at a fork in the road where the law seems to go one way, justice another. Warren is a practical man who knows where he wants to go and, having set out on the journey, is impatient to get there. His scholarly critics are more concerned with the route he takes, preferring at times to have him delay the trip rather than conclude it under a technically deficient flight plan.

"When decisions are too much result-oriented, the law and the public are not well served," says Dean Griswold of Harvard, and Robert Braucher, one of his colleagues, agrees: "Judges are supposed to focus on the case, rather than lawmaking or public administration."[40]

Five years after Warren disposed of the school-segregation cases in half a dozen pages, *Brown v. Board of Education* was still troubling Professor Herbert Wechsler of Columbia University Law School. As a man of goodwill, he wanted to reach the same desegregated position occupied by the Court, but he couldn't quite accept the route it had taken. The situation, as he described it in a Harvard lecture, was one in which a choice had to be made between two groups of individuals. One group wanted to associate with the other. The other wished to avoid the association. This put the Court in the quandary of having to decide whether association should be denied one group or imposed on the other. Professor Wechsler kept asking himself whether any constitutional basis existed for ruling in favor of the claim for association.

"I should like to think there is," he said, "but I confess that I have not yet written the opinion."[41]

This is all right for an academician. Five years after the Court has taken its stand, he can still continue to dissect the decision, but the Chief Justice and his eight brothers have to settle the matter in their Friday conference, then move on to the next case on their agenda. The pressure of work can be gauged by the report Warren gave the American Law Institute in mid-May, 1966. In less than eight months, with time off for Christmas, Easter and the opening of the baseball season, the Court had disposed of 2,145 cases. It had heard arguments in 131 cases in a period of 192 hours. All the while, of course, every member of the Court had not only had to take part in the discussion of each case, but also to turn out an opinion every ten days or so. A law professor may spend months or years picking the lint off of a single judicial doctrine, but not a Supreme Court Justice. He must rip off his coat, roll up his sleeves and get on with it.

"What do I *do?*" Warren has asked throughout his political life when experts have gathered around his desk to debate a certain course of action. As California's chief executive in a period of explosive growth he had no time for navel contemplation. Children were spilling out of rickety classrooms, while their parents killed one another on overcrowded highways. Elderly patients were sleeping on cots in hospital corridors. Then as now, he had to act.

"When he first became governor," says a former member of his staff, "the fire marshal came to him and said he was worried about some of the state's firetrap hospitals. 'Well, let's go take a look at them,' the Governor said, and they drove over to look at an old three-story hospital at Stockton. The Governor was shaken. He ordered the closing of the second and third floors immediately. The authorities said it was impossible, they had no place to put the patients. The Governor said, 'Get those people out of there,' and they did."

"Earl Warren never struck me as a crusader," says one of his early-day associates, expressing a familiar theme among California liberals, who find it difficult to square their memory of the bland, affable Governor with the controversial Chief Justice.

And yet, though he presides over a revolutionary tribunal, Warren is still a cautious man who carefully considers each step. He likes to quote Lincoln: " 'I am a slow walker, but I never walk backward.' " It may take him a maddeningly long time to reach a decision, but once he has listened to both sides of an argument and made up his mind, he can't be easily budged. On the hustings he was denounced by right-wing Republicans as a Socialist and by left-wing Democrats as a reactionary masquerading as a liberal. Actually, he has never thought in the black-and-white terms of any particular set of fixed certainties.

"No matter how thin you make a pancake," he is fond of saying, "it always has two sides."

According to the creed of many California liberals, Warren began his political life as a black reactionary. Somewhere along the road to Sacramento, they insist, he suddenly saw a blinding light, heard the voice of the people, and became a convert to the true faith. Those closest to the Chief Justice reject this doctrine. It is their belief that Warren has never made any abrupt change of course, but each step along the way has simply tried to do his job fairly, honestly and a little more efficiently than it had been done before.

In September, 1957, shortly before the start of his fifth term as Chief Justice, Warren spent three days in New York City listening to scholarly expositions of the Talmud at the Jewish Theological Seminary of America.[42] At the end of the first day he cited protections against double jeopardy and self-incrimination as examples of the debt common law owes to the Judaic code. When the conference ended, he gratefully accepted an English translation of the Talmud and promised to study it with the hope of arriving at "a better concept of justice and righteousness . . ."

Five years later he was back in New York, delivering the major address at a seminary banquet. "In civilized life," he began, "Law floats in a sea of Ethics. Each is indispensable to civilization."[43] He suggested some thought be given to the corporate use of ethics counselors. A large company, he pointed out, would not undertake a new business venture without consulting experts from various departments — law, engineering, sales, finance, personnel. Why not call in one other expert — "the expert in ethics who can suggest whether the whole plan as conceived was socially useful, was right, was appropriate under the circumstances . . . ?"

"The speech told a great deal about Earl Warren," James E. Clayton writes in *The Making of Justice.* "Ten years earlier he would never have dreamed of making it. In the fall of 1962 he was still the 'big, hearty, healthy Californian' whom newspapers had mentioned twenty years before as a likely Republican candidate for President. But internally Earl Warren was a different man now. The imprint of the Supreme Court on him had been deeper than his imprint on it. He was still the glad-handing politician with a firm handshake and a quick smile. But the opportunities to meet people were fewer now as he lived a 'sedentary life.' That life gave a man a chance to read and reflect that is normally denied to the active politician . . ."[44]

"No one really knows this man," says one of his more perceptive friends, and a former member of his gubernatorial staff agrees. "All day long we used to hear that booming voice, that belly laugh, that loud, 'How *are* you?' But sometimes in the evening when I worked late, I'd see him sitting in his office alone, his back to the door, his head bowed, and on that wall above him a sad, brooding picture of Lincoln. That's the Earl Warren few of us ever saw and none of us ever knew."

"He's like a man climbing a mountain," says a retired California official whose association with Warren goes back forty years. "When he started out as district attorney, he was standing at the foot of the mountain, a pleasant, hardworking fellow who couldn't see far beyond the problems of the county. He cleaned up the gambling joints, cleared the crooks out of the courthouse and tried to give the honest cop a little pride in his work.

"Then he got himself elected attorney general and, as the state's chief law-enforcement officer, he began to get a broader view of crime and punishment. As governor, he climbed to new heights where he had to deal with problems he had never faced before. He increased old-age pensions, reorganized the state prison system, provided modern medical care for the mentally ill, bucked the oil lobby to build new freeways and fought a losing battle for compulsory health insurance. Each step along the way, from county prosecutor to Chief Justice, his perspective has changed, but not the man. The man hasn't changed. He's simply grown."

On Friday mornings, when the Chief Justice takes his seat at the head of the Court's conference table, no one has worked harder to prepare himself for a discussion of the day's cases and no one has come into the handsome oak-paneled chamber with a more intimate knowledge of how laws are written in state legislatures and executed in county courthouses. His is not simply a law of books and briefs, statutes and citations. It is the living law of the police headquarters basement, the trial court, the back rooms where lobbyists set up drinks for state legislators.

The Warren Court has used the equal protection clause of the Constitution to set new standards for state and federal lawmakers. "Once loosed," writes Archibald Cox, former Solicitor General (1961–1965), "the idea of Equality is not easily cabined. In 1868 the proposal of a constitutional amendment forbidding racial discrimination in voting aroused wide support for a declaration of universal suffrage. Although the proposal was ultimately defeated, it attracted strong support in Congress. Similarly, revitalization of the constitutional prohibitions against racial discrimination under *Brown v. Board of Education* gives impetus to review of other inequalities in American life."[45]

"Ever since Hammurabi published his code to 'hold back the strong from oppressing the weak,' the success of any legal system is measured by its fidelity to the universal ideal of justice," Warren has written. "Theorists beset us with other definitions of law: that it is a mask of privilege, or the judge's private prejudice, or the will of the stronger. But the ideal of justice survives all such myopic views, for as Cicero said, 'we are born to it.' "[46]

Earl Warren was born to the beginnings of the American labor movement, when men risked a broken head and a hungry family for the right to join a union. His children grew up taking the Wagner Act for granted, and his grandchildren are equally casual about the Negroes in their classrooms. Each generation has to deal with its own inequities. The battle for equal justice under law can never be wholly won, but so long as courts are free and judges fair, it can never be wholly lost.

Acknowledgments

I WOULD like to record my appreciation for the assistance I received from former members of the staff of District Attorney, Attorney General and Governor Earl Warren. I am particularly grateful to Helen R. MacGregor, who served as confidential secretary in all three offices, and to Judge Folger Emerson, Oscar Jahnsen, Judge James H. Oakley, Verne Scoggins, Arthur Sherry, Merrell F. (Pop) Small, Judge William T. Sweigert and Judge Beach Vasey.

I also recall with gratitude the time I spent in San Francisco with Judge Oliver Carter, Judge Albert C. Wollenberg, Peter Mitchell and Newton B. Drury; in Oakland with John F. Mullins and Willard W. Shea; in Sacramento with Bartley Cavanaugh, Archibald M. Mull, Jr., Jack McDermott, Heman G. Stark and Edgar J. Patterson, and in Santa Barbara with Thomas M. Storke.

I would like to thank Mrs. Bernice Harrell Chipman, Walter Kane, James Day and Ralph Kreiser of the Bakersfield *Californian* for their reminiscences, their files and their many personal kindnesses. I am also indebted to Robert B. Powers, the community's philosophical former police chief, and to members of the Kern County High School class of 1908 who took time to chat with me about "the Warren boy": Miss Mary Ashe, Omar Cavins, Mrs. Ruth Smith Henley, Jean L. Phillip, Mrs. Ethel Robesky Simpson and Francis E. Vaughan.

I owe a special debt to Horace M. Albright, who lent me his files on the University of California Class of 1912; to Edythe Jacobs, who contributed neighborly legal guidance; to Judge Robert W. Kenny, who brightened so many dark days; to Lee D. Stephenson, who meticulously combed the manuscript for reversible errors, and to Kenneth Ziffren, who checked the chapters on the Court.

No book of this sort could have been written without the help of librarians. I have run up a formidable debt to Robert Vosper, Everett T. Moore and Wilbur J. Smith of the University of California at Los Angeles; Louis Piacenza and Sylvia Merritt of the UCLA Law School library; Willa Baum and Amelia Fry of the Regional Cultural History Project, University of California Library, Berkeley; Allan R. Ottley, California section library, California State Library, Sacramento; the Southern California Library for Social Sciences and Research, Los Angeles; and an especially heavy obligation to Romeo Carraro and Alfredo Sansoni of the Los Angeles *Times* library, who cheerfully tracked down so many elusive dates, spellings and clippings.

J.D.W.

Notes

Sᴏᴍᴇ variations from conventional legal methods of citation have been made to accommodate the general reader, but Supreme Court cases have been cited in the usual manner. Thus, the historic decision ending racial segregation in public schools is identified as *Brown v. Board of Education,* 347 U.S. 483 (1954), which means that the text of this 1954 decision appears in Vol. 347 of the *United States Reports,* beginning on page 483. If a particular passage from the decision has been quoted — one appearing on page 486, for instance — it is cited as 347 U.S. 483, 486, which means that the text begins on page 483 but the passage quoted is on page 486. Citations of law-review articles also follow this system of page reference.

All references to the *Congressional Record* are to the bound volumes unless otherwise stated.

The following short-form citations have been used:

Kefauver Hearings Hearings on S. Res. 202 Before the Special Committee to Investigate Organized Crime in Interstate Commerce, U.S. Senate, 81st Congress, 2d Session, 82d Congress, 1st Session, Part 2 (1950) and 10 (1951).

Kenny MS "My First Forty Years in California Politics, 1922–1962," the unpublished autobiography of Robert W. Kenny, Judge, Superior Court of California. 399 pp.

La Follette Hearings *Violations of Free Speech and Rights of Labor,* Hearings on S. Res. 266 Before a Subcommittee of the Committee on Education and Labor, U.S. Senate, 76th Congress, 3d Session, Parts 70 and 75 *Supplementary Exhibits* (1940).

Public Papers *The Public Papers of Chief Justice Earl Warren,* ed. Henry M. Christman (rev. ed.; New York: Putnam, Capricorn Books, 1966).

Stone Irving Stone, *Earl Warren: A Great American Story* (New York: Prentice-Hall, 1948).

Stone Papers Collection of notes, memoranda, drafts and manuscripts relating to Irving Stone's campaign biography of Warren. Special Collections, Library of the University of California at Los Angeles.

Sweigert Material A 141-page document, "Earl Warren: Biography and Record," and other material on EW which were provided Irving Stone by William T. Sweigert, Warren's executive secretary in 1948.

Tolan Hearings Hearings on H. Res. 113 Before the Select Committee Investigating National Defense Migration, House of Representatives, 77th Congress, 2d Session, Part 29, San Francisco Hearings, Feb. 21 and 23, 1942, *Problems of Evacuation of Enemy Aliens and Others from Prohibited Military Zones* (1942).

Warren Hearings *Hearings Before the President's Commission on the Assassination of President Kennedy* (Washington: Government Printing Office, 1964). 26 vols.

Warren Report *Report of the President's Commission on the Assassination of President Kennedy* (Washington: Government Printing Office, 1964). 888 pp.

When no documentary source of a quotation is given, it is to be assumed that the remark was made during one of the many interviews conducted during the period 1964 to 1967 in Washington and along the Warren Trail in California — Los Angeles, Bakersfield, Berkeley, Oakland, San Francisco and Sacramento.

CHAPTER 1

1. *U.S. News & World Report*, July 1, 1963, p. 72.
2. Negro children: *Brown v. Board of Education*, 347 U.S. 483 (1954). Impecunious defendants: *Gideon v. Wainwright*, 372 U.S. 355 (1963). Naturalized citizens: *Schneider v. Rusk*, 377 U.S. 163 (1964). Legislative districts: *Baker v. Carr*, 369 U.S. 186 (1962), opened federal courts to reapportionment suits; *Gray v. Sanders*, 372 U.S. 368 (1963), struck down the county-unit system used in Georgia to give additional weight to rural voters; *Wesberry v. Sanders*, 376 U.S. 1 (1964), ordered reapportionment of Congressional districts on the "one-man, one-vote"

principle; *Reynolds v. Sims*, 377 U.S. 533 (1964), applied the same principle to both houses of bicameral state legislatures.

3. Wilson, *U.S. News & World Report*, July 1, 1963, p. 72. Tuck, *Congressional Record*, 88th Cong., 1st Sess., Vol. 109, Part 6 (May 2, 1963), p. 7730.

4. Drew Pearson and Robert S. Allen, *The Nine Old Men* (New York: Doubleday, Doran, 1936), p. 14.

5. In a dinner talk at the Harvard Law School Association of New York, Feb. 15, 1913. *Collected Legal Papers* (New York: Harcourt, Brace, 1921), p. 292.

6. French films: Among others, *Les Amants* (*The Lovers*) in *Jacobellis v. Ohio*, 378 U.S. 184 (1964).

   Contraceptives: *Griswold v. Connecticut*, 381 U.S. 479 (1965).

   Fanny Hill: The book was cleared in *A Book Named "John Cleland's Memoirs of a Woman of Pleasure" v. Attorney General of the Commonwealth of Massachusetts*, 383 U.S. 413 (1966). On the same day, however, the Court upheld the conviction of Ralph Ginzburg, who had mailed his publications from Middlesex, New Jersey, after being unable to make use of the facilities of Intercourse, Pennsylvania. "Where the purveyor's sole emphasis is on the sexually provocative aspects of his publications," a majority of the Court ruled, "that fact may be decisive in the determination of obscenity." *Ginzburg v. United States*, 383 U.S. 463, 470 (1966).

7. *FTC v. Colgate-Palmolive Co.*, 380 U.S. 374 (1965). The commercial in question purported to show that even sandpaper could be shaved after it had been moistened by a cream called "Rapid Shave." A mock-up had been used to simulate sandpaper.

8. *Quinn v. United States*, 349 U.S. 155, 161 (1955).

9. *Engel v. Vitale*, 370 U.S. 421 (1962).

10. *Los Angeles Times*, Nov. 14, 1966.

11. *Washington Post*, Oct. 5, 1963; *San Jose Mercury*, Sept. 27, 1963. Both can be found in the *Congressional Record*, 88th Cong., 1st Sess., Vol. 109, Part 15 (Oct. 21, 1963), pp. 19852–19853.

12. *San Francisco Chronicle* quoted in *Congressional Record*, 88th Cong., 2d Sess. (Mar. 30, 1966), p. A1831 (unbound issue); *Washington Post*, editorial, Mar. 19, 1966.

13. *The Federalist*, No. 78.

14. 5 U.S. (1 Cranch), 137 (1803).

15. McCarthy quote from *Collier's*, Aug. 3, 1956; his political heirs' quote from *Inside the John Birch Society* by Gene Grove (New York: Gold Medal Books, 1961), p. 113.

16. *National Review*, Dec. 30, 1961, p. 442.

17. "Foreword: 'Equal in Origin and Equal in Title to the Legislative and Executive Branches of the Government,'" 78 *Harvard Law Review* 143, 176 (1964).

18. *Washington Star*, Mar. 19, 1966.

19. Inquiry about fairness from "New Look at the Chief Justice" by Anthony Lewis, *New York Times Magazine*, Jan. 19, 1964, p. 64. Question put to southern attorney general from an interview with one of EW's former law clerks.

20. *Sacramento Bee*, Dec. 17, 1966.

21. Irving Stone, *Earl Warren: A Great American Story* (New York: Prentice-Hall, 1948), p. 15. Hereafter referred to as *Stone*.

22. The amount EW receives from the California retirement system has been variously given. This figure was supplied by his executive secretary to Rep. William S. Mailliard of California, a former member of his gubernatorial staff. Cf. *Congressional Record,* 89th Cong., 1st Sess., Vol. III, Part 4 (Mar. 17, 1965), p. 5277.

23. *Ibid.,* p. 5275.

24. *Ibid.,* p. 5283.

25. *Ibid.,* p. 5280.

26. *Ibid.,* p. 5278.

27. *U.S. News & World Report,* June 10, 1963, p. 14. Rep. Neal Smith of Iowa: "I see so many Cadillacs around Washington that I could not believe there is only one in any Department."

28. San Francisco *Chronicle,* July 11, 1954.

29. John P. Frank, *The Warren Court* (New York: Macmillan, 1964), p. 27.

30. The decision day change was announced Apr. 5, 1965. EW's first public statement that the century-old custom had been abandoned to enable the press to do a better job of reporting the Court's rulings was made in his seventy-fifth birthday interview. Cf. John MacKenzie, Washington *Post,* Mar. 19, 1966.

31. Address delivered at the annual meeting of the American Law Institute, May 18, 1966.

32. Cf. Washington *Post,* Mar. 19, 1966. The Oakland *Tribune,* Jan. 8, 1932, carried a news item about Warren's admission to practice before the U.S. Supreme Court. He was sponsored by Rep. Albert Carter. The actual date was Jan. 5, 1932. On Jan. 7 he argued his first case, *Central Pacific Railway Co. et al. v. Alameda County et al.,* 284 U.S. 463 (1932). He won.

33. "It was because he took high performance for granted," says a long-time member of Warren's staff. "But he knew what we were doing. At times he thought appropriate he thanked us all. At our Christmas parties, he gathered the staff about him and told how their faithful work and loyal support had made possible his success. In August of 1954, a group of us whom he had appointed to judgeships or other important positions gave a dinner for him and Mrs. Warren in Oakland. We gathered staff from his whole career. When the C.J. spoke, he paid a moving tribute to all of us, and said that if we hadn't worked so faithfully and effectively from the beginning of our associations with him, he would not have been in a situation where he would have been considered for the position of Chief Justice of the United States. He gave his friendship to everyone on the staff, from the messenger to his executive secretary."

34. *Inside U.S.A.* (New York: Harper, 1947), p. 18.

35. *An Autobiography of the Supreme Court,* ed. Alan F. Westin (New York: Macmillan, 1963), p. 228.

36. "Mr. Justice Douglas," 73 *Yale Law Journal* 917 (1964).

37. Los Angeles *Times,* June 30, 1963.

38. "Our Presidents: A Rating by 75 Historians," *New York Times Magazine,* July 29, 1962, p. 12.

39. Cf. Anthony Lewis, *New York Times Magazine,* Jan. 19, 1964, p. 64. ("It is a delicious irony that the appointment of Chief Justice Warren may go

down in history as the single most important act of Eisenhower's presidency.")

CHAPTER 2

1. From the Kern County High School yearbook, *The Oracle*, p. 44.
2. Various versions of this anecdote turn up in contemporary clippings. It is told here as EW related it in a Sunday morning talk on "Law and Civilization" at the Wilshire Boulevard Temple in Los Angeles, Jan. 9, 1966.
3. *Stone*, p. 5.
4. "*Var* is a very ancient place-name element, going back even to pre-Gallic times, occurring in the names of several French rivers, and from them being transferred to towns. In particular, there is a small stream called Varennes or Warrenne in Normandy, and in the eleventh century a castle on it bore the same name. One of William the Conqueror's liegemen held that castle, and was known as William de Warrenne. After the Conquest, he was created Earl of Surrey, and the name was anglicized as Warren. Not only did the original earl leave descendants, but also many of his retainers, servants and serfs may have taken the name. There are other origins for this name also. Warin was a common given name among the Normans, and this became a family name, as Waring and Warren. Moreover, a warren was a piece of land which was enclosed and preserved for the breeding of game. These humble origins probably account for many more Warrens than does the name of the Norman lord." George Stewart, *New York Times Magazine*, Apr. 20, 1952, p. 17.
5. There is considerable confusion as to the given name of EW's mother. He confirms the correctness of "Christine," and spells "Chrystal" with an "h," although it often appears simply as "Crystal" (cf. *Stone*, p. 6). The Warrens are very casual about dates, which has also led journalists into error. At the time of their wedding, Matt was twenty-two (he was born Dec. 12, 1864), and his bride nineteen (she was born Jan. 1, 1867).
6. EW's birthplace is given as 458 Turner St. on p. 7 of *Stone* and on p. 19 of Luther A. Huston's *Pathway to Judgment* (Philadelphia: Chilton, 1966), but the Los Angeles City Directory, 1891, contains the entry (p. 658): "Warren, M., res. 457 Turner." In the *Stone Papers*, handwritten notes of Stone's interview with EW give the address correctly as 457, but it appears as 458 in the material prepared by William T. Sweigert.
7. The late Dr. Rebecca Lee Dorsey, who came to Los Angeles in 1883 and delivered some five thousands babies, left an unpublished autobiography containing the following passage given to the author by Dr. Dorsey's great-nephew, Robert Kellard: "I just wrote the sex and address of the babies until 1891, when the law required birth certificates. One of the first babies I registered under this new law was Earl Warren, former Governor of the State of California and now Chief Justice of the United States Supreme Court. The Chief Justice was born March 19, 1891 on what was then called 'Dingy Turner Street.'"
   The official records show that EW's birth was recorded by Mrs. A. Mueller, who was one of the six midwives listed in the city directory that year. Her mistake in spelling the names of the parents was corrected by an affidavit filled out by EW and his sister July 13, 1951.

8. *Stone*, p. 7. EW continued the tradition. Only one of the Warren children — Nina Elizabeth — has a middle name.
9. George E. Mowry, *The California Progressives* (Chicago: Quadrangle, 1963), p. 38. The hardcover edition was published by University of California Press in 1951.
10. Ray Ginger, *The Bending Cross: A Biography of Eugene Victor Debs* (New Brunswick, N.J.: Rutgers University Press, 1949), p. 88.
11. *Ibid.*, p. 116.
12. *Ibid.*, p. 130.
13. *Stone*, p. 9. Also *Sweigert Material* in *Stone Papers*, and interviews with EW and his sister.
14. *Stone Papers.*
15. Bakersfield *Californian*, Sept. 6, 1958.
16. The young ladies were Hazel Beebee Grandy, Little Dorrit Smith and Nona White. From the class yearbook, *The Oracle*, p. 44.
17. *The Daily Californian*, Apr. 20, 1903.
18. Oct. 14, 1906. Wallace M. Morgan, *History of Kern County, California* (Los Angeles, Historic Record Co., 1914), p. 165. Also, interviews with EW contemporaries in Bakersfield.
19. Welcoming address, June 11, 1952.
20. New York *Times*, Jan. 20, 1954.
21. Details of EW's high school years have been drawn from interviews with him and his classmates. Also, Mrs. Glendon Rodgers, widow of the dean of student activities at Bakersfield High School, made available the unpublished manuscript of her husband's history of the school's beginnings, which indicates that the orchestra was formed in the fall of 1906 and on Oct. 5 played at the dedication of the new school building at the corner of 14th and F streets.

   The name of the school often appears as "Kern County Union High School." James Day, managing editor of the Bakersfield *Californian*, straightened out this point in a letter to the author, May 9, 1966: "Before 1916, the official name was Kern County High School. In 1916 state legislation changed the name to: the Kern County Union High School district, an action affecting other high schools in this state under revised administrative and economic setups. Now as this particular high school district extends beyond county boundaries the official name is: Kern County Joint Union High School district, though no one uses this official patois."
22. First part of the quote in *Stone*, p. 6. Latter in handwritten notes, *Stone Papers.*
23. On Jan. 1, 1908 (*Rodgers MS* — see n. 21 above).
24. Los Angeles *Times*, Apr. 25, 1947.
25. *The Oracle*, Vol. II, 1907–1908, p. 20.
26. For details regarding Bakersfield's colorful history the author is indebted to the Kern County Centennial Edition of the Bakersfield *Californian*. The Withington story appears in the Apr. 2, 1966, issue, as related by Lawrence Weill. Other details have been drawn from the prodigious memories of two EW high school classmates, Omar Cavins and Francis Vaughan.
27. EW's appearance in the farce was recalled in the Bakersfield *Californian*, Apr. 24, 1958, when its director, the late Harold F. Hughes, sent a copy of the program to Mrs. Bernice Harrell Chipman, president of the news-

paper, who was graduated from Kern County High School a year ahead of EW. Mr. Hughes's widow has given the author a photocopy of the program which shows EW's name leading the cast of characters. The audience was entertained between the acts with "Take a Little Ride with Me" and "Kiss, Kiss, Kiss."

28. May 28, 1908.
29. Miss Ashe has often told this story, and one version appears in the Centennial Edition of the Bakersfield *Californian*, Apr. 2, 1966. She says Earl Warren, Reg Stoner and Al Lake were expelled, but Al Lake was not in the cast. EW is certain it was Reg Stoner, Tim English and himself.
30. According to some of EW's contemporaries in Bakersfield, Miss Millie was never actually his teacher, but on Apr. 25, 1956, his former private secretary, Helen R. MacGregor, wrote to her: "Many times, he has told me about your influence in his life and your excellent teaching. A tender smile always came to his face when he spoke of you or dictated a letter." Cf. "Her Pupil Became Chief Justice Earl Warren" in the *CTA Journal* of the California Teachers Association, Jan., 1956, p. 11, and Alda West, "The Chief Justice Called Her Teacher," *Independent Woman*, Nov., 1955, p. 7.
31. Quoted from EW's address at a seminar on "California and the Challenge of Growth," University of California, Berkeley, Sept. 27, 1963. Reprinted by Sen. Kuchel in *Congressional Record*, 88th Cong., 1st Sess., Vol. 109, Pt. 15 (Oct. 21, 1963), pp. 19848–19850.
32. *Ibid.*
33. Los Angeles *Times*, Apr. 24, 1946.
34. *Stone*, p. 19.
35. For details on the Class of '12 the author is particularly indebted to Horace M. Albright, who made his personal file available and rounded it out with reminiscences during leisurely luncheons at the UCLA faculty club.
36. *Stone*, p. 22.
37. EW recalled his law school days in a CBS-TV interview, "See It Now," Los Angeles *Times*, Oct. 7, 1953. His J.D. thesis is on file in the University of California library, Berkeley.
38. From the inscription on the photograph President Johnson gave EW on his seventy-fifth birthday.

CHAPTER 3

1. *Federal Bar News*, May, 1966, p. 153.
2. *Stone*, p. 24.
3. *Ibid.*, p. 28.
4. San Francisco *Chronicle*, Aug. 17, 1943.
5. *Stone*, p. 30.
6. *Ibid.*, p. 32.
7. *Sweigert Material, Stone Papers.*
8. *Stone*, p. 35.
9. *Ibid.*, p. 39.
10. *Ibid.*, pp. 39–40.
11. Los Angeles *Times*, Apr. 7, 1948. EW: "I am shocked by the sad news. Alameda County and California have lost a faithful, able servant and I have lost a lifelong friend who first interested and encouraged me as a young man to enter and remain in public service."

12. Oakland *Tribune*, Apr. 11, 1943.
13. Al Stump, "They Live in the Limelight," *American Magazine*, June, 1953, p. 103.
14. *Stone*, p. 46. Also, some details have been drawn from a memorandum written by Mrs. Stone after she interviewed Mrs. Warren in 1948, in *Stone Papers.*
15. Oakland *Tribune*, Oct. 15, 1925.
16. Stump, "They Live in the Limelight," p. 103.
17. Cameron Shipp, "The Golden Girls," *Redbook*, Nov., 1950, p. 70.
18. Stump, "They Live in the Limelight," p. 101.
19. Sidney Shalett, "The Warrens: What a Family!" *Saturday Evening Post*, Feb. 3, 1951, p. 74.
20. *Stone*, p. 1; Anthony Lewis, *New York Times Magazine*, Jan. 19, 1964, p. 63.
21. Notes, *Stone Papers.*
22. Oakland *Tribune*, June 29, 1926.
23. Ronald H. Beattie, *A System of Criminal Judicial Statistics for California* (Berkeley: University of California Press, 1936), p. 84.
24. *Stone*, p. 56.
25. Oakland *Tribune*, Feb. 19, 1925.
26. *Ibid.*, Jan. 20, 1925.
27. *Ibid.*, Oct. 24, 1930.
28. *Stone*, p. 63.
29. Quoted in an Oakland *Tribune* editorial, Sept. 20, 1931.
30. Oakland *Tribune*, Dec. 22, 1943.
31. From a copy in the files of Judge Earl Warren, Jr.
32. Oakland *Tribune*, Sept. 15, 1931.
33. *Ibid.*
34. *Ibid.*, Apr. 5, 1938.
35. *Ibid.*
36. *Ibid.*, Feb. 19, 1925.
37. From a letter of Aug. 23, 1965, to William J. Hays of Redwood City, Calif.
38. This account of the murder of EW's father is drawn from interviews with Jahnsen and Powers, and with various newspaper reporters who covered the story, particularly James Day of the Bakersfield *Californian*. Also from the files of the *Californian*, Los Angeles *Times*, and Oakland *Tribune*.
39. Oakland *Tribune*, May 17, 1938.
40. Estimates vary greatly. This figure is from a memorandum, drawn from court records, in the files of the Sacramento *Bee*.

CHAPTER 4

1. *Kenny MS*, p. 83.
2. *Stone*, p. 82.
3. Judge Kenny's files, which are invaluable to any student of California politics, produced a copy of the text sent to registered voters.
4. Oakland *Tribune*, May 16, 1934.
5. 380 U.S. 609 (1965).
6. *Stone*, p. 50.
7. EW's formal statement: "The primary and greatest objective of government is to make life and property secure, and I am convinced that the

future of our democracy depends on the quality of our local and State governments and on whether or not we have an honest, fearless and uniform enforcement of the law.

"Great problems of law enforcement now challenge the attention of all public officers and citizens of this state, and thirteen years as District Attorney of Alameda County have not only acquainted me with these problems but have also given me the sincere desire to strive for their solution." Los Angeles *Times*, Feb. 18, 1938.

8. From a campaign mailing piece supplied by Rollin McNitt, former chairman of the Los Angeles County Central Democratic Committee.

9. *Ibid.*

10. *Stone*, p. 65.

11. Cf. Alpheus Thomas Mason, *Harlan Fiske Stone* (New York: Viking, 1956), pp. 388–392, and Arthur M. Schlesinger, Jr., *The Politics of Upheaval* (Boston: Houghton Mifflin, 1960), pp. 255–260. The cases are: *Norman v. Baltimore & Ohio Railroad Co.*, 294 U.S. 240 (1935); *United States v. Bankers Trust Co.*, 294 U.S. 240 (1935); *Nortz v. United States*, 294 U.S. 317 (1935); *Perry v. United States*, 294 U.S. 330 (1935).

12. EW, Los Angeles *Times*, Apr. 21, 1936: "The unpledged delegation movement was started in an effort to harmonize the party so that it would be in a position to exert its full strength in the November election. We were trying to avoid the very factional differences which now exist. The personnel of the unpledged delegation slate was selected with the deliberate purpose of giving representation to all sides and factions. Members of the slate were not asked whether they were for Landon, Borah or anyone else.

"We wanted a cross-section of California Republicanism and believe we obtained it. I head the ticket merely because under California law it is necessary that someone assume that position."

13. Los Angeles *Times*, July 23, 1936.

14. Oakland *Tribune*, May 28, 1936.

15. Los Angeles *Times*, Sept. 13, 1936.

16. Oakland *Tribune*, Oct. 20, 1937.

17. To a trainside audience in Sacramento, where he had been warmly welcomed in EW's absence by Lieut. Gov. Goodwin J. Knight. Kansas City *Star*, June 12, 1948.

18. In Fresno, Calif., reported in Los Angeles *Times*, Oct. 5, 1948.

19. Joseph P. Harris, *California Politics* (Palo Alto: Stanford University Press, 1961, 3rd ed.), pp. 67–72. Cf. also, Winston W. Crouch, "Direct Legislation Laboratory," *National Municipal Review*, Feb., 1951, pp. 81–87; and Alfred F. Smith, "Can We Afford the Initiative?" *National Municipal Review*, Oct., 1949, pp. 437–442.

20. Bernadette Doyle ran as a nonpartisan for the office of State Superintendent of Public Instruction. *Time*, June 19, 1950, p. 21. Cf. Harris, *California Politics*, pp. 4, 18–19, 37–38. Also, Dean E. McHenry, "The Pattern of California Politics," *The Western Political Quarterly*, Mar. 1948, pp. 44–53, and "Invitation to the Masquerade," *National Municipal Review*, May, 1950, pp. 228–232.

21. *Sweigert Material, Stone Papers.*

22. Oakland *Tribune*, Oct. 21, 1942.

23. George E. Mowry, "The California Progressive and His Rationale: A Study in Middle Class Politics," *The Mississippi Valley Historical Review*, Sept., 1949, p. 250.
24. *Kenny MS*, p. 83.
25. Robert Glass Cleland, *From Wilderness to Empire: A History of California*, a combined and revised edition of *From Wilderness to Empire* (1542–1900) and *California in Our Time* (1900–1940), edited and brought down to date by Glenn S. Dumke (New York: Knopf, 1959), pp. 351–354.
26. Oct. 5, 1934.
27. Cleland, *From Wilderness to Empire*, p. 352.
28. EW quote, Los Angeles *Times*, Oct. 6, 1934; account of his selection, Oakland *Tribune*, Sept. 30, 1934.
29. Los Angeles *Times* editorial, Oct. 5, 1934.
30. Los Angeles *Times*, Oct. 6, 1934.
31. *Radicalism Exposed*, published by the Peace Officers of the State of California, 18 pp., 1934, p. 9.
32. Radio talk, Oct. 21, 1934; quoted next day in Sacramento *Bee* and Oakland *Tribune*.

CHAPTER 5

1. *La Follette Hearings*, Part 75 (1940), p. 27618.
2. *Kenny MS*, p. 113. Grant Cooper, a well-known Los Angeles attorney, was also present at the luncheon.
3. Kenny files. Also, Los Angeles *Times*, July 24, 1938.
4. Carey McWilliams, *California: The Great Exception* (New York: A. A. Wyn, 1949), p. 156. Also, same author's *Factories in the Field* (Boston: Little, Brown, 1939), pp. 231-263.
5. *La Follette Hearings*, Part 75 (1940), p. 27606.
6. *Ibid.*, p. 27640.
7. McWilliams, *California*, p. 162; *Factories in the Field*, p. 231.
8. *La Follette Hearings*, Part 75 (1940), p. 27632. Cf. also S. Rept. 398, 78th Cong., 1st Sess., Part 2 (1943), p. 1123, for summary.
9. McWilliams, *California*, p. 162.
10. S. Res. 226, 74th Cong., June 6, 1936, quoted in S. Rept. 1150, 77th Cong., 2d Sess., Part 1 (1942), p. 1n.
11. Length of hearings, S. Rept. 1150, p. 89; quote *ibid.*, p. 59.
12. *Ibid.*, p. 59.
13. *Ibid.*, Part 75 (1940), p. 27618.
14. Letter, Nov. 9, 1938. Reply in *La Follette Hearings*, Part 70 (1940), p. 25717.
15. *Ibid.*
16. *Ibid.*, p. 25719.
17. *Ibid.*
18. *Ibid.*, p. 25720.
19. *Ibid.*, pp. 25721–25722.
20. *Ibid.*, p. 25722.
21. *Ibid.*, pp. 25724–25725.
22. *Carlson v. California*, 310 U.S. 106, 113 (1940).
23. No official record was made of the dissent, and Justice McReynolds spoke so rapidly that not all of his words were caught by newspapermen. This

sentence is a reconstruction based on the report in the New York *Times*, Feb. 19, 1935; "Here he spoke of the Constitution, adding that it did not seem 'too much to say that it is gone.'"
24. *Home Building & Loan Assn. v. Blaisdell*, 290 U.S. 398, 426 (1934).
25. *Nebbia v. New York*, 291 U.S. 502 (1934). Dissent, *Tyson & Brother v. Banton*, 273 U.S. 418, 452 (1927).
26. *Panama Refining Co. v. Ryan*, 293 U.S. 388 (1935).
27. *Railroad Retirement Board v. Alton Railroad Co.*, 295 U.S. 330 (1935).
28. *Schechter Poultry Corp. v. United States*, 295 U.S. 495 (1935). Cf. Frank Freidel, "The Sick Chicken Case," in *Quarrels That Have Shaped the Constitution*, ed. John A. Garraty (New York: Harper & Row, 1964), pp. 191–209.
29. 295 U.S. 495, 543 (1935).
30. Press conference, May 31, 1935. From the transcript on file at the Franklin D. Roosevelt Library, Hyde Park (5:309–337). The "horse-and-buggy" phrase refers to a nineteenth-century case limiting the application of interstate commerce to goods in transit, *United States v. Knight*, 156 U.S. 1 (1895).
31. *Morehead v. New York ex rel. Tipaldo*, 298 U.S. 587 (1936); *West Coast Hotel v. Parrish*, 300 U.S. 379 (1937).
32. The cases were argued Feb. 10 and 11, 1937, and decided Apr. 2. *NLRB v. Jones & Laughlin Steel Corp.*, 301 U.S. 1; *NLRB v. Fruehauf Trailer Co.*, 301 U.S. 49; *NLRB v. Friedman–Harry Marks Clothing Co.*, 301 U.S. 58; *Associated Press v. NLRB*, 301 U.S. 103; *Washington, Virginia & Maryland Coach Co. v. NLRB*, 301 U.S. 142.
33. *La Follette Hearings*, Report No. 1150, Part 1 (1942), pp. 61–62.
34. *Ibid.*, p. 29.
35. Robert E. Burke, *Olson's New Deal for California* (Berkeley: University of California Press, 1953), pp. 211–212.
36. June 28, 1940.
37. Los Angeles *Times*, Oct. 25, 1938; Oakland *Tribune*, Feb. 26, 1936.
38. July 23, 1940.
39. Oakland *Tribune*, June 16, 1940.
40. June 28, 1940, editorial.
41. *Ibid.*, news story.
42. *NAACP v. Alabama*, 357 U.S. 449 (1958).
43. Los Angeles *Times*, June 14, 1940.
44. *Ibid.*
45. Oakland *Tribune*, July 23, 1940.
46. *Ibid.*
47. Downey, Stephen W., "Stephen W. Downey: California Water and Power Attorney," typed transcript of a tape-recorded interview conducted by Willa K. Baum, University of California General Library Regional Cultural History Project (Berkeley, 1957), pp. 235–236. In Bancroft Library.
48. Carter, Jesse W., "California Supreme Court Justice Jesse W. Carter," typed transcript of a tape-recorded interview conducted by Corinne L. Gilb, University of California General Library Regional Cultural History Project (Berkeley, 1959), p. 172. In Bancroft Library.
49. Cf. author's "Mr. Chief Justice Traynor," in *West*, the Los Angeles *Times* Sunday magazine, Dec. 11, 1966, pp. 28–32.

50. "Chief Justice Traynor and the Judicial Process," 53 *California Law Review* 11, 24 (1965).
51. *The New Republic*, Oct. 18, 1943, p. 516.
52. Cf. Olson Papers, letters of Feb. 24 and 27, 1940, in Bancroft Library.

CHAPTER 6

1. Los Angeles *Times*, Aug. 4, 1939.
2. From the files of the Los Angeles *Times*, which declared editorially, Jan. 7, 1939: "About the only bright spot in the whole affair is the determined effort of Attorney General Warren to get to the bottom of it, regardless of politics."
3. *Stone*, p. 97.
4. Los Angeles *Times*, June 20, 1939.
5. *Ibid.*, June 27, 1939.
6. *Ibid.*, June 24, 1939.
7. *Ibid.*, July 28, 1939.
8. *Ibid.*
9. *Ibid.*
10. *Ibid.*, July 29, 1939.
11. *Ibid.*
12. *Ibid.*
13. "Homespun Titan of the Law," *True* magazine, June, 1961, p. 24.
14. *Ibid.*
15. *Ibid.*
16. Los Angeles *Times*, Aug. 4, 1939.
17. *Ibid.*, Aug. 5, 1939.
18. *Ibid.*, Aug. 6, 1939.
19. *True* magazine, *supra*, p. 26.
20. Los Angeles *Times*, Aug. 11, 1939.
21. From Helen MacGregor's files.
22. 283 U.S. 473.
23. *Ibid.*, at 476.
24. Los Angeles *Times*, Nov. 30, 1939. Cf. also *People v. Stralla*, 14 Cal. 2d 617, 632, 96 P.2d 941,948 (1939).
25. Both letters from Helen MacGregor's files.
26. Los Angeles *Times*, Nov. 30, 1939.
27. *Ibid.* Also interview with Jahnsen.
28. Letter in Harry S. Truman Library, official file 1090.
29. Los Angeles *Times*, Aug. 1, 1955.

CHAPTER 7

1. Robert E. Burke, *Olson's New Deal for California* (Berkeley: University of California Press, 1953), p. 212.
2. *People v. King*, 30 Cal. App. 2d 185 (1938).
3. *Stone*, p. 86.
4. Los Angeles *Times*, Nov. 15, 1936. The figure of $7,000,000 a day is cited in the *Times*, Nov. 14.
5. *The Ship Murder: The Story of a Frameup*, published by the King-Ramsay-Conner Defense Committee, San Francisco, n.d., 23 pp.

6. *Ibid.*, p. 9.
7. 384 U.S. 436, 451 (1966).
8. *People v. King*, 30 Cal. App. 2d 185, 190 ff. (1938).
9. *The Ship Murder*, p. 11. Cf. also Carey McWilliams, "Warren of California," *The New Republic*, Oct. 18, 1943, pp. 515–516.
10. Oakland *Tribune*, Nov. 18, 1936.
11. *Ibid.*, Dec. 5, 1936.
12. *The Ship Murder*, p. 23.
13. *People v. King*, 30 Cal. App. 2d 185, 207–208 (1938).
14. Oakland *Tribune*, Oct. 5, 1953.
15. San Francisco *Chronicle*, Oct. 16, 1940.
16. Sacramento *Bee*, Oct. 16, 1940.
17. Los Angeles *Times*, Oct. 19, 1940.
18. *Ibid.*
19. *Ibid.*, Dec. 4, 1941.
20. Burke. *Olson's New Deal for California*, p. 157.
21. Los Angeles *Times*, Dec. 4, 1941.
22. *Ibid.*
23. Ellis Patterson, "Reflections of a California Liberal," recorded on tape in 1962, transcribed in 1965 as part of the oral history program at UCLA. In Special Collections, University Library, p. 76.
24. Los Angeles *Times*, Dec. 4, 1941.
25. Nov. 28, 1941.
26. Los Angeles *Times*, Nov. 28, 1941.
27. Burke, *Olson's New Deal for California*, p. 55.
28. *Ibid.*, p. 54.

CHAPTER 8

1. *Kenny MS*, p. 173.
2. *Stone*, p. 105; Robert E. Burke, *Olson's New Deal for California* (Berkeley: University of California Press, 1953), pp. 194–195. Cf. also Los Angeles *Times*, Aug. 15 and 23, 1940.
3. Los Angeles *Times*, Jan. 17, 1941.
4. *Ibid.*, June 11, 1941.
5. *Ibid.*, June 4, 1941.
6. *Ibid.*, June 11, 1941.
7. *Ibid.*, June 4, 1941.
8. *Ibid.*, March 13, 1941; Burke, *Olson's New Deal for California*, p. 157; *Stone*, p. 108.
9. Burke, *Olson's New Deal for California*, p. 157; *Stone*, p. 108.
10. Pp. 196–197.
11. Los Angeles *Times*, Apr. 10, 1942.
12. Oakland *Tribune*, Apr. 11, 1942.
13. Burke, *Olson's New Deal for California*, p. 216.
14. Los Angeles *Times*, Apr. 10, 1942.
15. Burke, *Olson's New Deal for California*, p. 212.
16. *Ibid.*, p. 220.
17. Richard Foote Pederson, "Governor Earl Warren, As Seen Through His Speeches," May, 1947, p. 7. Unpublished master's thesis. Stanford University Library.

18. Burke, *Olson's New Deal for California*, p. 226.
19. Los Angeles *Times*, Oct. 12, 1942.
20. 310 U.S. 586 (1940).
21. 316 U.S. 584 (1942). Cf. Alpheus Thomas Mason, *Harlan Fiske Stone* (New York: Viking, 1956), pp. 525–534, 598–599.
22. *Barnette v. West Virginia State Board of Education*, 47 F. Supp. 251, 252–253 (S.D. W. Va. 1942).
23. 319 U.S. 624 (1943).
24. The official totals of the Aug. 25th primary, as released by the secretary of state, were reported in the Los Angeles *Times*, Sept. 30, 1942.
25. Aug. 27, 1942.
26. Frank J. Taylor, "Man with a New Broom," *Saturday Evening Post*, Aug. 7, 1943, p. 90.
27. George Creel, *Rebel at Large: Recollections of Fifty Crowded Years* (New York: Putnam's, 1947), p. 326.
28. Los Angeles *Times*, Nov. 3, 1942.
29. Ellis Patterson, "Reflections of a California Liberal," p. 87 (see Ch. 7, n. 23).
30. *Kenny MS*, p. 166.
31. *Ibid.*, p. 173.
32. John Gunther, *Inside U.S.A.* (New York: Harper, 1947), p. 21.
33. Pederson, "Governor Earl Warren, As Seen Through His Speeches," p. 160.
34. Ernest Havemann, "Warren & His Court: Ten Crucial Years Have Made Them the Storm Center of Justice," *Life*, May 28, 1964, p. 117.
35. *Newsweek*, May 11, 1964. Also, a brief conversation with Salinger in Los Angeles at the Governors' Conference, 1966.
36. The author was present at this confrontation.
37. Letter from Helen MacGregor to author, Nov. 19, 1966.

CHAPTER 9

1. Los Angeles *Times*, Nov. 8, 1965.
2. Morton Grodzins, *Americans Betrayed: Politics and the Japanese Evacuation* (Chicago: University of Chicago Press, 1949), p. 94. (An Associated Press release, Jan. 30, 1942.)
3. *Ibid.* Cf. also EW's statement in *Tolan Hearings*: "Unfortunately, however, many of our people and some of our authorities and, I am afraid, many of our people in other parts of the country are of the opinion that because we have had no sabotage and no fifth column activities in this State since the beginning of the war, that means that none have been planned for us. But I take the view that that is the most ominous sign in our whole situation. It convinces me more than perhaps any other factor that the sabotage that we are to get, the fifth column activities that we are to get, are timed just like Pearl Harbor was timed and just like the invasion of France, and of Denmark, and of Norway, and all of those other countries" (pp. 11011–11012).
4. Lippmann, Feb. 12; Pegler, Feb. 16. Executive Order No. 9066, issued Feb. 19, 1942 (7 *Fed. Reg.* 1407). Bill was passed by Congress Mar. 19, signed Mar. 21 (56 Stat. 173).
5. Grodzins, *Americans Betrayed*, p. 1.
6. *Korematsu v. United States*, 323 U.S. 214 (1944).

7. Grodzins, *Americans Betrayed,* p. 127.
8. EW to Assemblyman Thomas A. Maloney, Feb. 7, 1942, Attorney General opinion NS4083, Feb. 7, 1942.
9. *Tolan Hearings,* Part 29, p. 11015.
10. *Ibid.*
11. *Ibid.,* pp. 10973, 11011.
12. *Ibid.,* pp. 11018, 11010.
13. *Final Report, Japanese Evacuation from the West Coast* (Washington: Government Printing Office, 1942), p. 34.
14. 263 U.S. 225, 229 (1923).
15. "The People Nobody Wants," May 9, 1942, p. 66. Attorney General Webb, in *Frick v. Webb,* had said the intent of the Alien Land Law was "to prevent ruinous competition by the Oriental farmer against the American farmer." 263 U.S. 326, 330 (1923). Cf. Dudley O. McGovney, "The Anti-Japanese Land Laws of California and Ten Other States," and Edwin E. Ferguson, "The California Alien Land Law and the Fourteenth Amendment," 35 *California Law Review* 7 ff., 61 ff. (1947).
16. Jan. 22, 1907. *Rodgers MS* (see Ch. 2, n. 21).
17. Before a House Naval Affairs subcommittee, Apr. 13, 1943. Quoted by Carey McWilliams in *Prejudice* (Boston: Little, Brown, 1945), p. 116.
18. June 25, 1945, p. 868.
19. *Proceedings of the Governors' Conference,* 1943 (Chicago, 1943), p. 10.
20. The assemblyman was Chester F. Gannon, Sacramento, who went on to add: "With the Japanese permitted to return, imperial Japan can carry out plans to smuggle Japs in by submarines from Tokyo to mingle with American Japanese permitted to return to the West Coast." *Los Angeles Times,* Dec. 19, 1944. Bowron quote, *ibid.*
21. *Ibid.*
22. *Ibid.*
23. 320 U.S. 81 (1943).
24. *Ibid.,* at 109. For argument, cf. Alpheus Thomas Mason, *Harlan Fiske Stone* (New York: Viking, 1956), p. 674.
25. *Hirabayashi,* at 111.
26. *Korematsu v. United States,* 323 U.S. 214, 233 (1944).
27. *Ibid.,* at 225.
28. *Ibid.,* at 219.
29. Eugene V. Rostow, *The Sovereign Prerogative: The Supreme Court and the Quest for Law* (paperbound; New Haven: Yale University Press, 1962), p. 261.
30. In a concurring opinion, *Ex parte Endo,* 323 U.S. 283, 307 (1944).
31. *Los Angeles Times,* Dec. 18, 1944.
32. *Ibid.*
33. *Ibid.,* Dec. 19, 1944.
34. *Ibid.*
35. *Ibid.,* Dec. 20, 1944.
36. *Proceedings of the Governors' Conference,* 1943, p. 9.
37. Grodzins, *Americans Betrayed,* p. 244.
38. San Diego (Calif.) *Union,* July 10, 1966.
39. *Los Angeles Times,* Nov. 8, 1965.
40. *Ibid.*

CHAPTER 10

1. P. 18.
2. Los Angeles *Times,* Jan. 9, 1943. Also interviews with Oscar Jahnsen, Helen R. MacGregor.
3. Los Angeles *Times,* Jan. 10, 1943.
4. *Ibid.,* Jan. 11, 1943.
5. *Ibid.,* Oct. 29, 1942.
6. Lawrence Arnstein, "Community Service in California Public Health and Social Welfare," typed transcript of a tape-recorded interview conducted by Edna T. Daniel, University of California General Library Regional Cultural History Project (Berkeley, 1964), pp. 160–161. In Bancroft Library.
7. *Stone,* pp. 121–122.
8. Robert Coughlan, "California's Warren & Family," *Life,* Apr. 24, 1944, p. 110. Purcell's appointment was reported in the Los Angeles *Times,* Dec. 17, 1942.
9. Mar. 7, 1943.
10. Oct. 18, 1943, p. 514. News of McWilliams's firing in Los Angeles *Times,* Jan. 6, 1943.
11. *Kenny MS,* pp. 184–186.
12. *Stone,* p. 141.
13. *Sweigert Material, Stone Papers.*
14. San Francisco *Call-Bulletin,* Aug. 17, 1943.
15. *Assembly Journal,* Jan. 4, 1943, p. 22.
16. *Ibid.,* p. 21.
17. Apr. 9, 1943. Miss Coontz fell into a common error, referring to Virginia as "Ginnie," a nickname the family never adopted. For a time she was called "Ia."
18. Farnsworth Crowder, "The Governor's Never Too Busy!" *Better Homes & Gardens,* Aug., 1947, p. 114.
19. The incident appears in various contemporary feature articles about the Warren family. This is Robert Warren's account of it in an interview in the fall of 1966.
20. Al Stump, "They Live in the Limelight," *American Magazine,* June, 1953, p. 101.
21. Oakland *Tribune,* Jan. 2, 1930.
22. *Ibid.,* Nov. 28, 1954.
23. *Ibid.,* Aug. 2, 1957.
24. *Ibid.,* Jan. 16, 1962.
25. *Ibid.,* July 26, 1962.
26. Sacramento *Bee,* Dec. 17, 1966.
27. Sidney Shalett, "The Warrens: What a Family!" *Saturday Evening Post,* Feb. 3, 1951, p. 74.
28. *Assembly Journal,* Jan. 4, 1943, p. 21.
29. Los Angeles *Times,* May 8, 1943.
30. *Ibid.,* Dec. 21, 1944.
31. Frank J. Taylor, "Man with a New Broom," *Saturday Evening Post,* Aug. 7, 1943, p. 23; Los Angeles *Times,* May 9, 1943.
32. *Stone,* p. 139.

33. "Youth Authority Services in California" by Karl Holton, *State Government*, Apr., 1946, p. 266 ff.; "The Youth Authority Way" by Anne Roller Issler, *The Survey*, May, 1951, p. 206 ff.
34. Taylor, "Man with a New Broom," p. 94.
35. *Assembly Journal*, Jan. 4, 1943, p. 23.
36. Address, "California's Sentencing and Correctional Methods," American Bar Association, Oct. 29, 1946, in *Public Papers*, p. 24.
37. Address, National Parole Conference, Washington, D.C., Apr. 18, 1939. Quoted in Pederson thesis (see Ch. 8, n. 17).
38. *Assembly Journal*, Jan. 4, 1943, p. 23.
39. *Public Papers*, pp. 22–23.
40. Robert A. Walker and Floyd A. Cave, *How California Is Governed* (New York: Dryden, 1953), p. 60.
41. Address, Annual Convention of Peace Officers, Oct. 6, 1939; quoted in Pederson thesis (see Ch. 8, n. 17).
42. Taylor, "Man with a New Broom," p. 90.
43. National Parole Conference address. In Pederson, p. 136.
44. Robert Glass Cleland, *From Wilderness to Empire* (New York: Knopf, 1959), p. 358.
45. Quoted in *Assembly Journal*, Mar. 22, 1943, p. 1121.
46. Los Angeles *Times*, June 22, 1942.
47. Taylor, "Man with a New Broom," p. 92.
48. Los Angeles *Times*, May 9, 1943.
49. *The New Republic*, Oct. 18, 1943, p. 517.
50. Los Angeles *Times*, Feb. 20, 1943.
51. *Time*, Jan. 31, 1944, p. 22.
52. *Ibid.*, p. 20.
53. Speech delivered June 26, 1944, reprinted in *Vital Speeches of the Day*, July 15, 1944, pp. 588–592.
54. Chester G. Hanson, Los Angeles *Times*, June 26, 1944.
55. Kyle Palmer, Los Angeles *Times*, June 28, 1944.
56. June 27, 1944.
57. Los Angeles *Times*, Dec. 30, 1944.
58. *Assembly Journal*, Jan. 8, 1945, pp. 18–20.
59. *Sweigert Material, Stone Papers.*
60. For opposite view, cf. Carey McWilliams, "Government by Whitaker & Baxter," *The Nation*, Apr. 14, 1951, p. 346.
61. Los Angeles *Times*, Feb. 20, 1945.
62. *Ibid.*, Mar. 25, 1945.
63. Richard Harris, *A Sacred Trust* (New York: New American Library, 1966), p. 34.
64. Harry S. Truman, *Memoirs*, (New York: Doubleday, 1956), Vol. I, p. 485; Vol. II, pp. 17–23, 29.
65. Los Angeles *Times*, May 21, 1947.
66. *Sweigert Material, Stone Papers.*
67. Los Angeles *Times*, May 14, 1949.
68. George E. Mowry, *The California Progressives* (Chicago: Quadrangle, 1963), p. 12.
69. *Ibid.*, p. 63.
70. Aug. 13 and 20, 1949. Quote, Aug. 20, p. 12.
71. Aug. 13, p. 13.

72. Los Angeles *Times*, Mar. 30, 1947.
73. *Ibid.*, Jan. 14, 1947.
74. *Ibid.*, June 3, 1947.
75. *Ibid.*, Mar. 20, 1947.

CHAPTER 11

1. Kansas City *Times*, Nov. 4, 1948.
2. Los Angeles *Times*, Feb. 7, 1945.
3. Farnsworth Crowder, "The Governor's Never Too Busy!" *Better Homes & Gardens*, Aug., 1947. EW quote taken from American Legion address, text printed in full in San Francisco *Call-Bulletin*, Aug. 17, 1943. It should read: "the dreams of every good man and woman," and ends: ". . . taught by a good mother the virtues of mankind as she might choose to interpret them from the Good Book and to feel the influence of those virtues in their daily lives and in their government."
4. *Fortnight*, Feb. 27, 1948, p. 15.
5. John Gunther, *Inside U.S.A.* (New York: Harper, 1947), pp. 20–21. In the revised edition (1951), Gunther added the word "liberalism" (p. 42).
6. *Ibid.*, p. 21.
7. Richard Blake Harvey, "The Political Approach of Earl Warren, Governor of California." Unpublished Ph.D. dissertation. Library of University of California at Los Angeles.
8. *Time*, Mar. 18, 1946, p. 22.
9. *Kenny MS*, p. 268.
10. Gunther, *Inside U.S.A.*, p. 22.
11. *Kenny MS*, p. 263.
12. *Ibid.*, p. 264.
13. Los Angeles *Times*, Apr. 13, 1946.
14. *Ibid.*, May 23, 1946.
15. Oakland *Tribune*, May 2, 1946.
16. *Sweigert Material, Stone Papers*.
17. "Building for the Future in the West," *State Government*, Jan., 1946, p. 5.
18. Los Angeles *Times*, June 2, 1946.
19. *Ibid.*
20. San Francisco *Call-Bulletin*, June 5, 1946.
21. Los Angeles *Times*, July 20, 1946.
22. From a text supplied by Robert B. Powers, retired police chief of Bakersfield, a friend and former associate of Judge Kenny.
23. *Newsweek*, Sept. 24, 1947, p. 23.
24. Los Angeles *Times*, Nov. 14, 1947.
25. *Ibid.*, Jan. 10, 1948.
26. Copy of EW's telegram in *Stone Papers*. Punctuation has been altered slightly.
27. *Time*, June 21, 1948, p. 23.
28. June 16, 1948.
29. From two articles with EW byline, San Francisco *Examiner*, Oct. 15 and 22, 1944.
30. Los Angeles *Times*, June 19 and 21, 1948.
31. *Ibid.*, June 24, 1948.

32. *Ibid.*, June 25, 1948.
33. *Ibid.*
34. EW said it was 11:30 A.M. when he made his decision. Los Angeles *Times*, June 26, 1948.
35. Kansas City *Times*, June 26, 1948.
36. Los Angeles *Times*, June 26, 1948.
37. *Ibid.*
38. Kansas City *Times*, June 26, 1948.
39. Kansas City *Star*, June 28, 1948.
40. Los Angeles *Times*, June 26, 1948.
41. *Newsweek*, July 12, 1948, p. 22.
42. Kansas City *Star*, June 12, 1948.
43. From interviews, press reports and Miss MacGregor's files, which contain, among other things, the daily travel notes.
44. Oct. 18, 1948, p. 31.
45. *Time*, Sept. 27, 1948, p. 20.
46. *Ibid.*
47. Sept. 21, 1948.
48. Sept. 22, 1948.
49. From a letter in Miss MacGregor's files.
50. Los Angeles *Times*, Nov. 1, 1948.
51. *Ibid.*, Nov. 2, 1948.
52. *Ibid.*, Nov. 3, 1948.
53. *Ibid.*
54. Cabell Phillips, *The Truman Presidency: The History of a Triumphant Succession* (New York: Macmillan, 1966), p. 246.
55. Kansas City *Times*, Nov. 4, 1948.
56. Los Angeles *Times*, Nov. 5, 1948.

CHAPTER 12

1. *Frontier*, Nov., 1953, p. 8.
2. Los Angeles *Times*, Sept. 17, 1949.
3. *Ibid.* EW, in reply: "This is not an election year. There is too much to be done as governor for me to be concerned about candidates. But candidacies or no candidacies, I don't intend to become a walkie-talkie. I'll just keep on working every day on California's problems of growth and congestion." *Ibid.*, Sept. 21, 1949.
4. Theodore H. White, "The Gentlemen from California," *Collier's*, Feb. 3, 1956, p. 40.
5. Los Angeles *Times*, Dec. 25, 1949.
6. *Ibid.*, Apr. 23, 1950.
7. December, 1966, p. 6.
8. Los Angeles *Times*, Nov. 17, 1949.
9. *Ibid.*, Aug. 31, 1950.
10. *Ibid.*, May 11, 1950.
11. *Ibid.*, May 28, 1950.
12. *Ibid.*, Nov. 4, 1950.
13. *Ibid.*
14. *Ibid.*, Sept. 13, 1950.

15. Sidney Shalett, "The Warrens: What a Family!" *Saturday Evening Post,* Feb. 3, 1951, p. 18.
16. *Ibid.,* p. 74.
17. *Ibid.,* pp. 18-19.
18. Los Angeles *Times,* Dec. 24, 1950.
19. *Kefauver Hearings,* Part 10 (1951), pp. 105–106. The committee met Nov. 16, 1950.
20. (Englewood Cliffs, N.J.: Prentice-Hall, 1960), p. 139.
21. Los Angeles *Times,* June 26, 1947.
22. *Ibid.,* June 29, 1947.
23. *Ibid.,* Mar. 1, 1951.
24. *Kefauver Hearings,* Part 10 (1951), p. 438.
25. "The long-simmering feud between Governor Earl Warren and Attorney General Fred N. Howser, both Republicans, has recently developed into the noisiest political brawl that California has seen in many a day. On the surface the issue is whether Howser has been an efficient and vigilant law enforcement official, but there is more to the feud than meets the eye.

"Some years ago Howser was appointed District Attorney of Los Angeles under circumstances that still excite amazement. His appointment was slipped through the Board of Supervisors before the public knew what had happened and almost before his predecessor's funeral rites had been performed. Howser was scarcely known at the time outside the Long Beach assembly district that he represented in the state legislature. The rumor still persists that Artie Samish, the king of the lobby in Sacramento, was largely responsible for this extraordinary appointment. In the 1946 campaign Governor Warren mentioned Howser, who had won the Republican nomination for Attorney General, as infrequently as possible and always with calculated coolness. In fact, Warren began to draw up plans for a Commission on Organized Crime, which the legislature approved in 1947, almost from the moment that he knew Howser would be the Republican nominee." Carey McWilliams, "Machines, Political and Slot," *The Nation,* May 28, 1949, p. 608.
26. *Kefauver Hearings,* Part 10 (1951), p. 107.
27. *Senate Journal,* Jan. 5, 1953, p. 41.
28. He appeared Aug. 16, 1950. His testimony: *Kefauver Hearings,* Part 2 (1950), pp. 215–241.
29. *Ibid.,* p. 218.
30. *Ibid.,* p. 219.
31. *Ibid.,* pp. 222–223.
32. *Ibid.,* pp. 229–230.
33. A favorite theme since his days in Alameda County. This particular quote from Los Angeles *Times,* Mar. 7, 1951.
34. *Kefauver Hearings,* Part 2 (1950), p. 227.
35. Los Angeles *Times,* Oct. 13, 1948.
36. *Ibid.,* Nov. 11, 1948.
37. *Ibid.,* Nov. 26, 1948.
38. Carey McWilliams, "Machines, Political and Slot," p. 609.
39. *Kefauver Hearings,* Part 2 (1950), p. 235.
40. *Ibid.,* p. 232.
41. Los Angeles *Times,* Mar. 12, 1949.
42. *Kefauver Hearings,* Part 10 (1951), p. 1189.

38. *Missouri ex rel. Gaines v. Canada,* 305 U.S. 337 (1938).
39. *Sipuel v. Oklahoma,* 332 U.S. 631 (1948).
40. 275 U.S. 78.
41. *Sweatt v. Painter,* 339 U.S. 629, 634 (1950).
42. Alfred H. Kelly, "The School Desegregation Case," in *Quarrels That Have Shaped the Constitution,* ed. John A. Garraty, pp. 254–255.
43. *Ibid.,* p. 254.
44. Robert Pearman in the Kansas City *Star,* May 17, 1964. Also background information in the *Star* files.
45. *Ibid.*
46. Quoted in *Brown v. Board of Education,* 347 U.S. 483, 494 (1954).
47. Kansas City *Star,* May 17, 1964.
48. *Ibid.*
49. Kansas City *Times,* Dec. 10, 1952.
50. *U.S. News & World Report,* Feb. 5, 1962, p. 86.
51. *Ibid.,* p. 87.
52. *Ibid.,* p. 88.
53. 347 U.S. 483 (1954).
54. *Ibid.,* at 492–493.
55. 339 U.S. 637 (1950).
56. 347 U.S. 483, 494, 495 (1954).
57. *Congressional Record,* 83d Cong., 2d Sess., Vol. 100, Part 5 (May 18, 1954), pp. 6750, 6777. Georgia attorney general quote, New York *Times,* May 24, 1954.
58. New York *Times,* May 18, 1954.
59. McCloskey, *The American Supreme Court,* p. 216.
60. *Brown v. Board of Education,* 349 U.S. 294, 301 (1955).
61. Sept. 3, 1957. *Public Papers* (1957), p. 640.
62. *Plessy v. Ferguson,* 163 U.S. 537, 551.
63. *Public Papers* (1956), pp. 758–759.
64. 40 *American Bar Association Journal* 956 (1954).
65. *Hamilton v. Alabama,* 376 U.S. 650 (1964).
66. *Johnson v. Virginia,* 373 U.S. 61 (1963).

Chapter 15

1. Oakland *Tribune,* Feb. 19, 1925.
2. *Gideon v. Wainwright,* 372 U.S. 335 (1963). Cf. Anthony Lewis, *Gideon's Trumpet* (New York: Random House, 1964).
3. 40 *American Bar Association Journal* 955, 956 (1954).
4. 316 U.S. 455.
5. 372 U.S. 335, 344 (1963).
6. *Weeks v. United States,* 232 U.S. 383, 392.
7. *Brown v. Mississippi,* 297 U.S. 278.
8. *Ibid.,* at 284.
9. *Ibid.,* at 287.
10. Address Feb. 8, 1965, dinner given by the Philippine Constitution Association in Manila.
11. *Irvine v. California,* 347 U.S. 128 (1954). Cf. Alan F. Westin, "Bookies and 'Bugs' in California," in *The Uses of Power,* ed. Alan F. Westin *et al.* (New York: Harcourt, Brace & World, 1962), pp. 118–171.

43. Los Angeles *Times,* Apr. 22, 1953.
44. *Ibid.,* Nov. 18, 1953.
45. *Ibid.,* Mar. 17, 1958.
46. *Ibid.,* May 11, 1949.
47. *Ibid.,* May 12, 1949.
48. *Proceedings of the Governors' Conference,* 1950 (White Sulphur Springs, W. Va. 1950), p. 76.
49. *Ibid.,* p. 45.
50. *Ibid.,* p. 77.
51. *Assembly Journal,* Jan. 8, 1951, p. 17.
52. *Ibid.,* p. 20.
53. James C. Derieux, "Will Warren Pivot to the Presidency?" *Collier's,* Jan. 19, 1952, p. 18.
54. *Ibid.,* p. 48.
55. *Ibid.,* p. 18.
56. Nixon remark in Labor Day speech, 1956. Cf. William Costello, *The Facts About Nixon, An Unauthorized Biography* (New York: Viking, 1960), p. 7. Lippmann quote, p. 8.
57. White, "The Gentlemen from California," p. 40.
58. George Creel, *Rebel at Large* (New York: Putnam's, 1947), p. 286.
59. July 13, 1959, p. 56.
60. Oakland *Tribune,* Sept. 11, 1949.
61. Los Angeles *Times,* Dec. 25, 1949.

Chapter 13

1. Sacramento *Bee,* Nov. 14, 1951.
2. Los Angeles *Times,* Nov. 15, 1951.
3. *Ibid.,* Nov. 16, 1951.
4. *The New Republic,* Dec. 17, 1951, p. 7.
5. Los Angeles *Times,* Jan. 16, 1952.
6. *Ibid.,* Mar. 6, 1952.
7. *Ibid.,* Mar. 5, 1952.
8. *Ibid.,* June 25, 1952.
9. Herbert L. Phillips in Sacramento *Bee,* July 4, 1952.
10. Robert W. Kenny, "The Crisis Nixon Forgot," *Frontier,* Apr., 1962, pp. 12, 17.
11. Richard M. Nixon, *Six Crises* (New York: Pocket Books, 1962), pp. 321, 323.
12. *Ibid.,* p. 323.
13. Theodore H. White, "The Gentlemen from California," *Collier's,* Feb. 3, 1956, p. 46.
14. Sacramento *Bee,* July 5, 1952.
15. Los Angeles *Times,* July 8, 1952.
16. *Ibid.,* Feb. 13, 1952.
17. Dwight D. Eisenhower, *Mandate for Change* (New York: Doubleday, 1963), Vol. I, p. 228.
18. Los Angeles *Times,* July 12, 1952.
19. Nixon, *Six Crises,* p. 323.
20. Earl Mazo, *Richard Nixon* (New York: Harper, 1959), pp. 82–83.

21. Richard Donovan, "Birth of a Salesman," in *The Political Yearbook, 1952* (New York: The Reporter, 1953), p. 93.
22. Los Angeles *Times*, Nov. 1, 1952.
23. *Ibid.*
24. Cf. Los Angeles *Times*, Jan. 6, July 20, and July 27, 1949.
25. *Ibid.*, Nov. 22, 1952.
26. *Senate Journal*, Jan. 5, 1953, p. 36.
27. *Ibid.*, p. 35.
28. *Ibid.*, statistics pp. 35–36; quote, p. 39.
29. Los Angeles *Times*, Mar. 6, 1953.
30. *Ibid.*, Feb. 24, 1948.
31. *United States v. California*, 332 U.S. 804 (1947).
32. Kansas City *Times*, Oct. 22, 1948.
33. *United States v. California*, 381 U.S. 139 (1965).
34. Los Angeles *Times*, Sept. 4, 1953.
35. *Ibid.*
36. *Ibid.*, Sept. 6, 1953.
37. Aug. 15, 1953, p. 123.
38. Los Angeles *Times*, Sept. 4, 1953.
39. Interview, Judge Earl Warren, Jr.
40. "I wouldn't submit a town marshal to this kind of charge," Sen. Knowland said, Feb. 19, 1954. EW was confirmed March 1 by a voice vote. "There were no audible 'noes,'" the Los Angeles *Times* reported next day.
41. Charles Warren, *The Supreme Court in United States History* (Boston: Little, Brown, 1960), Vol. I, pp. 128–139.
42. Eisenhower, *Mandate for Change*, Vol. I, pp. 226–227.
43. Los Angeles *Times*, Sept. 25, 27, 1953.
44. *Ibid.*, Sept. 28, 1953; Eisenhower, *Mandate for Change*, Vol I, p. 228.
45. Los Angeles *Times*, Oct. 2, 1953.
46. *Ibid.*, Oct. 1, 1953.
47. *Frontier*, Nov., 1953; Knight, p. 7: EW, p. 4.
48. Los Angeles *Times*, Oct. 3, 1953.
49. *Ibid.*, Oct. 4, 1953.
50. *Ibid.*, Oct. 5, 1953. Literally, of course, EW's political career began in 1926, when he ran for district attorney of Alameda County, but the *Point Lobos* case figured prominently in his first two campaigns for state office, and it was these victories that brought him to national notice.
51. Los Angeles *Times*, New York *Times*, Oct. 6, 1953.
52. Address to the California bar, Sept. 25, 1963, reprinted in *Congressional Record*, 88th Cong., 1st Sess., Vol. 109, Part 15 (Oct. 21, 1963), p. 19848.
53. Details from news stories, also *U.S. Supreme Court Journal*, October term, 1953, p. 1.
54. Los Angeles *Times*, Oct. 6, 1953.

CHAPTER 14

1. 39 *Connecticut Bar Journal* 220 (1965); reprinted *Case and Comment*, May–June, 1966, p. 1.
2. *Buchanan v. Warley*, 245 U.S. 60 (1917); *Missouri ex rel. Gaines v. Canada*, 305 U.S. 337 (1938).
3. *Crainquebille.*

4. Carl Sandburg, *Abraham Lincoln: The Prairie Years* (New York: Harcourt Brace, 1926), Vol. II, p. 131.
5. Irving Brant, *The Bill of Rights* (Indianapolis: Bobbs-Merrill, 1965), p. 337.
6. *San Mateo County v. Southern Pacific R.R.*, argued Dec. 19, 20, 21, 1882, decided Dec. 21, 1885 (116 U.S. 138). Cf. Howard Jay Graham, "The Conspiracy Theory of the Fourteenth Amendment," 47 *Yale Law Journal* 371–375 (1938).
7. *Connecticut General Life Insurance Co. v. Johnson*, 303 U.S. 77, 85 (1938).
8. *Wheeling Steel Corp. v. Glander*, 337 U.S. 562, 576–581 (1949).
9. Robert G. McCloskey, *The American Supreme Court* (paperback; Chicago: University of Chicago Press, 1963), p. 224.
10. *An Autobiography of the Supreme Court*, Alan F. Westin, ed. (New York: Macmillan, 1963), p. 431.
11. 32 U.S. (7 Peters) 243 (1833).
12. *Malloy v. Hogan*, 378 U.S. 1 (1964). Cf. *Griffin v. California*, 380 U.S. 609 (1965).
13. *Robinson v. California*, 370 U.S. 660 (1962).
14. *Gideon v. Wainwright*, 372 U.S. 335 (1963).
15. *Mapp v. Ohio*, 367 U.S. 643 (1961).
16. *Palko v. Connecticut*, 302 U.S. 319, 325 (1937).
17. *Snyder v. Massachusetts*, 291 U.S. 97, 105 (1934).
18. 332 U.S. 46, 89 (1947). Cf. Felix Frankfurter, "Memorandum on 'Incorporation' of the Bill of Rights into the Due Process Clause of the Fourteenth Amendment," 78 *Harvard Law Review* 746 (1965).
19. *Calder v. Bull*, 3 U.S. (3 Dallas) 386, 399 (1798).
20. *Boyce v. Anderson*, 27 U.S. (2 Peters) 150, 154 (1829).
21. *Dred Scott v. Sandford*, 60 U.S. (19 Howard) 393 (1857). Cf. Bruce Catton, "The Dred Scott Case, in *Quarrels That Have Shaped the Constitution*, ed. John A. Garraty (New York: Harper & Row, 1964), pp. 77–89.
22. Brant, *The Bill of Rights*, p. 347.
23. 83 U.S. (16 Wallace) 36 (1873).
24. 109 U.S. 3 (1883).
25. *Ibid.*, at 14.
26. Rocco J. Tresolino, *Justice and the Supreme Court* (Philadelphia: Lippincott, 1963), p. 59.
27. 109 U.S. 3, 62.
28. *Bradwell v. The State*, 83 U.S. (16 Wallace) 13 (1872). Cf. Charles Warren, *The Supreme Court in United States History* (Boston: Little, Brown, 1960), Vol. II, p. 50.
29. Cf. C. Vann Woodward, "The Case of the Louisiana Traveler," in *Quarrels That Have Shaped the Constitution*, ed. John A. Garraty, pp. 145–158.
30. 163 U.S. 537 (1896).
31. 59 Mass. (5 Cushing) 198 (1849).
32. 163 U.S. 537, 551 (1896).
33. *Ibid.*, at 559.
34. Woodward, "The Case of the Louisiana Traveler," p. 153.
35. 163 U.S. 537, 560 (1896).
36. Woodward, "The Case of the Louisiana Traveler," p. 158.
37. *Time*, Oct. 26, 1962, p. 52.

12. *Rochin v. California,* 342 U.S. 165 (1952); *Wolf v. Colorado,* 338 U.S. 25 (1949).
13. 338 U.S. at 26.
14. *Ibid.,* at 27.
15. *"Mapp v. Ohio* at Large in the Fifty States," 1962 *Duke Law Journal* 319, 327.
16. 342 U.S. 165, 172 (1952).
17. Address, California Bar, San Francisco, Sept. 25, 1963, *Congressional Record,* 88th Cong., 1st Sess., Vol. 109, Part 15 (Oct. 21, 1963), p. 19848.
18. William J. Brennan, "Inside View of the High Court," *New York Times Magazine,* Oct. 6, 1963, p. 100. Also, same author's "Working at Justice," in *An Autobiography of the Supreme Court,* ed. Alan F. Westin (New York: Macmillan, 1963), pp. 300–304.
19. Feb. 9, 1954.
20. *Mapp v. Ohio,* 367 U.S. 643 (1961).
21. *Olmstead v. United States,* 277 U.S. 438, 485 (1928).
22. *Mallory v. United States,* 354 U.S. 449, 454 (1957).
23. Cited by EW in footnote, *Miranda v. Arizona,* 384 U.S. 436, 482–483 (1966).
24. *McNabb v. United States,* 318 U.S. 332, 343 (1943).
25. *Ibid.,* at 340.
26. 287 U.S. 45, 68–69 (1932).
27. *Betts v. Brady,* 316 U.S. 455, 476 (1942).
28. Anthony Lewis, *Gideon's Trumpet,* p. 105.
29. 351 U.S. 12.
30. *Ibid.,* at 16.
31. From text released to the press at the Governors' Conference, 1966, Los Angeles.
32. *Escobedo v. Illinois,* 378 U.S. 478, 479 (1964).
33. *Ibid.,* at 480.
34. *Ibid.,* at 482–483.
35. 357 U.S. 433 (1958).
36. 357 U.S. 504 (1958).
37. *Escobedo v. Illinois,* 378 U.S. 478, 492 (1964).
38. Cited by EW in footnote, *Miranda v. Arizona,* 384 U.S. 436, 441 (1966). Cf. also *U.S. News & World Report,* Sept. 20, 1965, p. 12.
39. 378 U.S. 478, 490.
40. "Lawbreakers, Courts and Law-Abiders," 31 *Missouri Law Review* 181, 192–193 (1966). The cases cited by Chief Justice Traynor during the 1960's:
   Griffin v. California, 380 U.S. 609 (1965): Comment by prosecutor on defendant's failure to testify violates due process.
   Pointer v. Texas, 380 U.S. 400 (1965): Fourteenth Amendment makes Sixth Amendment's guarantee of defendant's right "to be confronted with the witnesses against him" applicable to the states.
   Escobedo v. Illinois, 378 U.S. 478 (1964): Right to counsel extended to police interrogations.
   Jackson v. Denno, 378 U.S. 368 (1964): Voluntariness of confession must be decided by someone other than jury that tries issue of guilt.
   Murphy v. Waterfront Commission, 378 U.S. 52 (1964): Compulsion

of testimony by one jurisdiction requires immunity from prosecution in all jurisdictions.

Malloy v. Hogan, 378 U.S. 1 (1964): Fifth Amendment's privilege against self-incrimination applicable to the states.

Massiah v. United States, 377 U.S. 201 (1964): Questioning of suspect after indictment in absence of counsel proscribed.

White v. Maryland, 373 U.S. 59 (1963): Sixth Amendment's right to counsel extended to preliminary hearing in state courts.

Fay v. Noia, 372 U.S. 391 (1963): Extension of federal habeas corpus for state prisoners.

Gideon v. Wainwright, 372 U.S. 335 (1963): Sixth Amendment's right to counsel made applicable to the states.

Townsend v. Sain, 372 U.S. 293 (1963): Extension of right to evidentiary hearing for state prisoners in federal habeas corpus proceeding.

Mapp v. Ohio, 367 U.S. 643 (1961): Fourth Amendment exclusionary rule extended to states.

Thompson v. City of Louisville, 362 U.S. 199 (1960): Conviction devoid of evidentiary support is invalid under due process.

41. *People v. Cahan*, 44 Cal. 2d 434, 274 P.2d 724 (1955).
42. *People v. Dorado*, 62 Cal. 2d 338, 351, 398 P.2d 361, 369–370 (1965).
43. 384 U.S. 436, 444–445.
44. *Ibid.*, at 469.
45. *Ibid.*, at 472.
46. *Ibid.*, at 481.
47. "Miranda and the Police: The Confession Debate Continues," *New York Times Magazine*, Oct. 2, 1966, p. 64.
48. 384 U.S. 436, 504.
49. *Ibid.*, at 542.
50. July 14, 1966.
51. Ronald J. Ostrow in Los Angeles *Times*, July 22, 1966.
52. *Ibid.*, Associated Press dispatch.
53. *U.S. News & World Report*, Sept. 20, 1965, p. 12. For more on Professor Kamisar, see "A Gifted Gadfly," *Time*, Nov. 11, 1966, p. 77.
54. Los Angeles *Times*, June 15, 1966.
55. *Wall Street Journal*, Nov. 26, 1965.
56. 332 U.S. 46.
57. 211 U.S. 78.
58. 332 U.S. 46, 69.
59. *Griffin v. California*, 380 U.S. 609, 614 (1965).
60. Oakland *Tribune*, May 15, 1934.
61. *Ibid.*, Sept. 11, 1932.
62. 360 U.S. 315, 320–321.
63. Quoted in an article by Wayne E. Green, *Wall Street Journal*, Nov. 26, 1965.

CHAPTER 16

1. 377 U.S. 533, 568 (1964).
2. In a speech at Merced, Calif., Oct. 29, 1948 (quoted in *U.S. News & World Report*, July 6, 1964, p. 34).
3. "The Reapportionment Struggle in California in 1948," *Western Political Quarterly*, 4 (June, 1951), 317.

4. "Urban vs. Rural in California," *National Municipal Review*, July, 1946, p. 353.
5. Sept. 27, 1963. Reprinted in *Congressional Record*, 88th Cong., 1st Sess., Vol. 109, Part 15 (Oct. 21, 1963), p. 19851.
6. "Elections and Reapportionment," a Report of the Assembly Interim Committee (1951), p. 36.
7. "A Case Study in Reapportionment — California, 1951," 17 *Law and Contemporary Problems* 440, 445 (1952).
8. *Colegrove v. Green*, 328 U.S. 549, 556 (1946).
9. Judge J. Frank McLaughlin in *Dyer v. Kazuhisa Abe*, 138 F. Supp. 220, 236 (D. Hawaii).
10. 175 F. Supp. 649, 652 (M.D. Tenn.).
11. *Baker v. Carr*, 369 U.S. 186, 237 (1962).
12. Los Angeles *Times*, Mar. 28, 1962.
13. Reprinted in Los Angeles *Times*, July 8, 1962.
14. *Newsweek*, Apr. 9, 1962, p. 32.
15. *Gray v. Sanders*, 372 U.S. 368 (1963).
16. *Ibid.*, at 379.
17. *Congressional Districting* (Washington, D.C.: The Brookings Institution, 1963), p. 121.
18. 376 U.S. 1.
19. *Ibid.*, at 20.
20. New York *Times*, Feb. 18, 1964.
21. *Wesberry v. Sanders*, 376 U.S. 1, 17 (1964).
22. 377 U.S. 533, 562.
23. Merced speech (see n. 2 above).
24. Everett McKinley Dirksen, "The Supreme Court Is Defying the People," *Saturday Evening Post*, Sept. 12, 1964, p. 12.
25. *Cook County v. City of Chicago*, 311 Ill. 234, 142 N.E. 512, 513 (1924).
26. 376 U.S. 1, 14 (1964).
27. "One Man, One Vote — Yes or No?" in *New York Times Magazine*, Nov. 8, 1964, p. 132.
28. 377 U.S. 533, 564–565 (1964).
29. Frank J. Taylor, "Man with a New Broom," *Saturday Evening Post*, Aug. 7, 1943, p. 94.
30. Los Angeles *Times*, Oct. 19, 1965.
31. *Ibid.*, Nov. 15, 1965.
32. *Ibid.*, Nov. 14, 1965.
33. Los Angeles *Daily Journal*, Oct. 28, 1965.
34. *Ibid.*, Oct. 26, 1965.
35. Los Angeles *Times*, Oct. 24, 1965.
36. Sept. 4, 1965, p. 36.
37. Dec. 1, 1965.
38. Los Angeles *Times*, Oct. 24, 1965.
39. *Ibid.*
40. *Ibid.*, news story, Jan. 12, 1967, and editorial page feature by Ray Zeman, Sacramento bureau chief, Jan. 19, 1967.
41. From an interview reported by Chalmers M. Roberts of the Washington *Post*, reprinted in the Santa Barbara (Calif.) *News-Press*, Sept. 16, 1956.
42. 369 U.S. 186, 270 (1962).
43. *Time*, Sept. 7, 1962, p. 15.

44. 319 U.S. 624, 646–647 (1943).
45. New York *Times*, Feb. 23, 1965.
46. *Baker v. Carr*, 369 U.S. 186, 267 (1962).
47. Nov., 1955, in *Public Papers*, p. 114.
48. *Time*, May 5, 1961, pp. 17–18.
49. *Newsweek*, May 8, 1961, p. 27. Also in Fred Rodell, "It Is the Warren Court," *New York Times Magazine*, Mar. 13, 1966, p. 96. The case was *Stewart v. United States*, 366 U.S. 1 (1961).
50. "F.F.: Frame for a Portrait," 76 *Harvard Law Review* 22 (1962).
51. *U.S. Supreme Court Journal*, Oct. term (1964), p. 181.
52. 328 U.S. 549, 554.
53. 377 U.S. 533, 566.

CHAPTER 17

1. *U.S. News & World Report*, July 9, 1962, p. 44.
2. *Time*, July 6, 1962, p. 7.
3. *U.S. News & World Report, loc. cit.* The case was *Manual Enterprises v. Day*, 370 U.S. 478 (1962).
4. Los Angeles *Times*, Feb. 13, 1966.
5. *Ibid.*, Jan. 20, 1966.
6. Kenneth Crawford, "Who's Against Prayer?" *Newsweek*, Aug. 8, 1966, p. 29. Also, Los Angeles *Times*, Mar. 2, 1966, quoting a liberal senator who told John H. Averill, "I think Dirksen might be trying to divert attention from his failure on reapportionment."
7. *Engel v. Vitale*, 370 U.S. 421 (1962).
8. *Ibid.*, at 425.
9. *Ibid.*, at 435.
10. *Ibid.*, at 436.
11. *Prayers in Public Schools and Other Matters*, Hearings Before the Committee on the Judiciary, U.S. Senate, 87th Cong., 2d Sess., S.J. Res. 205, 206, 207, S. Con. Res. 81, S. Res. 356 (Washington: Government Printing Office, 1963), p. 127.
12. *Ibid.*, p. 210.
13. Both quotes, *Time*, July 6, 1962, p. 8.
14. *School Prayer*, Hearings Before the Subcommittee on Constitutional Amendments, Committee on the Judiciary, U.S. Senate, 89th Cong., 2d Sess., S.J. Res. 148 (Washington: Government Printing Office, 1966), p. 615, nn. 3, 5.
15. July 6, 1962, p. 5.
16. *Engel v. Vitale*, 370 U.S. 421, 427–429 (1962).
17. 343 U.S. 306, 313.
18. 330 U.S. 1.
19. *Ibid.*, at 53–54.
20. *Engel v. Vitale*, 370 U.S. 421, 443 (1962).
21. The last sentence, omitted: "Such patriotic or ceremonial occasions bear no true resemblance to the unquestioned religious exercise that the State of New York has sponsored in this instance." *Ibid.*, at 435.
22. 374 U.S. 203 (1963).
23. New York *Times*, July 15, 1963.
24. *Cantwell v. Connecticut*, 310 U.S. 296. Cf. also, *Murdock v. Pennsylvania*, 319 U.S. 105 (1943).

25. *Murray v. Curlett,* 374 U.S. 203, 226 (1963).
26. *Ibid.,* at 319.
27. Address, Utah University School of Law, Feb. 27, 1963, reprinted in *Congressional Record,* 88th Cong., 1st Sess., Vol. 109, Part 23 (Mar. 19, 1963), p. A1569.
28. "Sunday in North America," 79 *Harvard Law Review* 54 (1965).
29. *Gallagher v. Crown Kosher Super Market,* 366 U.S. 617; *Braunfeld v. Brown,* 366 U.S. 599; *Two Guys v. McGinley,* 366 U.S. 582; *McGowan v. Maryland,* 366 U.S. 420 (quote at 448).
30. *Ibid.,* at 578.
31. *Arlan's Department Store v. Kentucky,* 371 U.S. 218, 219 (1962).
32. *Congressional Record,* Mar. 19, 1963, p. A1569 (see n. 27 above).
33. *Stein v. Oshinsky,* 348 F.2d 999 (2d Cir. 1965).
34. *Stein v. Oshinsky,* cert. denied, 382 U.S. 957 (1965).
35. New York *Times,* Dec. 14, 1965.
36. *Ibid.*
37. Los Angeles *Times,* Aug. 2, 1966.
38. *School Prayer,* Senate Judiciary Subcommittee Hearings (1966), p. 27.
39. *Ibid.,* pp. 7–22.
40. Los Angeles *Times,* Oct. 11, 1964.
41. *School Prayer,* Senate Judiciary Subcommittee Hearings (1966), p. 8.
42. As quoted by Dorothy McCardle, Washington *Post,* Mar. 24, 1966.
43. *Commonwealth v. Holmes,* 17 Mass. 335 (1821).
44. Leo M. Alpert, "Judicial Censorship of Obscene Literature," 52 *Harvard Law Review* 40, 47 (1938).
45. *Jacobellis v. Ohio,* 378 U.S. 184, 197 (1964).
46. Alpert, "Judicial Censorship of Obscene Literature," at 40–41.
47. L.R. 3 Q.B. 360, 371.
48. 209 Fed. 119 (S.D.N.Y. 1913).
49. *Ibid.,* at 120, 121.
50. *United States v. One Book Called "Ulysses,"* 5 F. Supp. 182, 183–184 (S.D.N.Y. 1933).
51. *An Unhurried View of Erotica* (paperback; New York: Ace, 1958), p. 109.
52. "A Wreath for the Gamekeeper," *Encounter,* Vol. 14 (Feb., 1960), p. 69.
53. "Sex . . . and the Supreme Court," *Esquire,* June, 1963, p. 82.
54. Thurman Arnold, *Fair Fights and Foul* (New York: Harcourt, Brace & World, 1965), p. 164.
55. *Joseph Burstyn, Inc. v. Wilson,* 343 U.S. 495, 505 (1952).
56. *Commercial Pictures Corp. v. Regents,* 346 U.S. 587 (1954).
57. 352 U.S. 380, 383 (1957).
58. Robert Antrim, "Sam Roth, Prometheus of the Unprintable," *Eros,* Vol. 1, No. 3 (Autumn, 1962), p. 26.
59. *United States v. Roth,* 237 F.2d 796, 825 (2d Cir. 1956).
60. 354 U.S. 476, 493–494 (1957).
61. *Ibid.,* at 487, 484, 489.
62. Arnold, *Fair Fights and Foul,* p. 184.
63. 355 U.S. 372 (1958).
64. 355 U.S. 371 (1958).
65. 355 U.S. 35 (1957).
66. *Newsweek,* May 11, 1964, p. 28.
67. 354 U.S. 476, 495 (1957).

68. *Ibid.*, at 495–496.
69. *Smith v. California*, 361 U.S. 147, 154 (1959).
70. "The Metaphysics of the Law of Obscenity," in *The Supreme Court and the Constitution: Essays in Constitutional Law from the Supreme Court Review*, ed. Philip B. Kurland (Chicago: University of Chicago Press, 1965), pp. 1–45, at 11. Cf. also "Free Speech and Obscenity: A Search for Constitutional Procedures and Standards," 12 *UCLA Law Review* 551 (1965).
71. *Kingsley Pictures Corp .v. Regents*, 360 U.S. 684, 688–689 (1959).
72. *Ibid.*, at 690.
73. Kansas City *Star*, June 24, 1964.
74. 378 U.S. 205 (1964).
75. Joe Lastelic in Kansas City *Star*, Apr. 2, 1964.
76. *A Quantity of Books v. Kansas*, 378 U.S. 205, 210 (1964), quoting *Bantam Books, Inc. v. Sullivan*, 372 U.S. 58, 66 (1963).
77. *Ibid.*, at 225.
78. Kansas City *Star*, June 24, 1964.
79. *Jacobellis v. Ohio*, 378 U.S. 184 (1964).
80. *Ibid.*, at 201.
81. *Ibid.*, at 197.
82. Vol. 78, p. 208 (1964).
83. 378 U.S. 184, 200 (1964).
84. *Ibid.*
85. Vol. 78, pp. 209–210.
86. New York *Times*, Dec. 8, 1965.
87. *Ibid.*, Dec. 9, 1965.
88. In his concurring opinion in the *Fanny Hill* case, *Memoirs v. Massachusetts*, 383 U.S. 413, 427 (1966).
89. *Mishkin v. New York*, 383 U.S. 502 (1966).
90. *Ginzburg v. United States*, 383 U.S. 463 (1966).
91. *Ibid.*, at 470.
92. *Ibid.*, at 500.
93. *Ibid.*, at 482.
94. Apr. 4, 1966, p. 379.
95. Apr. 3, 1966, pp. 5–6.
96. Arnold, *Fair Fights and Foul*, p. 170.
97. *Playboy*, July, 1966, p. 42.
98. Los Angeles *Times*, July 19, 1966.
99. 383 U.S. 463, 498 (1966).
100. Apr. 4, 1966, p. 21.
101. 383 U.S. 413, 432 (1966).
102. Los Angeles *Times*, Apr. 7, 1966.
103. *Commonwealth v. Gordon*, 66 Pa. D. & C. 101, 110 (1949).

CHAPTER 18

1. Santa Barbara (Calif.) *News-Press*, Aug. 29, 1957.
2. *U.S. News & World Report*, Feb. 6, 1959, pp. 40–41.
3. *The Blue Book of the John Birch Society* (third printing, 1959), pp. 86, 91.
4. *The Dan Smoot Report*, Vol. 7, No. 5, Jan. 30, 1961, p. 33.
5. *Nine Men Against America: The Supreme Court and Its Attack on American Liberties* (New York: Devin-Adair, 1960), p. 37.

6. George R. Stewart, *The Year of the Oath* (New York: Doubleday, 1950), p. 24, quoting San Francisco *Chronicle*, Mar. 1, 1950.
7. *Elfbrandt v. Russell*, 384 U.S. 11 (1966).
8. Mar. 13, 1966.
9. New York *Times*, Apr. 19, 1966.
10. *Baggett v. Bullitt*, 377 U.S. 360.
11. Los Angeles *Times*, Jan. 5, 1967.
12. *Ibid.*, Jan. 6, 1967.
13. New York *Times*, Jan. 24, 1967.
14. *Keyishian v. New York Board of Regents*, 35 *United States Law Week* 4152 (Jan. 23, 1967).
15. Jan. 29, 1967.
16. *Sweezy v. New Hampshire*, 354 U.S. 234, 250.
17. *Nine Men: A Political History of the Supreme Court of the United States from 1790 to 1955* (New York: Random House, 1955), p. 321.
18. 341 U.S. 494 (1951).
19. *Ibid.*, at 581.
20. Distributed by *The Independent American*, as "Tax Fax No. 27."
21. *Watkins v. United States*, 354 U.S. 178; *Yates v. United States*, 354 U.S. 298; *Sweezy v. New Hampshire*, 354 U.S. 234.
22. P. 61.
23. 354 U.S. 178, 187.
24. *Ibid.*, at 185.
25. *Ibid.*, at 215.
26. 354 U.S. 298, 324–325.
27. 354 U.S. 234, 250.
28. 71 *Harvard Law Review* 85, 91 (1957).
29. 360 U.S. 109 (1959).
30. 360 U.S. 72 (1959).
31. 360 U.S. 109, 134 (1959).
32. *Ibid.*, at 141, 143.
33. *DeGregory v. New Hampshire*, 383 U.S. 825, 829 (1966).
34. 351 U.S. 345 (1956).
35. *Ibid.*, at 367–368.
36. *Ibid.*, at 361.
37. Delivered Sept. 22, 1950.
38. 350 U.S. 497 (1956).
39. *Ibid.*, at 505.
40. Los Angeles *Times*, Aug. 23, 1965.
41. *The Reporter*, July 18, 1963, p. 22. Also, Brooks Atkinson, New York *Times*, July 16, 1963.
42. *Lamont v. Postmaster General*, 381 U.S. 301.
43. Quoted in Washington *Post* editorial, June 1, 1962.
44. 357 U.S. 116, 127. Cf. *Bauer v. Acheson*, 106 F. Supp. 445 (D.D.C. 1952); *Nathan v. Dulles*, 129 F. Supp. 951 (D.D.C. 1955); *Schachtman v. Dulles*, 225 F.2d 938 (D.C. Cir. 1955).
45. 378 U.S. 500, 514.
46. *Zemel v. Rusk*, 381 U.S. 1.
47. *Ibid.*, at 22.
48. *United States v. Laub*, 35 *United States Law Week* 4125 (Jan. 10, 1967), and *Travis v. United States*, 35 *United States Law Week* 4129 (Jan. 10, 1967).

49. 381 U.S. 437, 461 (1965).
50. Los Angeles *Times*, Dec. 19, 1965.
51. 382 U.S. 70 (1965).
52. The Court is going to take another look at this situation, having granted certiorari in a case involving the tax, *Costello v. United States*, 383 U.S. 942 (1966). Cf. also, *Lewis v. United States*, 348 U.S. 419 (1955), and *United States v. Kahriger*, 345 U.S. 22 (1953).
53. Los Angeles *Times*, Nov. 16, 1965.
54. *Ibid.*, Nov. 28, 1965.
55. Nov. 27, 1965, p. 4. Cf. Frank A. Warren III, *Liberals and Communism: The "Red Decade" Revisited* (Bloomington: Indiana University Press, 1966); Earl Latham, *The Communist Controversy in Washington: From the New Deal to McCarthy* (Cambridge: Harvard University Press, 1966); Milton R. Konvitz, *Expanding Liberties: Freedom's Gains in Postwar America* (New York: Viking, 1966).

CHAPTER 19

1. *Warren Hearings*, VI, 456.
2. New York *Times*, Nov. 21, 1963.
3. Senate Document No. 46 (Washington, D.C.: Government Printing Office, 1963), in *Public Papers*, pp. 107–108.
4. *Warren Hearings*, XV, 727.
5. *Who Killed Kennedy?* (New York: Macfadden-Bartell, 1964), pp. 142, 144.
6. New York *Times*, Nov. 24, 1963.
7. *Ibid.*, Nov. 26, 1963.
8. Harrison E. Salisbury in the paperback edition of the *Warren Report* prepared by the New York *Times* (New York: Bantam, 1964), p. xvi.
9. Eulogy, Senate Document No. 46 (1963).
10. Arthur M. Schlesinger, Jr., *A Thousand Days* (Boston: Houghton Mifflin, 1965), p. 1028.
11. New York *Times*, Sept. 28, 1964.
12. Edward Jay Epstein, *Inquest: The Warren Commission and the Establishment of Truth* (New York: Viking, 1966), p. 15.
13. *Warren Report*, p. 21.
14. Norman Mackenzie, Oct. 2, 1964, p. 476.
15. Nov. 2, 1964, pp. 295, 297, 299.
16. Los Angeles *Times*, Nov. 24, 1966.
17. *Sunday Times* (London), Dec. 20, 1964, replying to Hugh Trevor-Roper, *ibid.*, Dec. 13, 1964.
18. Malcolm O. Couch, *Warren Report*, p. 65.
19. *Warren Hearings*, VII, 108.
20. Los Angeles *Times*, Nov. 27, 1966, taken from transcript of a panel discussion at the Associated Press Managing Editors Convention, San Diego, Calif., Nov. 17, 1966.
21. *Warren Hearings*, IV, 206.
22. *Ibid.*, VII, 299.
23. *Ibid.*, I, 74.
24. *Ibid.*, X, 297.
25. *Ibid.*, I, 68–69.
26. *Ibid.*, II, 226.

27. *Ibid.*, II, 248.
28. *Warren Report*, p. 134.
29. *Ibid.*, p. 136.
30. *Ibid.*, pp. 118–119.
31. *Warren Hearings*, VII, 228.
32. *Warren Report*, pp. 181–182.
33. *Warren Hearings*, VII, 231.
34. *Ibid.*, I, 15.
35. *Warren Report*, p. 127.
36. *Warren Hearings*, IV, 187.
37. *Ibid.*, XIII, 231.
38. *Ibid.*, XIII, 212.
39. *Warren Report*, pp. 352–357.
40. *Warren Hearings*, XIV, 358–359, 341.
41. *Ibid.*, V, 199.
42. Los Angeles *Times*, Dec. 20, 1966.
43. P. 373.
44. Oct. 2, 1964, p. 49.
45. *Warren Hearings*, V, 212.
46. *Ibid.*, V, 191.
47. *Ibid*, XIII, 215.
48. *Ibid.*, V, 192.
49. Alexander M. Bickel, "The Failure of the Warren Report," *Commentary*, Oct., 1966, p. 37.
50. *Warren Hearings*, V, 184.
51. *Ibid.*, V, 209.
52. *Ibid.*, V, 196.
53. *Ibid.*, V, 210.
54. *Ibid.*, V, 211.
55. Sept. 25, 1966.
56. Bickel, "The Failure of the Warren Report," p. 38.
57. Los Angeles *Times*, Oct. 19, 1966.
58. Richard Warren Lewis, "The Scavengers," in *World Journal Tribune* Sunday Magazine, Jan. 22, 1967.
59. *Warren Hearings*, VI, 213.
60. *Ibid.*, VI, 214.
61. *Ibid.*, VI, 215; *Warren Report*, pp. 334–335.
62. Mark Lane, *Rush to Judgment* (New York: Holt, Rinehart & Winston, 1966), pp. 348–349.
63. In a note to the author.
64. *Warren Hearings*, VII, 495, 496.
65. *Ibid.*, III, 191.
66. Los Angeles *Times*, Nov. 13, 1966.
67. Epstein, *Inquest*, p. 150.
68. Los Angeles *Times*, Nov. 24, 1966; cf. *Life*, Nov. 25, 1966, p. 48.
69. Lane, *Rush to Judgment*, p. 47; Washington *Post*, Nov. 23, 1964; *Warren Hearings*, III, 373.
70. *Warren Report*, p. 543.
71. Lane, *Rush to Judgment*, p. 59.
72. *Warren Report*, p. 55.
73. *Warren Hearings*, II, 371.

74. *Look*, July 12, 1966, p. 66.
75. Epstein, *Inquest*, p. 62.
76. *Warren Hearings*, Commission Exhibit No. 3025, XXVI, 573.
77. *Look*, July 12, 1966, p. 71.
78. *Ibid.*, p. 67.
79. *Ibid.*, p. 71.
80. Oct. 10, 1966, pp. 48–63.
81. Epstein, *Inquest*, p. 49.
82. "The Warren Commission Report and Its Critics," *Frontier*, Nov., 1966, p. 18.
83. New York *Times*, Nov. 26, 1966.
84. Epstein, *Inquest*, p. 53; *Warren Hearings*, Commission Exhibit No. 397, XVII, 45.
85. Epstein, *Inquest*, pp. 54–58.
86. Los Angeles *Times*, Nov. 25, 1966.
87. From transcript of Associated Press Managing Editors Convention, Nov. 17, 1966 (see n. 20 above).
88. June 13, 1966, p. 37.
89. Los Angeles *Times*, July 10, 1966.
90. *Newsweek*, Nov. 14, 1966, p. 31.
91. *U.S. News & World Report*, Nov. 14, 1966, p. 81.
92. Penn Jones, Jr., editor of the Midlothian (Texas) *Mirror* has been the chief exponent of the Kennedy Curse. He has collected his columns in *Forgive My Grief*. Cf. also *Ramparts*, Nov., 1966, pp. 29–50; *Time*, Nov. 11, 1966, pp. 33–34.
93. Refuted in *Warren Report*, p. 663. Cf. Mark Lane testimony, *Warren Hearings*, II, 38.
94. Cf. Richard H. Popkin, *The Second Oswald* (New York: Avon, 1966).
95. *Warren Report*, pp. 315–325.
96. *The Oswald Affair* (New York: World, 1966).
97. *Warren Report*, p. 662.
98. Los Angeles *Times*, Sept. 29, 1964.
99. *Warren Hearings*, XV, 738–739.
100. Los Angeles *Times*, Nov. 6, 1964.
101. Jean Stafford, *A Mother in History* (New York: Farrar, Straus & Giroux, 1966), p. 12.
102. New York *Times*, Jan. 12, 1964.
103. *The Nation*, Sept. 14, 1964, p. 112.
104. *Warren Hearings*, II, 56, 57, 59.
105. Dwight Macdonald, "A Critique of the Warren Report," *Esquire*, March, 1965, p. 128.
106. *Warren Report*, p. xiv. Mr. Craig's name does not appear in the report's index.
107. Bickel, "The Failure of the Warren Report," p. 38.
108. "A Lawyer's Notes on the Warren Commission Report," Vol. 51, pp. 39–43 (Jan., 1965).
109. *Warren Hearings*, I, 22.
110. *Warren Report*, p. 423.
111. *Warren Hearings*, IX, 321, 309.
112. *Ibid.*, I, 1.
113. *Ibid.*, I, 13.

114. Gerald R. Ford and John R. Stiles, *Portrait of the Assassin* (paperback; New York: Ballantine, 1965), p. 496.
115. *Warren Hearings*, V, 607.
116. Ford and Stiles, *Portrait of the Assassin*, p. 496.
117. *Warren Hearings*, I, 130.
118. Ford and Stiles, *Portrait of the Assassin*, p. 62.
119. *Warren Hearings*, I, 250.
120. *Ibid.*, I, 176.
121. *Ibid.*, I 210.
122. *Ibid.*, II, 29.
123. *Ibid.*, I, 500.
124. Stafford, *A Mother in History*, p. 35.
125. *Warren Report*, p. 326.
126. *Los Angeles Times*, Oct. 4, 1964.
127. Epstein, *Inquest*, p. 22.
128. June 13, 1966, p. 37.
129. *Los Angeles Times*, Nov. 22, 1966.
130. P. 22.
131. Lane, *Rush to Judgment*, Introduction, p. 19.
132. *Stone*, p. 110.
133. Popkin, *The Second Oswald*, Introduction, p. 10.
134. *Warren Hearings*, VIII, 235.
135. *Ibid.*, IV, 232.
136. Dec. 13, 1964.
137. Macdonald, "A Critique of the Warren Report," p. 131.
138. *Los Angeles Times*, Oct. 3, 1966.
139. *Look*, Feb. 7, 1967, p. 45. (From the book, published by Harper & Row, 1967).
140. *Los Angeles Times*, Nov. 19, 1964.
141. "Death of a President: The Established Facts," *Atlantic Monthly*, Mar., 1965, p. 112.
142. *Warren Hearings*, I, 76.
143. R. W. Lewis, "The Scavengers" (see n. 58 above).
144. *Los Angeles Times*, Sept. 30, 1964.
145. *Ibid.*, Sept. 25, 1964.
146. *Washington Post*, Oct. 13, 1966.
147. The remark was not intended for publication, but it was printed by *Newsweek*, Nov. 28, 1966, p. 19. It is substantially correct.

CHAPTER 20

1. Dana Bullen in the Washington *Star*, Mar. 19, 1966.
2. Robert Cahn in the *Christian Science Monitor*, Mar. 21, 1966.
3. John MacKenzie in the Washington *Post*, Mar. 19, 1966.
4. *Christian Science Monitor*, Mar. 21, 1966.
5. "It Is the Earl Warren Court," Mar. 13, 1966, p. 100.
6. Ronald J. Ostrow in the Los Angeles *Times*, Mar. 19, 1966.
7. New York *Times*, Mar. 25, 1966.
8. Dorothy McCardle in the Washington *Post*, Mar. 24, 1966.
9. *Brown v. Louisiana*, 383 U.S. 131 (1966). New York *Times*, Feb. 24, 1966.
10. New York *Times*, Feb. 24, 1966.

11. Mar. 7, 1966, p. 2.
12. 385 U.S. 39 (1966).
13. *Ibid.*, at 47.
14. *Ibid.*, at 52, 56.
15. "The Court v. the Demonstrators," Dec. 26, 1966, p. 704.
16. 385 U.S. 39, 41 (1966).
17. *Hague v. C.I.O.*, 307 U.S. 496, 515 (1939).
18. *Brown v. Louisiana*, 383 U.S. 131, 162.
19. *Griswold v. Connecticut*, 381 U.S. 479, 521 (1965).
20. *Harper v. Virginia Board of Elections*, 383 U.S. 663, 676 (1966).
21. Feb. 27, 1966.
22. June 20, 1966, p. 48.
23. Mar. 21, 1966.
24. *South Carolina v. Katzenbach*, 383 U.S. 301, 337 (1966).
25. The custom goes back to 1955, when Lucian Warren (no relation) became president of the club. The Chief Justice was amused by the coincidence of names and cheerfully agreed to administer the oath of office. In January, 1967, he was given a gold membership card by the incumbent president, Win Booth, who said of him, "All of us know a great man when we see one."
26. John P. Frank, *The Warren Court* (New York: Macmillan, 1964), p. 22.
27. Address, California bar, Sept. 25, 1963.
28. From text supplied by EW's office.
29. From text as released for Mar. 21, 1966.
30. *U.S. News & World Report*, Feb. 6, 1959, p. 40.
31. Address before a meeting of the Life Insurance Association of America, New York City, Dec. 9, 1964, reprinted in *U.S. News & World Report*, Dec. 21, 1964, p. 61.
32. James C. Derieux, "Will Warren Pivot to the Presidency?" *Collier's*, Jan. 19, 1952, p. 48.
33. *Ibid.*
34. Los Angeles *Times*, June 26, 1943.
35. Sept. 25, 1963 (see n. 27).
36. *Newsweek*, June 27, 1966, p. 17.
37. "Is the Warren Court Too 'Political?'" *New York Times Magazine*, Sept. 25, 1966, p. 31. Cf. Alexander M. Bickel, *Politics and the Warren Court* (New York: Harper & Row, 1965).
38. Sept. 11, 1966, p. 49.
39. *Ibid.*, p. 152.
40. *U.S. News & World Report*, June 20, 1966, p. 52.
41. "Toward Neutral Principles of Constitutional Law," 73 *Harvard Law Review* 1, 34 (1959). Cf. rebuttal by Ira Michael Heyman, "The Chief Justice, Racial Segregation, and the Friendly Critics," 49 *California Law Review*, 104–125 (1961).
42. New York *Times*, Sept. 14, 15, 16, 1957.
43. Quoted from James E. Clayton, *The Making of Justice* (New York: Dutton, 1964), pp. 95–96.
44. *Ibid.*, p. 99.
45. 80 *Harvard Law Review* 91 (1966).
46. *Public Papers*, p. 115.

Table of Cases

Index